7/00

The
Great Radio
Soap Operas

— The — Great Radio Soap Operas

BY JIM COX

McFarland & Company, Inc., Publishers
Jefferson, North Carolina, and London

Cover photograph: Vivian Smolen and Karl Swenson
of Our Gal Sunday, 1950 (Photofest)

British Library Cataloguing-in-Publication data are available

Library of Congress Cataloguing-in-Publication Data

Cox, Jim, 1939–
    The great radio soap operas / by Jim Cox.
       p.   cm.
    Includes bibliographical references and index.
    ISBN 0-7864-0589-9 (case binding: alkaline paper) ∞
    1. Radio serials — United States — History and criticism.   2.
Soap operas — United States — History and criticism.   I. Title.
PN1991.8.S4C69   1999
791.44'6 — dc21   99-29045
                                          CIP

Manufactured in the United States of America

McFarland & Company, Inc., Publishers
  Box 611, Jefferson, North Carolina 28640

For my family, who experienced this book vicariously,
and for the memory of my mother and father,
who inspired it

Contents

Acknowledgments

A host of individuals deserve some acknowledgment in a project like this, for no author acts alone. I fear that I shall inadvertently overlook someone.

I am particularly obliged for the practical contributions of George Ansbro, Tom DeLong, Florence Freeman, Jack French, Dan Haefele, Jay Hickerson, the late Mary Jane Higby (whose observations I acquired in 1969), Howard Mandelbaum, Bob Mott, Arthur C. Nielsen, Jr., Bob Sabon and Vivian Smolen.

I shall be forever indebted to the competent and tireless staff of the Louisville (Kentucky) Free Public Library, who provided an ongoing wealth of research for me more times than I can enumerate and did so willingly, cheerfully and meticulously with every request.

I'm also appreciative of several vintage radio club newsletter editors — Jim Adams, Peter Bellanca, Bill Davies, Jack French, Dan Haefele, Ken Krug and Jim Snyder — who perpetuate this avocation and who encouraged me to complete the project by publishing some related vignettes that I contributed.

Finally, from the very beginning, my family members resigned themselves to my escape into solitude for interminable hours to complete this dream. I appreciate their recognizing those requirements and giving me the space to satisfy them.

Preface

What strong, mysterious links
enchain the heart
To regions where the morn
of life was spent.
— James Grahame, *The Sabbath*

Did you ever play "What do you want to be when you grow up?"

I was a teenager in the summer of 1955, the year our family took a vacation to Florida. On the way there, we made a detour to visit some lifelong friends of my parents. Their children were close to my age, and I remember that during that stopover we of the younger set discussed our vocational choices. I recall admitting publicly for the first time that I intended to go to New York City to become an announcer or an actor in radio drama. The other children asked me a lot of questions about it, for they had never talked to anyone with an ambition like mine. I was probably equally stunned by the disclosure, although I had every intention of making good on it. It was something I had considered for a long time but simply hadn't found the right moment to admit.

How little I discerned about the fickleness of public tastes and the shifting fortunes of an industry! At that very instant some of the programs I hoped to conquer were being abandoned wholesale by listeners who were readily adapting to the newer medium of television. The radio networks were, sometimes reluctantly, reducing their programming to permit local affiliates to sell time more profitably nearer home. But in the summer of 1955, I simply couldn't know that — nor that before I could collect a college diploma in mass communications and the performing arts, my window of opportunity would be shut forever. The first medium to simultaneously entertain and inform millions of Americans wouldn't be broadcasting any drama when I was ready for it. I'd find myself searching for another career.

Journalism, which I ultimately selected, provided some rewarding challenges. At the same time, it never substituted for my lifelong love affair with radio. An emotional link with "furniture that talks," as Titus Moody once defined radio, was implanted in me early. Although I couldn't appreciate its value at the age of four or five, I observed my parents as they roared with laughter over the antics of Fred Allen, Jack Benny, Edgar Bergen, Red Skelton and Fibber McGee and Molly. Only someone who reacted similarly could appreciate my growing fondness for that large mahogany box filled with audio delights.

In time, I performed as an announcer, sometimes alone and sometimes before small groups in "pretend" shows that I wrote. I corralled friends into taking parts in my productions. As I grew a little older, my extracurricular pursuits came to the attention of my

teachers, and I found myself writing radio plays — adaptations for *The Lux Radio Theater,
The FBI in Peace and War* and *Mr. Keen, Tracer of Lost Persons* were three — which my class-
mates performed as in-school productions.

For me, the serials were shrouded in some aura of mystique, so much so that I didn't
tune in to them during my early years. My mother called them "silly," yet she could name
virtually all of them and their major characters. I wondered if she didn't hear some of them
on the sly, and she admitted that she had listened regularly before I was born. It was only
when I hit ten or eleven that her secret came out: She tuned to *Wendy Warren and the News*
every day while preparing lunch, ostensibly to "catch the news." But I quickly discerned
that she never turned the radio off when Douglas Edwards was finished delivering the headlines. Instead, she was dropping the names of Wendy, Mark, Gil and Anton into conversations now and then. That broke the ice; I, too, became an addict to those intriguing plots
about scurrilous anti-government enemies.

That was only the beginning. I soon began tuning in during the late afternoons to
some of the dramas on NBC (*Stella Dallas, Young Widder Brown* and *Front Page Farrell*). In
the summers and on infrequent days I was home ill from school I could catch *Our Gal Sunday, Perry Mason* and *This Is Nora Drake* on CBS. One summer I had an afternoon newspaper delivery route. Homes weren't air conditioned then, and most women were still at
home. I rode my bike from house to house throwing my papers on porches while picking
up almost every word of *Backstage Wife* as it filtered through open windows. To say I was
affected by all that exposure to daytime drama would be an understatement! Can you see
why I wanted to invest my life in it?

After the Golden Age of radio (roughly 1930–1960) ended, I began to seriously collect materials from the era. Over the years I acquired an extensive library of recordings,
tapes, books, autographs, correspondence, photographs and other memorabilia. One item I
doggedly sought was a collection of factual information flavored with anecdotes and
obscure details about the daytime serials that had been missed by other authors, or hadn't
surfaced all in one place. I wanted some glimpses into the lives of favorite performers
beyond single shows. And I wanted some perspectives on how those dramas they appeared
in made it to the airwaves. Such information, I felt, would be fascinating to many who had
come under radio's spell, particularly those who were drawn to daytime
programming.

As the years rolled by I ascertained that no such work had come on the market. It
occurred to me that it might be up to me to write such a book as a service to present and
future radio enthusiasts. This volume is my attempt to scratch my long-standing itch to
make some kind of contribution to the radio field. With apologies to an advertising copywriter for a popular brand of syrup, I'm asking myself: "Mr. Cox, why did you wait so
long?"

The passionate fan of the Golden Age who included weekday programming as part of
a steady listening habit may have acquired a particular favorite among the serials. I hope
that fan will find that favorite in this collection. Thirty-one of some 200 dishpan dramas
have been selected for examination in these pages. If your preference was omitted, I hope
you'll understand that my choices were limited by the dictates of space. In making them, I
followed a simple formula.

Programs with very long runs on the air were obvious choices for inclusion, but longevity was not the sole criterion. A serial must also have established a distinction unique to itself; or it must have significantly influenced the genre; or it must have gained a strong and decidedly loyal following. Some of the serials could boast a combination of those factors. I believe all of the prominent serials appear. Others, which were not assigned separate chapters, are mentioned in the text and also noted in Appendix B. A look at the Table of Contents will reveal whether your particular favorite is included.

Just who was tuning in to these dramas? Well, in the middle of radio's Golden Age, researcher Herta Herzog found that the average serial listener was between 18 and 35 years old, female, middle-class and high school educated and lived in a rural setting. She preferred activities at home over amusements outside her home. Surprisingly, studies made nearly two decades later turned up comparable data, so the audience didn't shift a lot.[1]

In 1948 an estimated 20 million listeners were tuning in the soap operas on a regular basis. The typical daily quarter-hour episode cost $3,600 to produce. Of that amount, $600 went to talent, $540 (15 percent) to the advertising agency producing the show and the remaining $2,460 for network time. In all, sponsors were spending nearly $35 million annually on the daytime serials.[2]

I've attempted to give you some idea of the numbers who were listening to these dramas each day. The audience figures cited in each chapter refer to the practices of determining a program's popularity, which profoundly affected the sale of a serial's advertising time. For many years these figures were provided by the firm of C. E. Hooper, Inc., which kept tabs on the audience response to radio shows using a method known as "coincidental ratings." Hooper made random telephone calls to people living in 36 metropolitan areas. Respondents were asked to name any program they were listening to at the time of the phone call. The sampling resulted in an estimate of audience size for a given program. Unfortunately, its scope disenfranchised people living in rural communities and smaller and medium-sized towns.

A "Hooperating" of 6.2 for a drama meant that out of every 100 telephone calls placed, 6.2 respondents said they were listening to that specific program at that time. (A rating of 100 would have been impossible, incidentally, for it would have meant that radios in all households were on and tuned to a single show. At no time was every set on simultaneously.) A "share" of the total audience was determined by dividing a program's rating by all the sets then in use. A daytime show with a respectable rating of at least 5.0 (which was generally high enough to keep a drama on the air) might net an audience "share" of 22 percent or higher.

When the A. C. Nielsen Company began producing radio audience estimates in the 1940s, it embarked on a different method. Nielsen outfitted thousands of households with audiometers, an electronic device intended to offer a more accurate picture of what Americans were hearing. Using paper tape, the audiometer continuously printed out records of every moment a radio was turned on, graphically depicting the station to which the radio was tuned. The numbers obtained often turned out to be similar to those that the Hooper firm had gained with its method. (In later years Nielsen purchased Hooper, and the firms' efforts were combined to measure the nation's television-viewing habits.)

The discerning reader should note that the ratings in this treatise are based on *estimates* derived from such sampling and are never absolute measurements. The figures reflect what Americans were listening to in the daytime during the winter months (usually mid to late January each year). Ratings may have been a little higher then than in the warmer months, for people spent more time indoors in winter and were entertained more often by their radios. (The transistor set had not yet arrived, and portability was generally limited to vehicles that had radios installed, an option that was out of reach for many.) Although this is a rather protracted explanation, it is offered to help the reader understand the audience-measurement data that appears in these pages.

Another point that might be confusing to the novice is the naming of the networks. From its earliest days the National Broadcasting Company (NBC) owned two radio networks. They were easily illustrated on a U.S. map by red or blue lines that connected affiliates. The dual systems thus became commonly known as the Red and Blue networks. In the early 1940s the Federal Communications Commission ruled, primarily for competitive reasons, that networks could not be jointly owned. The requirement forced NBC to sell one of its webs. It kept the Red network, which from that time forward was known simply as NBC. The Blue network was renamed the American Broadcasting Company (ABC). You will find references to NBC (properly interpreted as the Red network), NBC Blue, the Columbia Broadcasting System (CBS), the Mutual Broadcasting System (MBS) and finally ABC.

If some of your favorite performers are missing from the text, some of mine are too. Again, there was no way to do justice to all who merited recognition. In determining who was featured in the 158 brief profiles included, I chose actors who played the roles of series heroes and heroines. Occasionally I was able to enlarge the scope to add some of the more prominent announcers and authors. Once in a while a series had more "equals" than individual "stars" (e.g., *One Man's Family*), requiring biographical data on several cast members. I wish there had been space for more of them.

Nearly all of these actors and actresses played in more than one show. In most cases an artist's biography appears in the chapter discussing his or her most prominent role. (Those who played leads in several series sometimes made this difficult!) If you need help locating a biography, check the index.

I make no claim of infallibility. Every human effort has been made to produce correct data and avoid perpetuating falsehoods that sometimes creep into print to be repeated by others. Still, the discerning reader may discover an inconsistency here and there. I have relied on some sources that occasionally conflicted with others. If I found obvious errors or questionable statements, I examined multiple sources. Accounts proving to be unreliable were simply discarded.

Most of the people who were directly associated with these dramas are no longer with us. The passing of time has left others with fuzzy memories. Be assured that any mistakes you find are mine alone and are of the head and not the heart. The possibility of error weighs on me heavily, and I beg your indulgence.

I agree with the scholars who identify *Painted Dreams* as the first daytime serial. I'm also convinced that we do a disservice if we disregard the contributions of a handful of earlier shows that displayed serial-like qualities. In his wonderfully insightful volume *The Serials: Suspense and Drama by Installment*, Ray Stedman leads readers through a discussion of the soap opera's ancestral tree. In the 1920s several Chicago stations offered listeners programs that, though not branches of the tree, could be called the seedlings from which that timber surely sprang.

Sam 'n' Henry, first appearing on WGN on January 12, 1926, may be the precursor of the genre. It was a humorous portrayal of the southern black who had moved North and was played by a couple of white actors from the South. The pair, Freeman Gosden and Charles Correll, were to entertain the nation for four decades. The following year WENR premiered *The Smith Family*, an open-ended family drama that was presented one night weekly. It featured Jim and Marion Jordan, whose names would also become household words a little later as *Fibber McGee and Molly*. Their first radio effort was labeled the "great-granddaddy of soap operas" by radio historian Francis Chase, Jr.

By 1928 *Sam 'n' Henry* had vanished, the result of a dispute between actors and station owners. But those characters appeared that same year under new names, *Amos 'n' Andy*, at competitor station WMAQ. From those humble origins, Gosden and Correll would command the largest audiences in radio's fledgling history — so much so that theaters would halt their films for fifteen minutes nightly to air the enormously popular duo's capers.

In late 1929 in New York, also at night, a folksy ethnic drama made its appearance on WJZ. It was called *The Rise of the Goldbergs*. Another seven years would pass before *The Goldbergs* (as it was retitled) would transfer to a daytime network lineup.

Then there was *Clara, Lu 'n' Em*, a comic dialogue among three women. This initially appeared on WGN in June 1930 as a nighttime feature. The series was soon picked up by NBC Blue for airing to a national evening audience. An important precedent was set on February 15, 1932, when the network transferred the show to the morning hours. Without notoriety the drama became, indisputably, the first *network* daytime serial. A potent trend was chartered!

In addition *Moonshine and Honeysuckle*, a half-hour, continuing tale featuring the earthy colloquialisms of southern mountaineers, premiered on NBC's Sunday afternoon lineup in 1930.

Each of these shows was a forerunner of coming attractions.

By the time the daily episodes of *Painted Dreams* arrived in October 1930, the groundwork had been laid to the far reaches of those giant broadcasting towers in the Windy City and the Big Apple for daytime programming that included continuing action. These shows took critical initial steps toward what would become soap opera. In doing so, they discovered vast audiences just waiting to be entertained on the installment plan.

James Thurber's definition of the genre, issued in the late 1940s, seemed inspired: "A soap opera is a kind of sandwich, whose recipe is simple enough, although it took years to compound. Between thick slices of advertising, spread twelve minutes of dialogue, add predicament, villainy, and female suffering in equal measure, throw in a dash of nobility, sprinkle with tears, season with organ music, cover with a rich announcer sauce, and serve five times a week."[3]

In 1967 Jim Harmon recalled his love affair with radio: "How many times did I make my cold last longer so I could stay home to follow kindly old Ma Perkins' courtroom trial for mass murder? Radio listening was as much a part of life as running water, runny noses, and recesses. How could you do without it?"[4]

I confess, I wouldn't know. It was an obsession for me. The reader who shares that fond remembrance will return to the pages of yesteryear in the chapters to follow and relive the great radio serials once again. I invite you to join me in celebrating the heroes and heroines who brought to our lives daily visits with pathos, pain, anxiety, encouragement, mayhem, jealousy, rage, humor, love, dissension and discord. Were I asked to typify the genre in a single word, however, I wouldn't hesitate for a moment to offer this answer: *joy*!

> *Ah! happy years! once more who would not be a boy!*
> — Lord Byron, *Childe Harold's Pilgrimage*

1
Aunt Jenny's Real Life Stories

(The Ultimate Conclusion)

The format for this soap opera assumed a closed-end story line, a feature shared by few other serials that were considered successes. The number of thriving daytime dramas with terminating story lines could be counted on the fingers of one hand. Ongoing series — with central characters whose lives were affected by other figures — were prolific and usually attracted far more fans. But *Aunt Jenny* proved there was an audience for drama dispensed in only five chapters. For nearly two decades the show confounded the odds, drawing one of daytime radio's biggest audiences and becoming the most successful drama of its kind. The series typically focused on romantic tales involving citizens of the rural community of Littleton. As narrator, Aunt Jenny provided a link between the daily installments and the weekly story changes. In her perky kitchen — where she baked warm delicacies from the recipes of the longtime sponsor, Spry — she spun yarns while interacting with announcer Dan Seymour and other townsfolk. The stories themselves were little more than vignettes, of course, when compared with other soap operas. But they were intriguing to serial lovers with short attention spans and to those whose schedules wouldn't permit their involvement in serials with continuing plots.

Producers: Ruthrauff and Ryan advertising agency
Directors: Ralph Berkey, John W. Loveton, Bill Steel, Robert S. Steele, Thomas F. Vietor Jr., Tony Wilson
Writers: Eleanor Abbey, Carl Alfred Buss, David Davidson, Edwin Halloran, Doris Halman, Lawrence Klee, Eleanor Lenz, Douglas McLean, Elizabeth McLean, Bill Sweets
Music: Elsie Thompson
Sound Effects: Jim Dwan, Harold Forry
Announcers: Dan Seymour, others unidentified
Aunt Jenny: Edith Spencer (1937–51), Agnes Young (1951–56)
Others: Peggy Allenby, Alfred Corn, Toni Darnay, Virginia Dwyer, Maurice Franklin, Franc Hale, Ed Jerome, Nancy Kelly, Ed MacDonald, Eddie O'Brien, Ann Pitoniak, Helen Shields, Ruth Yorke, more

Theme: "Believe Me, If All Those Endearing Young Charms"

Sponsors: Ruthrauff and Ryan, which became one of the most successful ad agencies in producing radio serials, packaged this show for Lever Brothers Co. specifically as a vehicle to promote Spry shortening. Lever underwrote the series for more than 18 years (Jan. 18, 1937–March 18, 1955). The firm dropped sponsorship for awhile in 1955, then picked up partial sponsorship for the remaining 10-plus months the program was on the air (Jan. 2–Nov. 16, 1956). Commercials during that final interval (Jan. 2–March 30, 1956) were shared with Campbell Soup Co. Despite the brief commercial interruption, *Aunt Jenny* was so strongly identified with Spry that many fans may later have argued there was never a time the product *wasn't* advertised. The durable program-sponsor association was one of the most effective in daytime radio marketing.

Ratings: In the 1949–50 season *Aunt Jenny's Real Life Stories* placed a tenth of a point behind third-place *Wendy Warren and the News*, which immediately preceded it on CBS. (Numbers 1 and 2 were CBS features *The Romance of Helen Trent*, which followed *Aunt Jenny*, and the morning variety series *Arthur Godfrey Time*.) The ultimate conclusion formula, applied to a midday audience, with a strong lead-in (*Warren*) and an even stronger show following it (*Trent*), worked well for *Aunt Jenny*. Ratings exceeded 6.0 in 13 of the 20 seasons it was on the air. The numbers topped 7.0 during four of those years. Its lowest figure, 3.7, occurred in 1955–56 after losing its long-held lunchtime quarter-hour.

On the Air: Jan. 18, 1937–July 2, 1937, CBS, 1:45 p.m. ET; July 5, 1937–June 21, 1946, CBS, 11:45 a.m.; June 24, 1946–July 1, 1955, CBS, 12:15 p.m.; Jan. 2, 1956–Nov. 16, 1956, CBS, 2:45 p.m.

In *Aunt Jenny's Real Life Stories*, we were given an on-air cast of only five "regulars," three of whose names weren't revealed on the air:
  • A sound effects specialist (Jim Dwan or Harold Forry)
  • A whistling canary (wildlife imitator Henry Boyd)
  • The customary musician (organist Elsie Thompson, who played the theme "Believe Me, If All Those Endearing Young Charms" at the start and close of each broadcast and the bridge music between scenes)
  • The obligatory announcer (a job held for most of those years by Dan Seymour, who interacted daily with the show's host, especially when commercial time arrived)
  • A storyteller (Aunt Jenny herself, a genteel, soft-spoken matron played initially by Edith Spencer, then by Agnes Young)
The show's premise was that homespun philosopher Aunt Jenny, who lived in the small mythical village of Littleton, would spin engaging yarns via a closed-end soap opera. Situated in her cheery, homey kitchen, she would invite listeners and passersby to join her daily for another installment of a five-part tale that would be completed by the week's end.

Helping her launch a new tangent, friends and neighbors wandered into her kitchen, pausing to share some obsessive grief from their troubled lives. By any calculation, in

Edith Spencer originated the role of Aunt Jenny in 1937 and carried it until illness forced her retirement in 1951. Each day she whipped up a delicacy in her kitchen with the sponsor's product while spinning yarns about incidents in the lives of citizens in the mythical hamlet of Littleton. (Photofest)

nearly two decades Aunt Jenny's faithful listeners must have heard exposés of every citizen in the minuscule hamlet of Littleton many times over.

For 15 minutes each day over the background din of a boiling teakettle, frying skillet or whistling canary, Aunt Jenny would narrate a chapter of the current week's drama. Then she furnished cooking hints unabashedly tied to her sponsor, Spry, a top-selling shortening. While delivering the pitch about the sponsor's product, she was aided and abetted by "Danny" (announcer Seymour), whose most frequent and familiar line across those years was "For all you bake and fry, rely on Spry!" He sprinkled conversations with the line liberally. Finally, Aunt Jenny would offer listeners a piece of positive philosophy at the close of every weekday session.

The show was affectionately known by several different appellations over its long tenure. The shortened version, *Aunt Jenny*, was the most popular and widely accepted. Yet for perhaps half the life of the series its proper designation was *Aunt Jenny's True Life Stories*. Sometime around the late 1940s this moniker was altered slightly to *Aunt Jenny's Real Life Stories*. And in Canada, where the program was also aired, listeners knew it by the name *Aunt Lucy*.

The program's format, using a closed-end story line, wasn't shared by very many other successful soap operas. Several had tried similar tactics but had met swift and dismal ends. To be certain that all of us are working from the same page, it is probably wise to define and differentiate between open- and closed-end dramas before proceeding.

Open-ended serials, including the vast majority of all soap operas, carried story lines that extended indefinitely. When, for instance, *Stella Dallas* displaced an ugly maverick who attempted to rain on her daughter Laurel's parade, another just as vile villain would be waiting in the wings for a turn at dispelling "Lolly-Baby's" happiness. It was, as announcer Frank Gallop assured listeners, "a *continuation* on the air of the true-to-life story of mother love and sacrifice." So it was with the preponderance of *Stella Dallas'* peers — ongoing tales that could never be quite finished, except, of course, when the networks canceled them and the loose ends had to be hastily tied together.

On the other hand, the closed-end type of serial, sometimes called the ultimate conclusion drama, did have sporadic final climaxes at appropriate intervals. And though both open- and closed-end forms are referred to in the present chapter, the primary emphasis is on the handful of soap operas that neatly fit into the latter category.

In the late 1930s, a period of accelerated radio serial growth, some modest attempts were made to vary already established soap opera patterns. Among them was to add mysteries with continuing story lines, series plots that evolved from the Bible and a few fictionalized narratives that actually came to an end. Although no permanent new trends resulted, a refreshing measure of diversity and creativity was injected into daytime drama. A brief history should put this in perspective.

An intriguing 1940 dramatic series introduced radio audiences to acclaimed novels like *Of Human Bondage, Jane Eyre, My Man Godfrey* and *Wuthering Heights.* Called *Wheatena Playhouse* for a leading breakfast cereal of the day (its sponsor), this transcribed experiment enjoyed moderate success for a couple of seasons.

Not to be outdone, however, within a year General Mills, a prominent Wheatena competitor, offered a similar program of literary works titled *Stories America Loves.* Yet by 1942 a single project offering, "Kitty Foyle," garnered such interest that its producers decided to drop the rotational story concept. *Kitty Foyle* was carried as a soap opera with a continuing story line.

General Mills wasn't as successful with its 1941 offering, *The Mystery Man.* This series aired reenactments of well-known suspense novels. By 1942 the show left the air, the victim of mediocre ratings.

A year earlier one of *Aunt Jenny's* contemporaries in an ultimate conclusion format, *By Kathleen Norris,* met a similar fate. Two shows that attempted to put mystery on the daytime agenda, *Follow the Moon* (1937) and *Thunder Over Paradise* (1939), abruptly bit the dust too. By then, death in the afternoon was commonplace among serials that ventured away from traditionally accepted formulas.

By 1959, the final full calendar year of the radio soap opera, one radio historiographer observed that 35 percent of the open-ended serials commercially underwritten for radio and television remained on the air five or more years. But of those serials featuring an ultimate conclusion format, only 11 percent (two serials) were still aired five years later. This duo, *The Light of the World* and *Aunt Jenny's Real Life Stories,* had favorable qualities working for them. More about them shortly.

A few words are probably in order regarding the continuing series *Front Page Farrell*. Though its peculiar variation is addressed in its own chapter, it should be included in any serious discussion of open- and closed-end dramas. *Farrell* may not have been labeled a true closed-end drama (it isn't included in the tally reported above, for instance), yet in its later years the program became an ultimate conclusion serial. During the 1950s the show successfully evolved into a five-chapter crime series — murder on Monday, solution on Friday. Thus, it turned into a prime example of a thriving closed-end serial, albeit late in the run.

The Light of the World, which aired throughout the 1940s, was based upon the Holy Scriptures. For obvious reasons its sequences always came to an end. Actors played Old Testament figures while biblical accounts were reenacted through daily episodes. Because millions in the audience were already familiar with the narratives, most listeners could readily adapt to the characters and plots on this show.

Yet *Aunt Jenny's True Life Stories*, introduced on January 18, 1937, easily became the most successful of all the closed-end ventures. The series lasted until November 16, 1956, and employed a continuing narrator to bridge the gaps between changing story lines. The device singularly offered listeners a sense of continuity, whether real or imagined.

The program provided an outlet for fans whose situations dictated shortened attention spans by choice or by circumstance — over a brief vacation period, illness or other confinement, job layoff, rotating shifts in work schedules, etc. Such listeners often found a story they could follow in its entirety. Another advantage the series enjoyed was that it aired during much of the nation's lunch hour, undoubtedly increasing its audience size.

In 1950 the show carried a feature about the benevolence of a wife who endangered her own health to reach her husband's goals of financial security. She labored incessantly in the family business, failing to disclose to her mate the gravity of her illness. In the end her silence nearly cost her her life. Fortunately, her husband learned the truth in time. She recovered, they prospered and the couple presumably went on living normal lives.

The following year another Littleton couple desperately sought adoption when they were informed they couldn't have a biological child. At last the pair came upon the "right" little boy, with whom they quickly fell in love. But they were dismayed to learn that the boy had a sister from whom he was not to be separated. The young couple, convinced they could afford only one child, faced an awful dilemma. Their story found a happy solution too, when a method of caring for both children surfaced in a surprise conclusion.

Popular recording and radio singer Lanny Ross arrived in Littleton in 1946 to guest star in a production of the operetta "Naughty Marietta." He also stepped into the middle of an aspiring actress's love trial. The girl had been offered a radio audition in New York. Yet her heart was clearly in Littleton with a local stagehand who was pulling for her success in New York. Lanny got the pair together, telling the young man to ask the would-be actress: "What do you want more than anything in the world?" When the stagehand popped that question, the girl admitted it was to stay in Littleton and marry him. Lanny signed off the week's final episode singing "Ah, sweet mystery of life, at last I've found you" to thunderous applause from the operetta's audience.

Then there was the story, in 1939, of the girl who couldn't get over her lost love. Her honey had flown to South America, his plane had crashed and parts of his plane had been recovered from the sea. A year later, she followed her mind but not her heart. Proposed to by another young man, she accepted, still pining for the other guy. Three months after their wedding a cable arrived, telling her that the love of her life was on his way home. Although she didn't want her husband to suffer, she claimed she loved the other man "more than life itself." How could these three possibly live happily ever after? Listeners couldn't turn it loose until the week's exciting climax found a way to make that possible.

In 1952, when a 16-year-old girl and a 19-year-old boy fell in love, the girl's mother did everything she could to break them up. Recalling a similar situation from her own youth that had strong negative impact, the mother took drastic measures to prevent such heartache for her daughter. Before the week ended, however, she had come to terms with the fact that the young man her daughter was seeing was totally unlike the man who had brought her so much grief years before.

And on and on the yarns were spun.

Aunt Jenny's Real Life Stories gave particular attention to battle-related subjects during World War II. On one broadcast Mrs. Franklin D. Roosevelt, wife of the president, visited in *Aunt Jenny's* kitchen. Speaking on behalf of the national military effort, she appealed to American women to unite behind the troops. On another day WAVES Commander Mildred H. McAyer did the same thing. During the conflict, death in military action was included in some of *Aunt Jenny's* dramatizations. This helped the series remain in touch with reality, critics felt.

By its very design, this serial had the distinct advantage of providing opportunities for work for scores of actors and writers. It also offered exposure for new talent. In general, new casts were assembled every week, although some individuals were called fairly often.

The part of Aunt Jenny was initiated by Edith Spencer, whose resume listed no distinguishing radio credits when she began the role. The actress made an early and distinct impression on future soap opera queen Mary Jane Higby (*When a Girl Marries*). On one of Higby's first days in New York, she observed Spencer at the CBS lunch counter. Higby had arrived in "Gotham" in the late 1930s with one mission in mind—to become a serial heroine. Aunt Jenny, she recalled, was dressed in mink-topped galoshes, hat, muff and coat on the very first chilly day of fall. "Come hell or high water," Higby wrote years later in her autobiography, "I intended to join that furry line-up at the lunch counter!"

Only an unexplained, debilitating illness forced Spencer to eventually relinquish her role as Aunt Jenny. The part was awarded in 1951 to Agnes Young, who carried it to the end of the run. Young had enjoyed recurring roles in several series—*Meet Me in St. Louis, Mrs. Wiggs of the Cabbage Patch, Mother o' Mine, My Son and I, Snow Village* and *Young Widder Brown*. She also appeared in the acting company for *The March of Time Quiz*. In 1972–73 she would have a bit part in television's *The Guiding Light*.

Dan Seymour, the gregarious announcer who was readily available to taste anything cooking in Aunt Jenny's kitchen, was a veteran of numerous radio series. As narrator for the infamous October 30, 1938, broadcast of the "War of the Worlds" on Orson Welles' *Mercury Theatre on the Air*, he probably worked the single best-remembered radio program ever broadcast. He also announced for *Bobby Benson and the B-Bar-B Riders, Bulldog Drummond, Dick Tracy, Tommy Riggs and Betty Lou, The Aldrich Family, The Henry Morgan Show, Mystery Theater, Young Man with a Band, Major Bowes and His Original Amateur Hour* and more.

Seymour hosted the quiz show *Sing It Again* and the human-interest anthology *We, the People* (the latter show also appeared as a nighttime series on NBC-TV in 1950–52). For three months in 1952–53 he was host of a CBS-TV Tuesday/Thursday daytime half-hour talk show, *Everywhere I Go*. He received large amounts of fan mail from women who, hearing him on radio, claimed he sounded like "the perfect American male."

Born on February 22, 1915, in New York, Seymour graduated from Amherst College in 1935. Entering radio as a staff announcer at a Boston station, within a year Seymour joined CBS in a similar capacity. By his 30th birthday, insiders said his salary topped $100,000.

An entrepreneurial spirit led him to drift from the microphone into production, supervising a wartime series, *Now It Can Be Told*, and later *We, the People*. Seymour claimed never to like being a performer: "The process of simply reading lines became a bore. I became fascinated with the whole business of mass communication and mass persuasion." In the early 1950s he supervised television programming for the Young & Rubicam advertising agency. He joined a rival agency, J. Walter Thompson, in 1955, heading its radio-TV work. Within nine years he was president and chairman of the firm's executive committee. That allowed him to heavily influence both advertising and programming on the tube. The announcer-turned-marketer died on July 27, 1982, in New York City.

Lever Brothers Co., the makers of Spry, underwrote *Aunt Jenny's Real Life Stories* for more than 18 years. Narrating her stories in the setting of her inviting kitchen was a natural extension of the sponsor's product. In a typical commercial on October 17, 1946, Aunt Jenny shared the secret of broiling fish fillets "so they have such a grand flavor." Brush them with lemon juice, then melted Spry, and broil to a golden brown, she advised.

Petunia, Aunt Jenny's domestic helper who was in the kitchen that day, commented: "Ummm-ummm, that sure do sound good, Aunt Jenny." (It was an era, the reader will recall, when minorities weren't treated with the dignity, respect and equality they deserved.)

In the same commercial, Petunia cited a problem many companies like Lever Brothers and their competitors were facing during the war and postwar years. "Lawsy, sure is disappointin' when you can't git Spry," she complained.

Danny rushed to the rescue: "Both your grocer and the Spry folks have a world shortage to reckon with, as well as an ever-increasing demand for Spry. So if you can't get it the first time you ask, keep Spry on your marketing list until you do get it."

He concluded the commercial with that familiar Seymourism: "For all you bake and fry, rely on Spry!"

When Fred, the mailman, arrived in Aunt Jenny's kitchen on September 21, 1939, he was weighed down with a heavy load of letters from thousands of her admirers. It gave Aunt Jenny and Danny yet another chance to talk about a current premium offer soon set to expire. For one Spry disc off the can label and ten cents in coin, Aunt Jenny would mail her latest recipe book coupled with six flavors of frosting tints. Danny proclaimed that the book included two-crust pies, one-crust pies, deep-dish pies, apple fritters, baked apple dumplings, Dutch apple cake and many more kitchen delights that listeners couldn't afford to miss. And for his burden, postman Fred got a slice of apple crumb cake that Aunt Jenny had baked only that morning. (If listeners kept track, they may have wondered who was eating all that stuff she baked every day for she seemed to have no family nearby to share it with. After all, the parish bazaars could accommodate only so much, no matter how worthy her delicacies!)

At the end of every show, Aunt Jenny offered her "golden thought for today," a quotation or succinct piece of advice to listeners, such as: "Our Creator would never have made such lovely days and have given us the deep hearts to enjoy them above and beyond all thoughts unless we were meant to be immortal."

The radio comedians Bob Elliott and Ray Goulding ("Bob and Ray"), whose improvisations endeared them to millions on network radio, developed sundry routines based on "Aunt Penny's Sunlit Kitchen." In the spoof sketches, "Aunt Penny" philosophized and told a tale while announcer Danny visited her kitchen, mostly to eat.

In one, Danny was introducing Aunt Penny when she urged him to "cut it short" because he had talked so much on the previous show she "couldn't finish my story." He told her he'd merely like a handful of cookies. She chastised: "Well take 'em Danny, and dry up!"

In another, Aunt Penny informed Danny that the raisin cookies she had just baked in chicken fat were completely digestible. "If it's in chicken fat, it's saturated with fat!" she declared.

What advantages and characteristics of the ultimate conclusion drama distinguished it from open-ended serials? Several can be cited.

• Action was in short doses, appealing to those favoring its style or those whose situations precluded their immersion into open-ended story lines.

• Listeners intimately identified with the storyteller, offering a consistent technique despite the fact that the stories changed after every fifth broadcast day.

• Ratings remained high, at least during the run of this series. Airing it at midday was probably an enhancing factor.

• The rotational format gave many more professionals an opportunity to participate in working on the show — both in the cast and behind the scenes.

It might all have been done better, of course. But why tamper with success? *Aunt Jenny's Real Life Stories* was unlike anything else in radio. And for 20 years, it proved its time had come.

2
Backstage Wife
(The Perfectly Named Serial Heroine)

One of numerous success stories of the prolific serial creators Frank and Anne Hummert, *Backstage Wife* ultimately made the rounds of all four networks. The series embodied a Hummert motif: taking a fragile but persistent heroine of humble origin, wedding her into status, prosperity or both, then delivering her into contemptible situations in which she must fend off an endless procession of demented females hell-bent on capturing her mate for themselves — at the risk of bodily injury to her. Mary Noble, an office clerk from the Midwest, married notoriety in Broadway matinee idol Larry Noble, "dream sweetheart of a million other women." For 23 years she fought bravely, defending her happiness against a perpetual parade of resolute damsels. And in the meantime, a mélange of unbalanced men was just as committed to separating the Nobles for their own trysts with Mary. After two decades — retaining a single NBC quarter-hour for 17 consecutive seasons — that network gave *Wife* the boot. But because the drama sustained such a strong following, CBS extended its life an additional three years.

Producers: Frank and Anne Hummert
Directors: Lou Jacobson, Richard Leonard, Joe Mansfield, DeWitt McBride, Les Mitchel, Blair Walliser, Fred Weihe
Writers: Robert Hardy Andrews, Marie Baumer, Ruth Borden, Ned Calmer, Doris Halman, Lawrence Hammond, Anne Hummert, Frank Hummert, Phil Thorne, Elizabeth Todd
Music: Chet Kingsbury
Sound Effects: Frank Blatter, Michael Eisenmenger, Chet Hill, Tom Horan, John Katulik, Bob Graham
Announcers: Edward Allen, Pierre Andre, Sandy Becker, Ford Bond, Bob Brown, Harry Clark, Stuart Dawson, Roger Krupp
Mary Noble: Vivian Fridell (1935–45), Claire Niesen (1945–59)
Larry Noble: Ken Griffin (1935–45), James Meighan (1945–51), Guy Sorel (1951–59)
Larry Noble, Jr.: Wilda Hinkel (child impersonator)
Maude Marlowe: Henrietta Tedro, Ethel Wilson
Tom Bryson: Frank Dane, Mandel Kramer, Charles Webster
Others: Charme Allen, Hoyt Allen, George Ansell, Anita Anton, Luise Barclay, Anne Burr, Helen Claire, Donna Creade, Leo Curley, Joseph Curtin, Susan Douglas, Patricia Dunlap,

Virginia Dwyer, Louise Fitch, Dorothy Francis, Don Gallagher, Maxine Gardenas, Norman Gottschalk, Joyce Hayward, Rod Hendrickson, Gail Henshaw, John M. James, Ginger Jones, Carlton KaDell, Bonita Kay, Charlotte Keane, Eloise Kummer, John Larkin, Paul Luther, Ken Lynch, Alan MacAteer, Charlotte Manson, Sherman Marks, Bess McCammon, John McGovern, Malcolm Meecham, Marvin Miller, George Niese, Ethel Owen, Eileen Palmer, George Petrie, Kay Renwick, Bartlett Robinson, Elmira Roessler, Dorothy Sands, Betty Ruth Smith, Dan Sutter, George Tiplady, Phil Truex, Vicki Vola, Andree Wallace, Lesley Woods, more

Theme: "Stay as Sweet as You Are"; "The Rose of Tralee"

Sponsors: From its inception, Blackett-Sample-Hummert governed for Sterling Drugs, a conglomerate that sponsored all of NBC's serials in the four o'clock ET hour (*Backstage Wife, Stella Dallas, Lorenzo Jones* and *Young Widder Brown*) into the early 1950s. Among Sterling's brand names were Astring-O-Sol mouthwash, Bayer aspirin, Campho-Phenique canker sore medication, Double Danderine shampoo, Energine cleaning fluid and Energine Shoe-White polish, Fletcher's Castoria laxative, Haley's M-O mineral emulsion oil laxative, Ironized Yeast vitamin supplement tablets, Lyons' toothpaste and Dr. Lyons' tooth powder, Mulsified Coconut Oil shampoo, Phillips' Milk of Magnesia laxative, antacid tablets, toothpaste, tooth powder and face creams, ZBT baby powder, and other remedies. When Sterling bowed out on June 8, 1951, Procter & Gamble picked up *Backstage Wife* on June 11, 1951 (for Cheer detergent, Spic 'n' Span cleanser and other personal and household goods), carrying it to July 1, 1955, when the series left NBC. The show was sold to participating sponsors in the following years.

Ratings: The audience fell below 6.0 only three times in 17 seasons while airing at 4:00 p.m. (1941–42, 5.9; 1942–43, 5.9; 1954–55, 5.2). It achieved a median of 7.0 in those years (1938–55), earning its highest figure (9.6) in 1939–40.

On the Air: Aug. 5, 1935–Mar. 27, 1936, MBS, 9:45 a.m. ET; Mar. 30–June 26, 1936, NBC Blue, 4:15 p.m.; 1936–38, NBC Blue, 11:15 a.m.; 1938–July 1, 1955, NBC, 4:00 p.m.; July 4, 1955–Jan. 2, 1959, CBS, 12:15 p.m.

Now, we present once again, Backstage Wife, *the story of Mary Noble, a little Iowa girl who married one of America's most handsome actors, Larry Noble, matinee idol of a million other women — the story of what it means to be the wife of a famous star.*
— Epigraph to *Backstage Wife*

As "The Rose of Tralee" faded, Ford Bond, voted by listeners as the eighth "best announcer on radio" in the early 1940s, introduced the venerable *Backstage Wife* with its seemingly timeless message. Mary Noble, an ignoble stenographer from the sticks, met and married the man after whom 98 percent of American women lusted, so one historiographer of the genre conjectured.[1]

The serial was pure formulaic, offering one of the most widely celebrated themes of the Hummert tradition. The heroines of *Backstage Wife, Our Gal Sunday, Amanda of Honeymoon Hill, Lora Lawton, Kitty Foyle* and others of their ilk started out as simple nobodies. But when fortune smiled, each one married above her station in life. Their stories revolved around conflicts in making the adjustment to a world they had never known. It was one of the favorite premises of serial moguls Frank and Anne Hummert. And because the duo adopted it so frequently on shows that amassed impressive audiences, one can assume that the formula also appealed to the fans at home.

Mary Noble gained eminence by linking with America's heartthrob of the stage. It was apparent soon enough, however, that she would spend the rest of her days thwarting the advances of "a million other women" who unashamedly threw themselves at her man. Complicated plots hinted at unfaithfulness, jealousy and confusion on the part of both Nobles. But Larry needn't have worried: for Mary, there was but one man, and she would remain forever loyal to her wedding vows. This woman's gentleness of spirit and her supreme devotion to her mate earned her the appellation as "the perfectly named serial heroine."[2]

Backstage Wife sported a myriad of psychotics, many of them men, who simply coveted Mary. Whereas Helen Trent had to resist some perverted nuts, those targeting Mary Noble sometimes appeared in more immediate need of psychiatric help. They endangered her life, tossed acid in her face, drugged her and left her to die in desolate territories. Deceit, extortion and even homicide were her constant companions as the result of her obsessive pursuers.

Larry Noble, on the other hand, could be viewed from a perspective absolutely counter to Mary's. Although he erratically professed abiding love for Mary, he often was unable — or unwilling — to spurn the overtures of a succession of women who trailed him. He was no different, of course, from the men in other Hummert soap operas. He could be classified as a rather powerless boob, just as they were. Larry and his contemporaries proved that — on programs created specifically for homemakers — it didn't take rocket science to distinguish which gender was the superior one. On a Hummert soap opera, if a man wasn't ineffective (as Larry was), he was usually maladjusted, or perhaps both.

Not surprisingly, when Larry's best friend, Tom Bryson, wrote a play called "Blackout," what novice with minuscule acting experience tried out for the feminine lead, won it and earned unprecedented critical acclaim for it? Mary Noble, of course. It was soon obvious to everybody that her oaf of a mate couldn't match her abilities in his own profession! The serials were definitely "women's territory." Entering their domain usually meant playing by their rules. (So mortified was Mary over her unexpectedly favorable reviews — and her coincidental triumph over Larry — that she hastily beat a path to the wings. The self-effacing spouse remained a backstage wife from that day forward. How typical of a perfectly named heroine!)

Before continuing, it will be well to digress for the purpose of more fully introducing Frank and Anne Hummert. The pair unquestionably influenced radio soap opera more than anyone else associated with it, whether measured by sheer volume of their work or by the magnitude of their innovations. Their predominance across the decades of radio's Golden Age can be observed in almost every chapter of this text. Their powerful influence simply cannot be ignored. To comprehend their contributions, one must first become acquainted with the Hummerts themselves.

Born in St. Louis in 1882, Frank Hummert became a journalist for his hometown's *Post-Dispatch*. He later operated a writing school and finally focused his efforts in advertising. Joining the ad agency of Lord and Thomas in New York in 1920 as its $50,000-a-year chief copywriter, he coined dual slogans that granted him widespread recognition in the industry. Each captured the public's imagination: *Bonds or Bondage* touted liberty bonds in the World War I era; *The Skin You Love to Touch* originated for a soap manufacturer. The latter was a prelude to the phenomenal success he would earn from several clients who made soap. Hummert joined Chicago's Blackett and Sample advertising agency in 1927 and saw his name added to the firm's. Although he wasn't a partner and held no stock, he shared a percentage of the profits as creative genius and director of the production unit. He was once characterized physically as the "thin, unmuscular type, thoughtful, sensitive, quiet to the point of shyness."

Meanwhile the future Mrs. Hummert — Anne S. Ashenhurst — was a Goucher graduate. Married and the mother of a young son, John, she applied to Hummert for a job in 1930. Born in Baltimore in 1905, Ashenhurst had a journalistic background too, having reported for her native city's *Sun* and the Paris *Herald*. She had met her husband, John, also a reporter, while working for the latter paper. She was small and dressed neatly; like Hummert, she had an inventive mind. Hired as his assistant, ostensibly as office manager, she professed to know "what women wanted." What Anne Ashenhurst wanted for herself, it turned out, was Frank Hummert. The two were wed in 1935.

Frank Hummert said it was merely a lucky guess when, in 1931, it occurred to him that radio drama might be as appealing to housewives as serialized fiction. Such narratives had become popular in magazines and newspapers in the 1920s. To implement his notion, Hummert employed still another journalist, Charles Robert Douglas Hardy Andrews (one person!), who had authored serialized features for the *Chicago Daily News*. Andrews' first assignment for Blackett-Sample-Hummert was to write a radio serial called *The Stolen Husband*. Its plot was to be about (a) a handsome young businessman, (b) a voluptuous secretary, eager to advance her boss' career and (c) a dense but attractive wife who would learn too late that a man spending nights at the office with a gorgeous assistant could become preoccupied beyond his occupation.

The Stolen Husband couldn't be declared a phenomenal success, but it gave Hummert, Ashenhurst and Andrews invaluable insights. And in a short while it led to three extremely successful serials against which almost all others could be measured for a couple of decades: *Just Plain Bill* (1932–55), *The Romance of Helen Trent* and *Ma Perkins* (both 1933–60).

By the end of 1943 Hummert had withdrawn his services from the ad agency and he and Anne created Hummert Radio Productions. (They had previously produced serials under the name Air Features, Inc., and a subsidiary, Featured Artist Service, Inc., while being compensated by Blackett-Sample-Hummert.) In the first half-dozen years of radio soap opera, the couple significantly multiplied their assets, controlling virtually half of the serials broadcast. By 1938 they were buying one-eighth of all commercial radio time at $12 million annually. Soon the Hummerts would have 36 programs airing concurrently.

By every measure, Air Features (Hummert Radio Productions) was unique. From their spacious home in Greenwich, Connecticut, the Hummerts presided over their vast empire. To themselves alone credit was given for the concepts, plot lines and words uttered on the programs they produced. Below them, laboring dutifully, were a half-dozen editors, a score of writers and five dozen clerical workers. Their employees endured assembly-line methods autocratically run with sweatshop tactics and offering little tolerance to those who broke well-publicized codes. It was, in every sense, a soap opera factory.

Salaries became a major bone of contention among the Hummerts' underlings. Artists were paid about half of what they would have received for working on other serials. By 1938 scriptwriters earned only $25 for each 11-minute script. Actors on Hummert serials were then commonly paid $15 per show and $5–$6 dollars per hour of rehearsal. In that organization, rehearsal time was kept to an absolute minimum to reduce expenses. The Hummerts often achieved that by having their directors employ seasoned actors exclusively.

The Hummerts maintained that the salaries made the writers their employees but never their designers. Any scribe who challenged the system, adding his or her own name as creator of such material, would be seeking employment elsewhere. The pair dictated the outlines for each series, suggesting characterization and dialogue. Writers took the couple's ideas and created action and conversations to flesh out the scripts. As a precaution, to prevent dialoguers from becoming too identified with a given program, the Hummerts scuttled the line-up at random, moving writers from show to show. Scriptwriters were required to stay three weeks ahead at all times. Moreover, weeks of approved episodes sitting on a shelf for broadcast could be instantly jeopardized when Anne Hummert had a change of thought about a plot's direction. On a whim, such notions often sent writers scrambling to revise finished chapters while keeping three weeks ahead.

In true assembly-line tradition, the writers created some of the most hackneyed dialogue that was broadcast on the serials. Hummert programs were almost always sequence-plotted: a small band of permanent characters was harassed by figures brought into the plot for that sequence. As the sequence drew to a close at least eight weeks and, more likely, many months later, the crafty rabble-rousers were dispersed, only to be replaced by a new group of malefactors. On many of these shows there were two scenes daily: a "recap" from one or more previous episodes and a scene featuring new action. Such techniques were applied repeatedly in the Hummert factory. As a result, transferring writers from show to show could be accomplished rather smoothly.

Directors who worked for the Hummerts met inflexible guidelines too. Anything not in a script was forbidden, like overlapping speeches, background music or sounds not already approved. To the Hummerts, proper enunciation and clarity were of utmost importance. A basic requisite was that the listener must always be able to tell who was speaking and who was being addressed. To achieve this in a Hummert serial, characters had to call one another by name every few seconds so that there could never be any doubt about who was talking to whom.

Despite the dark picture already painted, working for the Hummerts had its attractive points too. For example Julie Stevens, heroine of one of the Hummerts' most durable soap operas, *The Romance of Helen Trent*, was unprepared for the menial salary figure that appeared on her contract when she originally signed for the part of Helen. The Hummerts' attorney, however, assured her that she would work on all their serials. That would translate into a banner income. She — and others who told about those days — attested that they found this to be true.

In addition, in the late 1940s, when a Communist scare swept the land, agencies, sponsors and networks panicked. Any writer or actor suspected of ties to leftist causes was suddenly blacklisted — out of work. Since overt accusations were seldom made, a defense was often impossible. But the Hummerts alone defied all of it. Going about their business as usual, they ignored the call to ferret out subversives and continued employing actors, directors and writers as if nothing was going on. If for no other reason than that one, they were revered above most other producers. Their open-mindedness brought unswerving allegiance from many in the industry, including Hummert employees and those who worked for others.

The Hummerts also infused soap opera with common sense, basic efficiency, advertising expertise and production competence. From them the genre gathered its purest and most durable traditions. Without them, much of the success it enjoyed might never have been realized.

A list of Hummert features is included below, although it may not be exhaustive. Numbers in parentheses indicate the year of each program's network debut.

American Album of Familiar Music (1931)	*Mr. Keen, Tracer of Lost Persons* (1937)
The Stolen Husband (1931)	*Second Husband* (1937)
Skippy (1931)	*Alias Jimmy Valentine* (1938)
Judy and Jane (1932)	*Valiant Lady* (1938)
Betty and Bob (1932)	*Young Widder Brown* (1938)
Marie, the Little French Princess (1933)	*Stella Dallas* (1938)
Easy Aces (1933)	*Those Happy Gilmans* (1938)
Just Plain Bill (1933)	*Houseboat Hannah* (1938)
The Romance of Helen Trent (1933)	*This Day Is Ours* (1938)
Ma Perkins (1933)	*Central City* (1938)
Manhattan Merry-Go-Round (1933)	*Doc Barclay's Daughters* (1939)
Waltz Time (1933)	*The Carters of Elm Street* (1939)
Painted Dreams (1933)	*Caroline's Golden Store* (1939)
Lavender and Old Lace (1934)	*The Man I Married* (1939)
Mrs. Wiggs of the Cabbage Patch (1935)	*The Trouble with Marriage* (1939)
Five Star Jones (1935)	*Orphans of Divorce* (1939)
Backstage Wife (1935)	*Beyond These Valleys* (1939)
Molly of the Movies (1935)	*Amanda of Honeymoon Hill* (1940)
David Harum (1936)	*The Light of the World* (1940)
Rich Man's Darling (1936)	*Lone Journey* (1940)
Modern Cinderella (1936)	*Front Page Farrell* (1941)
Love Song (1936)	*Helpmate* (1941)
Sweetest Love Songs Ever Sung (1936)	*American Melody Hour* (1941)
John's Other Wife (1936)	*Lonely Women* (1942)
Our Gal Sunday (1937)	*Chaplain Jim, U.S.A.* (1942)
The Couple Next Door (1937)	*Lora Lawton* (1943)
Lorenzo Jones (1937)	*Dreft Star Playhouse* (1943)
Arnold Grimm's Daughter (1937)	*Mystery Theater* (1943)
Kitty Keene, Incorporated (1937)	*Real Stories of Real Life* (1944)

Strange Romance of Evelyn Winters (1944)   *Nona from Nowhere* (1950)
Mr. Chameleon (1948)   *Hearthstone of the Death Squad* (1951)

Frank Hummert died on March 12, 1966, at the age of 84. His wife, Anne, died on July 5, 1996, at 91.

The Hummerts viewed their serials as "successful stories about unsuccessful people."[3] By "unsuccessful," they referred only to their figures' wealth. Their characters certainly weren't failures in realms other than material.

Such was the case of the Nobles, who never seemed to possess many of the world's physical goods. Despite that fact, for years they could afford a maid at their Rosehaven, Long Island, farm home, an irony that must have been an oddity to listeners. Often, had it not been for Mary's frugalness in devising ingenious methods of cutting back, supplementing their income and paying their bills, the Noble clan (including a son, Larry, Jr.) might have gone hungry. Their money woes were directly tied to Larry's infrequent bouts with unemployment, his penchant for making poor business investments and a proclivity for lending money to people with little or no history of repaying debts.

Yet Larry took Mary for granted. Though happy to receive her financial assistance, he never seemed to understand when it came to a reality check on the reasons for their economic ills. Bless Mary's heart: her fans never once remembered hearing her criticize the poor galoot for his ineptness in fiscal responsibility. She was an angel of mercy, supportive of her mate in every way.

Their money problems were a sidelight to the main issue, however. Faithful listeners over a long period soon realized that — once a crisis involving a third party had been resolved — within a few days, another star-crazed temptress (or tempter) would arrive to drive a wedge between the erstwhile happy couple.

During World War II Larry honored the nation by serving as a lieutenant in the Coast Guard. For a while during the time he was away, announcer Ford Bond introduced the series as *Mary Noble, War Wife.* This highlighted Larry's extended absence, of course, and temporarily gave the show an altered focus.

Shortly after returning from active duty, Larry encountered wealthy, attractive Virginia Lansing, with whom he had once starred in a play. A widow by the time of their second meeting, she waged a subtle campaign to weaken his confidence in himself. By consoling him, she figured she might replace Mary. But her plans were stymied by a most unexpected source — her engaging sister, Irene, who was several years her junior and with whom she shared a Park Avenue apartment.

Irene had become friendly with both Nobles during the time Mary was in rehearsal for Tom Bryson's play. Irene's current suitor, the actor Cliff Caldwell, was in the same play. Cliff didn't realize that, years before, Virginia had claimed an earlier love of Irene's for herself and had married him. Virginia intimated that she would have little hesitancy in a repeat performance should Irene fail to help her achieve her intended conquest of Larry Noble.

When it was Mary's turn to be courted, multimillionaire Frederic Dunbar, who had seen Mary in the same stage play, became obsessed. In the episode airing on August 10, 1945, he invited Mary and Larry to dinner at his palatial home overlooking the East River. There Dunbar unveiled a portrait of a long-lost lover. To the Nobles' surprise and confusion, the woman in the picture could have passed for Mary's identical twin. For weeks

Mary fought bravely, trying to deflect Dunbar's amorous advances. Eventually her admirer was put to rest, but not before he entangled them in some chilling moments of suspense.

Sometime after Virginia Lansing was dispatched, Larry sheepishly returned home late one night, having spent long hours with a "wealthy benefactress." Regina Rawlings was footing the bill for the next play in which he would star. Mary, meanwhile, waited up for her man. Unlike some wives in similar situations, Mary was attentive, comforting and ready with his slippers so that he could relax in his favorite easy chair. But in the installment broadcast on August 21, 1947, Larry — misguided fool that he was — had the audacity to ask if, behind his back, Mary was keeping company with playwright Eric Jackson. His devoted mate assured him, perhaps for the umpteen-jillionth time: "Just keep telling yourself that I've never cared for anyone but you." Millions of listeners knew she spoke the truth. Only Larry didn't get it.

Within moments, having returned home apologetically, he questioned his faithful spouse again about his doubts. Seeing a thick envelope she had set aside to mail to Eric Jackson, he blindly protested: "I've been a fool all over again! Sorry I walked in unexpectedly and interfered with your romance by picking up your letter. What letters — how much you must have to say!"

Larry stormed out of the house, unwilling to hear Mary's explanation that she was returning a play that Jackson had sent. She didn't want any involvement with the playwright. In an episode that had begun with the promise that the couple might mend their rift, the gap was wider than ever by the close of the quarter-hour.

Regina Rawlings, meanwhile, was to have an even greater influence on the Nobles in the months and years ahead. So infatuated with Larry did she become that she built her own mansion at the end of the country road on which the Nobles lived. Her estate was but a quarter of a mile from the Nobles' modest residence, in fact.

After moving into her new digs, in the chapter broadcast on May 5, 1948, Regina confided to her maid, Margo: "I won't have Mary Noble interfering with my life…. You've *got* to think of something to get rid of her! If you don't want me to do something desperate, you'll have to help me!" A few days later, on the broadcast of May 13, she assured Margo: "If something doesn't happen soon, I'll go mad. I'll do anything— even to violence."

The very next day a sinister-looking man appeared at her door. Listeners would soon learn that she had summoned him to, as he put it, help "get rid of Mary Noble." Identified only as Captain Arthur Duncan, this schemer posed as Regina's cousin while fostering a diabolical plan to eliminate Mary. Regina's goal was to have the undivided attention of Larry. For a while, it appeared as if her assault would succeed. Millions followed their story for months to determine how Arthur's plan, Regina's resolve, Mary's courage and Larry's weakness would collide.

At mid-century, after Regina Rawlings was finally dispatched, Anne Burr (the actress who played her) left the show. But Burr returned only a short time later, playing aspiring actress Claudia Vincent. Claudia too had an affinity for making life hell for Mary Noble. To Mary's dismay, at Larry's invitation, this damsel in distress moved in under the Noble roof— for a whole summer! And she brought as much anguish to Mary as any other female afforded during the run of the show.

Was it merely coincidence that one day, weeks later, another character in the durable series compared Claudia Vincent to the aforementioned Regina Rawlings? Perhaps by then most listeners had forgotten the similarity of the two women's dialects (they were, after all, the same actress). Their modus operandi, however, was inherently the same. Then again, their methods could be applied to almost every villainess introduced on this show!

Claudia Vincent was as tenacious as her predecessor in getting her hooks into Larry Noble. Even though she was an acting lightweight, when the leading lady of Larry's current play bowed out, Claudia persuaded him to go to bat for her with the drama's producer. She and Larry spent long hours in private rehearsals, developing her talent to allow her, to Mary's surprise, to assume the feminine lead.

In the meantime Mary had become the object of millionaire playboy Rupert Barlow's affection. He hired a glamorous publicist, Beatrice Dunmore, to promote the production he had financed in which Larry was starring. But it was instantly apparent that his real motive was to urge Beatrice to use her wily charms on Larry and to separate the Nobles. He intended to win Mary for himself. (The Nobles were so infatuating that almost everybody wanted to marry them.) But when Rupert's scheme dwindled to dismal ends, he fired Beatrice. Then Claudia Vincent, the next diversion, surfaced.

Although Rupert and Claudia had shared a not-so-pleasant history years before, Rupert was thrilled to have her occupy Larry's time. Even though Mary was turned off by Rupert's advances, Larry became enraged over the mere mention of the wealthy business tycoon's name. Perfectly innocent situations involving his devoted Mary typically resulted in gross overreactions by Larry.

When Julia Dixon, Rupert's longtime lady friend and executive housekeeper, returned from vacationing in Bermuda accompanied by a penniless young swain, Oliver Wilson, the plot took an unusual twist. Thanks to Mary's close confidante Maude Marlowe, Oliver gained the impression that Claudia Vincent was a wealthy dowager. And thanks again to Maude, Claudia made the erroneous assumption that Oliver was loaded too. Acting on their perceptions, the misguided pair eloped. After they learned the truth, however, their "romance" turned to bitter hatred for one another.

A short time later Mary discovered Oliver Wilson's body backstage at the theater where Larry and Claudia were performing. By then Oliver had alienated several characters; almost all had a reason to want him dead. The plot thickened. With the focus shifted, the notion of a permanent split between Mary and Larry was temporarily sidetracked. But as soon as Claudia was dispatched, the Nobles revisited their old haunts.

In 1951 Larry Noble took an acting job on the West Coast, leaving Mary and Larry Jr. on Long Island. Rupert Barlow, still committed to breaking up their home, interested producer Harold Ramsey in reopening a play in which Larry had starred. By mid–1952, in a convoluted sequence that Larry believed had been plotted by Rupert, Larry was kidnapped. After years of unsuccessfully chasing Mary, Rupert had at last become a desperate man.

The following year Larry was pursued by actress Elise Shephard. Mary once more desperately sought to save her troubled marriage. Meanwhile, a newly introduced character, Lucius Brooks, set his sights on Mary, threatening not only her home but also Larry's Broadway career. Ardent devotees of the serial probably thought: If not for Elise and Lucius, then somebody else. When the Hummerts struck a chord, the listeners could be pretty sure of consistency.

Only two actresses played the role of Mary Noble during the washboard weeper's long run. When the show was broadcast from Chicago during its first decade (1935–45)—

Claire Niesen and James Meighan (as Mary and Larry Noble) were the sidelined spouse and the "dream sweetheart of a million other women" in *Backstage Wife*. Although other actors shared those anguished parts, Niesen and Meighan may be better recalled for these roles than for any others they played. (Photofest)

before production was moved to New York — a Milwaukee woman, Vivian Fridell, won the part. Breaking into radio on her local campus station, Fridell later earned recurring roles in *Road of Life* and *The Romance of Helen Trent*. She died at age 85 on August 20, 1998, at Wilmette, Illinois.

But in fans' minds, veteran radio actress Claire Niesen is perhaps best associated with the part of Mary Noble. To her portrayal she brought an empathy that exuded virtue, selflessness, devotion, tenderness and compassion. From her characterization the audience could acquire a sensitive caring for Mary Noble. Only 25 years old when, in 1945, she assumed the lead in *Backstage Wife,* the Phoenix native was experienced, having captured the part of Peggy O'Neill Kayden in *The O'Neills* as a mere 16-year-old.

Niesen initiated the role of another radio heroine, *The Second Mrs. Burton,* in 1946. She was a regular in *Life Can Be Beautiful, The Right to Happiness* and *Her Honor, Nancy James.* She also infrequently appeared in *The March of Time Quiz* and on *The Light of the World.* She died at the age of 43 on October 4, 1963, at Encino, California. The credits she earned in a scant few years in the industry were seldom matched.

Three radio actors portrayed Mary Noble's handsome, deficient spouse, Larry. Ken Griffin, in Chicago, was a familiar voice on several other serials: *Woman in White, Road of Life, Myrt and Marge, Kitty Keene* and *The Guiding Light.* He was also a regular on *The Chicago Theatre of the Air, Armstrong of the SBI* and *Peter Quill.*

The best-remembered Larry Noble followed Griffin. James Meighan was born on August 22, 1906, in New York and became a perennial daytime lead. The nephew of silent-film star Thomas Meighan first appeared with the Yonkers Stock Company in several Eugene O'Neill dramas, including *Desire Under the Elms.* He performed on Broadway in *Hamlet in Modern Dress* and *My Maryland.* By 1936 he was playing on radio opposite Helen Hayes. During a World War II broadcast of *These Are Our Men,* Meighan portrayed General Dwight David Eisenhower.

From 1945 to 1951, he played Larry Noble. But for many years he slipped out of the studio following that performance to attend rehearsals of *Just Plain Bill* down the hall. On that serial he was Kerry Donovan, Bill's son-in-law. He was the lead, or male lead, on at least ten other series: *Lora Lawton, The Falcon, Flash Gordon, Alias Jimmy Valentine, City Desk, I Love Linda Dale, Dot and Will, Special Agent, Orphans of Divorce* and *Marie, the Little French Princess.* Other shows in Meighan's repertoire included *Death Valley Days, Mohawk Treasure Check, Against the Storm, By Kathleen Norris, Lone Journey, The Romance of Helen Trent* and *Second Husband.* He died in Huntington, New York on June 20, 1970.

The last Larry Noble was Guy Sorel, husband of the serial actress Mary Jane Higby (heroine of *When a Girl Marries*). Sorel played the lead on *Twenty Thousand Years in Sing Sing.* He was the only permanent actor on *You Are There* while maintaining running parts on *Just Plain Bill, Road of Life* and *Superman.*

Larry Jr. was more often mentioned than heard. After all, a woman (child impersonator Wilda Hinkel) played the role. When the child did enter the plot, it was often at a most opportune moment. Once, while Mary was distressed over Larry's attention to one of those glamour girls who swooned over him, the lad observed that hussy kissing his father. The youngster promptly carried his eyewitness account to his mother, who wondered if that wasn't confirmation of the doubts she harbored.

There were at least two other prominent characters featured in *Backstage Wife.* Both were friendly to the Nobles; neither sought to break up their marriage, something of an exception on this drama. Aging, matronly character actress Maude Marlowe lived with the Nobles on several intermittent occasions in their Rosehaven, Long Island home. The Nobles also kept a guest room available for frequent visitor Tom Bryson, Larry's best friend and theatrical manager.

Tom and Maude were perpetually waiting in the wings of the story line, ready to come on stage when summoned. So protective of the Nobles was Maude, in particular, that she could easily be compared to a lioness guarding her cubs. She and Tom valiantly defended Mary and Larry's honor again and again, even though at least once Larry became suspicious of Tom's motives around Mary. Larry wouldn't trust any male who so much as looked at his sweet Mary, the rose of Tralee! Tom and Maude surely gained the respect of series fans if for no other reason than that millions cheered anyone who released the unhappy Nobles, even briefly, from their eternal confinement in misery.

While a large number of announcers served *Backstage Wife*, none is better remembered than Ford Bond, who narrated the show from the mid–1940s through the early 1950s. A native of Louisville, Kentucky, Bond was born October 23, 1904, and broke into radio as a singer on his hometown's 50,000-watt WHAS. At 18 he was elevated to program director. By 1929 he became general program executive in New York for NBC's program department. From 1930 to 1956 he held what was regarded as broadcasting's longest sponsor-announcer association. As the voice of the Cities Service Oil Company, he announced *The Cities Service Concert* (1930–44), *Highways in Melody* (1944–48) and *The Cities Service Band of America* (1948–56). From 1932 to 1949 he was the interlocutor for *The Manhattan Merry-Go-Round*, proclaiming "lyrics sung so clearly you can understand every word."

Bond filled similar slots on *The Collier's Hour, David Harum, Lora Lawton, Nona from Nowhere, Easy Aces, Stella Dallas, The Kraft Music Hall, Believe It or Not, Just Plain Bill, Alias Jimmy Valentine, Orphans of Divorce, Your Family and Mine* and several more shows. Married to soprano vocalist Lois Bennett, he developed and built resorts after his radio career. Bond died on August 15, 1962, in St. Croix, Virgin Islands.

On *Backstage Wife*, Bond's deep, resonant voice bellowed such familiar commercial slogans as "Keep it clean with Energine!" Perhaps he could be forgiven that, but maybe not "pityrosporum ovale," which daily rolled off his tongue with ease. He said the disease, a malady that most people didn't know they had, was a common cause of dandruff. What to do? For years Bond assured listeners that Double Danderine would kill the stuff on contact.

For several seasons Frank Gallop announced for NBC's *Stella Dallas* immediately following *Backstage Wife*— both programs underwritten by Sterling Drugs. After Bond delivered *Wife's* daily opening line, "Next, *Backstage Wife*," the organist played a few chords. Gallop then appeared before the microphone, reading a cowcatcher commercial for one of Sterling's products. Afterward, he would retreat to the *Dallas* rehearsals in a nearby studio.

At least once Gallop opened with this line of copy on *Wife*: "Many fastidious women know that hair must be washed frequently and thoroughly to keep it not only lustrous, but — what's more important — fresh and cleanly fragrant." The missive, for Mulsified Coconut Oil shampoo, probably sent millions to their dictionaries to discover what a "fastidious" woman was. She wasn't living in the fast lane, as they might have postulated. According to *Webster*, she was critical and discriminating, not easy to please. Was the level of intellect among the homemaking faithful so high that most of those in *Wife's* audience had little difficulty grasping Gallop's meaning? Or, just perhaps, was this the reflection of an overzealous copywriter run amok?

Wife, which originally floated onto the air to an organ arrangement of "Stay as Sweet as You Are," soon dropped both instrument and tune in favor of a piano rendition of "The Rose of Tralee." By the early 1940s, when the piano was supplanted by a studio organ, fans grew accustomed to their favorite serial making hefty use of the latter instrument. With three or four commercials in a quarter-hour, the bridges between sponsors' messages and the transitions between scenes filled nearly as much time as the dialogue itself!

Announcer Ford Bond's staccato delivery was instantly recognizable to the practiced ears of *Backstage Wife*'s audience and fans of the other serials and musical programs he hosted. Bond gained broadcasting's longest sponsor-announcer link as spokesman for a major oil firm from 1930 to 1956. (Photofest)

In 1941, six years after the series' inception, subscribers to one of the popular national fan magazines, *Movie-Radio Guide*, named *Backstage Wife* "Radio's Best Daytime Serial Program." In the same decade, readers of another widely read consumer publication, *Radio Mirror*, chose it as their "Favorite Daytime Radio Serial"—for five consecutive years. The lives of dysfunctional families were obviously stimulating to the homemakers even then.

Bob and Ray, erstwhile radio comedians who made it to the big time in the 1950s spoofing everything and everybody, capitalized on this soap opera. *Mary Backstayge, Noble Wife* turned into a series of running on-air vignettes. These are still being heard today via widely circulated tapes. The exploits of "America's favorite family of the footlights"—the Backstayges of mythical Skunkhaven, Long Island—were retold through the escapades of Mary Backstayge, her husband, Harry, their friend Calvin and Pop Beloved. The announcer identified himself as Word Carr, of course a takeoff on Ford Bond.

Backstage Wife remained on the air from its debut on MBS on August 5, 1935, until CBS cut the show from its daytime roster on January 2, 1959. Departing also that day were three other long-running daytime dramas—*Our Gal Sunday, Road of Life* and *This Is Nora Drake*. This quartet collectively aired more than three-quarters of a century, with *Wife* boasting the longest tenure among them.

Backstage Wife was a kind of play-within-a-play, for it dealt with the performing arts. Its hypothesis—that virtually everyone wanted to be married to one or the other of the Nobles—was a farce. But homemakers listened intently anyway, even though they knew the tale would be reprised. For a gentle noblewoman, you see, had cast them under her spell.

3
Big Sister
(John's Other Wife)

Ruth Evans was the sister of a pair of younger siblings who were little more than emotional cripples. The three were orphaned sometime before the series went on the air in 1936. As the eldest, Ruth took charge of Neddie, who was also physically crippled, and Sue. As the trio grew older, the younger pair became so dependent on Ruth that they turned to her with virtually every concern. After Dr. John Wayne restored Neddie to health, the doctor divorced his wife and married Ruth. But the troubles she had experienced earlier were a mere prelude to what was to follow. John had a wanderlust that Ruth hadn't detected before. One day he quit his medical practice, announcing he was going to New York City to find himself, without Ruth and their young son, Richard. In addition to her patients, Ruth — a nurse — still had Neddie, Sue and Richard to cope with while staving off the amorous advances of Dr. Reed Bannister, who saw qualities in her that Dr. Wayne ignored. Even when the couple attempted to reconcile, John was plagued by intermittent bouts of amnesia, depression, rage, lust, jealousy and physical ailments. Despite her own forced isolation, Ruth was able to rise to every occasion, remaining an even-tempered counselor no matter how complicated the issue. Surprisingly, the program was sold only to rival soap manufacturers over its long run, a rarity in the annals of radio serials.

Producers: Ruthrauff and Ryan advertising agency
Directors: Mitchell Grayson, Theodore T. Huston, Thomas F. Vietor, Jr.
Writers: Carl Bixby, Julian Funt, Lillian Lauferty (the drama's creator), Robert Newman, Bill Sweets
Music: Richard Leibert, William Meeder
Sound Effects: Bill Brown, Walt McDonough, Lavern Owens
Announcers: Jim Ameche, Nelson Case, Clayton (Bud) Collyer, Hugh Conover, Howard Petrie, Lee Stevens, Fred Uttal
Ruth Evans Wayne: Alice Frost, Nancy Marshall, Marjorie Anderson, Mercedes McCambridge, Grace Matthews (1946–52)
Dr. John Wayne: Martin Gabel, Paul McGrath, Staats Cotsworth
Ned Evans: Michael O'Day
Sue Evans Miller: Fran Carden, Peggy Conklin, Helen Lewis, Dorothy McGuire, Haila Stoddard

Richard Wayne: Jim Ameche, Jr., Ruth Schafer
Dr. Duncan Carvell: Santos Ortega
Dr. Reed Bannister: David Gothard, Berry Kroeger, Ian Martin, Arnold Moss
Others: Mason Adams, Vera Allen, Ed Begley, Ralph Bell, Teddy Bergman, Horace Braham, Anne Burr, Patsy Campbell, Guy de Vestel, Susan Douglas, Eric Dressler, Helene Dumas, Elspeth Eric, Louise Fitch, Arlene Francis, Charlotte Holland, Joe Julian, Teri Keane, Alexander Kirkland, Adelaide Klein, Richard Kollmar, Elizabeth Love, Agnes Moorehead, Erin O'Brien-Moore, Zasu Pitts, Oscar Polk, Carl Benton Reid, Ann Shepherd, Everett Sloane, Chester Stratton, Joan Tompkins, Evelyn Varden, Harold Vermilyea, Charles Webster, Ned Wever, Richard Widmark, more

Theme: "Valse Bluette" (Drigo)

Sponsors: From Sept. 14, 1936 to June 21, 1946, Lever Brothers Co. underwrote the show, primarily as a merchandising vehicle for Rinso detergent. Lifebuoy deodorant soap also was featured. When Lever bowed out, the show was sold to rival consumer goods manufacturer Procter & Gamble, which carried it the rest of the way for Ivory soap (June 24, 1946–Dec. 26, 1952). *Big Sister* also sold Dreft detergent, Joy dishwashing liquid and Spic 'n' Span cleanser.

Ratings: Surpassed 8.0 in one-fourth of its 16 seasons; topped 7.0 in nine seasons. High: 9.3 (1949–50); low: 5.7 (1939–40).

On the Air: Sept. 14, 1936–Aug. 22, 1941, CBS, 11:30 a.m. ET; Aug. 25, 1941–June 21, 1946, CBS, 12:15 p.m.; June 24, 1946–Dec. 26, 1952, CBS, 1:00 p.m.

> ANNOUNCER: Ninety-nine and forty-four one-hundredths percent pure...
> MUSIC: A few bright notes
> ANNOUNCER:...enjoyment! That's *Big Sister*, compliments of Ivory soap...
> MUSIC: Dual notes
> ANNOUNCER: The most famous soap in the world.
> MUSIC: A few notes to signify end of commercial melody
> ANNOUNCER: And now by transcription, Ivory's own *Big Sister*, written by Julian Funt and Robert Newman.
> MUSIC: First few bars of theme

The fact that the program was transcribed indicates that it could not have been broadcast before the late 1940s or early 1950s. Before then, there was a network ban on prerecording most series. A dictate from on high mandated that dialogue must be spoken as it was heard.

There were some good reasons for this. For many years the quality of recording equipment wasn't equal to the discerning demands of radio's perceptive ear. There was also a pervading belief that realism could be achieved if the actors speaking the lines of characters did so at the very moment those figures were being heard by an audience. Eventually, the networks relaxed their long-standing prohibition against prerecording features as better sound equipment arrived and preconceived notions died.

Recording more than music and commercials was a technique just coming into vogue at midcentury. Its possibilities seemed endless on shows where, in the past, every minute of action had been performed live. As a byproduct, for the first time whole casts could take extended vacations at the same time — and plan them in advance. (In the summer of 1950, *Ma Perkins'* troupe prerecorded two weeks' worth of episodes before disbanding to parts unknown. Unless listeners caught the announcer's "by transcription" during the fortnight the performers were away, no one was the wiser.)

For the last half-dozen years of its life, when it reached its largest audiences, *Big Sister* was underwritten by Procter & Gamble (P&G) on behalf of Ivory soap. So associated was Ivory with the shows on which it was pitched (*The Right to Happiness, Road of Life, Life Can Be Beautiful* and others) that the mere mention of an Ivory serial by name brought product recognition to many minds.

Big Sister's venerable, mellow-toned narrator, Nelson Case, had long been associated with Ivory soap and was termed "the original 'soft-sell' announcer."[1] Case's rhapsodic timbre meant instant voice-identification with "the most famous soap in the world." P&G paid him to convince listeners of Ivory's attributes without resorting to high-pressure, hard-sell tactics. When *Big Sister* left the air at the end of 1952, Case remained on the job, pitching Ivory to the audience of *Road of Life,* which inherited the time period. It was a high tribute to Case's soft-spoken effectiveness as P&G's chief Ivory spokesman.

In those days, the commercials often featured singing jingles. One of the ditties, which a female vocalist sang to a lilting tune each day, went like this:

> Oh, your hands aren't made of china;
> They need a soap for the skin.
> In your dishpan, float I'vry...
> You'll admit your hands ... aren't made ... of china!

Earlier, *Big Sister* had been sponsored by one of P&G's most formidable competitors, Lever Brothers Co. In those days announcer Jim Ameche introduced the soap opera without "compliments of Ivory Soap." Instead, the quarter-hour opened like this:

> WHISTLER: Three notes up the scale whistled and quickly
>   repeated
> ANNOUNCER: Rinso presents ... *Big Sister.*
> SFX: Tower clock strikes first four notes of Westminster
>   Chimes
> ANNOUNCER: Yes, there's the clock in Glen Falls town hall,
>   telling us it's time for Rinso's story of *Big Sister,* brought to
>   you by the new, soapy-rich Rinso.... (Spells slowly) R-I-N-
>   S-O. (Delivers first Rinso commercial)

Did loyal listeners notice the change in sponsors on Monday, June 24, 1946? On the previous Friday, an announcement had been made that the program would move to a different time period on the following Monday. But no mention was made that Lever was relinquishing its decade-long association. On Monday the program shifted from 12:15 p.m.

to one o'clock. And the rhyming commercial singer (Beverly Silverman, who later changed her name to Beverly Sills as a diva on the opera circuit) wasn't chirping "Rinso white, Rinso bright, happy little washday song" any more. Instead, a new girl urged homemakers to "float I'vry" in their dishpans. Although such about-face changes occurred among sponsors of long-running radio serials, they were rare.

In earlier years Lever had been a major purveyor of soap operas, controlling several quarter-hours daily. But by 1946 it had reduced its span to only one weekday serial, *Aunt Jenny's Real Life Stories*. P&G, on the other hand, continued to underwrite daytime drama to the tune of eleven quarter-hours every day! Meanwhile, Lever remained a strong supporter of nighttime radio. *Lux Radio Theater* was one of the most persuasive, and costly, programs in its arsenal.

The protagonist in *Big Sister*, Ruth Evans, lived in the small town of Glen Falls, probably located in upstate New York. The tale often centered on the dilemmas she faced in nurturing her two younger siblings: a lame brother, Ned (most often referred to as "Neddie"), and a sister named Sue. The three Evans children had been orphaned several years before. Ruth, the eldest, possessed the ability and intellect to guide her brother and sister through all sorts of tempests.

Soap opera creators learned an important lesson near the beginning of their craft: as a device for making a continuing story possible, a central helping-hand character was an invaluable aid in connecting several subplots. Suspense could ebb and flow without resolution while continuity was sustained. Ruth Evans, (Just Plain) Bill Davidson, Ma Perkins and *Life Can Be Beautiful*'s Papa David could have earned fortunes if they had acquired licenses to dispense their plentiful advice.

In this quartet Ruth was the only counselor-in-residence who was still young and single when she was elevated to a saintly perch by family members. From a very practical sense, it was a rather dangerous predicament for a never-married soap opera heroine to be in. Such formulas had not often generated high ratings elsewhere. *Big Sister* was among a handful that successfully broke with tradition.

Though Neddie may have been physically distorted, he and his younger sister came across to the radio audience as mental weaklings. Fans who tuned in over a protracted period must have felt that neither Sue nor Neddie could ever mature well enough to be capable of running their own lives. They were lucky to have Ruth to address their worries and heartaches. Whether she did them a good turn by allowing the pair to run to her for advice on everything is debatable. She left little for them to figure for themselves. But then — in the early years — without her assistance, there would have been no plot ... and no drama.

Neddie was eventually restored to physical health by the brilliant young surgeon Dr. John Wayne, who was fond of Ruth. (Note his well-recognized designation. Soap opera creators had no bias against naming their characters after celebrities. Thus, Joan Davis was the leading lady of *When a Girl Marries*.) Audience interest had lagged until Ruth became involved with John, a married man whose wife, Norma, was insane. To save Norma's life after an automobile crash, John operated on her, unintentionally damaging her mind forever. He then divorced Norma and in October 1939 married Ruth. (In reality, Ruth became John's *other* wife, coincidentally the title of another soap opera then on the air.)

Ruth and John soon became parents of a son, Richard. In addition to guiding him as well as her younger siblings, Ruth had enough domestic problems to keep a sane woman permanently occupied. There was a prolonged separation during World War II when John was held captive in a Japanese prison camp. A few years later the couple became estranged when he boldly resigned his medical practice and moved to New York City to "think life through"—to "find himself" during a mid-life crisis (although it wasn't identified as such in those days).

John had been working alongside the aging Dr. Duncan Carvell while Ruth was their nurse. To physician Reed Bannister, however, John's best friend who later joined their practice, Ruth was womanhood perfected—an impossible, unattainable love, though worth salivating over.

The stock heartaches of serialdom were all introduced. Bouts with amnesia persisted. John was struck blind, the result of an explosion aboard a ship. And when he could see, he had a roving eye for a pretty leg. To his credit, he rebuffed the come-hither advances of Dr. Carvell's stunningly attractive daughter, Diane. The girl had a flighty, uneven temperament and seemed totally clueless to any deep meaning to life. Both she and John lived in New York City for a while, which could have given John the chance to pursue her had he been so inclined.

He saved himself, instead, for a torrid affair with Hope Evans, Neddie's young wife, his own sister-in-law. Hope was a deceptively spoiled brat who was constantly plotting something behind her spouse's back. She often lied with a straight face to every member of the family, never considering the consequences or damages to her own failing reputation.

By 1950 Reed and John's friendship, in which an element of rivalry had always existed, was badly strained. John became influenced by a power-hungry millionaire, Millard Parker, whom everybody else disliked and distrusted. Cultivating Parker's friendship, John saw him as a resource for funding the Glen Falls Health Center, which he and Reed had given much of their energy to. But Reed rejected a $50,000 gift from Parker, since he suspected Parker's motives. As a result, John resigned from the center. Only Ruth, ever the peacemaker, could persuade him to reconsider his hasty decision.

Relationships soured further when Dr. Kenneth Morgan arrived. John disliked him from the start. But Reed, viewing Morgan as a brilliant physician, added him to the health center's staff. The wedge between the two medicos dug even deeper.

Parker, meanwhile, was to remain a powerful figure through this serial's final days. Neddie and Hope Evans' marriage was nearly shattered by his influence. Ruth uncovered diabolical schemes instigated by Parker against several of Glen Falls' citizens. In his twisted mental state, he somehow confused Ruth with his late wife, Selena.

Thanks to Parker's continuing villainy, Ruth and John's marriage was left hanging by a thread. Parker tried convincing John that Reed was deeply in love with Ruth. (Listeners, of course, had known this to be true for years.) Was is possible for Ruth to tell John that Reed was not in love with her? It was a tough call.

John was suffering with a serious siege of pneumonia in 1952. Worse, he had lapsed into yet another bout with depression. Ruth had to rescue her man again and return him to a tolerable emotional level. By then *Big Sister*'s days were numbered. The drama had but a few months to tie the loose ends together, closing the book on the Waynes, Bannister, Parker, Morgan, the Carvells and others in Glen Falls.

Big Sister enjoyed a couple of treats most of its contemporaries didn't. The drama was copied in at least two ways. It became the very first serial to be televised, albeit only once. Though this 1946 experiment was of little consequence in itself, it certainly gave those early viewers a clue of what was ahead. Bringing a single episode of the soap opera into a TV studio for a broadcast test opened a vision for the future that wouldn't have been foreseen much earlier. The Dumont network's short-lived *A Woman to Remember*, the first serious effort at a televised soap opera, appeared in 1949. *Big Sister's* experiment had paved the way.

Big Sister was also complimented when one of its characters, Michael West, left the show in 1941 to become the protagonist in a spin-off series, *Bright Horizon*. West played a bistro singer in the plot. This drama was also sponsored by Lever Brothers and was slotted into *Big Sister's* original 11:30 a.m. quarter-hour. At the beginning it drew Ruth Wayne into its story line to help it become established with listeners.

Richard Kollmar portrayed West on the parent serial while Joe Julian inherited the role in the new one. In 1945 the drama was altered slightly and renamed *A Woman's Life*. Under neither title did the spin-off achieve the success of its long-running big sister, however, and the series faded from the air in 1946.

Lillian Lauferty, the author who created *Big Sister*, also lent her writing talents to the daytime serial *Your Family and Mine* (1938-40). This tale of an impractical inventor who dreamed of making a fortune on his gadgets while married to a practical woman enjoyed moderate success. The concept was more widely embraced by listeners when pursued by the lovable character in *Lorenzo Jones*.

Of more than a half-dozen announcers on *Big Sister* broadcasts, none was better identified with it than Jim Ameche in the Lever Brothers years and Nelson Case in the Procter & Gamble era.

The versatile Ameche was the announcer for *Here's to Romance, Amos 'n' Andy* and *Welcome Travelers* and was master of ceremonies on *Woodbury Hollywood Playhouse*. He played the lead in *Silver Eagle, Mountie* and the title roles in *Attorney-at-Law* and *Jack Armstrong, the All-American Boy*. He regularly appeared in dramatic companies on *Grand Hotel, Grand Marquee* and *Lux Radio Theater*. Born on August 6, 1915, at Kenosha, Wisconsin, in 1933 Ameche was summoned by his older brother Don, already established in radio, to audition for the part of Jack Armstrong. Jim won the part, maintaining it until 1938. He eventually became a disc jockey, moving to Tucson, Arizona, in 1975, where he announced for station KCEE. He died on February 4, 1983, at Tucson.

Case, born on February 3, 1910, at Long Beach, California, formed his own orchestra for a local station before joining NBC as a staff announcer in San Francisco in 1931. Moving to New York three years later, he introduced Lowell Thomas on nightly newscasts and the big band shows of Guy Lombardo, Ray Noble, Wayne King and the NBC Symphony Orchestra. His announcing duties included *Marriage Club, Hour of Charm, New Carnation Contented Hour, Charlie & Jessie* and *Ford Theater*. Case supplied narration for several other serials: *Against the Storm, Lone Journey, Road of Life* and *The Story of Mary Marlin*. He died on March 24, 1976, in Doylestown, Pennsylvania.

Five actresses played the heroine in *Big Sister*. Several were widely known as popular radio celebrities. Alice Frost, best remembered for her role as Pam North on the radio detective series *Mr. and Mrs. North*, originated the part of Ruth Evans Wayne. Frost was also the female lead in *Woman of Courage*. She was born August 1, 1910, in Minneapolis,

Minnesota; her credits included frequent appearances on *Buck Rogers in the Twenty-Fifth Century, The Fred Allen Show, Famous Jury Trials, The Mercury Theater on the Air, Town Hall Tonight, Suspense, Columbia Workshop* and *Stoopnagle and Budd*. She had recurring roles in *Lorenzo Jones, Bright Horizon, Maverick Jim, Mrs. Wiggs of the Cabbage Patch* and *David Harum*. Frost launched her career on Broadway in a 1931 production of *Green Grow the Lilacs*. She appeared as Aunt Trina Gunnerson in the TV dramatic series *Mama* (1949–57). She died on January 6, 1992.

Nancy Marshall, the next Ruth Evans Wayne, also appeared in the serials *Lone Journey* and *The Story of Bess Johnson*. She was followed by Marjorie Anderson, who became the announcer on *Big Sister*'s spin-off show, *Bright Horizon*, and who portrayed Margo Lane in *The Shadow*. She also had running roles in *Mrs. Wiggs of the Cabbage Patch, The O'Neills, The Parker Family* and *Portia Faces Life*.

Mercedes McCambridge, whom Orson Welles called "the world's greatest radio actress," was the fourth Ruth. She also played the title role in *Defense Attorney*, female leads in *Betty and Bob* and *Abie's Irish Rose* and leads in *The Guiding Light* and *Family Skelton*. She had recurring parts in *Midstream, Girl Alone, A Tale of Today* and *This Is Nora Drake*. She also infrequently acted in *Studio One* and *Ford Theater* and a host of mystery series: *Bulldog Drummond, The Adventures of Dick Tracy, The Thin Man, Inner Sanctum Mysteries, Gangbusters, I Love a Mystery* and *Lights Out*. She made occasional appearances on the early TV religious program *Lamp Unto My Feet*. McCambridge was born in Joliet, Illinois, on March 17, 1918. She won an Academy Award for her role as best supporting actress in the movie *All the King's Men*. Her autobiography, *The Quality of Mercy*, was published in 1981.

Grace Matthews carried the role of Ruth Evans Wayne from 1946, when Procter & Gamble took over the serial's sponsorship, to its conclusion in 1952. She also played leads on *The Brighter Day, Hilltop House, Soldier's Wife* and *The Story of Dr. Susan*. For a while she was Margo Lane on *The Shadow* and had a recurring role on *Just Plain Bill*. She was in the cast of television's *The Guiding Light* (1968–69). In the 1970s she appeared sporadically on *The CBS Mystery Theater*. Matthews was born in Toronto, Ontario, Canada, on September 3, 1910. She died on May 15, 1995, at Mount Kisco, New York.

Martin Gabel, Paul McGrath and Staats Cotsworth, all well-known radio luminaries, portrayed the role of Dr. John Wayne on *Big Sister*. Gabel, who originated the part, was the real-life husband of actress-celebrity Arlene Francis. Francis had a running part in the drama in its early days. Gabel was among several carrying the title role in *The Case Book of Gregory Hood*, a mystery series. He was in several repertory companies, appearing steadily on *The Mercury Theater on the Air, The March of Time Quiz, Everyman's Theater, Norman Corwin* dramatic specials and *Columbia Presents Corwin*. In the latter days of the long run of the TV game show *What's My Line?*, on which his wife was a panelist (1950–67), Gabel often appeared as a guest panelist. Born in Philadelphia in 1912, he died on May 22, 1986.

Paul McGrath's most memorable performance was undoubtedly as a host on *Inner Sanctum Mysteries*. He also played the male lead in *The Affairs of Dr. Gentry*, one of the dying gasps of radio's daytime serials (1957–59). The Chicago native, born on April 11, 1904, acquired many roles in soap operas (*This Life Is Mine, Lora Lawton, When a Girl Marries, Young Doctor Malone*). For several years he was on *Crime Doctor*. On television, McGrath appeared briefly on two serials, *First Love* (1955) and *The Guiding Light* (1967). He died in London on April 13, 1978.

The third and final John Wayne was Staats Cotsworth, whose name dominates in the annals of radio history. His contributions appear with his most notable serial — *Front Page Farrell* — for which he was the title character for many years.

An entertainment trade publication observed in 1947 that *Big Sister* had a powerful social effect on its audience.[2] The serial curbed neuroticism, strengthened marriages, offered help for coping with emotional problems, improved the sense of importance and security in women and had a "positive effect" on the personalities of its listeners, an inquiry revealed.

In a subsequent study, analysts William Henry and Lloyd Warner reported that *Big Sister* strengthened and stabilized society.[3] As an example they cited a housewife comparing herself to a career-girl achiever and seeing herself as coming up short. But in Ruth Evans, she found a resourceful make-believe homemaker who added demonstrable assets to daily living. Henry and Warner's conclusions led them to view *Big Sister* as a morality play with idealized symbols of good and evil patterned after listeners' beliefs. While the soap opera condemned neurotic behavior, it constructively dealt with normal and adaptive anxiety. Logical solutions were offered for problems occurring in the plot line, they found.

Almost nothing surfaced in either of these studies to suggest that *Big Sister* — or radio serials in general — had harmful effects. Such dramas expressed the hopes and fears of their largely feminine audiences, helping listeners integrate their lives into their own environment. The conclusions suggest that fantasyland wasn't very far away for most listeners. And residing there for a little while was perfectly harmless to visitors.

4
The Brighter Day
(Falling Leaves)

This was the final radio contribution of Irna Phillips, one of the earliest and most powerful influences of soap opera. After this show was introduced in 1948, her attention turned to a new medium, television, where her legacy continues today. On *The Brighter Day*, which for eight years also made it to TV, the central character was a widowed parson with a large brood of children. The story was set in the rural community of Three Rivers, where Reverend Dennis tended a nonsectarian flock. Over time listeners learned that the Dennis family was no different from others; its members had feet of clay too. Yet guided by the sweet-spirited eldest sister, Liz — who filled many of the gaps in the absence of a mother — the younger offspring were molded into caring, responsible citizens. Liz unselfishly put aside her own romantic interests for a while to be available to her siblings. One of the clan, Althea, maintained a resolute aloofness. She often defied the high moral plain that Reverend Dennis had set for his family and that Liz attempted to imbue in the others. The challenge of meeting Althea's needs while positively channeling her energies became a compelling focus of the drama. The fact that the serial maintained a respectable rating for most of its life indicated the public was receptive to a story imprinted with high moral values and family traditions.

Producer: David Lesan
Directors: Ted Corday, Arthur Hanna, Edwin Wolfe
Writers: John Haggart, Irna Phillips, Orin Tovrov
Music: William Meeder
Sound Effects: Jack Anderson, Bill Brown
Announcers: Ron Rawson, Bill Rogers, Len Sterling
Rev. Richard Dennis: Bill Smith
Liz Dennis: Margaret Draper, Grace Matthews
Althea Dennis: Jay Meredith
Barbara (Bobby) Dennis: Lorna Lynn
Grayling Dennis: Billy Redfield
Patsy Dennis: Pat Hosley
Others: Inge Adams, Joan Alexander, Joe De Santis, Ann Hilary, John Larkin, Dick
    Lockser, Charlotte Manson, Paul McGrath, Bob Pollock, John Raby, Dick Seff, more

Theme: "At Dawning" (Cadman)

Sponsors: From Oct. 11, 1948 to July 1, 1955, Procter & Gamble underwrote the show, first for Dreft dishwashing suds and then for its "new blue" Cheer laundry detergent. Beginning on Aug. 1, 1955, the program was heard under multiple sponsorship (for Hazel Bishop lipstick and others).

Ratings: Surpassed 5.0 in five of its eight seasons, and 6.0 in three. High: 6.6 (1949–50); low: 3.8 (1948–49).

On the Air: Oct. 11, 1948–July 8, 1949, NBC, 10:45 a.m. ET; July 11, 1949–Dec. 30, 1955, CBS, 2:45 p.m.; Jan. 2, 1956–June 29, 1956, CBS, 2:15 p.m.

Our years are as the falling leaves — we live, we love, we dream, and then we go. But somehow, we keep hoping — don't we? — that our dreams come true on that brighter day.
—Epigraph to *The Brighter Day*

Was it possible to achieve a decent following for a continuing drama about life in a small town, with a clergyman as the protagonist? If you have any doubts, check this out: acclaimed creative genius Irna Phillips was able to do it — not once but *twice* during her lifetime.

In 1937 Phillips successfully brought Dr. John Ruthledge, the minister of a nonsectarian parish in Five Points, to daytime radio listeners. His story became the early backdrop for her six-decades-old radio and television serial, *The Guiding Light.* Although the action long ago departed from its focus on the Ruthledge clan, the popular serial is unequaled in longevity among all broadcast dramas. That simply couldn't be termed a shabby start.

Missing the feel of a religious serial, in 1948 Phillips conceived another show in which a pastor was the central figure. His name was Rev. Richard Dennis, a widower with four daughters and a son. The clergyman served an interdenominational congregation in the rural hamlet of Three Rivers.

Phillips named her final radio story *The Brighter Day.* It was one of only three successful postwar soap operas introduced to audiences in the late 1940s. (The other two were *Wendy Warren and the News* in June 1947 and *This Is Nora Drake* in October 1947.)

Phillips is another of those ubiquitous soap opera figures whose commanding influence on the genre demands extensive examination. Because her contributions were so vast, let's pause to herald her achievements. A native Chicagoan, Phillips was one of ten children growing up in a German-Jewish family that manifested strong traditional values, the kind that the leading characters were to display in her dramas. She was raised by a widowed mother, who became the inspiration for at least two of her early serials.

Educated at the University of Illinois, Irna temporarily abandoned a dream of becoming an actress to pursue the more practical occupation of schoolteacher in Dayton, Ohio. But performing was never far from her thoughts, and in the summertime she returned to Chicago to find seasonal work in local radio.

One day in 1930 this schoolmarm wandered into Chicago's WGN, seeking a job. She was hired as an actress, and one of her early assignments was to host an extemporaneous talk show, *Thought for the Day*. But her role soon expanded — literally. In the earliest forerunner of the impressively lengthy legacy she was to leave in broadcasting, Phillips "starred" as Sue in *Sue and Irene*. She and Ireene *(sic)* Wicker, another teacher-turned-thespian — Irene in the show — were featured in all of the drama's speaking parts.

The fascinating story of Phillips' first attempt at writing a serial, *Painted Dreams*, and its ultimate evolution into *Today's Children* is recounted later. But despite some legal difficulties, Phillips gained valuable experience, which she applied to future efforts: *The Guiding Light* and *Road of Life*, both 1937 entries; *Woman in White*, debuting in 1938; and in 1939 *The Right to Happiness*, her first spin-off, from *The Guiding Light*. For a while she and others scripted *Young Doctor Malone*, which also premiered in 1939. She introduced *Lonely Women* — a second reincarnation of *Painted Dreams* — in 1942 and *Masquerade* in 1946. Neither of this latter duo gained the stature of her earlier serials, however. Finally, her radio antecedents ended with *The Brighter Day* in 1948.

Moving to television, Phillips penned *These Are My Children* (which lasted less than a month in 1949), *The Guiding Light* (introduced to TV audiences in 1952), *The Brighter Day* (1954), *As the World Turns* (1956), *Another World* (1964), *Days of Our Lives* (1965), *Our Private World* (a short-lived 1965 prime-time spin-off of *As the World Turns*) and *Love Is a Many Splendored Thing* (1967). Some of these series were cocreated with other writers, whom she strongly indoctrinated.

When Phillips no longer wrote *The Guiding Light* and *Another World*, a protégé, Agnes Nixon, became head writer on both soap operas. (Nixon had cocreated *Search for Tomorrow* in 1951.) In 1968 Nixon unveiled her own TV serial, *One Life to Live*. It was followed in 1970 by an even more popular Nixon property, *All My Children*. Finally, in 1983 she cocreated *Loving*, later retitled *The City*.

In 1973 William Bell, another Phillips apprentice who learned his craft by writing for *The Guiding Light*, introduced a new hit serial, *The Young and the Restless*. Fourteen years later he brought a second successful daytime drama to TV, *The Bold and the Beautiful*.

As a new millennium approached, several of these dramas were still being televised every weekday afternoon.

One of Phillips' idiosyncrasies was that she refused to address actors and actresses by their real names, preferring to use the names of their characters. In the early radio years she dictated as many as six scripts daily, amounting to 60,000 words weekly and three million words annually. Phillips was depicted as a good storyteller but not an especially effective dialoguer. As a result, her performers often attempted to rewrite many of her lines.

In her private life, she fell in love with a married man, who refused to marry her when she told him that she could not bear children. Although she never married, Phillips later adopted two children — a son, Thomas, and a daughter, Katherine. The latter, who helped her mother write *As the World Turns* for a while, created the TV serial *A World Apart*, which ran for fifteen months in 1970-71. Based on a figure similar to her mother, it concerned a soap opera writer who adopted a son and a daughter. Unlike her mother, however, this heroine eventually married.

Phillips died on December 23, 1973 at the age of 72, but her influence is seen beyond the shows she created. Several of her protégés have carried her traditions forward, continuing to implement ideas that worked well for her.

Phillips placed strong emphasis on characterization, revealing details over time about the figures in her stories and allowing audiences to closely relate to those individuals. Two of her subjects would often spend a quarter-hour on radio dialoguing with one another. Such a phenomenon would seldom be heard on serials written by other authors.

She was also the first writer to focus on the career professional as a protagonist in daytime drama, including clergymen, physicians, nurses, attorneys and similar fields in her serials. She realized that they made interesting targets for stories, and she capitalized on an area that most others missed. The preponderance of such characters in daytime TV serials now is an outgrowth of her astute vision.

Even though *The Brighter Day* didn't attain the status enjoyed by its venerable creator's earliest serials, its uniqueness — based on values and beliefs traditionally held by most Americans — may have given it the impetus to sustain a loyal following. It was a heart-warming, compassionate drama. Phillips' strong reliance on character development meant that the situations those characters encountered were seldom out of the ordinary. No one could be accused of stretching the typical listener's imagination beyond belief in a Phillips drama, another major contribution to the genre.

The Brighter Day premiered on the NBC network on October 11, 1948. But it was actually rolled out on another drama some time before that. For more than three years, NBC carried *Joyce Jordan, M.D.*, the story of a surgeon at Hotchkiss Memorial Hospital in mythical Preston. The serial originated on CBS in 1938 under the title *Joyce Jordan, Girl Interne*. (Did adding the "e" qualify the show's name as the feminine expression of a possibly perceived masculine *Intern*?) Five years later Jordan passed her qualifying medical exams, altering the program's name. Fans of her series recall that she opened her program with this aphorism: "The sick in body, I try to heal; the sick in soul, I try to comfort; For to everyone — rich or poor, young or old — a doctor's hand is a helping hand."

By 1948, however, she was doing more telling about her achievements than performing them. Dr. Jordan had been relegated to duties as hostess of her long-running program, merely narrating the stories of her make-believe patients. Into this setting came Elizabeth (Liz) Susan Dennis. At 25, she was the eldest of five children of the widowed Rev. Richard Dennis. The Dennises lived in a parsonage in the nearby village of Three Rivers.

That autumn Dr. Jordan became better acquainted with the members of the Dennis household while providing medical attention to Liz. Thus, simultaneously, she introduced the radio audience to the Dennis clan. By the time Dr. Jordan said "good-by" on her final broadcast on Friday, October 8, 1948, the fans were already acquainted with the family that would replace her. The following Monday listeners could easily connect with the new series growing out of the show they had been hearing for so long.

To make the change even more transparent, *Jordan's* sponsor — Procter & Gamble's dishwashing powder, Dreft — and its durable announcer, Ron Rawson, moved to *The Brighter Day* with the Dennis clan in the old time period on the same network. The transition could hardly have been smoother, creating a virtually captive audience. It was the stuff that sponsors, ad agencies and network executives dreamed of.

Two later attempts to reprise (resuscitate?) *Joyce Jordan, M.D.* — by ABC in 1951–52 and NBC in 1954–55 — failed. Each experiment lasted less than six months.

In addition to Liz, the siblings in the Dennis family included Althea, the glamorous and tempestuous one; Patsy (whom Poppa Dennis called "Patricia"), the family genius;

Barbara (referred to by everybody as "Bobby"), the ever-hungry adolescent; and Grayling, the only son, tall, lanky, handsome and reserved. (In a later TV series based on the Dennises, he would become an alcoholic, but that was several years hence.)

Liz had become engaged to a young physician, Jerry Forrester, as the serial began. She was an obvious stand-in for her mother, who had died a brief while before that. Accepting the responsibilities and challenges that went with the role, she counseled and encouraged her younger siblings. She also was a listening post for her preacher-father as he faced trials in ministering to his small flock.

If it seems strange that Irna Phillips, with Jewish heritage, created two dramas around Protestant ministers, there is a credible explanation. Early in life she was impressed by the values espoused by Dr. Preston Bradley, a Chicago nondenominational Protestant clergyman. Unable to dismiss his outspoken philosophy regarding brotherhood and peace, a philosophy that she shared, she based the central figures of *The Guiding Light* and *The Brighter Day* around characters who held similar ideals. Bradley's beliefs, in fact, were incorporated into *Light*'s early epigraph:

> There is a destiny that makes us brothers;
> None goes his way alone.
> All that we send into the lives of others...
> Comes back into our own.

Although not spelled out in those precise terms, that intent was apparent in *The Brighter Day* too. It was characterized daily in the form of Rev. Richard Dennis of the nonsectarian flock in Three Rivers and those who related to him.

Mrs. Kennedy, a housekeeper, performed the tasks of preparing the meals, washing, cleaning and maintaining a tidy home for the Dennis family. Thus relieved of the routine chores, Liz concentrated on the dilemmas facing her sisters and brother. She sought to be a friend to each member of the household while living the examples about which her father instructed.

While Poppa Dennis was the basis for the soap opera's premise, there was little doubt that a feminine presence — as on nearly every successful serial — was at the core of its action. In many ways this story was more about Liz Dennis than the reverend.

The Dennis family encountered a major crisis in one of its earliest broadcasts. Announcer Ron Rawson set the scene:

> ANNOUNCER: Well, the blow has fallen — Poppa Dennis has lost his church. Poppa is a clergyman and the other day one of Poppa's many daughters got her picture in the papers under circumstances not-too-pleasant, and now the vestrymen have decided that ... Poppa must go. Well, the reverend hasn't yet heard the bitter, bitter news, but Liz has heard it.... Dr. Jerry Forrester, Liz's fiancé, bites his lip at Liz's tears. Listen....
>
> LIZ: (Cries softly in the background)
> JERRY: (Over crying) Liz, Liz — oh, but there's nothing to be said ... go ahead ... cry....
> LIZ: When Poppa walks down the street even the little kids tag along after him. In the middle of the night, let someone call

us, say somebody's sick, ... and Poppa goes out. One day I
stopped at the church and there he was on his hands and
knees trying to sew up a rip in the carpet. People ... know
he cares about them. Even Mr. Bliss. Mr. Bliss calls himself
an atheist. He tips his hat to Poppa. Atheist! He's a truer
believer and a better man than the people who've done this
to Poppa.
JERRY: There's no question about that, Liz. Your father is a ...
saint.

A short while later Poppa Dennis arrived and Liz realized that he had already learned
the news. But even in divisiveness, the man of God was true to his call. After Jerry
departed, Poppa confronted a bewildered Liz and Patsy and offered apologies for his failures.

While Poppa Dennis ultimately did not leave the church, neither did Liz marry Jerry
Forrester. A year later, having felt for a while that romance in life was over, Liz became
restless and was drawn toward her new employer, lawyer Sam Winship. Actually, Winship's
own motherless brood — young Toby and Tallulah — appealed to her initially. When Tallulah fell ill, Liz could not help noticing what a caring father Sam was. She began to regard
his judgment with high praise, seeking him out when weighty matters surfaced.

To complicate the situation, yet a third prospect entered Liz's life after a brief while.
Nathan Eldredge was a Hollywood producer who had nearly lost his life in a tragic accident. He favorably impressed every member of the Dennis family, including Poppa. Liz too
grew to genuinely love and appreciate him. But she turned down his marriage proposal, to
her family's complete surprise. Again she found solace in Winship, where she confided the
cares of her heart. He had become her best friend; would he become something more?

Althea, "the problem child," consistently proved that ministers' children are little
different from their peers. While a student at an eastern university situated an ample distance from Three Rivers, she married wealthy Bruce Bigby. At first it appeared to be the
proverbial marriage made in heaven. Not until the charming Dennis sister paid a visit
home from her college town did the family learn that Althea had married Bruce solely for
money, not love. She provoked her father-in-law on that occasion; he even ordered her out
of his house! Althea was nonplussed, however. She set about coercing Bruce into fighting
his family for every penny that was "rightfully his."

Even Liz, who worked overtime to find the good in humanity, was convinced that
Althea was an opportunist — a gold digger whose hooks were imbedded in schemes to
relieve the Bigbys of a major portion of their assets and provide an endless stream of cash
to satisfy her personal whims.

Later — after Althea became a mother — her unbridled ambitions led her to pursue an
acting career, at her family's expense. She intended to sacrifice her baby to achieve it, asking Liz to raise the child while she followed her heart. It was a bit much and proved once
more that ministers' families have feet of clay too.

A couple of years before the radio serial left the air, CBS added a televised version.
The drama aired from January 4, 1954, until September 28, 1962. Initially a quarter-hour
soap opera, it was allotted twenty-five minutes daily in its final three months. On TV the
Dennises moved from Three Rivers to New Hope to Columbus. Liz had married and
moved away, but the other family members remained in the story line. Of the radio cast,

only Bill Smith (Poppa Dennis) joined the program on television, but he departed the TV show when the radio series ended in 1956.

Smith maintained another durable radio role as *Stella Dallas'* longtime confidante Phil Baxter. Earlier he was heard as the title character's father in *Ellery Queen*.

The first Liz Dennis was Margaret Draper. She played *Ma Perkins'* younger daughter, Fay, until that series ended on radio soap opera's final day (November 25, 1960), and had few other major roles. Canadian-born actress Grace Matthews followed as Liz. She already had experience as a family counselor; from 1946–52 she was also playing the elder sibling in *Big Sister*.

The Brighter Day was an appealingly heartwarming story of a low income family's struggles to maintain the unconditional love of its members for each other. It was a welcome addition in many homes, signifying lofty ideals shared by the majority of its listeners. Did Irna Phillips succeed in her mission of introducing ministers as protagonists in some of her serials? The loyalists tuned here could only respond in the affirmative.

5
David Harum

(Bab-O's *Own* Program)

This program baited its audience with the sponsor's frequent premium offers by having serial characters unabashedly refer to giveaway items within the story line. Other dramas generally did it less obtrusively (and, perhaps, less effectively), but here the hook for selling wares was often an integral part of the plot. It was an abstraction that sent some in the industry into spasms. The show itself offered plenty of promise, meanwhile. Its hypothesis involved a small-town New England banker, never married, who was as adept at helping people in trouble as at protecting their investments and loaning money. He followed in the footsteps of a parade of soap opera characters whose destinies included dispensing practical advice out of their bountiful wisdom. Like several of his counterparts, David Harum also had his share of mystery encounters: he would search for kidnapped damsels in distress, nail an occasional scoundrel and expose diabolical schemes the police didn't know existed. The common sense he employed, along with the perceptive abilities that he acquired and that everybody else in Homeville missed, turned the banker-hero into a trusted friend of the righteous and a hated nemesis of evildoers. His exploits supplied adventure and inspiration while capitalizing on premiums that turned lukewarm listeners into faithful fans.

Producers: Frank and Anne Hummert
Directors: Martha Atwell, Himan Brown, John Buckwalter, Arthur Hanna, Ed King, Lester Vail
Writers: Peggy Blake, John DeWitt, Noel B. Gerson, Charles J. Gussman, Johanna Johnston, Mary W. Reeves
Music: Stanley Davis
Sound Effects: Jack Anderson, Bill Brown
Announcer: Ford Bond
David Harum: Wilmer Walter, Craig McDonnell, Cameron Prud'homme (1944–47, 50–51)
Polly Benson (Aunt Polly): Charme Allen, Eve Condon
James Benson: Bennett Kilpack
Susan Price Wells: Peggy Allenby, Joan Tompkins, Gertrude Warner
Others: Ray Bramley, Donald Briggs, Joseph Curtin, Marjorie Davies, Ethel Everett, Roy Fant, Paul Ford, Florence Lake, Arthur Maitland, Junius Matthews, Richard McKay,

Claudia Morgan, Billy Redfield, Philip Reed, William Shelley, Paul Stewart, Zeke Swinney, Ken Williams, more

Theme: "Sunbonnet Sue" (initially hummed by Stanley Davis to his own guitar accompaniment, later played on the organ)

Sponsors: This program's 15-year run was supported by B. T. Babbitt, Inc., primarily for Bab-O cleanser. Its hitchhike commercials (brief announcements for other products made by the sponsor) at the end of the broadcast plugged Babbitt's Lycons home soap-making recipes, farm products and Best soap. It was governed by the Blackett-Sample-Hummert agency and Duane Jones for Babbitt.

Ratings: Spectacular in 1939–40, when it reached 9.0. In only five of 14 seasons for which numbers were posted did the series climb above 5.0, however (median: 4.6). Lowest was 2.3 (1944–45). Frequent shifts in networks and broadcast times may have frustrated marginal fans, who perhaps had difficulty locating the series.

On the Air: Jan. 27, 1936–Mar. 27, 1936, NBC Blue, 10:45 a.m. ET; Mar. 30, 1936–Sept. 27, 1940, NBC, 11 a.m.; Sept. 30, 1940–Jan. 10, 1947, NBC, 11:45 a.m.; Jan. 13, 1947–June 25, 1948, CBS, 10:45 a.m.; June 28, 1948–Jan. 6, 1950, CBS, 3:00 p.m.; Jan. 9, 1950–Jan. 5, 1951, NBC, 11:45 a.m. Also: 1937–38, MBS, 3:45 p.m.; Feb. 2, 1942–May 14, 1943, CBS, 3:00 p.m.

Once again we present David Harum, *one of the most beloved stories in American fiction, for David Harum is America. It's the story of every one of us — of our search for love ... for happiness ... and the good way of life.*

— Epigraph to *David Harum*

"Sweeten the swill!" was — as radio serial heroine Mary Jane Higby recalled in her book of memoirs — the opening line of a commercial often repeated on *David Harum*.[1] Delivered by announcer Ford Bond in an emotionless, staccato style on behalf of sponsor Benjamin Talbot Babbitt, Inc., the ad espoused a farm animal feed.

It was probably an appropriate match for a show featuring "the kindly little country philosopher," as Harum was dubbed. While homemakers listened, the mystery and intrigue offered here — frequently at lunchtime, just as the "hands" were returning to farmhouses up and down the eastern seaboard — could easily persuade critics to think this series might have been targeted to a rural male audience. The following commercial, which Bond issued on one mid–1940s *Harum* broadcast a couple of minutes before high noon, is typical:

> *Now, all of you hog raisers ... helping supply America with fine pork ... accept this free offer: Write today for a new 48-page book on farm sanitation. It gives practical, low-cost methods for sanitizing yards and pens. Includes methods that can help make your hogs grow sturdier ... heavier ... so you can market more pounds of pork. Write for your copy today. Address Lycons, L-Y-C-O-N-*

S, care of this station. Ask for free Lycons farm book.

Lycons, a Babbitt brand name, was a flake commodity to be turned into the consumer's own laundry detergent at home. Recipes for using it were printed on the product labels.

At least one radio historiographer believed that this soap opera — it did regularly advertise a soap product, Babbitt's flagship commodity, Bab-O, a grease-dissolving household cleanser — may have been remembered more for its promotional stunts than for its program content.[2] No other serial integrated the mailhook into its story line more frequently or more effectively than *David Harum*. Its messages were often straightforward appeals to listeners to respond in order to receive a premium offer. The commercial above is an example.

Harum was one of three dramas underwritten by B. T. Babbitt. The others were *Lora Lawton* (1943–50) and the short-lived *Nona from Nowhere* (which succeeded *Lawton*, 1950–51). All vigorously exploited the premium derivation, but *Harum* was the champion at consistently and unabashedly combining it into the story line to beef up (no pun intended) marketing efforts. For ten cents and a label from the sponsor's product, listeners might receive a packet of flower seeds "just like those planted by David Harum in his very own garden." The response to that bait brought about some unanticipated pandemonium: the show's fans mailed in over 275,000 labels, each accompanied by a dime. Certainly this was all the assurance Babbitt needed that it was doing something right.

In one of the show's typical stunts, listeners heard the drama's characters discussing David's horse, Xanthippe, over an extended period of time. Then, individually and collectively, they arrived at the conclusion that Xanthippe — named for the rumormongering, nagging spouse of the Athenian philosopher and instructor Socrates — was a lousy moniker for a thoroughbred steed. Who could argue that? Harum's friends and neighbors suggested that he sanction a new appellation.

Bingo! In a short while announcer Ford Bond was urging fans to participate in a contest to rename the mount. To simplify matters, listeners could write proposed names on the back of Bab-O labels and mail them in. More than 400,000 labels arrived, underscoring not only the listeners' level of interest in the program and the contest but also the marketing power of such efforts. In an ironic twist on the animal's former name, the contest officials declared "Town Talk" as the winning entry.

For several weeks, in another competition, the show gave away a horse a week to a different, presumably lucky, listener. On *Harum*, the giveaways were an accepted part of doing business.

Long before this, Babbitt, a maker of household and personal cleansing products, had earned a reputation for adopting unusual and flamboyant techniques to create recognition for some of its goods. The firm was the first to gain the confidence of women who, in the midnineteenth century, were dubious about buying wrapped soap bars. By returning the soap wrappers to Babbitt, consumers were offered a series of highly prized illustrations. This tactic was sanctioned as the first time that premium advertising was used, certainly on a grand scale. It became a harbinger of multiple schemes that the company would use to increase trade.

In another ploy, thousands of spectators were drawn to New York City to view huge cauldrons filled with precious soap ingredients. Babbitt estimated the vessels to be valued at a quarter of a million dollars. People flocked, reporting far and wide what they had seen, a phenomenon to marvel over in that prebroadcasting era.

Another time Babbitt flabbergasted journalists by spending $70,000 for a breed of large, fast-trotting draft horses for yet another promotion. These great steeds pulled carriages to riverbanks, where they were linked with ferryboats. On shorelines in metropolitan centers, samples of Babbitt's Best soap were given to passengers and crews as the media looked on. This captured the public's attention and imagination far beyond their locales.

In the twentieth century, Babbitt's fascination with premium-baiting gained a mammoth infusion on the resignation of advertising executive Duane Jones from the Blackett-Sample-Hummert agency. After he launched his own outfit, one of Jones' first moves was to court and win the Babbitt account. Before the innovations he would launch on the *Harum* radio series, premiums were linked to soap operas only as marginal tools. Heretofore they had merely indicated an approximate number of listener-consumers for a given serial.

As Jones was being introduced to the Babbitt promotional mix, the firm's product popularity had sunk to a low ebb. Bab-O, its best-known commodity, could muster only a seventh-place showing among competitors. Jones decided to revitalize its sales by concentrating on a medium that he knew plenty about as a Blackett-Sample-Hummert alumnus: radio. As a start, he would focus on the heavily populated metropolitan areas of New York and nearby environs.

In the mid–1930s he bought the rights to an 1898 best-selling novel on which a 1934 motion picture had been based starring America's legendary superhero entertainer Will Rogers. The novel, *David Harum*, and the movie featured a homespun New England banker who offered practical advice on a variety of subjects while providing vigilant surveillance over his clients' finances. Jones enlisted the aid of Frank and Anne Hummert, two of his most trusted former business associates, to adapt the tale to a serialized radio play. When the drama debuted in 1935 on New York City's powerful station WOR, it acquired an immediate following.

Encouraged, Jones decided there was potential for a much larger market beyond the confines of New York. He planned to broaden the audience by taking the series to network radio. *Harum* debuted nationally on NBC Blue (forerunner of ABC) on January 27, 1936. Babbitt underwrote the serial for the next 15 years, the full length of the run.

Bursting with the success of attempts to gain customers through its initial premium offers, Babbitt added similar marketing ploys to its programs. For years the firm would announce a new offer every three or four months. Sales of Bab-O and other goods began to climb. Many first-time users of these products became repeat buyers, significantly increasing Babbitt's market share.

Meanwhile, *Harum*'s success with premium offers was closely monitored by producers of other washboard weepers. Few of them permitted the dramas in their trusts to become conduits serving little more than their sponsors' prize promotions — a ploy the Jones-Hummert duo had so brazenly embraced on *Harum*. While serials like *Ma Perkins, Today's Children, Aunt Jenny's Real Life Stories, The Romance of Helen Trent, One Man's Family* and others dangled flower seeds, photo albums and other trinkets at fans, only the trio of Babbitt serials resembled a premium lover's paradise.

Ford Bond provided continuity to the Babbitt dramas as the announcer on all three. Although only two aired at any given time, Bond's rapid-fire delivery for the same advertised commodities emitted a compelling urgency about buying them. "Compare grease-dishwashing Bab-O with your former lazy cleanser," he'd proclaim. "Then see if you could ever go back to any less modern method!" If listeners missed his bid on one show, they could catch it on another, for the commercials were about the same. The repetition was obviously effective: Bab-O sales flourished.

David Harum became an important crusader "for love ... for happiness ... and the good way of life." A lifelong bachelor, he resided in the home of his sister, Polly Benson (called Aunt Polly on the show), and her husband, James, who operated the local hotel. As president of the Homeville Bank, Harum was in a position not only to dispense financial assistance but also to become actively involved in the personal lives of the townsfolk. They looked to him as one of their leading citizens and readily sought his sage counsel. As a shrewd businessman, David also earned the reputation of being as penurious as Silas Marner.

Offering large doses of grandfatherly advice and helping folks out of trouble was his forte, however. An early epigraph introduced the program as "the story that has thrilled America for generations — the true-to-life story of David Harum, the kindly little country philosopher who makes life worth living by helping those who need help, and by outwitting those who are too clever in scheming in helping themselves."

In a manner befitting *Just Plain Bill* (the barber of Hartville), the banker of Homeville — "the Will Rogers of radio soap operas"[3] — projected values that were considered "all-American." Kind and benevolent, Harum was generous to a fault, often going out of his way to assist a troubled neighbor, relative or friend. Sometimes his involvement in their lives brought difficulty and danger to himself. But just like all of his philosophical peers in radio soapland — Bill Davidson of *Just Plain Bill,* Ma Perkins, Ruth Evans Wayne of *Big Sister*, Papa David Solomon of *Life Can Be Beautiful,* Dr. John Ruthledge of *The Guiding Light* and others — he had the innate ability to stay levelheaded. Those about him might be losing their capacities for holding everything in proper perspective, but not David. He could free himself — and everybody else, if needed — from the hopeless calamities that beset much of the local citizenry.

On the broadcast of August 10, 1945, Harum landed in one of those trying situations. Harum and Susan Price Wells — who often assisted him in his exploits of "do-goodism" — had tracked a young kidnap victim, Jenny Gray, to the estate of Jonathan Blake. There Gray was being detained against her will. Shortly after their arrival on the lawn of the secluded mansion, Harum and Wells found themselves face-to-face with one of Blake's big, burly thugs who was brandishing a Colt-45.

"I got orders to ask questions after I shoot," he informed them. Having been down similar roads before, Harum's fans must have viewed it as just another day in the life of a rural banker. Their hero would think of something to overturn the tables on Blake's security man — and to release Jenny Gray from her unwelcome confinement before further disaster struck.

Nearly all of the really dastardly rogues who appeared in serials that were fixed in rural settings were émigrés from metropolitan areas. Such curious eccentricities as unnatural moms, white-collar criminals, professional hit men, cold wives, designing women and men who were simply rich, ruthless and rotten were usually imported from the big towns. Invariably, they soon encountered sagacious personalities who could outsmart or eliminate them, or win them over to new perspectives in heart and mind.

In one sequence in the late 1940s, David injected himself into the lives of Elaine

Dilling, a former Homeville resident, and her daughter, Dorothy. The bank president had some legitimate reasons for becoming involved in their dilemma. The two women had temporarily returned to Homeville to see about some financial concerns. Accompanied by Jack Wallace, Dorothy's fiancé, they arrived to claim an inheritance that legally belonged to Dorothy. The matter so piqued David's interest and empathy that he invited the ladies to stay at Aunt Polly's house on Catalpa Street while they were in town.

What David didn't know was that, at that very moment, he was being played for a fool. Dorothy Dilling was an impostor. With Wallace and a third accomplice — the crafty Hilda Jackson, who arrived in town posing as Mrs. Bradshaw, Elaine Dilling's mother — she mixed deception and mayhem. Hilda Jackson was keeping close tabs on the real Dorothy Dilling, whom she was holding against Dorothy's will at the former Dilling mansion. Listeners knew that none of it portended pleasantness for David after he suspected that something was amiss.

One of his first clues surfaced when he discovered that Elaine Dilling was frightened by her "daughter." Yet with Elaine powerless to help herself, it appeared that Jack, "Dorothy" and "Mrs. Bradshaw" would succeed in their scheme — to gain the inheritance that belonged to the hostage, Dorothy Dilling — unless David Harum could learn the truth and find a way to prevent them from carrying out their fiendish plan. By then, of course, he had already earned a rather widespread reputation for saving damsels in distress — particularly those tied up in knots in old estates. Longtime fans knew that they had little cause to start sweating.

On another occasion the banker-hero turned his attention to his old friend Ed Brice. Brice was experiencing marital discord with his wife, Ina. (Let's face it: although David Harum was a lifelong, self-proclaimed bachelor, he had the right answer for *everybody!*) Fortunately, Harum was able to reunite the couple after passing along the information that the man who had so aroused Ina, Denny Elkins, earned his living operating a stolen-car ring.

Things weren't really that simple, however. When Ina returned to Ed's waiting arms, their daughter, Lucy, fell romantically for (can you guess?) Denny Elkins. Of course, it took David Harum to help her work through her obsession. She had to be led to see that Herbert Elkins, Denny's brother, cited for unquestioned honesty and integrity, would make a much better choice for a husband. (Why the Brices were hell-bent on marrying into the Elkins family was never explained; it seemed enough that there were *two* eligible bachelors in Homeville at that moment — *three* if you count wily old David Harum.)

World War II exerted a heavy influence on this serial, just as it did on many others. At one point David relinquished his horse trading and ledger sheets to serve his country as the manager of a plant manufacturing secret weapons for the government. Though he had no prior experience, the fans forgave that, since he was doing his part for the nation. The genteel financier wasn't alone among soap opera figures in his quest. Pepper Young's daddy, Sam, professed a similar occupation in about the same time period. Lolly-Baby's mama, Stella Dallas, always of modest means, merely worked in a war plant. In addition to Ma Perkins' son, John, and others who went off to the battlefront, other serial characters — on *Kitty Foyle, Front Page Farrell* and *The O'Neills* — worked wartime jobs too.

Early in the conflict several programs (including *David Harum*) dwelled on homefront complexities by having younger men enroll or be drafted into the armed services. Within three months after the bombing of Pearl Harbor, characters on *Harum* and *Amanda of Honeymoon Hill* were rejected for service because of health-related deficiencies. Such situations injected a hint of realism into the uncertainties faced by their heroes and heroines.

At one point *Harum* wafted onto the airwaves with the familiar strains of its theme song, "Sunbonnet Sue," hummed by Stanley Davis while he plucked the notes on a guitar. Davis must have made a nice living at this, since he also hummed the theme for *The Romance of Helen Trent* and whistled the melody for *John's Other Wife*, both while accompanying himself on the guitar. By the mid–1940s, however, the hums and plunks were discarded on *Harum* and were replaced by the customary studio organ. Though "Sunbonnet Sue" still ushered in the serial, it was played to a lively beat on the console. This gave the drama a greater sense of urgency while complementing the staccato delivery of Ford Bond's narration and commercials. ("Once again we present Bab-O's *own* program, *David Harum*," he imparted.)

The role of David Harum was played by three radio thespians: Wilmer Walter, Craig McDonnell and Cameron Prud'homme. The first two portrayed leads on shows that built their reputations on pulp fiction. Walter, the initial Harum, was Andy Gump in the 1934–37 radio adaptation of *The Gumps*. That series was based on a prominent comic strip of the era. His credits are brief, since he died at age 57 on August 23, 1941, at the apex of radio's Golden Age. McDonnell, who also announced for another serial, *The O'Neills*, was a principal in both *Under Arrest* and *Official Detective*. The latter show was loosely drawn from stories appearing in a magazine of the same name. McDonnell also appeared in *Bobby Benson's Adventures*, *Bringing Up Father*, *Daddy and Rollo*, *The Adventures of Dick Tracy*, *The Second Mrs. Burton* and *Valiant Lady*.

Prud'homme, who played the Harum role from 1944 to 1947 and again in 1950–51, sounded so much like Arthur Hughes — the actor who dispensed advice in the small town of Hartville on *Just Plain Bill* — that listeners might have easily confused the two. Since their air traits, missions and personalities were so similar, the enunciations of one actor might easily have passed as the other's. Some fans probably thought that the two were the same individual, never knowing the difference. Actors' names were seldom revealed to audiences on most soap operas.

Prud'homme was born on December 16, 1892, at Auburn, California, and earned distinguished recognition for his work in at least three mediums — stage, film and radio. In all of them he frequented roles as a father, offering counsel based on his maturity and depth. He was dad to such stage and screen luminaries as Shirley Booth, Tammy Grimes, Katharine Hepburn and Geraldine Page. And after breaking into radio in San Francisco in 1931, Prud'homme landed parts in such series as *Stella Dallas*, *A Woman of America*, *One Man's Family*, *Backstage Wife*, *Life Can Be Beautiful*, *Young Widder Brown*, *Cavalcade of America* and *Theatre Guild on the Air*. He also penned scripts for *Hawthorne House*, a regional serial drama heard in the West. The accomplished actor died on November 27, 1967, at Pompton Plains, New Jersey.

The supporting role of Aunt Polly was handled by Charme Allen and Eve Condon. Allen also played the feminine lead in a short-lived comedy dialogue series, *Mother and Dad* (1943-44). She frequented the repertory company of *Columbia Presents Corwin*. Aside from another situation comedy, *Abie's Irish Rose*, her strength was in the serials. She carried running parts in *Backstage Wife*, *County Seat*, *The O'Neills*, *Pretty Kitty Kelly*, *The Story of Mary Marlin*, *Valiant Lady* and *We Love and Learn*. She died at age 89 on October 4, 1980.

Condon had only one other recorded radio credit, but it was a biggie. She portrayed the title character in the popular 1930s serial *Mrs. Wiggs of the Cabbage Patch*. Incidentally, if David Harum's voice sounded like (Just Plain) Bill Davidson's, there seemed to be a lot of similarity (albeit in a singsongy, whiny petition) between Aunt Polly and another of radio's distaff do-gooders, Ma Perkins. Could both have been cut from the same bolt of cloth?

David Harum was a ray of sunshine to the downtrodden masses in his community. Never bewildered by those who used evil means to gain fortune at the expense of the weak, he vigilantly pursued piety. He was the epitome of rectitude within the heart and soul of small-town America. Even those incessant giveaways that brought his shows into listeners' homes could never diminish the character that personified this kindly little country philosopher. In him, perhaps, his most devoted fans saw something that they too had always wanted to be.

6
Front Page Farrell
(The Unforgettable Radio Drama)

Centering on a newspaper reporter and his wife, David and Sally Farrell, *Front Page Farrell* was launched as a melodrama, heavy on domestic crises while thin on journalistic exposes — precisely what anyone would expect from the Hummert production factory. Somewhere in the late 1940s, however, the serial took a bolder stance toward thugs in the Big Apple. David's efforts intensified, his persistence in uncovering the truth turning relentless as he sought to unveil legions of evildoers and place them behind bars. Perhaps in an effort to combat audience slippage to television, this "get-tough" policy became even more pronounced as time went on, moving almost exclusively from matters of the heart to hysteria and homicide. By the 1950s new five-part episodes were launched every Monday. David was on a tear to solve mysteries, expose corruption and deal with crooks of every persuasion. By Friday evening he and Sally had helped remove that week's culprit from the streets, giving him another page-one byline. Infrequent listeners who missed an episode now and then found it simpler to keep up with the story line when the serial offered a new case every week. Because *Farrell* aired well within the hearing range of millions of men, it enjoyed the added benefit of being listened to by commuters.

Producers: Frank and Anne Hummert
Directors: John Buckwalter, Arthur Hanna, Frank Hummert, Richard Leonard, Ed Slattery, Bill Sweets, Blair Walliser
Writers: Alvin Boretz, Harold Gast, Bob Saxon, Robert J. Shaw
Music: Rosa Rio
Sound Effects: Ross Martindale, Manny Segal
Announcers: Bill Bond, Larry Elliott, Ed Fleming, Don Hancock
David Farrell: Richard Widmark, Carleton Young, Staats Cotsworth
Sally Farrell: Virginia Dwyer, Florence Williams
Others: Peter Capell, Frank Chase, Robert Donley, Katherine Emmet, Elspeth Eric, Betty Garde, Sylvia Leigh, Athena Lorde, James Monks, William Shelley, Eleanor Sherman, Vivian Smolen, George Sturgeon, James Van Dyke, Evelyn Varden, more

Theme: "You and I Know"

Sponsors: Blackett-Sample-Hummert introduced this serial for American Home Products Corp. (AHP), a firm for which it already governed three other long-running soap operas: *Just Plain Bill, Our Gal Sunday* and *The Romance of Helen Trent.* AHP rotated its goods in commercials on its serials. From its packaged drug division, the Whitehall Pharmacal Co., it advertised Kolynos toothpaste and tooth powder dentifrice, Anacin pain reliever, Kriptin antihistamine, Bi-So-Dol analgesic, Freezone corn remover, Heet liniment, Dristan and Primatene cold remedies, Preparation H hemorrhoid medication, Neet hair remover, Infrarub balm, Sleep-Eze calmative and more. From its household products division, Boyle-Midway, it promoted Black Flag insect repellent, Aerowax and Olde English floor cleaners, Wizard room deodorizer, Sani-Flush toilet cleanser, Easy-Off oven cleaner and others. AHP was the serial's only sponsor, from inception to cancellation.

Ratings: Though ratings were never phenomenal, they often hovered in the "high 5s." In nine out of 13 seasons, the numbers reached or exceeded a highly respectable 5.5. The lowest figure (2.0) occurred in the program's first year, 1941–42, as it sought an audience. Its peak season (6.8) was 1948–49.

On the Air: June 23, 1941–Mar. 13, 1942, MBS, 1:30 p.m. ET; Sept. 14, 1942–June 29, 1951, NBC, 5:45 p.m.; July 2, 1951–March 26, 1954, NBC, 5:15 p.m.

We now present the exciting, unforgettable radio drama Front Page Farrell, *the story of a crack newspaperman and his wife — the story of David and Sally Farrell.*
— Epigraph to *Front Page Farrell*

Would you believe … this many crimes to solve?
• *The Deep-Freezer Murder Case:* The body of a department store executive is found in a refrigeration unit. Ace newspaper reporter David Farrell of the *New York Daily Eagle* and his wife Sally, uncover frantic efforts by the guilty party to conceal facts that would expose him.
• *The Fountain of Youth Murder Case:* While having a rejuvenation treatment, a former beauty queen is killed. David and Sally aid the police in uncovering a quest to retrieve lost youth and beauty, a story so fantastic that it can hardly be believed.
• *The Blinding Light Murder Case:* When a modeling agency owner is murdered, the police expect an open-and-shut case against a young model who threatened the owner within hearing range of a waiting room of applicants. But David and Sally's own examination soon points the skeptics elsewhere.
• *The Interrupted Wedding Murder Case:* With the murder of the bride's father and the disappearance of a wedding gift that was alleged to contain a large sum of money, David and Sally have their hands full. Nor are they helped by the fact that the murderer has blended into a sea of guests.

All of this occurred on one serial? Yes, and all of it took place within four weeks (not a misprint) — including crime, investigation and solution. Impossible in soap opera? So many heinous assaults on any other dishpan drama might have easily required a year and a half. But on *Front Page Farrell*, with its 1950s upbeat tempo, at least 52 different evildoers were brought to justice *every year*. No other show in daytime radio could boast the resolution of a crime a week. David Farrell was on a roll, aided and abetted by producers who decided to help him grab more and more of those page-one bylines.

By midcentury *Front Page Farrell* had a couple of devices working in its behalf, devices that most other serials lacked. Five daily installments based on a single criminal act was one such device. This allowed selective listeners, and those who couldn't become involved in continuing, open-ended story lines, to tune in for a few days, perhaps catching an entire sequence. They knew that with this serial, unlike all others except *Aunt Jenny's Real Life Stories* (which seldom delved into serious mystery), they could hear a crime committed on Monday and solved on Friday. In between, David and Sally discovered clues that led to the perpetrator. Everything was tied up in a neat package by week's end; the no-accounts were exposed and carted off to prison — no muss, no fuss.

A second stroke of good fortune lay in the fact that, for most of its life, this serial was broadcast in the late afternoon — well within the scope of many a male listener. Whereas some men may have found other forms of soap opera repulsive, *Farrell's* contemporary setting and emphasis on quick action likely drew the attention of many males. This factor contributed to a portion of the drama's audience.

Front Page Farrell didn't start out as a vibrant thriller series, however. In 1941 it became the first live serial on the Mutual Broadcasting System to air from New York City. It was also one of the first pieces of business that the Blackett-Sample-Hummert advertising agency gave to Mutual.

Remember the Hummerts? Frank and Anne were the same creatives whose characters wallowed elsewhere in matinee goo. Just because David Farrell was a "crack newspaperman," he couldn't hope to escape the domestic crises that flowed out of radios across the land — infiltrating virtually all daytime soap operas during their heyday. One would hardly think a serial was a Hummert property if the melodrama was missing.

Throughout the 1940s, this serial fashioned a conflict between home and work, intersecting the Farrells' personal lives with David's not-so-relentless pursuit of good stories. The Hummerts decided that women might welcome some spine-tingling distraction in the midst of their daytime sagas, especially if it arrived wrapped in the cloak of familiar soap opera devices. Writing a news story was what David did for a living, just as Larry Noble was an actor and Jerry Malone earned his income as a physician. In this serial's formative years, however, David's occupation got no more than equal billing with the domestic issues that the Hummerts believed homemakers wanted to hear.

David's marriage to Sally Howard, in fact, was one of the strangest in the annals of daytime serials. David had had affairs with several glamorous, even famous, women before meeting Sally. Yet in the early weeks of the soap opera, David — to prevent her from marrying a middle-aged multimillionaire whom her family had picked out for her — virtually kidnapped the inexperienced 20-year-old. Following a whirlwind courtship, they were wed. The trite epigraph in those days suggested that theirs was "the unforgettable story of a handsome, dashing young star reporter on one of New York's greatest newspapers, and the girl he marries on impulse, to save her from throwing herself away on a rich man twice her age."

Within a brief time a fan magazine suggested that David's widely publicized encounters with other women cast a dark shadow over his vows to Sally.[1] "She thinks she is inferior to women he's known in the past and women he meets in his daily work," a journalist calculated. "In her heart she fears that some day he will meet a beautiful woman writer and, if this happens, she will lose him."

Are we still talking about the serial that focused on "The Deep-Freezer Murder Case" and all those other chiller-thrillers? Yep, same one. But that was a few years into the future.

This silly period occurred, coincidentally, at about the time of America's involvement in World War II. David wrote some stories about war production efforts at home. In the fall of 1943 he covered wartime topics that had been selected by the serial writers with the help of the U.S. Office of War Information. Sally did her part by laboring in a war factory, as did some of her peers, such as the heroine of *Kitty Foyle*.

Maybe to prove something to himself — or to prove his manliness to his young wife — David decided to enlist in the army. The couple pondered their fate shortly before he was to report for duty. Summing up their dialogue, the announcer dawdled while the syrup flowed: "And so David and Sally Farrell stand on the doorstep of their little home facing the future, not knowing what it will bring them, but knowing in their hearts that they have kept faith with themselves ... their country ... and their God. They stand there beneath the stars, ready to do their part to bring back to this world the everlasting right which belongs to each and every one of us — the right to live in love, security and peace!" It was a tender moment, and there probably wasn't a dry eye above the onions that many a homemaker was peeling for supper that night.

In the serial's second season, when the show advanced to NBC, much of the tripe was abandoned; the epigraph was replaced by a softer, mellower inscription (included at the start of this chapter). But on many days the journalistic crusades continued to play second fiddle to the problems at home. Sally's mother, for one, remained an omnipresent dynamic in their lives. They also had a son, Jimmy, who — though seldom heard — was good for a domestic crisis now and then.

As the 1940s played out and television began to erode radio's ability to retain large audiences, some serials were discontinued. The producers of those that remained decided to add more action to their stories, to move them along more swiftly to try to hold the fans to traditional listening habits. Murder became a favorite sport, cropping up 30 times on 15 serials in a single calendar year! Attempted murders, fatal accidents and other violent tragedies contributed to the serials' new, action-packed image.

Possibly at the forefront of all of this carnage stood *Front Page Farrell*, a drama that could shed its staid domesticity rather easily to concentrate on fighting crime. Off with Jimmy! The devil with Mother Howard! The chance for another woman in David's life could be damned! There were hoodlums to be separated from civilized society and Sally could help her man track them down! (She too was a newspaper reporter when they met, although never a great writer. Her forte was in assisting David, gathering details and checking leads. Occasionally she became a maniac's foil, cornered in an effort to thwart David's scrutiny as he got too close to fingering a dispassionate killer.)

For three or four years after reinventing itself, this series resulted in a hard-hitting investigative phenomena. Though the change didn't ultimately save the show, it probably staved off its demise, squeezing out a few extra years of dialogue and fast-paced action. The drama focused on such weekly case titles as "The Man Who Knew All the Angles," "The Case of the Mysterious Killer," "High Explosives" and "Fatal Smile."

In a typical plot sequence, David rented a room at a hotel where a world-famous scientist had been killed. At the time of his death the researcher was working on a secret formula that had international import. David gradually pieced together a succession of clues that led him to the identity of a cold-blooded assassin whose intentions went much further.

In another case, David was scheduled to interview an author whose latest published exposé cast several socially prominent individuals in a poor light. Arriving for his appointment at her home, he followed a taxi pulling up to the front door. Inside he found the author's body. Before the escapade ended he was thrust into a daring robbery and encountered a blackmail ring.

It was rough-and-tough stuff, not the dainty doings most daytime audiences were accustomed to. And as radio's final adult serial of the afternoon, it set the tone for *Mr. Keen, Tracer of Lost Persons; Big Town; The FBI in Peace and War; Mr. Chameleon; Casey, Crime Photographer; Hearthstone of the Death Squad; Mr. and Mrs. North* and other crusading sleuths who would occupy the airwaves a short time later, during the evening hours.

Richard Widmark, later of Hollywood cinema fame, was the first to play David Farrell. Born in Sunrise, Minnesota, on December 26, 1914, he attended Lake Forest College in Illinois and for a couple of years taught speech and drama. For nearly a decade, starting in the late 1930s, he cut his acting teeth on radio drama. In a 1977 newspaper interview, he affirmed that this period was the best time of his life. "It was a very nice living, and completely anonymous," he remembered. "I worked with some marvelous people — Joe Cotton, Arlene Francis, Agnes Morehead [*sic*], Orson Welles, Art Carney. It took me the longest time to realize that Art Carney was funny, because we were always doing *Gangbusters* together on Saturday night."

Widmark appeared on *Home of the Brave, Helpmate, Suspense, Cavalcade of America, March of Time, Gangbusters, Ethel and Albert, True Confessions, Big Sister, Mystery Theater, Inner Sanctum Mysteries, The Mercury Theatre of the Air, Meet the Dixons* and *Joyce Jordan, Girl Interne.*

He won an Academy Award nomination for his portrayal of a depraved gangster in 1947's *Kiss of Death*, launching his motion-picture career. He was typecast as a villain or spoilsport in numerous cinema roles. Widmark returned to radio in the late 1970s as host and occasional star of a CBS adventure series, *Sears Radio Theatre.* In the late 1990s he appeared sporadically in television specials and films.

Carleton Young, the second actor to play David Farrell, gained leads in *The Count of Monte Cristo, Ellery Queen, Trouble House* and *Hollywood Mystery Time.* He carried running roles in *Carol Kennedy's Romance, Stella Dallas, Society Girl, Second Husband, Hilltop House, Life Begins, Portia Faces Life* and *Our Gal Sunday.* Young died at age 64 on July 11, 1971.

The actor best associated with the part of David Farrell was Staats Cotsworth, who is probably even better remembered for another mystery series in which he played the title role: *Casey, Crime Photographer.* This veteran of the microphone was on so many shows, in fact, that in 1946 he was designated "radio's busiest actor."[2] At the time he had appeared on 7,500 broadcasts over a dozen years. His average day included an 8:30 a.m. rehearsal for *Lone Journey* and ended at midnight after the West Coast repeat of a live broadcast of *Mr. and Mrs. North.* He played Lieutenant Bill Weigand in that mystery series.

Some of Cotsworth's other radio credits included *Lorenzo Jones, Stella Dallas, When a Girl Marries, Marriage for Two, Amanda of Honeymoon Hill, Big Sister, The Man from G-2, Mark Trail, The Cavalcade of America, The Right to Happiness, The Second Mrs. Burton, The March of Time Quiz* and *Rogue's Gallery.*

Born in Oak Park, Illinois, on February 17, 1908, Cotsworth was an accomplished photographer, painter and Shakespearean and repertory actor. Shortly before he died on April 9, 1979, in New York City, the versatile artist returned to the microphone to star in Himan Brown's *The CBS Mystery Theater.*

In a 1948 magazine interview, Cotsworth, provided, apparently unintentionally, some fascinating insights into the compensation of radio actors.[3] The prospect certainly existed for some rather lucrative incomes in this business; most outsiders had no idea just how rewarding those were, however, until the newsmagazine hit the stands.

One day over a few drinks on the terrace of his penthouse apartment, Cotsworth loosened up to a *Newsweek* reporter's pertinent inquiry. Just how had an actor who began his career in the repertory theater of Eva Le Gallienne, and who had also played on Broadway with such luminaries as Judith Anderson, Maurice Evans and Flora Robson, turned to *Casey, Crime Photographer* and *The Second Mrs. Burton* for a livelihood? When the full-page text of his answer appeared under the banner "Cotsworth in the Chips," radio actors everywhere cringed. The deep, dark secret surrounding their rather generous occupational recompense, a matter they had closely guarded across the years, suddenly came to light. As a consequence, a few who weren't intimidated by all the publicity decided to meet the press too, sharing similar accounts of large salaries.

The periodical estimated Cotsworth's weekly income at $1,000, an immense sum in 1948 when incomes from all trades and professions were considered. He flatly acknowledged that he received $250 weekly for the half-hour *Casey* series. In addition, he portrayed the title role in *Front Page Farrell* every day and was the male lead in the daily *Lone Journey.* An average of three times weekly his recurring role was written into the story line of *The Second Mrs. Burton.* Beyond that, he appeared each week, without billing, on one or more other nighttime shows. With union scale then at $18.15 plus $7.26 for each hour of rehearsal per fifteen-minute show, anyone could easily calculate his approximate income.

So why did he act on soap operas? "Giving up a daytime show is like turning in your insurance policy," Cotsworth freely admitted. Although he hadn't intended to release a financial statement to the press, his comments offered fresh insights into a gray area that the public could only speculate about until then. After all, those penthouses, servants and Cadillacs were coming from somewhere!

The part of David's wife, Sally, was played by two well-known radio actresses: Virginia Dwyer and Florence Williams. Dwyer, the first, also had running roles in *Second Husband, Houseboat Hannah, Backstage Wife, Aunt Jenny's Real Life Stories* and *Joyce Jordan, Girl Interne.* In late 1954 she was cast as the heroine, Jocelyn McLeod Brent, wife of Dr. Jim Brent, in a six-month trial at televising radio's popular *Road of Life.* (Her real-life husband, Walter Gorman, directed the experiment.) Though it failed, it was the first of several TV serials to extend Dwyer's career another two decades. She was cast in *The Secret Storm* (1955–56), *Young Doctor Malone* (1958–59), *The Guiding Light* (1959–60), *As the World Turns* (1962) and *Another World* (1964–75). In the last she played the feminine lead.

The actress best identified with the part of Sally Farrell was Florence Williams, who

Staats Cotsworth played the title role of newsman David Farrell in *Front Page Farrell*. David was assisted by his wife, Sally, played by Florence Williams. David Farrell's front-page bylines were a natural outgrowth of the couple's relentless pursuit to put New York's vilest behind bars. (Photofest)

took turns in the casts of *Barry Cameron, The Light of the World* and *Roses and Drums*. The St. Louis native became a popular stage actress following her radio career, appearing on Broadway and in regional theater productions.

Front Page Farrell, broadcast over 13 years, was like two dramas in one. Filled with domestic crises in its formative years, the soap opera gradually turned into a daytime version of nighttime radio's hard-hitting journalism crime series *Big Town*. The transition resulted in a more contemporary drama, injecting it with very real issues that affected Americans beyond their own doorsteps.

7

The Guiding Light

(The Longest Narrative Ever Told)

The most durable drama in the history of broadcasting (including both radio and television) was launched with a minister as its central figure. Dr. John Ruthledge, the kindly cleric of rural Five Points, pastored an interdenominational flock. His inspirational qualities were infectious, for the soap opera that swirled about him has survived for more than six decades. Drama-mama Irna Phillips, working through a succession of ministerial appointments to Five Points, expanded this tale into one of character development (a Phillips hallmark), eventually centering on the Bauer family. Papa, Meta, Trudy, Bill, Bertha and others became the focus for three decades. By the early 1950s, as the serial entered television with an enlarged cast, it had long since turned from its humble origins. Yet many of the sustaining qualities that Phillips imbued in it continue to influence *The Guiding Light* and other serials in the modern era. Early on, the program had a penchant for attracting and retaining audiences with contests loaded with substantial prizes. Each competition required proof that entrants had purchased the sponsor's product. Product sales soared and the number of listeners multiplied. Some of those respondents would become lifelong fans, passing their deep devotion to this show from generation to generation.

Producer: Carl Wester and Company
Producer-Director: Joe Ainley
Directors: Harry Bubeck, Gil Gibbons, Gordon Hughes, Howard Keegan, Ted MacMurray, Charles Urquhart
Writers: Emmons Carlson, Art Glad, Irna Phillips
Music: Bernice Yanocek
Sound Effects: Ralph Cummings, Hamilton O'Hara
Announcers: Herb Allen, Clayton (Bud) Collyer, Chet Kingsbury, Fort Pearson
Dr. John Ruthledge: Arthur Peterson
Mary Ruthledge: Mercedes McCambridge, Sarajane Wells
Rose Kransky: Ruth Bailey, Charlotte Manson
Ned Holden: John Hodiak, Ed Prentiss
Papa Bauer: Theodore Goetz
Bertha Bauer: Charita Bauer
Bill Bauer: Lyle Sudrow

Meta Bauer: Jone Allison
Trudy Bauer: Laurette Fillbrandt
Ted White: Arnold Moss
Others: Betty Arnold, Frank Behrens, Bill Bouchey, Sidney Breese, Muriel Bremner, Phil Dakin, Frank Dane, Susan Douglas, Sam Edwards, Laurette Fillbrandt, Margaret Fuller, Betty Lou Gerson, Sharon Grainger, Tarry Green, Ken Griffin, Annette Harper, Gladys Heen, Gail Henshaw, Raymond Edward Johnson, Eloise Kummer, Mary Lansing, Phil Lord, Sunda Love, Carolyn McKay, Marvin Miller, Bret Morrison, Herb Nelson, Michael Romano, Beverly Ruby, Alma Samuels, Mignon Schreiber, Hugh Studebaker, Henrietta Tedro, Sam Wanamaker, Leonard Waterman, Willard Waterman, Jane Webb, Lesley Woods, Seymour Young, more

Theme: "Aphrodite" (Goetzl)

Sponsors: Jan. 25, 1937–Dec. 26, 1941, Procter & Gamble (P&G) for P&G White Naptha soap; March 16, 1942–Nov. 29, 1946, General Mills for Wheaties and other products; June 2, 1947–June 29, 1956, Procter & Gamble primarily for Duz detergent. Governed by Compton Advertising, Inc., for P&G.

Ratings: High: 8.7 (1949–50); low: 4.7 (1955-56). In 10 of 16 full broadcast seasons, the program earned 6.0 or more. For six seasons it reached 7.0 or higher.

On the Air: Regretfully, dates haven't been preserved by radio historians for some of this series' life. Rather than presume without fact, this material is offered with gaps. Debuting on Jan. 25, 1937, at 4:15 p.m. ET on NBC, the serial soon shifted to 3:45 p.m. Although sources don't agree, evidence suggests that the program was off the air briefly during its second year. But by the 1939–40 season it had resurfaced on NBC at 11:45 a.m. The following year it moved to 10:45 a.m. When P&G canceled on Dec. 26, 1941, the drama left the air, netting 75,000 protest letters from fans. The serial resumed 11 weeks later, on March 16, 1942, on NBC at 3:30 p.m., moving in 1942–43 to 2:30 p.m. and in 1943 to 2:00 p.m. When General Mills canceled on Nov. 29, 1946, the series again left the air. It returned 26 weeks later, on June 2, 1947, on CBS at 1:45 p.m. The radio version was withdrawn on June 29, 1956.

Its resilience may account for its longevity. The fact that *The Guiding Light* has adapted to change across the years may be reason enough for it to have sustained legions of fans for a lifetime.

The serial, which debuted from Chicago on the NBC Red radio network on January 25, 1937, is in its seventh decade of broadcasting. Although *The Guiding Light* has omitted a few broadcasts, it is one of a handful of radio soap operas to successfully transfer from that medium to television. And it has been a staple of CBS-TV's daytime schedule since its initial telecast on June 30, 1952. No other drama, daytime or prime time, can begin to challenge *Light's* impressive record. In one sense, it is the longest narrative ever told.

The program was contrived in the mind of the grandame of daytime drama, Irna Phillips — the creator, author and inspiration for more than a score of radio and television serials. Surprisingly, by 1946 Phillips found herself in a legal mire over the origins of *The Guiding Light.* One of her former writers, Emmons Carlson, claimed he had helped spawn the popular serial nearly a decade earlier. Phillips dismissed his allegations as falsehoods, claiming Carlson only penned a few of its early scripts. She pronounced him "a lying bastard," then went against the advice of counsel and refused to settle outside the hall of justice. That cost her. Carlson sufficiently satisfied the court that he had contributed more than a few scripts, and he was awarded $250,000.

Despite her temporary setback, the seldom-rattled Phillips maintained ownership rights to *Light* until she sold the soap opera to Procter & Gamble soon after. William Ramsey, the firm's agent in charge of broadcast productions, purchased the series for a reported $50,000. P&G also acquired the rights to a pair of other popular Phillips dramas: *Road of Life*, for $50,000, and *The Right to Happiness*, for $75,000.

For a woman of Phillips' stature, clearing in excess of $5,000 every week after paying casts, production crews, writers and advisors (including an attorney and two physicians on retainer), the proceeds ($175,000) for the trio of shows may seem paltry. But during its long radio association with Procter & Gamble, *Light* was introduced to listeners every day as "*The Guiding Light*, created by Irna Phillips." Wouldn't such a reminder of the program's origins be payment enough for Irna Phillips, who could afford just about anything money could buy? It had to be gratifying to be able to maintain her upfront name recognition for many years after she no longer owned the drama. Having earlier turned out as many as six scripts daily, by 1948 she was still hacking away on *The Guiding Light*, the only serial she was still writing. P&G was then paying her $200 per episode for each quarter-hour script.

Just two years into that drama, after the characters and story line had acquired a strong following, Phillips decided to transfer one of its major figures into another dramatic vehicle. One of radio's earliest spin-offs, this was the first true spin-off of a daytime serial. Rose Kransky, then a prominent figure in *Light*, became the initial protagonist in *The Right to Happiness,* which debuted on October 16, 1939. The focus on *Happiness* would soon shift, however, to the plights of yet another fictionalized character, Carolyn Allen. Allen was destined to spend the remainder of her waking hours in unnerving distress. She eventually gained notoriety as the "most married heroine on radio," and deservedly so. She was a bride four times before the show was discontinued two decades later.

Shortly before selling *Light*, Phillips was involved in a rather unique exercise. During the 1943–44 radio season, three of her serials — *The Guiding Light, Woman in White* and *Today's Children*, all sponsored by General Mills — were aired in adjacent quarter-hours on NBC. In an exercise that would be repeated several times but would never work again quite as well, she employed a "crossover" effect. Phillips allowed her figures to move freely between the trio of serials. For instance, Dr. Jonathan McNeill, a character in *Light*, wandered through *Woman in White's* Municipal Hospital while visiting some of his patients. Later, he consulted with Dr. Paul Burton on *Today's Children* about a case involving both medics.

This forty-five-minute variation was couched under the banner "The General Mills Hour." (A fourth serial, *The Light of the World*, was produced by the Hummerts. Also sponsored by General Mills, it was otherwise unrelated to the Phillips programs but rounded out the "Hour.") To pull this off, Phillips selected actor Ed Prentiss, who — almost from

Light's start — played a major character, Ned Holden. He would be the adhesive tying the segments together. As host-narrator, he narrated the three serials while continuing to be an active member of *Light's* cast.

Chicago was the mecca for soap opera production in the genre's earliest days. By 1946, however, production of most of the daytime dramas on the air, controlled largely by advertising agencies, had moved from Chicago to New York. (This was nearer many agency and network headquarters and offered a larger pool of talent.) Because an active broadcasting center was also developing on the West Coast, a decision was made to transfer "The General Mills Hour" serials to Hollywood.

Because *The Guiding Light* was then embroiled in the court case over Phillips' claim as its sole creator, that serial never moved to the West Coast. Instead, in November 1946, General Mills bowed out as sponsor, and the drama left the air. A new Phillips serial, *Masquerade*, which replaced *Light*, was the first to move to California. It was soon followed by *Woman in White* and *Today's Children*.

When *Light* returned to the air six months later, it was owned by Procter & Gamble and had shifted to CBS. Five years later it was extended to a televised version. Irna Phillips was so certain that the serial could successfully transfer from an audio to a video medium that she paid production costs from her own pocket for a couple of pilot episodes. That convinced P&G, and the series initially appeared on CBS-TV on June 30, 1952.

While the radio version continued, scripts were taken directly from the audio performances and acted out in front of a camera. By then the radio enactment was taped a day before airing, giving the cast an unusual format to rehearse the televised series. During much of this period the live TV performance was broadcast from 12:45 to 1:00 p.m. at the CBS television studios at Liederkranz Hall. Following that, the cast and crew reassembled a short time later at the CBS Radio studios on East 52nd Street. There they recorded the next day's radio show. The next morning, they met at Liederkranz to rehearse and block the live TV show. This went on for four years, until the radio version was discontinued.

P&G hired Phillips to personally oversee the casting of all new characters on the TV show. This, of course, helped her maintain a measure of control, guaranteeing that no radical departures would occur in the theme or story line. Production costs for the TV series were initially pegged at $8,000 weekly.

While several radio soaps were transplanted to the tube during this era (e.g., *Valiant Lady*, *Portia Faces Life*, *Road of Life*), *The Guiding Light* alone survived. The experiment of carrying an audio narrative to a visual medium in almost every case met with misfortune. Some speculated that *Light's* prosperity resulted from the fact Phillips knew what audiences wanted and gave it to them.

To perform the writing, she employed a cadre of nameless scribes, similar to the Hummert soap opera assembly line. Phillips' dialogue was far less banal, however. Her writers churned out five scripts for about $500 per week for their efforts. In 1938 the Hummert underlings typically received about $125 for the same number of scripts, possibly intimating a difference in perceived quality.

While Phillips maintained ownership of the serials she created, the ad agencies, sponsors and networks had little control over them. She appointed Carl Wester and Company to produce them, allowing that firm the privilege of selecting the announcers and casts. The Phillips dramas were sold to sponsors individually and offered to networks as whole packages.

The Guiding Light, at its inception, swirled around the Reverend Dr. John Ruthledge, a kindly cleric of a nonsectarian congregation in the small town of Five Points. Representing the spiritual strength of suburbia, his mission was to demonstrate how to live a good life through understanding and patience. The pastor of the Little Church of Five Points became a champion of life's enriching qualities and the humanitarian ideals of the American way. Some of his sermons, which were popular features in the show's early days, were collected in a book, purchased by more than 250,000 readers.

The show's title was a direct link to the example offered by Ruthledge himself as he became the community's "guiding light." A widower whose daughter moved with him to Five Points, Ruthledge offered helpful advice while displaying an attitude of caring and selflessness.

These formative years revolved around a succession of ministers including Doctors Ruthledge, Gaylord, Matthews, Andrews, Keeler and — by the early 1950s — Reverend Marsh. When the actor portraying Ruthledge was called up by the armed services in 1944, the character of Ruthledge departed with him. Phillips sent him overseas as a chaplain in the armed forces, replacing him with Dr. Richard Gaylord. Although Ruthledge returned to Five Points two years later, his influence had greatly diminished. Never again did he carry the weight that had burdened him during his pre-war days. When the actor (Arthur Peterson) playing him refused to relocate following the decision to send the show's production from Chicago to Los Angeles, Phillips removed the character entirely rather than replacing him.

Several devices sustained a sure connection between the character of the current clergyman and the principles of the "guiding light." During the 1940s the program opened with a prayer or homily delivered by the pastor. In a June 1947 episode, for instance, Dr. Matthews offered this intercession.

> Almighty God ... help us to realize that it is not enough to be
> good merely for the sake of being good; not enough to do good
> to others, merely because of an abstract ideal of brotherhood.
> Help us to understand that goodness and brotherhood must be
> meaningless unless they are practiced in your name and
> through your light — the light which alone can show us the
> way and the truth ... the light which is our guiding light.

The announcer added: "Let us all join hearts in the sentiment expressed by Dr. Charles Matthews in his prayer for today." Following some unnerving chords from the organ, he announced: "And now, *The Guiding Light*."

Annually, and sometimes more often, the current clerical character delivered a sermon for the duration of the daily installment. On Good Friday during the final decade on radio, "The Seven Last Words" sermon was preached by the resident minister. On March 30, 1956, the last time the sermon was aired, Reverend Marsh delivered it in the fictionalized story line by way of a national radio broadcast. This allowed some of the soap's characters then living in New York to hear it from their vantage point.

In the early days, in addition to Dr. Ruthledge, the cast included his daughter Mary and an orphan son, Ned Holden. The minister had adopted Ned when the boy was eight; the child would grow up to become Mary's husband. (A similar sequence transpired on *Life Can Be Beautiful* when Papa David Solomon's two wards married each other.) There was also Rose Kransky, Mary's best friend, a Jewish girl whose father, Abe, was a local merchant.

More characters would be introduced for a limited time, then faded from the plot. There was Rose's employer, Charles Cunningham, whose marriage ended in a scandalous divorce as the result of his liaison with Rose. A mystical character referred to as "Mr. Nobody from Nowhere" brought intrigue to the story. He lived in the same apartment building as the Kranskys. And Ned's biological mother briefly became the focus. She killed her husband, Paul, and reached the threshold of the electric chair before a governor's pardon spared her life.

With the serial's loftier ideals greatly diminished by the time it got to TV, about the only carryover beyond the characters was the organ music. In the radio story line the organ had been played by the parson's daughter. For years the instrument supplied bridges and background on the tube version, too.

The console virtuoso (in real life, Bernice Yanocek on radio) labored over the keyboard for a thunderous rendition of Goetzl's "Aphrodite" near the opening of each chapter. One observer discounted her sharp intrusions into an otherwise reflective performance, noting: "No program in heaven or earth could match *The Guiding Light* in ominous chords, stings and cadences."[1] In the broadcast of January 10, 1950, for instance, the organ's erratic exclamations jarred fans 23 times. Such unexpected and disarming outbursts interrupted every episode in those days, possibly keeping some of its listeners on unnerving edge.

Around 1947, a decade after the program debuted, *Light*'s focus shifted to the Bauer family of nearby Springfield. Despite their numerous tragedies and personal dilemmas, the Bauers provided the fusion that bound listeners to the show for decades. In fact, after an absence of 22 years from the story line, the character of Meta Bauer — by then an elderly woman — reentered the plot in late 1996. The actress selected to play her was a veteran of TV soap opera: Mary Stuart had portrayed the invincible Joanne Gardner Barron Tate Reynolds Vincente Tourneur, oft-married heroine of *Search for Tomorrow*, from 1951 to 1986.

The Bauers included Bill and his wife, Bertha; Bill's widowed father, who was affectionately known as Papa Bauer and who lived with his son and daughter-in-law; Bill's sisters, Meta and Trudy, and their mates and offspring. Meta conceived a child, Chuckie, out of wedlock.

By the late 1940s Chuckie was adopted by Ray and Charlotte Brandon. Meta then decided to reclaim him. This devastating sequence extracted a heavy toll on the Brandons. Straining their marriage beyond repair, it pushed Charlotte into the waiting arms of theatrical agent Sid Harper, whose affections toward her had been well documented previously.

Meanwhile, Chuckie expressed his preference for Aunt Trudy over his mother, Meta. And Meta professed romantic interest in Trudy's current heartthrob, Ross Boling, a promising young physician. Ted White, Chuckie's dad, at last persuaded Meta to marry him so that Chuckie could have a home with both biological parents. The result was a loveless marriage. Trudy was ecstatic over the turn of events, seeing it as her chance to win Ross' affections. But Ross had other plans; he announced that he was in love with Meta.

A short time later Chuckie was injured in an accident that resulted from his father's ideas about raising a child. Ted was determined to moderate the unyielding control that Meta displayed over their son. He saw the boy's interest in painting as something sissies did, and he tried to emphasize the boy's masculine developmental needs. But the child responded with neither the desire nor the personality for such strenuous activity. Once Meta threatened her husband: "You're talking to a woman who'd rather see you dead before she can trust a small boy into your care. I'd kill you first, Ted. I'd kill you! I'd kill you!"

Sometime after the accident, Meta returned home from one of many visits to her son's hospital bedside. At about three o'clock in the morning, unable to sleep, she confided in Trudy:

> Ted White! ... I didn't think I was capable of hating him any more than I have.... What's he done to me? To Chuckie? To my family? He's tried to destroy us! ...All of us ... Bill — just an innocent bystander.... Trudy, someday ... someday Ted White is going to meet up with something that'll destroy him! Yes, really destroy him!

The two sisters spent the entire 15-minute episode discussing the current issues affecting the Bauer family. The fact that only a couple of people appeared in the cast was not unusual for a Phillips drama. Hers were unlike the Hummert serials, where several characters normally gathered on any given day in a rather complex, sometimes disjointed maze of scenes. Instead, Phillips' slower action, combined with fewer people in a single chapter, was another trademark. *Light* frequently presented a single scene featuring dialogue by two, or seldom more than three, characters.

These long, slow discussions with plenty of time for developing personalities offered an added benefit, though perhaps not one the audience perceived. By using fewer cast members in an episode, Phillips minimized a drama's expenses and maximized her own profits. Fewer performers required a lower payroll. Phillips became a shrewd businesswoman who capitalized on opportunities that added to her own net worth.

The action involving Chuckie reached a climax in 1950 when — instead of healing from his injuries — he died unexpectedly. Meta was overcome with grief and blamed Ted for Chuckie's death. Strained beyond endurance by the unforeseen turn of events, she lost control. In a rage she picked up a gun and shot Ted to death. But a jury acquitted her of the crime, determining that she was temporarily insane.

Meta was soon off on a new tangent, chasing Joe Roberts, a newspaper reporter who helped her gain her freedom during the trial. Roberts' children by a previous marriage resented Meta so deeply that they posed a threat to any serious intentions. Despite their threats, the couple married. Within months they were on the brink of divorce as a result of ongoing family disputes involving the children. At about the same time, the marriage of Meta's brother, Bill, and his wife, Bertha, began to unravel as a result of Bill's unfaithfulness and alcoholism.

By then the drama had arrived on television. In making the decision to air a televised version of its popular radio serial, Procter & Gamble recognized the possibility that it would lose millions of loyal radio fans. To avoid that, P&G offered the concurrent episodes on both mediums.

Within 18 months, *Light*'s TV audience had increased to 3.5 million viewers while only 2.6 million were following the show by radio. As many as four million fans had been listening on radio at the inception of the televised series. There could be no mistake which way mass audiences were turning as TV became accessible to millions of potential new viewers. The decision was made in 1956 to discontinue the radio series, focusing exclusively on the visual one. *Light* aired on radio for the last time on June 29 of that year.

Irna Phillips may be credited with another idea that was to profoundly influence the soap operas aired today. Realizing that televised serials were the wave of the future, in 1954 she launched a new crusade. Appealing to Procter & Gamble, she made a strong pitch to extend the show from a quarter-hour to a half-hour.

P&G was stunned. The firm was quite dubious that American homemakers would be willing to lay aside their chores for as long as 30 minutes to watch the unfolding saga of any soap opera. Could a drama really be that engaging? Phillips insisted that it could. For two years she fought indefatigably to change P&G's mind. In the end, the determined creative won the battle — as she most often did — without outright winning the war. That too would come soon enough.

While P&G wouldn't agree then to let her tamper with the format of *Light*, it gave her the green light to create a new 30-minute serial. Then, at virtually the eleventh hour, P&G decided to launch not one but a *pair* of 30-minute soap operas on the same day. CBS premiered both live half-hour weekday dramas on April 2, 1956: *As the World Turns*, created by Irna Phillips, and *The Edge of Night*, created by Irving Vendig and written by Henry Slesar.

These two dramas set a new standard for a long-established soap opera format, one that other serials would soon sanction (or else find themselves banished from TV). The change established a pattern that would lead to a full hour for most soaps. By then, P&G's earlier fears had been put to rest. Those homemakers may not actually have been doing many of the chores in their households any more, since a well-kept house was no longer an ideal of many young moderns. And audiences had shifted, populated more and more by singles, students, men and working moms with schedules that allowed them to be at home part of some workdays — as well as by homemakers who had children, had paid help or had significant others to assist with household duties. On September 9, 1968, *Light* expanded to a daily half-hour on TV; on November 7, 1977, it was seen for an hour.

Viewers in the 1990s would find light-years of difference between the program's contemporary commercials and what radio listeners heard. Typically in the late 1940s and early 1950s, the rhythm of a washing machine cycle clued listeners that their serial was on the air. After a few seconds of agitator action, announcer Bud Collyer intoned: "Now D-U-Z has a guarantee." A young female vocalist then belted out a commercial jingle, with the washing machine agitator swishing in the background while she sang.

> With extra duty Duz in your machine...
> Clothes come out so white and clean;
> With Duz-backed guarantee for you,
> When Duz does everything for you!

Then, in a somber-sounding mood, Collyer announced: "The new Duz presents *The Guiding Light*, created by Irna Phillips." And the familiar sharp organ cadences rolled again.

Meanwhile, on May 16, 1938, when the serial had been on the air for less than 15 months, P&G announced a competition that was designed to identify the audience of that era. After those infamous, infernal and eternal organ chords and announcer Fort Pearson's introduction of the program's name came more chords and this tagline: "Brought to you by the makers of P&G White Naptha soap, largest selling bar soap in America today." Listeners heard more music and then a familiar voice — the drama's protagonist — Dr. Ruthledge:

> I suppose most of you kind people recognize my voice. If you don't, I would like to introduce myself. I'm Dr. John Ruthledge, a minister in the community of Five Points. Now, as you know, we have been telling our story of *The Guiding Light* to you for over a year. Still, in all this time, it has never been our good fortune to show you how much we appreciate your most thoughtful loyalty. You can well imagine, therefore, how happy we are to tell you that with the program today, you are to hear some news about which we are all genuinely excited … because it brings you such a splendid opportunity. Obviously, I can't go into all of the details, so I'm going to ask a gentleman I have come to admire, Fort Pearson, to tell you about this opportunity. Would you do that, Fort?

Then it was Pearson's turn:

> Thank you, Dr. Ruthledge. And indeed, I am happy to tell our thousands of loyal listeners about this thrilling opportunity we are offering. So listen carefully, please. Every day for thirty days the makers of P&G White Naptha soap will give away ten of the finest automatic refrigerators made. Yes, ten beautiful new Servel Electrolux refrigerators will be given away in the easiest contest ever. That's ten refrigerators … every day for thirty days, beginning Friday, May 20th, and continuing through July 1st, excepting Saturdays, Sundays and holidays.

Typical of radio contests of that day, Pearson asked listeners to complete this statement in 25 words or less: "I like P&G White Naptha soap because…." To help underwrite the contest, he asked them to attach the front panels from five packages of White Naptha soap to their entries. P&G and other sponsors launched scores of similar competitions over the years to increase the fervor for their shows and wares. In subsequent contests on *The Guiding Light* during the early P&G era, the prizes were sometimes diversified but the reactions of listeners remained intense. For one similar event a $1,000 bill, five $500 bills and 60 Servel Electrolux refrigerators were given away each week for several consecutive weeks, leading up to Mary and Ned Holden's wedding date. Marketing genius obviously isn't confined to contemporary times.

A little-known thespian who had played in stage productions before making his radio debut in Minneapolis, Arthur Peterson was tapped to portray Dr. John Ruthledge. Born in Mandan, North Dakota, in 1912, Peterson was only 24 when he won the role of the Five Points cleric. During his radio career he earned credibility on *Bachelor's Children, Girl Alone, The First Nighter, The Story of Mary Marlin, Woman in White, The Barton Family,*

Tom Mix and *Silver Eagle, Mountie.* At the start of the television era, in 1949, Peterson appeared in a weekly quarter-hour sitcom, *That's O'Toole.* It lasted 13 weeks. He was in the cast of the TV serial *Hawkins Falls* in 1952. Peterson died on October 30, 1996, at age 83.

Mercedes McCambridge, who was more prominently featured in *Big Sister,* and Sarajane Wells portrayed Dr. Ruthledge's daughter, Mary. Wells had running parts in three other Phillips dramas — *Woman in White, Road of Life* and *The Right to Happiness* — plus *Jack Armstrong, the All-American Boy.* She died on January 11, 1987, at age 73.

Making the transition from the radio to the televised drama were Charita Bauer (Bertha Bauer), Lyle Sudrow (Bill Bauer), Theodore Goetz (Papa Bauer), Jone Allison (Meta Bauer), Susan Douglas (Kathy Roberts Holden), Herb Nelson (Joe Roberts) and Tarry Green (Joey Roberts).

Of these, Charita Bauer (whose name was coincidental to the part she played) left a lasting impression on the series, from 1950 to 1984. "Bert," who was married to Bill, became the family matriarch on TV, a role that grew softer as the years progressed.

Charita Bauer was born on December 20, 1923 in Newark, New Jersey. At age nine she debuted on Broadway in Christopher Morley's *Thunder on the Left.* As a teen, she launched her radio acting career on *Let's Pretend.* She played in many serials, including *David Harum, Front Page Farrell, Our Gal Sunday, Stella Dallas, Lora Lawton, Young Widder Brown, Orphans of Divorce, Second Husband* and *The Right to Happiness.* She was cast in *The Aldrich Family, The FBI in Peace and War, Maudie's Diary* and *Johnny Presents.* Health problems forced her retirement late in 1984, and she died a short time later, on February 28, 1985, in New York.

Announcer Clayton (Bud) Collyer, who serviced this show on radio for years, was a popular Duz pitchman on several other P&G series: *The Goldbergs, Road of Life* and *Truth or Consequences.* A native New Yorker, Collyer was born June 18, 1908. Intending to be a lawyer, he attended Williams College and Fordam University's law school. After two years as a clerk for a law firm, a job he labeled "dull," Collyer decided radio offered more promise. In college he sang on New York's WABC (now WCBS) and later said actors and announcers he met made as much in a month as he could in a year before the bar. At a 1935 NBC audition he won a part in a show, a life-changing experience. In 1936 he earned $85 weekly as a CBS vocalist, later confessing he made up to $7,000 annually for as many as 30 shows weekly — "big dough at that time," he allowed.

He frequented many other shows as announcer: *Big Sister, The Cavalcade of America, House in the Country, The Philip Morris Playhouse, The Raleigh Room, Schaefer Revue, Silver Theatre, Stage Door Canteen* and *The Story of Mary Marlin.* Unlike most announcers, Collyer could act too, and he maintained running parts in *Just Plain Bill, Life Can Be Beautiful, Terry and the Pirates, Young Widder Brown* and *Chick Carter, Boy Detective.*

He also won leading parts, the title role in *The Adventures of Superman* being among the most prominent. Collyer's ability to speak as Clark Kent in a high-pitched voice while successfully altering his tone to maximum power and depth when it was time for Superman to speak was imposing. The difference between the two speech patterns was curiously distinct. Other shows in which Collyer played leads or male leads included *Abie's Irish Rose, High Places, Kitty Foyle, The Man I Married, Pretty Kitty Kelly* and *Kate Hopkins, Angel of Mercy.* He hosted *Listening Post,* a drama anthology series, and a variety show, *By Popular Demand.*

As versatile as his infectious smile and gregarious personality, Collyer soon came before live audiences as host-quizmaster-emcee of a string of game shows. On radio, where he married radio actress Marian Shockley on *Bride and Groom*, an audience participation show, he presided over *Break the Bank, On Your Mark, Three for the Money, Times A-Wastin'* (a.k.a. *Beat the Clock*) and *Winner Take All!* On TV, he welcomed contestants to *This Is the Missus* (1948), *Break the Bank* (1948–53), *Feather Your Nest* (1954–56), *Beat the Clock* (1957–61), *Number Please* (1961) and *To Tell the Truth* (1962–68). He did voice-overs on *Superman* (1966–69), a Saturday-morning cartoon, reprising his old radio role. Collyer appeared on more than three dozen radio and TV series combined, possibly setting a record among all performers.

A firm believer in Sunday school, he took his children to High Ridge (Connecticut) Methodist Church weekly. For years he was the parish's Sunday school superintendent. He was president of the New York chapter of the American Federation of Radio Artists. Collyer died at Greenwich, Connecticut, on September 8, 1969.

The Guiding Light— or *Guiding Light,* as it was renamed in 1977 to "modernize" its image — has given new generations of Americans a direct link with an era in which the nation was primarily informed and entertained by the theater of the mind. Although the humble origins of the radio play may radically depart from the glitz and glamour of the fast-paced sequences of the 1990s, the fact that this longest-running narrative of daytime drama survived for over 60 years is a milestone. Those who owned, wrote, produced, directed, sponsored and gave air time to it were willing to sacrifice traditions to move with the times.

In doing so, Irna Phillips's most important radio creation lives on, a testament to the enduring qualities that she brought to a form that entertains billions of people around the globe every weekday. Could she — in her wildest imagination — have dreamed of a more befitting legacy than this?

8
Hilltop House
(To the Women of America)

In this serial, unlike most others, without the kids, there wouldn't have been a plot. The strife was often predicated on the interaction of adults with children who were placed in an orphanage and on the attempts to iron out the problems that had put those youngsters there. Of course, such a theme by itself wouldn't have had staying power either; the love life of the home's superintendent, Julie Erickson, was added to give a steady diversion. There was also occasional friction between the staff and board members over how the home was run. Sometimes financial concerns threatened to shut the orphanage down. Ultimately, this was a tale of one woman's dilemma in offering herself to the emotional care of sometimes unwanted, occasionally unruly adolescents while concerned with matters of her own heart. Listeners — most of them mothers themselves — related to the tenderness with which this tireless servant went about her tasks. After the program left the air, it made two comebacks following long absences. An actress who played the lead was so popular with audiences that she was able to transfer to a spin-off series, using her own name for its title. That was surely the ultimate in character identification.

Producer: Edwin Wolfe
Directors: Carlo De Angelo, Jack Rubin
Writers: Adelaide Marston (pen name for Addy Richton and Lynn Stone)
Music: Chester Kingsbury
Sound Effects: John McCloskey, Hamilton O'Hara
Announcers: Frank Gallop
Bess Johnson: Bess Johnson
Julie Erickson: Grace Matthews, Jan Miner
Grace Dolben: Vera Allen
Others: Spencer Bentley, Donald Briggs, Edwin Bruce, Helen Coule, Joseph Curtin, Margaret Curtis, Lilli Darvas, Jimmy Donnelly, Jeanne Elkins, Maurice Ellis, Ethel Everett, Janice Gilbert, Richard Gordon, David Gothard, Mitzi Gould, Irene Hubbard, Gee Gee James, Leon Janney, Lamont Johnson, Jay Jostyn, Jackie Kelk, Estelle Levy, Ronald Liss, Dorothy Lowell, Iris Mann, Norma Jane Marlowe, John Moore, Nancy Peterson, Jack Roseleigh, Evelyn Streich, Alvin Sullum, Alfred Swenson, Jimmy Tansey, Susan Thorne, Jerry Tucker, James Van Dyke, Ray Walker, Wallace Warner, Dickie Wigginton, Carleton Young, more

Theme: "Lullaby" (Brahms), played on the xylophone

Sponsors: Nov. 1, 1937–Mar. 28, 1941, Colgate-Palmolive-Peet, Inc., for Palmolive soap,
initially under the auspices of Benton and Bowles advertising agency; May 17,
1948–1954, Miles Laboratories, Inc., for Alka-Seltzer stomach-distress reliever, Bactine
antiseptic, Tabcin heartburn antidote, One-A-Day multiple vitamins, Miles Nervine
anxiety calmative and Chooz antacid gum; 1954–July 1, 1955, Pharmaco, Inc., for Feen-
A-Mint chewing gum laxative and other products; Sept. 3, 1956–July 30, 1957, participating sponsors.

Ratings: High: 8.0 (1939–40); low: 2.4 (1948–49). Audience levels fell below 5.0 in only two
seasons for which records are available, each time in years when the program was introduced or reintroduced. Higher numbers might have been achieved had the show not
departed for seven years.

On the Air: Nov. 1, 1937–Aug. 12, 1938, MBS, 11:30 a.m. ET, also Nov. 1, 1937–April 22,
1938, CBS, 5:45 p.m.; April 25, 1938–April 5, 1940, CBS, 10:30 a.m.; April 8,
1940–March 28, 1941, CBS, 4:30 p.m.; May 17, 1948–Jan. 5, 1951, CBS, 3:15 p.m.; Jan. 8,
1951–July 1, 1955, CBS, 3:00 p.m.; Sept. 3, 1956–July 30, 1957, NBC.

What's in a name? If for no other reason, the appellations of the fictional characters
and real people associated with this serial made it unique. Adding into the mix the fact that
the program was on the air in three widely separated segments — and that its central theme
revolved around caring for homeless, sometimes unwanted juveniles — and the result is a
rather curious drama.

Consider the unusual names:

• One character in *Hilltop House* was Tiny Tim. This Tiny Tim was neither the one
of "God bless us every one!" nor the one of "Tiptoe Through the Tulips" fame. Instead, he
was one of the youngest residents — and perhaps among the most outspoken — at Hilltop
House, an orphanage set in the mythical town of Glendale.

• When the lead character married in 1953, her name-change resulted in the moniker
Julie Nixon. Though that was not a common name, it gained widespread recognition years
later. (Julie Nixon, a U.S. president's daughter, earned international renown when she was
married while her father was in office.)

• The authors of *Hilltop House*, Addy Richton and Lynn Stone, combined their real
names under the pseudonym Adelaide Marston.

• The part of the drama's earliest protagonist was named for the actress portraying
the role. Bess Johnson later achieved the ultimate in character recognition when a washboard weeper on which she appeared was named for her.

At its inception, *Hilltop House* was produced by Edwin Wolfe, one of the most
respected and practiced artisans during radio's infancy. He maintained quality standards
that were not often equaled in the industry. Wolfe directed *Ma Perkins* for many years.
When actor Charles Egleston — who was Shuffle Shober in that drama for a quarter-century —

died unexpectedly in 1958, Wolfe took on the role, playing it until the end of the run. He directed *The Brighter Day* and *Pepper Young's Family* and branched into scriptwriting for *The Parker Family*. This versatile professional, who was instrumental in introducing some new talent (novice actors and actresses) to soap opera, died on September 22, 1983, at age 90.

On *Hilltop House,* Wolfe freed authors Addy Richton and Lynn Stone ("Adelaide Marston") from much of the formality required in writing other daytime serials. The result was superior literary quality, which was widely recognized by others throughout the industry. But when sponsor Palmolive soap shifted to another advertising firm, agency moguls decided to adjust priorities. The literary quality would be forsaken in favor of lower production costs. Wolfe was displeased. Determined that the serial's luster would not tarnish, he withdrew the program from the air.

Meanwhile, the new agency was committed to building a strong following generated by actress Bess Johnson, who played the orphanage caseworker. To keep her on its payroll, they transferred her into a new series built around her, *The Story of Bess Johnson*. It was the most shameless character flattery ever contrived for a daytime serial star.

On Friday, March 28, 1941, Bess Johnson served her final day as the social caseworker on *Hilltop House*. On Monday, March 31, 1941, she was starting a new soap opera adventure as superintendent of a boarding school. Her series aired on CBS at the same time as the just-departed *Hilltop House*. It was also carried on NBC at 10:00 a.m. by a new sponsor, Kimberly-Clark Corporation, for Kleenex tissues. Thirteen weeks later it disappeared from the CBS program logs. The series finally ran out of gas at NBC on September 25, 1942.

But never say die. Although *The Story of Bess Johnson* was gone forever, six years later CBS revived *Hilltop House* when Miles Laboratories came looking for a vehicle to plug its wares. With little improvising, the character of Julie Erickson replaced Bess Johnson, becoming assistant to Grace Dolben, the orphanage superintendent. (Dolben was sometimes referred to as the "head matron," conjuring up images of a prison or — at best — a detention center for wayward youths. This wasn't the case at all.) The recalled *Hilltop House* arrived on May 17, 1948. Miles Labs footed the bill for six years, and Pharmaco stepped in for another year. At that point the series again left the air.

Even then, it wasn't dead. After an absence of over a year, *Hilltop House* turned up for a third run — on NBC. Under multiple sponsorship, the program's final effort aired for 11 months. It had made a valiant attempt to stem the tide of daytime audiences flowing to television. But local affiliates were swimming like sharks. Having gained the upper hand, they were turning out the lights on daytime drama. *Hilltop House* wouldn't be rescued again.

The show's story line challenged one woman's choices by pulling at her heartstrings. Should she give herself unselfishly in the service of others or concentrate on her own emotional psyche? It was a question the protagonist of *Hilltop House* never fully answered. Instead, she lived in the best of dual worlds, pursuing a career while concurrently following her own romantic quests.

An early epigraph — "A child crying in the night; a child crying for light" — was quickly discarded in favor of a more characteristic and reflective missive: "*Hilltop House* is dedicated to the women of America ... the story of a woman who must choose between love and the career of raising other women's children."

That was the dilemma fraught with irony for both Bess Johnson and Julie Erickson. As professional social workers, they attempted to practice the intellect that years of formal training and experience, plus their own predispositions, afforded. Simultaneously, their desires of the flesh urged them to separate from the rudimentary confinement of a children's home.

Johnson was diligently pursued by at least three suitors: wealthy explorer Captain John Barry, Dr. Robby Clark and Steve Cortland, the latter two staff members at the orphanage. When John Barry succeeded in winning her heart, the couple set a wedding date for December 1939. In the meantime they had to work through a convoluted plot involving John's sister-in-law, Gwen — a wretch who had married his late brother — and an 11-year-old son, Roy. John was convinced that Gwen had killed her husband. It was a domestic mess but provided the trifles that made for good soap opera.

In subsequent action, an airplane on which John was traveling vanished from the radar screens. Normally a strong young woman, Bess was shattered by the experience. Unknown to her, the plane had crashed in a remote area inhabited by Native Americans. John was alive, but he had amnesia, the bane of many a soap opera figure. Would he ever find his way to Glendale and Bess? As *Hilltop House* departed the airwaves in 1941, she was still Bess Johnson; those two poor souls never made it down the aisle.

When the show returned in 1948, Julie Erickson's maternal instincts assisted the head matron at the orphanage. (She was affectionately called "Miss Julie" by residents and staff members.) This girl wasn't about to let sisters-in-law or plane crashes stand between her and a man. While she exuded all the elements of a loving, compassionate social practitioner, she often had a love interest on the side.

To wit, early in the rejuvenated series' life, she became the bride of a respected attorney, Michael Paterno. But a love triangle emerged when one of her former suitors, Kevin Burke — and his five-year-old son, David — turned up in Glendale. Kevin told her he was about to have a potentially fatal operation. In the meantime, he urged Julie to accept his motherless child as a resident. While the situation brought up some unpleasant memories for her, she could hardly refuse, having by then succeeded Grace Dolben as head matron.

For Michael, however, it was a different story. His hostility flared as he questioned why Julie should help a man who had, years before, badly hurt her. Michael became even more outspoken when he learned that Kevin refused to leave Glendale for the operation that was to save his life. Kevin admitted that he preferred to gamble for the year of life that his physicians said he would have. But Michael pondered: was Kevin merely using a gimmick to bid for Julie's empathy, to try to break up their marriage?

Not to worry: Michael wouldn't be around to concern himself with such matters for long. In late spring 1950, the writers allowed Michael to die unexpectedly. Julie was devastated; she took a short leave of absence to put her life together, leaving Mrs. Dolben in charge at the orphanage. (Coincidentally, the occasion gave Jan Miner, the actress playing Julie, a wonderful opportunity for an extended summer hiatus from the daily confines of the microphone.)

We've noted that Julie wasn't the kind of girl to put her love life on the shelf. Soon after returning to work, she again became the object of several salivating males. A few months later she was prepared to marry a widower, Dr. Jeff Browning, who also had a young son, Bill. (Notice how the heroines on this show gravitated toward men with young kids. The writers found a theme they liked and wore it out.) But Julie's cousin Nina entered the plot, sweeping the physician off his feet. Nina took him to the altar almost before Julie realized what had landed. Later, Nina did such a poor job of looking after Bill that the child ran away from home to Hilltop House and Miss Julie. As a result, the boy's father had to step in and send the boy home.

Then there was Reed Nixon, another ex-beau, who reentered Julie's life through the adolescent troubles of his adopted daughter. In a short while a rekindled courtship led to marriage, with Julie becoming Julie Nixon, a designation that would later acquire some fleeting historical fame.

As for the clinical aspects of the job, the caseworkers at Hilltop House never lacked for something to do. Once Julie was caught in a web involving a 14-year-old precocious youngster named Pixie. Pixie had challenged the norms by trying to make all of her own decisions. One of those decisions was to become involved with a boy who had run afoul of the law.

Looking for a peg to develop reader interest, a popular fan magazine proposed a letter-writing contest based on Julie's dilemma with Pixie.[1] "How Much Trust Should You Place in Your Teen-Age Daughter?" offered a grand prize of $25 to the writer of the letter judged best. Writers of the next five best letters received $5 each. It was one of many methods of interrelating readers and listeners.

One day Bess Johnson solved a less serious dilemma for a couple of adolescents, twins who were brother and sister. They had been arguing over the meaning of love. "I've always found that people ridicule things they don't understand," she explained. "Love is the greatest and finest emotion that can come into anyone's life. Without it, life can be very empty. If you love someone very deeply, it can change your whole outlook on life. Love should be a sacred thing…. That's why I don't like to see you poking fun at it."

Without embellishment, she succinctly stated an important cornerstone in her philosophy about living. In these juveniles, she hoped to instill values to penetrate their thinking for the rest of their lives. Hers was a work in progress; she didn't assume her mission lightly.

The intrepid Bess worked diligently to ward off those who would deter the orphanage from reaching its goals. As a shrewd businesswoman, she toiled mercilessly to make sure Hilltop House could pay its creditors on time. She was thwarted in her good deeds by the head of the home's board, Frank Klabber, and his fiancée, Thelma Gidley. Each had personal reasons for wanting Bess to step aside. Yet staff members stood by her; even Tiny Tim, one of the home's youngest residents, spoke persuasively on her behalf. As a result, she was able to hang on.

Recognized as the highest-paid radio actress of that era, Bess Johnson (the actress) was a Chicago native. She became the spokesperson for Lady Esther skin-care products, which allowed her to appear on *The Lady Esther Serenade* and *The Lady Esther Screen Guild Players*. She had running parts in *The Story of Mary Marlin* and *Today's Children* and starred in the serial *True Confessions*. Following her radio work, she played on television's *Search for Tomorrow* (1951–54, 1960–61). Johnson died on January 3, 1975, at age 73.

The role of Julie Erickson was briefly played by Grace Matthews, a heroine of *Big Sister*. For most of the run of *Hilltop House*, however, the peerless actress Jan Miner portrayed Julie Erickson Paterno Nixon. This widely celebrated thespian, veteran of stage, film, television and radio, was born in Boston on October 15, 1917. She entered New York radio in 1946 via a local station in Hartford, Connecticut. A short time later, Miner landed the title role in *Lora Lawton*. She gained running parts in *Boston Blackie, Perry Mason, I Love Linda*

Dale and *Casey, Crime Photographer.* Appearing regularly in *My Secret Story* and *Radio City Playhouse*, she was in the big-screen releases of *Lenny* and *The Swimmer.*

On Broadway, Miner was in *Watch on the Rhine.* Her television credits included *The Robert Montgomery Playhouse.* In 1997 she appeared on the AMC cable series *Remember WENN.* Miner is also remembered by millions as Madge the manicurist, the product spokesperson on long-running TV commercials aired internationally for Palmolive dishwashing liquid. There's a touch of irony in that, for Palmolive was the original sponsor of *Hilltop House* — in the years *before* Jan Miner was tapped for the show.

Hilltop House announcer Frank Gallop, born on June 30, 1910, in Boston, was often mistaken as an Englishman due to a liberal voice inflection. His announcing credits included *The Milton Berle Show, Monitor, Stella Dallas, Gangbusters, The New York Philharmonic Orchestra, Abbott Mysteries, Amanda of Honeymoon Hill, The Hour of Charm, The Prudential Family Hour, Quick as a Flash, When a Girl Marries, Cresta Blanca Carnival, Texaco Star Theater* and *Her Honor, Nancy James.* On TV he announced for *The Perry Como Show*, providing the bass voice, booming out of nowhere to the star: "Oh, Mr. C...."

Authors Addy Richton and Lynn Stone ("Adelaide Marston") collaborated twice more, writing the serial dramas *This Life Is Mine* and *Valiant Lady.* Yet their most durable achievement was *Hilltop House.* It became a model for dealing with trifling youngsters in uncommon situations while simultaneously meeting the personal traumas that beset our daily lives. Attempting to meet dual objectives, Richton and Stone maintained a healthy respect for each one. And as their widely acclaimed plaudits would attest, they covered both territories well.

9
Just Plain Bill
(A Giant of the Air)

The "haircutter of Hartville" just didn't cut it. The "barber of Hartville" seemed more fitting. Nor was the first name given to this series, *Bill the Barber*, satisfying to the future Mrs. E. Frank Hummert. Anne S. Ashenhurst, one of the serial's creators, replaced the title with *Just Plain Bill*. So why would homemakers be inspired by the story of a small-town barber anyway? Because Bill Davidson, a good-natured, soft-spoken, homespun country philosopher, sensitive to the needs of friends and relatives, offered level-headed advice to help them straighten out their tangled lives. Listeners identified with people like themselves, just as the serial's familiar epigraph espoused. Here was a man among them who was all-wise and all-heart. He gave reassurance that even when the clouds are darkest, there is a silver lining if one searches diligently for it. The dilemmas he solved frequently focused on his little family: his daughter, Nancy; her lawyer-husband, Kerry Donovan; and Bill's grandson, Wiki. Leaving fiction behind, however, the most significant thing about this show was the distinction it held in the annals of radio soap opera. Debuting in 1932, *Just Plain Bill* was easily the first serial to make a lasting impression on far-flung audiences. It continued doing so for 23 years — initially as a nighttime feature and soon as a daytime quarter-hour. Against this classic series many of its followers came to be measured, with some lacking the quality that made it an enormous favorite.

Producers: Frank and Anne Hummert
Directors: Martha Atwell, Gene Eubank, Arthur Hanna, Ed King, Norman Sweetser, Blair Walliser
Writers: Robert Hardy Andrews, Barbara Bates, Peggy Blake, Evelyn Hart, Jack Kelsey
Music: Hal Brown, on harmonica and banjo
Sound Effects: Max Miller
Announcers: Andre Baruch, John Cornell, Fielden Farrington, Ed Herlihy, Roger Krupp
Bill Davidson: Arthur Hughes
Nancy Davidson Donovan: Ruth Russell (1932–51), Toni Darnay (1951–55)
Kerry Donovan: James Meighan
Wiki Donovan: Sarah Fussell, Madeleine Pierce
Elmer Eeps: Joe Latham
Others: Curtis Arnall, MacDonald Carey, Cliff Carpenter, Ray Collins, Clayton (Bud) Collyer,

Elizabeth Day, Audrey Egan, Charles Egleston, Anne Elstner, Ara Gerald, Teri Keane, Elaine Kent, Charlotte Lawrence, Bill Lytell, Bill Quinn, Ann Shepherd, Guy Sorel, George Tiplady, Helen Walpole, William Woodson, more

Theme: "Darling Nellie Gray" (early opening and bridges); "Polly Wolly Doodle" (closing, also later opening)

Sponsors: Blackett-Sample-Hummert introduced this serial to nighttime radio listeners as a sustaining feature. After 17 weeks (Jan. 16, 1933), the show was picked up by American Home Products Corp. (AHP), which carried it for the next 21 years except for brief interruptions. The series was a major commercial vehicle for AHP's packaged drug division, Whitehall Pharmacal Co. Major brands included Kolynos toothpaste and tooth powder dentifrice, Anacin pain reliever, Kriptin antihistamine, Bi-So-Dol analgesic, Freezone corn remover, Heet liniment, Dristan and Primatene cold remedies, Preparation H hemorrhoid medication, Neet hair remover, Infrarub balm, Sleep-Eze calmative "and many other dependable high-quality drug products," as the announcer reminded listeners every day. Sometimes AHP's Boyle-Midway household products division advertised brands like Black Flag insect repellent, Aerowax and Olde English floor cleaners, Wizard room deodorizer, Sani-Flush toilet cleanser and Easy-Off oven cleaner. When AHP canceled on March 25, 1954, the serial left the air, returning on Sept. 26, 1954 for Miles Laboratories, Inc., a major pharmaceutical firm. Miles made Alka-Seltzer acid-indigestion reliever ("Listen to it fizz") and other drugs (Tabcin, One-A-Day, Bactine, Miles Nervine, Chooz). Miles carried the show until July 1, 1955. Oddly, this earliest serial among the durable soap operas was never sponsored by a soap manufacturer.

Ratings: The series enjoyed both ups and downs, although there were more ups. Its lowest point, 2.9 (1941–42), was never recorded again. The very next season, the serial shot up to 6.5. With negligible competition in the early 1930s, its evening audience was larger, often topping 9.0. As a daytime feature, the numbers most often approached or exceeded 6.0. In 1948–49 the serial climbed to 7.2.

On the Air: Sept. 19, 1932–June 16, 1933, CBS, 6:45 p.m. ET; June 19, 1933–1935, CBS, 7:15 p.m. Nighttime performances were discontinued in 1935. The daytime version was added Oct. 16, 1933, CBS; 1935–June 12, 1936, CBS, 11:45 a.m.; Sept. 14, 1936–March 15, 1940, NBC, 10:30 a.m.; March 25, 1940–July 31, 1942, NBC Blue, 3:45 p.m.; Sept. 14, 1942–June 29, 1951, NBC, 5:30 p.m.; July 2, 1951–March 25, 1954, NBC, 5:00 p.m.; Sept. 26, 1954–July 1, 1955, NBC, 5:00 p.m.; July 4, 1955–Sept. 30, 1955, NBC, 3:45 p.m.

Now, to the many friends who wait for him ... we present Just Plain Bill, barber of Hartville, the story of a man who might be living right next door to you — the real-life story of people just like people we all know.

— Epigraph to *Just Plain Bill*

Those who study such things offered many descriptive terms signifying this serial's place in history. It was "the first smash hit network soap," one said.[1]

It was the Hummerts' "first hardy perennial," another added.[2] It was "the first day-time serial with lasting power," someone else suggested.[3] Yet another proclaimed it "a fifteen-minute giant of the air."[4] It was all of those. And more.

It was the first of three highly successful serials against which nearly all others would be weighed in the decades to follow. Besides *Just Plain Bill*, the next year (1933) would witness the premiers of *The Romance of Helen Trent* and *Ma Perkins*, durable soap operas that lasted until the genre ran out of gas (electricity?) in 1960.

Bill Davidson, the central figure (yet not the protagonist) of *Just Plain Bill*, was one of several "helping hands" among the serial leads. Deeply concerned about the lives of others, these characters had little dramatic life of their own. Aptly referred to as a "male Ma Perkins,"[5] Bill was right at home among the serials' helping hands (*Ma*, Papa David Solomon of *Life Can Be Beautiful*, Ruth Evans Wayne of *Big Sister*, the character of *David Harum*, the reverends of *The Brighter Day* and *The Guiding Light* and others). Goodness, kindness and a desire to help other people get out of trouble were definitely among soap opera's strongest themes.

The philosophizing tonsorial artist of Hartville was once compared to a super-seltzer tablet in relieving people in distress.[6] (One of his sponsors, coincidentally, was Alka-Seltzer.) This widower maintained a combination of qualities that perfectly suited him for his tasks. "Calm and quiet and gentle and sympathetic and tolerant and understanding and kind, but still firm and strong and wise,"[7] Bill's attributes matched the role he had selected for himself. Here was a man folks could go to in time of need, assured that — without pretension — he would give them sound advice and the personal assistance within his power. Most of their troubles were none of his business, and he seldom entered into their concerns unless invited. But there were many people in Hartville who needed help in running their lives and who didn't hesitate to ask for it.

For two bits, coiffeurs normally cut and washed hair and offered shaves while talking about the weather, sports and politics. But the proprietor of the Hartville barbershop seldom had time to lather many faces — he was too busy patching up marriages, stifling the urges of citizens to commit suicide or murder, solving crimes of major and minor proportions and, in essence, being the guardian of his community.

Bill Davidson was trusted by Americans for decades before Walter Cronkite ever saw the eye of his first television lens. Viewed as a God-fearing proponent of the Golden Rule, Bill could find good in the town's sorriest blackhearts. As a result, thousands in his audience responded by writing to the actor who played him, seeking his counsel and sage advice concerning very real problems — their own and sometimes those of relatives and friends. He was held in such esteem, in fact, that about 175,000 fans over a ten-day engagement paid the unlikely sum of a dime and a box top to see him at New York's Roxy Theatre.

The dramatist, Arthur Hughes, was among the most extraordinary in the business. To the role of Bill Davidson, as well as others, he brought a professionalism seldom equaled. A graduate of the Academy of Dramatic Arts, Hughes distinguished himself in such Broadway productions as *Elizabeth the Queen*, *Golden Boy*, *Idiot's Delight* and *Mourning Becomes Elektra*. Born in Bloomington, Illinois, on June 24, 1893, the actor was in his mid-30s when he played the host-editor and lead character, Fu Manchu, of radio's *Collier's*

As Bill Davidson in *Just Plain Bill,* Arthur Hughes brought a wealth of professionalism to his role, even memorizing his lines before airtime! He was there for all of the series' 23-year run. Ruth Russell, as daughter Nancy Davidson Donovan, remained in the cast until illness forced her departure after 19 years. (Photofest)

Hour. At 39 he was tapped for the role for which he would be remembered for the rest of his life — Bill Davidson, whom he would play for almost 6,000 broadcasts. His radio acting repertoire would include the title role of *Mr. Keen, Tracer of Lost Persons* and running parts on *Stella Dallas, The Orange Lantern, Jungle Jim, East of Cairo* and *I Love Linda Dale.*

Considered by colleagues "an actor's actor," Hughes used to take a radio script, mark his lines in red pencil and go off to a corner by himself to memorize those lines before broadcasts. Unlike most other soap opera performers, he was very much like the character he portrayed in *Just Plain Bill*: serious, thoughtful, depicting an "old school." As he aged in real life he became even more like Bill Davidson, observers noted.

When *Just Plain Bill* left the air, Hughes and his wife, the former Geneva Harrison, who had been a Broadway actress when they wed in 1933, continued living quietly on West End Avenue in Manhattan. They had no children and kept in touch with several artists with whom they had worked, among them Ruth Russell, who played Bill's daughter, Nancy, for most of the run. Another was Anne Hummert, who moved to Manhattan after the death of her husband, Frank, in 1966. Insiders felt that even though no favoritism was shown, *Just Plain Bill* was the Hummerts' personal favorite among their soap opera creations.

Hughes continued his acting career, amusing audiences with uproarious laughter in the part of an eccentric millionaire in the 1968 Broadway hit musical *How Now Dow Jones?* The accomplished actor died at age 89 in New York City on December 28, 1982. A half-century had elapsed since he had inaugurated his most famous role.

Ruth Russell, who played Nancy Davidson Donovan until illness forced her to leave the cast in 1951, was one of the children appearing on *The American School of the Air*, an early radio series. She also played in *Our Gal Sunday*.

Her successor as Nancy, actress Toni Darnay, had earlier played title roles on two other serials, *The Strange Romance of Evelyn Winters* and the short-lived *Nona from Nowhere*. Darnay's other radio credits included parts on *When a Girl Marries* and *Aunt Jenny's Real Life Stories*. From 1963 to 1965 she was in the cast of TV's *As the World Turns*. The actress died at age 61 on January 5, 1983.

James Meighan, as Kerry Donovan, appeared on scores of dramas all over the radio dial. His best-remembered role was as stage actor Larry Noble, husband of Mary, on *Backstage Wife*. For years he would leave that drama to cross to the NBC studio where *Just Plain Bill* was about to rehearse. Thus, on most afternoons within a short time frame, listeners to that network heard Meighan at least twice — and more, when he had running parts elsewhere.

After it occurred to Frank Hummert in 1931 that homemakers might be interested in some sort of serialized fiction broadcast on a daily basis, he hired a young man who had been writing such material for the *Chicago Daily News*. Charles Robert Douglas Hardy Andrews, commonly known as Robert Hardy Andrews, was assigned to write a radio serial about a love triangle and the consequences of blending work and pleasure. Titled *The Stolen Husband*, completely giving the premise away, it involved a handsome young businessman, his voluptuous secretary and a dense but attractive wife who didn't consider what was going on during those nights her husband worked late until it was *too* late.

By subsequent standards *The Stolen Husband* wouldn't be declared a phenomenal success. Yet it gave Hummert, Ashenhurst (the future Mrs. Hummert) and Andrews tremendous insights, leading them to produce the three highly successful serials already mentioned, which became the early standards of soap opera. Andrews' first daytime network sagas, *Betty and Bob* and *Judy and Jane*, both debuted on October 10, 1932, on NBC Blue, although the latter was aired only in the Midwest.

Earlier that year Andrews was given the task of creating a folksy drama for Chicago's WMAQ. It would be broadcast in the early evening, just as was the already established comedy serial *Easy Aces,* which had premiered on CBS on March 1, 1932. (Like *Just Plain Bill, Easy Aces* later moved to daytime. But unlike *Bill, Easy Aces* returned to the evening schedule in 1935 and remained there.)

Andrews recalled a rather gregarious barber from his younger days — friendly, bordering on nosy, yet a veritable reassuring presence to customers. The prolific writer would create situations that were set in a small town around this character, allowing him to become the conscience of the community. Andrews titled his drama *Bill the Barber*. But Ashenhurst, claiming to understand what women wanted, corrected him: "*Just Plain Bill,*" she injected.

On September 19, 1932, a group of actors converged around a microphone in New

York's CBS Studio 5. *Just Plain Bill* debuted. A new radio institution that was destined to leave a tremendous legacy on the medium had begun.

Years later, in the only public speech she is known to have made, Anne (Ashenhurst) Hummert explained that Hartville was situated somewhere in the Midwest because "people seem to like characters from that section best." The geography alone made Bill Davidson "a great favorite," she suggested. The Hummerts maintained that the speech of characters from that area wasn't identified with any particular dialect that might show partiality or distract listeners.

As noted earlier, the Hummerts made a mint by pursuing an assembly-line approach to scripting their shows. And Charles Robert Douglas Hardy Andrews, labeled a writing "syndicate" by one journalist, may have been their original inspiration. Born at Effingham, Kansas, on October 19, 1903, he produced a 100,000-word serialized story for a newspaper contest by age 16. At 20 he was the city editor of the *Minneapolis Journal.* Until he moved to New York in 1932, he kept his day job with the *Chicago Daily News* while hammering out five radio scripts per night, astounding skeptics with an amazing fluency and stamina. This was only a warm-up for the main attraction, however.

For a decade, until he acknowledged that he "got tired," he kept anywhere from four to seven daily radio shows going, most of them soap operas. Working in a penthouse apartment on New York's Central Park West, Andrews consumed 40 cups of coffee and chain-smoked 100 cigarettes between the hours of noon and midnight, seven days a week, while typing scripts. His weekly production rate typically surpassed 100,000 words. And as a diversion, he wrote numerous novels and dozens of movies, either alone or jointly with other writers. Of course, the Hummerts never replaced him, and when he died on November 11, 1976, it was surely the passing of an era among scribes.

Andrews offered some valuable insights when he elaborated on the success of his soaps in a magazine interview. He claimed that he pursued a "Cinderella story" theory:

> Cinderella is the spirit of make-believe. She is the princess of
> dreams-come-true.... She represents what every man, woman,
> and child, deep down in their hearts, really want.... Cinderella
> represents life as people would like to see it lived. In her never-
> ending story, justice overcomes cruelty and injustice, riches
> supplant poverty, virtue is rewarded, and romance comes to
> complete the dream.[8]

The formula for *Just Plain Bill* (which Andrews relinquished to others in October 1942, the last of his serials) fit that description precisely. Even its theme songs fostered the image of the good-natured country philosopher. During part of the long run, two different songs opened and closed the show. At the beginning, the versatile instrumentalist Hal Brown plunked a countrified chorus of "Darling Nellie Gray" on his banjo. Before the sign-off, he ripped out a rousing version of "Polly Wolly Doodle" on the harmonica. Both tunes suggested the traditionalism and familiarity that were synonymous with the soap opera. Later, "Darling Nellie Gray" became an informal bridge played on guitar, with "Polly Wolly Doodle" reserved for the opening and closing themes.

The plot itself was often convoluted. In one sequence Bill offered advice to a head-strong Karen Ross, who was determined that the wealthy Wesley Franklin would not destroy her father—Bill's longtime friend John Ross. When Franklin arrived in Hartville, he engaged Bill's son-in-law, Kerry Donovan, to oversee his business interests. Franklin's ultimate objective was to gain control of a factory owned by John Ross. Within a short while, Kerry realized that he was compromising his own convictions by working for Franklin while helping this man undermine Bill's friend. Kerry withdrew from Franklin's employ.

Karen Ross, however, was another story. Despite Bill's warnings, she intervened in the stand-off between her father and Franklin, even flirting with Franklin. Her goal was to distract him from putting her father out of business. Eventually she realized that Bill's concerns were justified—Franklin forced her to promise she would marry him when he divorced his wife, Vera. John Ross, who made no secret of his disdain for Franklin, confronted him. In a rage he ordered Franklin to stay clear of his daughter.

A short while later Franklin mysteriously disappeared, leaving the townsfolk to wonder if John knew more about it than he was admitting. Not long afterward, Franklin was found murdered. If John Ross ever needed a friend, that was the time, and Bill Davidson was the man. As listeners had long come to expect, Bill rallied to the rescue, exposing the real killer while restoring his friend's reputation.

Kerry Donovan, a wealthy socialite, was often perceived as a jealous, moody highbrow who occasionally piddled in politics. Sometimes he became the focus of blind hate and vicious backbiting. Campaigns against Bill or his family could result when Kerry was involved in intensive disputes.

Sparing the little family from those who would snare and lead them astray was all in a day's work for Bill. Family came first; he could cut hair some other day. Dialoguing with him between crises was his pal Elmer Eeps, proprietor of the Hartville general store. The chums mused often over the day's events.

Sometimes Bill had to face far more dangerous situations than the usual domestic crises on which he thrived. In one sequence he discovered that an operator of rest homes for the aged was finishing off clients for their insurance. Bill's own life was threatened.

In the mid–1940s Bill became the target of vicious Judith Seymour and Leslie Groves, her son-in-law. At one point he was knocked unconscious and nearly killed. Evelyn Groves, Seymour's daughter and Leslie Groves' wife, drowned under mysterious circumstances. Finally Bill was given a basket of poisonous fruit, some of which his grandson ate, resulting in a near-fatal tragedy. Bill's personal philosophy continued to see him through, however, even in his most trying situations. "You have to stand up to evil and fight it. You have to be ready for it when it strikes, and never give in to it. If you do them things, … you can never be whipped by evil men," he allowed. (Even though his English was sometimes atrocious, he got his point across.)

Just Plain Bill was a forerunner of radio drama-by-installment. It was, for all intents and purposes, the first serial with staying power, a permanent model for all other soap opera. Because its setting was a small country town, *Bill* probably lacked some of the gripping action and flagrant absurdities that crept into most other daytime serials. But its central character was so strong that it commanded a loyal following and endured into the mid–1950s, long beyond the time most serials arriving after it had faded.

Recognizing Arthur Hughes' name on the playbill credits of *How Now Dow Jones?* in 1968, a patron exclaimed: "I never peel potatoes for dinner that I don't miss that program."

Years of habit, listening to a "story of a man who might be living right next door to you," had left an indelible imprint. For this woman, as she prepared the evening meal in earlier years, it had been a pleasant association. Millions of other housewives must have felt the same thing as they peeled potatoes too.

10
Life Can Be Beautiful
(A Beam of Hope in a Dark World)

Every episode of this soap opera opened with a snippet from a great thinker who advocated a positive frame of mind. It worked well; in essence, this was what the serial was about. The philosophical proprietor of the Slightly Read Book Shop, Papa David Solomon, waxed eloquently on a recurring theme to his young wards: take charge of present circumstances and turn them into something valuable. An oft-repeated message that "life can be beautiful" spoke to the hearts and minds of Carol (Chichi) Conrad and Stephen Hamilton. Obviously, it also spoke to the millions of listeners who kept this serial near the top of the weekday charts for most of its long run. Destined from the start to become husband and wife, Stephen and Chichi saw their lives take radical departures from the past sometime after their marriage and the birth of a child. The serial, in fact, took a near 180-degree turn for a while, entering a dark period that no one could have predicted. Despite that, writers Carl Bixby and Don Becker, speaking through Papa David, never rescinded their exhortations about the happy life. In the end, Chichi — inspired by the greatly admired patriarch's teachings — kept the faith, practicing most of what the old man had espoused.

Producer-Director: Don Becker
Directors: Oliver Barbour, Chick Vincent
Writers: Don Becker, Carl Bixby
Music: Herschel Leucke
Sound Effects: Bill Brown, Art Zachs
Announcers: Bob Dixon, Ralph Edwards, Don Hancock, Ed Herlihy, Ron Rawson
Papa David Solomon: Ralph Locke
Carol (Chichi) Conrad: Alice Reinheart (1938–46), Teri Keane (1946–54)
Stephen Hamilton: John Holbrook, Earl Larrimore
Others: Peggy Allenby, Ed Begley, Clayton (Bud) Collyer, Humphrey Davis, Roger DeKoven, Carl Eastman, Gavin Gordon, Mitzi Gould, Vinton Hayworth, Elsie Hitz, Joe Julian, Waldemar Kappel, Adelaide Klein, Richard Kollmar, Ian Martin, John Moore, Agnes Moorehead, Dick Nelson, Ethel Owen, Minerva Pious, Sidney Smith, Paul Stewart, Charles Webster, Ruth Weston, Ruth Yorke, more

Theme: "Melody in C" (Becker)

Sponsors: The Compton advertising agency governed the show for Procter & Gamble (P&G) from its inception; P&G remained the serial's only sponsor throughout the run. Advertised brands were Ivory and Camay soap, Spic 'n' Span cleanser, Crisco shortening and Ivory Flakes, Ivory Snow and Tide detergents.

Ratings: For several years the drama held third or fourth place among all daytime features. Combining listeners on dual networks pushed it to 14.7 (1940–41). Broadcasting once daily, it reached 9.0 (1941–42). In only two of 16 seasons did numbers fall below 5.0. Low: 3.8 (1953–54).

On the Air: Sept. 5, 1938–Sept. 27, 1940, CBS, 1:15 p.m. ET; 1939–40, NBC, 9:45 a.m.; 1940–41, NBC, 5:45 p.m.; Sept. 30, 1940–June 21, 1946, CBS, 1:00 p.m.; Aug. 5, 1946–June 25, 1954, NBC, 3:00 p.m.

It was a rarity for most soap operas to arrive each day accompanied by less than a fixed epigraph, the easily recognized strains of a time-worn theme and a billboard delivered by an announcer's familiar voice. Those epigraphs — verbal inscriptions of prologue repeated over long periods of time — reassured a serial's audience that the fundamental nature of the play was still intact. This was typical on other serials: "We give you now ... *Stella Dallas* ... a continuation on the air of the true-to-life story of mother love and sacrifice...." And: "Once again, we present ... *Our Gal Sunday* ... the story of an orphan girl named Sunday from the little mining town of Silver Creek, Colorado, who ... in young womanhood ... married England's richest, most handsome lord."

Life Can Be Beautiful was an exception to the familiarity rule. For most of its existence, it did maintain an epigraph, albeit an abbreviated one: "*Life Can Be Beautiful* is an inspiring message of faith drawn from life." But that phrase was almost like an afterthought, an appendage to a variable and rather brief epithet that opened each day's program.

Thus, one day announcer Don Hancock, over the program's theme (an original composition — "Melody in C" — by series creator-author-composer-director-producer Don Becker), spoke the first words:

> John Ruskin wrote this: "Whenever money is the principal
> object of life, it is both got ill and spent ill, and does harm
> both in the getting and spending." When getting and spending
> happiness is our aim, life can be beautiful. *Life Can Be Beauti-*
> *ful* is an inspiring message of faith drawn from life, written by
> Carl Bixby and Don Becker, and brought to you by Spic 'n'
> Span. No soap ... no other cleaner ... nothing in America
> cleans painted walls, woodwork and linoleum like Spic 'n' Span.

On December 30, 1946, announcer Ron Rawson offered this homily at the show's inception:

> If, now and then, you become depressed over the condition of
> the world and feel inclined to condemn the actions of its leaders

... try recalling Philip James Bailey's words: "Men might be
better if we better deemed of them; the worst way to improve
the world is to condemn it." And you might also remember
this short stanza by Michael Wentworth Beck:

> This world is not so bad a world
> As some would like to make it;
> Though whether good, or whether bad,
> Depends on how we take it.

No, don't let the words or actions of others discourage you. If
you keep faith, your life can be beautiful.

Long before *Truth or Consequences* and *This Is Your Life* made his name a household
word to American audiences, Ralph Edwards, another announcer on *Beautiful,* told listeners on September 21, 1939:

> If you wonder what to do about a certain problem that's trou-
> bling you today, why not sit down and ask yourself: "When
> tomorrow comes, what will I wish I had done today?" ...That
> will help you believe that ... life can be beautiful.

And on another day, an unidentified announcer delivered this moral bromide:

> Longfellow expressed the opinion that the Sabbath is the
> golden clasp that binds together the volume of the week.... By
> the way, how long has it been since you've been to church,
> where you'll find new assurances that life can be beautiful?

Writers Carl Bixby and Don Becker saw their mission as providing "a beam of hope
in a dark world." As they implied in a 1953 magazine interview, no matter how foreboding
mortality might become, "this, too, shall pass."

Their series was a warm-hearted attempt to offer eternal optimism to those suffering
setbacks. Each wrote the drama by himself for a few weeks before turning it over to the
other for a while. In the interim, they conferred by telephone on the show's direction.

In the plot line — perhaps to a greater extent than in almost any other soap opera — a
single character's perspective embodied the norms of the text as a whole. Without Papa
David Solomon, an elderly, compassionate Jewish intellect who operated the Slightly Read
Book Shop, the drama might never have succeeded in conveying the moral platitudes to
which Becker and Bixby were so strongly committed. But through Papa David — called
"radio's wisest man" by one industry observer[1] and "the kindliest of all daytime sages" by
another[2] — day after day for almost 16 years the pair validated that "life is indeed precious"
and should be treated with respect.

Just as Dr. John Ruthledge represented the spiritual strength of suburbia on *The
Guiding Light,* so Papa David was the conscience of a metropolis. No matter how dismal
things might seem, on this soap opera he reminded the disconsolate *ad nauseum* that life
could be beautiful again, repeating the phrase thousands of times. It was an upper that millions of middle-class Americans trying to recover from the economic catastrophes of the

Great Depression, and facing the ravages of world war and the Korean conflict, reflected upon again and again.

At the start of one show, the day after D-Day in August 1945, the narrator allowed nothing more than this brief appellation: "Here is Papa David." The old man invoked these thoughts, obviously from Becker and Bixby's hearts.

> Yesterday we heard the news for which the entire world has
> been waiting.... The day has come ... D-Day.... We are invad-
> ing Europe. In your hearts and in mine, there ain't any doubt
> but what it's going to be successful. But in your heart I know
> like in mine is one big prayer that the invasion will be success-
> ful quickly and our losses won't be too great. Would ... would
> I be out of order at a time like this to suggest that ... right now
> ... we have a few seconds of silence ... so that we can all offer
> up such a prayer? [A 13-second lapse of silence followed.]
> Amen. And may it come soon, when life is beautiful again!

It was only natural for this series to directly confront a crisis that was then riveting the world's attention. And Papa David could hardly allow the crisis to pass without his trademark phrase becoming a moving part of it.

Once in a while, that theory went askew. Usually it was the consequence of a script-reading slip. On January 20, 1943, Papa David deliberated: "Love ain't something you can throw out of your heart like bucket from a water."

A radio drama could hardly be carried by a single figure, of course. A second character—a homeless waif, a product of street gangs—provided a human form for Papa David to engage in conversation over the years. Tumbling into his isolated island of serenity within the city one day, Carol Conrad, whom Papa David would call "Chichi," was someone with whom he could share his sound logic. And in her he could manifest the compassion and kindness that was a part of himself. This washboard weeper then became their tale—two opposites who meshed extremes, developing over the years a warm and affectionate respect for one another.

Chichi, whom Papa David took in as the series debuted on September 5, 1938, arrived as a teenager, a victim of urban ghettos. Seeking safety from a street-gang hooligan, Chichi was relieved when Papa David created a space where she could sleep on a cot in a rear room of his small shop. (The impropriety of it would surely raise eyebrows if such an act of generosity were offered today. Of course, zoning laws would first have to be changed to provide for residential use of a business. How much simpler life was in the 1930s!)

As Chichi's self-esteem returned, and her admiration grew for the man who had taken her in and offered her a new course for living, she remained a permanent resident in the little book shop. While she cried buckets of tears over the times when life wasn't so beautiful, Papa David was an enduring source of inspiration and encouragement. To him, this young girl—and the events and people that invaded her life—became a foremost concern in his waning years.

He faithfully offered Chichi the wisdom of his experience. "The future is like a thick veil between us and the tomorrows that are yet to come," he reminded her one early autumn day in 1939 as she was having difficulty finding a steady job. "What's coming, we don't know ... only what we can see and touch and put our hands on.... Don't sit down and hold the hands and wait for life to get beautiful. You got to do something!"

Papa David also instilled his values into young Stephen Hamilton, physically crippled but bright in mind and spirit. Stephen had come to work for Papa David when other opportunities for employment evaporated. He was already helping at the little book shop when Chichi arrived. For much of Stephen's life, he aspired to a law-related career, and he gave some promise of achieving it.

Confined to a wheelchair, Stephen lacked a sufficient stimulus to push him into undertaking a surgical procedure that might reinstate his mobility. But in Chichi, Stephen found the incentive he needed. Even though his operation was a success, he was soon back in that wheelchair once more. In saving Chichi from an accident shortly after his recovery, he put himself in harm's way. As a result he lost his legs and was crippled forever.

Yet it must have gladdened Papa David's heart when the relationship between his two young wards eventually blossomed into love. It certainly surprised Chichi that a man of such intellect as Stephen's would consider someone with as simple a background as hers. But before long, the pair set a wedding date.

Serial writers Bixby and Becker had been hesitant from the start to promote such a marriage. They were concerned that the union would create a plot device that would impair the story line rather than buoy it. Alas, they succumbed to listener sentiment, and the nuptials took place late in 1945. Very soon Bixby and Becker realized that they had erred badly — so much so, in fact, that they would eventually have to take steps to correct their mistake. Regretfully, the sequences leading in that direction didn't provide a satisfying conclusion for many of the show's listeners.

In the interim, however, Chichi and Stephen became parents of a happy, healthy baby boy, born on Christmas Day 1946. The audience eavesdropped on the conversation between Papa David and Chichi that day in Chichi's hospital room:

> PAPA DAVID: Well, you're glad that Christ was born a baby.
> CHICHI: Uh-huh.
> PAPA DAVID: Instead of coming into the world in a chariot with trumpets blowing and acting like a king.... You're glad that Mary had a baby, because ... you understand Mary now. And you're beginning to understand that everything that's big was once small ... that greatness grows like a flower ... and that the truest king, the most understandable expression of a kind and loving God ... was a baby ... a son ... who grows to be a fine man ... who through all the centuries, all people, like the angel said, "All people ... will revere and love."
> CHICHI: That's what I was trying to say....
> PAPA DAVID: By understanding Mary ... you got a better understanding of Christ.
> CHICHI: Yeah. And you know something else? I'm also glad my son was born on Christmas for another reason, too. On Christmas from now on for the rest of my life every year I'll have a Christmas present. First, right now, a little baby, and ... then after a while, a son born ... and then a man....
> PAPA DAVID: Yes, and God grant that his life will be beautiful, Chichi....

CHICHI: Oh, I'm gonna try, Papa David. Oh I hope my son's life
can be beautiful.

The dialogue probably wasn't what the random listener turning the dial that day might have expected from a Jewish elder. But Papa David's moral horizons allowed him to combine Judeo-Christian ethics, beliefs, customs and traditions without raising a furor from any disparate group. In the first half of the twentieth century — unlike the second half — there would be few, if any, calls for "equal time" on the part of offended or disgruntled listeners. And the threat of lawsuits over airing one's convictions wasn't a popular practice; it might not even have been thought of. We've come a long way since. Could Papa David's opinions on *any* subject go unchallenged before almost *any* crowd today?

After an appropriate interval, Becker and Bixby — still convinced they had painted themselves into a corner with no honorable means of exit — cast a dark spell over their crowd-pleasing series. First, Stephen, acting foolhardy, carried the infant into a cold rain without benefit of proper clothing. As might be anticipated, the baby contracted pneumonia and died. At about the same time, Stephen drifted toward another woman and, subsequently, participated with others in a jewel heist. If this wasn't pain enough for Chichi and Papa David, then Stephen died unexpectedly, a victim of a heart attack.

Suddenly, in a brief period, one of the great empathy characters of daytime drama had turned 180 degrees from the righteousness that Papa David had instilled in him. Showing tremendous promise, although forever unfilled, this third-most-important figure in the drama came to an abrupt and dishonorable end by preferring unfaithfulness and corruption. It was a crushing defeat for Chichi and Papa David and millions of fans.

As a result, Becker and Bixby created an opportunity, similar to one that the writer of *Young Doctor Malone* offered at the start of each new daily episode of *that* serial: "This is a new page in the life of Ann Malone and her husband, Jerry." *Beautiful's* authors had a fresh start — "a new page" — and a chance to return their beloved serial to the affectionate relationships that characterized it in its formative years. Free once more, Chichi would be pursued by some of the more eligible men in her city. The cries of anguish from an unhappy radio audience would soon be vanquished. Everybody could again concentrate on proving that life can be beautiful. And Bixby and Becker would show them how.

Chichi kept one friend from her street gang days. He was there for her during the hardships she endured — or at least until he was shipped off to Korea by the army in 1952. Toby Nelson realized he had little chance at a serious romance with Chichi. Yet he was determined to be her pal, helping her pick up the fragments of her shattered dreams. Affectionately calling her "Cheech," he was around when she needed a shoulder to cry on. As the two became inseparable chums, they celebrated many joys and sorrows.

In 1949 Chuck Lewis, a menacing youth-gang leader, crossed paths with Chichi and Papa David. Lewis was responsible for acts of vandalism at a local recreation center. While community leaders were wringing their hands, Chichi — a product of just such an environment — drew on her former life to turn things around. She had been a tough, defiant youngster at the time she met Papa David. Now she used her experience to help quell the disturbance, sharing her insights with local officials.

Brushing aside a romantic entanglement with the newspaper publisher Douglas Norman, Chichi soon fancied herself in love with a rural Texas vocalist who was adept at using other people to advance his own career. She had a rude awakening when she asked a stage-and-screen glamour girl, Lise Martain, to give him a boost. The singer, Cal Duncan, quickly dropped Chichi in an effort to charm Martain. Chichi's reaction was to conclude that, aside from Papa David, no man was trustworthy.

Chichi later became a temporary cripple when an accident left her unable to walk, suffering psychosomatic paralysis. Returned to normal a few months later, she was engaged to two men in the last couple of years of the serial. It wasn't exactly the finale that listeners might have expected.

Life Can Be Beautiful was one of the top-ten programs that "most faithfully portrayed American life."[3] The acclaim resulted from a 1947 poll of almost all Protestant churches in the United States by the International Council of Religious Education. The top-ten shows included four soap operas: *Life Can Be Beautiful, Ma Perkins, One Man's Family* and *Pepper Young's Family*.

Another distinction that *Beautiful* enjoyed was recognition from a series of monthly magazine articles. Published by a popular fan journal, the features presumably sold magazines while increasing audience size and listener identification. A writing competition sponsored by the magazine allowed readers to submit original experiences of how their lives were turned into something beautiful. The following solicitation appeared:

> Have you sent in your *Life Can Be Beautiful* letter yet? If, some time in your life, there was a moment when the meaning of happiness became clear to you, won't you write your story to Papa David? For the letter he considers best each month, *Radio Mirror* will pay one hundred dollars. For each of the other letters received which we have space enough to print, *Radio Mirror* Magazine will pay fifteen dollars. Address your letters to Papa David, care of Radio Mirror Magazine, 205 East 42nd Street, New York 17, New York. No letters can be returned.[4]

In one issue the editors explained, "This month's group of letters is the most heartwarming proof we have ever had to one odd little fact about happiness: there is no age that is the right age to discover one's own way to it. Every age is right, if we make it so." Three letters had arrived in the editorial offices sharing stories "so moving that it was impossible to say which of them should be placed above the others." One was from a teenager, one from a grandmother and a third from a young adult. Each posed widely diverse problems that their authors had conquered. The publication printed the trio and sent each writer a check for $35. Five other letters, presumably at $15 each, were included in the same issue.

Because the show had a long title, people in the industry shortened it to a nickname, "Elsie Beebe," based on the soap's acronym (LCBB). Many performers and writers kept small pocket diaries in which they recorded names of shows and rehearsal times for which they were to appear. Notations about "Elsie Beebe" were well understood by those in the trade. The radio audience, of course, never heard the program referred to by that name.

The part of Papa David Solomon was played for the entire run by Ralph Locke. Locke was an Eastern European native who was on the Broadway stage and active in Yiddish theater in New York before entering broadcasting. During the 1930s and 1940s he was awarded many ethnic-Jewish parts in radio. Though he is best remembered as Papa David, he also

Chichi Conrad (Teri Keane) and Papa David Solomon (Ralph Locke) admired one another deeply in *Life Can Be Beautiful*. Locke went the distance, playing the optimistic operator of the Slightly Read Book Shop for 16 years. Keane was his idolizing young ward in the final half of the run. (Photofest)

had recurring roles in the serials *Dot and Will* (1935–37) and *Second Husband* (1937–46). He died in 1956 at about age 71, two years after *Beautiful* left the air.

Two seasoned radio actresses played the part of Chichi Conrad, each for about half the series' 16-year life. Alice Reinheart took the first turn, from 1938 to 1946. Born in San Francisco in 1910, she became a star of four mediums — stage, screen, television and radio. She appeared in Broadway productions of *Parapet* at age 12 and *The Mask and the Face* at 14. She returned in 1940 for *Journey to Jerusalem* and in 1944 for *Leaf and Bough*. Reinheart's film credits included roles in *The Lieutenant Wore Skirts* (1956) and *A House Is Not a Home* (1957). She was featured in guest shots on TV's *Make Room for Daddy* (1955–60), *The Donna Reed Show* (1958–66) and *I Dream of Jeannie* (1965). For a few months in 1965–66 she appeared in the short-lived TV serial *Paradise Bay*.

But it was in radio that Reinheart worked most often. Among scores of regular assignments, she appeared on *The Adventures of the Abbotts*; *Gangbusters*; *One Man's Family*; *Casey, Crime Photographer*; *John's Other Wife*; and *Her Honor, Nancy James*. Reinheart and her husband, actor Les Tremayne, aired a six-day-a-week breakfast talk-show, *The Tremaynes*, on New York's WOR. She died on June 10, 1993, at age 83.

The other Chichi, Teri Keane, heroine of *The Second Mrs. Burton*, is discussed in chapter 24.

Announcer Ron Rawson, like Clayton (Bud) Collyer, was a favorite of Procter & Gamble as a pitchman for its wares. In addition to this serial, he worked on *The Brighter Day*, *The Right to Happiness*, *Road of Life* and *Young Doctor Malone* for the consumer goods manufacturer. Other announcing duties included *Portia Faces Life*, *The Adventures of Topper*, *The Hour of Charm*, *The Thin Man* and *Mystery of the Week*. Rawson died on July 18, 1994, at age 76.

The creators-writers of *Beautiful* — Carl Bixby and Don Becker — had numerous other radio credits, some jointly. Bixby's writing duties included scripts for *Big Sister*, *Mrs. Miniver*, *Radio Reader's Digest* and two other serials that he also cowrote with Becker —*This Day Is Ours* (1938–40) and *The Man I Married* (1939–42)— during the period the duo was writing *Beautiful*. Bixby died at age 83 on June 29, 1978.

In addition to the serials on which they collaborated, Becker wrote scripts and composed the original theme music for *Beyond These Valleys*. He was creator-producer of *The Light of the World* and *The Parker Family* and producer-writer of *We Love and Learn*. Few were as diverse as he.

In *Life Can Be Beautiful,* the audience found that the eternal optimism of a single figure — Papa David Solomon — permeated the expressions of all its characters for more than a decade and a half. The serial affectionately penned by the gifted Bixby and Becker and eloquently verbalized by the endearing Ralph Locke offered time-honored messages that lifted Chichi Conrad from the depths of despair.

In time, she became a disciple, believing that life could be beautiful once more. By adopting Papa David's watchwords, she gladdened the old man's heart. For in Chichi, he saw a woman who was not only a daughter but a protégée to transport the maxims of his soul. What greater tribute could he gain than that?

11
The Light of the World

(An Eternal Beacon)

Few would have guessed that a soap opera based on the Good Book would ever have been created and that if it had, it would have gotten on the air. Fewer still would have believed that such a serial could have lasted for more than a few weeks. But public response can be a surprising barometer. When *The Light of the World* gained a berth at NBC, large numbers of listeners liked what they heard and kept it on the air for a decade. Its action was based on the narratives of the Old Testament, most of them recounted in multipart dramatizations. Casts were constantly changing, requiring a rather large repertory company to remain "on call" for short-term acting assignments. Many of the "regulars" who appeared in *World* maintained running parts in other serials. This was one of a few closed-end radio dramas, with each story arriving at a natural terminating point. One of the byproducts of the ultimate conclusion was that the audience could drift in and out of the plots as listening habits allowed; the brevity of such story lines didn't mandate the total attentiveness that was required for some open-ended dramas broadcast over long periods of time. The fact that this biblical series was sponsored throughout its run (and by a single advertiser, no less!) said a great deal about its quality and its commitment to faithfully interpret the scriptural context. Because a large portion of the audience was familiar with the plots, many of them readily followed the story lines, resulting in listener identification at an optimum level.

Producers: Frank and Anne Hummert
Creator-Producer: Don Becker
Producer-Director: Basil Loughrane
Directors: Oliver Barbour, Don Cope
Writers: Don Becker, Noel B. Gerson, Margaret E. Sangster, Adele Seymour, Katharine Seymour
Music: Clark (Doc) Whipple
Sound Effects: Jack Anderson
Announcers: Ted Campbell, James Fleming, Stuart Metz
The Speaker: David Gothard, Bret Morrison, Arnold Moss
Others: Bill Adams, Inge Adams, Peggy Allenby, Jack Arthur, Sanford Bickart, Philip Clarke, Richard Coogan, Humphrey Davis, Eric Dressler, Louise Fitch, Barbara Fuller,

Mitzi Gould, Ernest Graves, Albert Hays, William Hollenback, Mandel Kramer, Bernard Lenrow, Iris Mann, James McCallion, James Monks, Virginia Payne, Eleanor Phelps, Lynne Rogers, Elaine Rost, Chester Stratton, Daniel Sutter, Florence Williams, more

Theme: Original music

Sponsors: Blackett-Sample-Hummert governed this serial for General Mills. Softasilk and Gold Medal flours were among advertised commodities. When a nationwide flour shortage erupted in 1946 in the aftermath of World War II, General Mills canceled, and the series left the air. But the response from listeners was so vocal and persistent that when the shortage eased a few months later, General Mills returned the program to the air.

Ratings: In ten seasons *World's* ratings averaged 4.8 annually. High: 7.3 (1940–41); low: 2.9 (1944–45). When the serial returned as an afternoon feature, its numbers jumped, never falling below 4.5.

On the Air: March 18, 1940–March 21, 1941, NBC, 2:45 p.m. ET; March 24, 1941–1943, NBC, 2:00 p.m.; 1943–June 2, 1944, NBC, 2:30 p.m.; June 12, 1944–March 1946, CBS, 10:15 a.m.; Dec. 2, 1946–June 2, 1950, NBC, 2:45 p.m.

Could a soap opera attract a passionately loyal following among religious groups — and have them apply the serial as Bible study? The literary radio critics had predicted as early as 1934 that a drama with a high moral message couldn't last long. The public wouldn't buy into the idea of treating the Holy Scriptures as a castaway chip from a soap urn, they contended.

But once again the prophets of doom were out of touch with the pulse of an important segment of the radio audience. Not only did such a series with high principles arrive and remain on the air, but it landed a sponsor and generated a respectable audience, to the surprise and perhaps the consternation of naysayers. And the series was closely monitored by students of the Scriptures as a kind of educational affirmation of their faith.

Sincerely and simply worded, dramatized in contemporary settings, the biblical tales on *The Light of the World* included the typical soap opera melees of other programs. With doses of crises and heartbreaks, *World's* plots often resembled those of its distant cousins, companion serials with story lines couched in real time. Yet the sponsor discovered — almost too late — how much *World* really was appreciated by strong adherents of multiple faiths who tuned in every day.

When the nation experienced a flour shortage soon after World War II, General Mills, which had underwritten this radio series for six years, withdrew its sponsorship. As a result, in March 1946, *World* abruptly left the air. But public outcry is an amazing thing. Persistent fans have saved — or returned to the air — many a television series that didn't establish a sufficiently large share of the viewers to avoid cancellation. In *World's* case, this was a successful program that had an audience but lacked a sponsor.

An overwhelming call for the serial's return could not be ignored. When the flour scarcity eased a few months later, General Mills brought *World* back to the airwaves. On resumption, the soap opera regained not only its lost audience but also 50 percent more fans than it had before it left. *World* was able to maintain an increased share of listeners almost to the end of the run.

An announcer opened the show over an organ droning in the background. Employing an echo effect, the announcer exhorted: *"The Light of the World...! The story of the Bible, an eternal beacon lighting man's way through the darkness of time ... brought to you by General Mills."*

Following a commercial, the drama unfolded as a serialized version of an Old Testament narrative. Ancient characters were drawn out and offered as personalities set in modern applications.

The program initially presented the story of Adam and Eve portrayed by Albert Hays and Eleanor Phelps and set in the Garden of Eden. When *The Light of the World* returned after its eight-month hiatus in 1946, it was relaunched with the tale of Adam and Eve. This time the story was told as an 11-part adaptation. Philip Clarke (radio's *Mr. Keen, Tracer of Lost Persons*) played Adam while Eleanor Phelps reprised her role as his mate. Their sons, Cain and Abel, were portrayed by the venerable actors Mandel Kramer and Chester Stratton.

In addition to Adam and Eve, the scriptural accounts of the lives of David, Jezebel and Samson proved especially popular with *World*'s audience. The biblical series consistently drew heavy fan mail, much of it positive.

The show was brought to radio from the serial production factory of Frank and Anne Hummert. In a five-year period, 1937–42, the Hummerts introduced 22 new serials, including this one, to network radio. No one matched the volume of dramas they devised during this period or any other.

World was created by the enormously talented Don Becker, whose credits included *Life Can Be Beautiful*. The series went on the air on March 18, 1940. A pair of sisters, Adele and Katharine Seymour, wrote most of *World*'s scripts. If the siblings had other radio credits, they were lost to history.

In addition to the program's announcer, there was also a narrator. For a while serial veterans David Gothard and Arnold Moss filled that slot. But the name most often associated with the drama — its narrator for most of the run — is Bret Morrison. In addition to playing the title role of *The Shadow* (1945–54), the actor, who was born on May 5, 1912, in Chicago, hosted *The First Nighter* (1937–41), his initial foray into radio. He carried roles in *Arnold Grimm's Daughter, Great Gunns, The Guiding Light, Road of Life, The Romance of Helen Trent, Stella Dallas, The Story of Mary Marlin* and *Woman in White*. He also worked on the *Carnation Contented Hour, Best Sellers* and *Listening Post*. During the 1970s Morrison appeared infrequently on *The CBS Mystery Theater*. He had just completed an episode for a rejuvenated radio drama in 1978, *Heartbeat Theatre*, when he collapsed on Hollywood's Vine Street. A heart attack victim, he died on September 25, 1978.

In an effort to maintain as much authenticity as possible for their radio play, the producers of *The Light of the World* submitted story lines to several respected theologians for advance review. A nonsectarian advisory board offered suggestions for maintaining biblical integrity in the scripts. And a noted biblical scholar, Union Theological Seminary's Dr.

James B. Moffatt, was on retainer to confer with scriptwriters. Congregants of various faiths were consulted in an effort to yield the highest-possible levels of quality and integrity.

Attempting to lend further credibility, producer-director Basil Loughrane gained an egregious reputation for holding lengthy auditions for each drama's speaking roles. He was determined that voices on the air would closely approximate what many listeners might have envisioned in the original experiences. Such determination pushed purity almost to the limit but was applauded by religious groups for its thoroughness.

The Light of the World and *Aunt Jenny's Real Life Stories* were the only ultimate-conclusion serials (stories that had permanent endings) to be rated as highly successful over an entire run. At least 16 other soap operas attempting the closed-end formula never reached such distinction.

Although some may have viewed *World* as a novelty in network programming, it daily delivered sizable audiences to its sponsor and networks. Doubtlessly it raised the level of Americans' interest in the Scriptures. Basing its story lines on events that occurred at the beginning of the human race, the series offered an attractive format for recalling major biblical themes. Thus, at least for a decade, society's moral fiber was raised a notch as a unique soap opera sought to light man's way "through the darkness of time."

12
Lora Lawton
(Where So Few Dreams Come True)

Let it be inscribed in marble that when soap opera creators found a theme they liked, they often beat it to death. All serial originators were guilty of this to some extent, but the Hummerts took special delight in bringing to audiences the same time-worn hypotheses. Each serial approached a given premise in just a little different vein from that of the others. To wit, one of their favorite notions was to take a young, single woman from Podunk and marry her to a man who was much higher on the social register and then watch them both squirm. The twist in *Lora Lawton* was that the heroine initially became the housekeeper for a shipping magnate. Wealthy, devilishly handsome and oh-so-single Peter Carver was the object of every ambitious duchess, debutante and just plain damsel on the East Coast. Sometimes it wasn't clear whether they were after his money or his body, but these vixens would stop at nothing to gain both. Even when Peter and Lora fell in love and were married — as in every other Hummert drama with this theme — it made no difference to those temptresses who were determined to get their claws into him. Such obsessive attitudes prevailed on *Backstage Wife, Our Gal Sunday* and several other serials of this stripe. Things got a little crazy at times, and Lora was occasionally the intended object of violence. The serial was one of three on which the sponsor, B. T. Babbitt, trotted out numerous premium offers, unceremoniously weaving them into plot lines as if they were part of the action.

Producers: Frank and Anne Hummert
Directors: Martha Atwell, Arthur Hanna, Fred Weihe
Writers: Jean Carroll, Elizabeth Todd, Helen Walpole
Music: Ted Steele
Announcer: Ford Bond
Lora Lawton: Joan Tompkins (1943–46), Jan Miner (1946–50)
Peter Carver: James Meighan, Ned Wever
Others: Charita Bauer, Fran Carlon, Marilyn Erskine, Walter Greaza, William Hare, Elaine Kent, Alan MacAteer, Kate McComb, Paul McGrath, Carol Summers, James Van Dyk, Ethel Wilson, Lawson Zerbe, more

Theme: "Just a Little Love" (originally a vocal, later played on the organ)

Sponsors: Blackett-Sample-Hummert and Duane Jones governed this serial for B. T. Babbitt, Inc., primarily for its Bab-O cleanser. The program was also a conduit for Lycons soap-making recipes.

Ratings: High: 4.2 (1943–44); low: 2.5 (1948–49); median: 3.1. Some explanation for the low ratings appears in the chapter.

On the Air: May 31, 1943–1945, NBC, 10:00 a.m. ET; 1945–Jan. 10, 1947, NBC, 10:15 a.m.; Jan. 13, 1947–Jan. 6, 1950, NBC, 11:45 a.m.

While developing new serials for radio, producers and writers were smitten with the premise of romantically linking a common girl with a man well above her station in life. The formula was used so frequently that it became an underlying theme of at least a dozen washboard weepers. (One serial took an opposite approach: an unsteady, indolent male married a highly successful woman in *Portia Faces Life*. And in *When a Girl Marries*, a young law graduate considered himself inferior to his wife's family, which included an esteemed attorney father.)

Whether listeners took the time to discover the similarity of the threads weaving through some of their favorite dramas is unknown. Surely the repetition must have been noticed by some. But in each serial using the blueprint, a unique twist was offered so that the story wouldn't come off as a mere duplicity of another. The variations, in some cases, were minimal.

• *Betty and Bob* (1932–40) was about a poor but beautiful secretary who married her boss; the pair was then cut off by his millionaire father.

• In *Peggy's Doctor* (1934–35), a well-to-do physician working in a remote Kentucky village wooed the daughter of a penniless horse breeder.

• In *The Story of Mary Marlin* (1935–45, 1951–52), a small-town Iowa girl rose in the world of politics after her husband, elected a U.S. senator, disappeared a short time later. The heroine was named to complete his unexpired term, moving in circles for which she was never prepared.

• *Backstage Wife* (1935–59) was also about a lowly Iowa girl, this one a former stenographer: "The story of Mary Noble and what it means to be the wife of a famous Broadway star, dream sweetheart of a million other women."

• In *Rich Man's Darling* (1936–37), a 20-year-old newspaper reporter at a fairly low end of the wage scale married a 45-year-old millionaire. The title says it all.

• *Modern Cinderella* (1936–37) was a contemporary version of the fairy tale, in which a pauper struck it rich via matrimony.

• *Our Gal Sunday* (1937–59) asked this question about its average, orphaned heroine: "Can this girl from the little mining town in the West find happiness as the wife of a wealthy and titled Englishman?"

• *Linda's First Love* (1939–50) was a nonnetwork series wherein a "shop girl" (modern rendering: store clerk) was diligently pursued by a wealthy playboy.

• *The Man I Married* (1939–42) involved the disinherited son of a millionaire and his wife as they attempted to make a fresh start in a new city.

• *Amanda of Honeymoon Hill* (1939–46) concerned the bickering families of a blue-collar redhead and a southern aristocrat who married and moved to his magnificent estate on Honeymoon Hill.

• In *Lora Lawton* (1943–50), a nobody from the Midwest was domestic help for — then the wife of — a billionaire tycoon from the East.

• *The Strange Romance of Evelyn Winters* (1944–48) was the tale of a young woman who just completed her formal education and became infatuated with her guardian, a well-established Broadway playwright 15 years her senior.

Some other serials modified the concept. One of Carolyn Allen's four husbands on *The Right to Happiness* rose to become governor of Mississippi, carrying her from virtual obscurity to the limelight of the state's highest office. *Stella Dallas*, a seamstress who lived in a Boston rooming house, never enjoyed prosperity and fame herself, but her epigraph reminded listeners that "she saw her beloved daughter, Laurel, marry into wealth and society, and — realizing the differences in their tastes and worlds — went out of Laurel's life." Slightly revised, the popular formula could be pressed into service wherever scriptwriters needed a tangent to diversify story lines.

The dramatic device of romantically involving a commoner with a man of power and wealth permitted audiences to contemplate the opulence resulting from such influence and affluence. At the same time, serial writers were cautious not to carry the new environment to extremes. They usually allowed their protagonists to adapt to new surroundings over a period of time, gradually accepting the trappings that went with them.

Lora Lawton was dubbed "the story of what it means to be the wife of one of the richest, most attractive men in all America." At the same time it cautiously advised that the serial was "the story of love and riches in a world so many dream of, but where so few dreams come true."

Lawton was the narrative of a young woman from the Midwest who became the housekeeper for a shipping magnate in Washington, D.C. The handsome Peter Carver was also one of that area's most pursued and eligible bachelors.

Lora, on the other hand, had survived one marriage already — to Harley Lawton, who had died in an airplane crash within hours of asking Lora for a divorce. Their union had been an unhappy one almost from the day of their nuptials. It had left Lora soured on the institution of marriage. In Harley's death she saw an opportunity to make a fresh start in life. When Peter Carver's invitation arrived for her to leave behind her sad memories and move to Washington to manage his household staff, she welcomed it as a chance to begin anew.

It didn't take astute listeners long to determine the direction in which this soap opera was headed. In a brief time Lora became the object of Peter's affections. But her unhappy past prevented her from readily accepting the proposal of marriage he proffered. In due time, Lora found in Peter positive qualities that she had never witnessed in Harley. Gradually, her resolve against remarriage melted. After a while the pair became sweethearts and, later, husband and wife.

Even though Lora was then mistress of Peter's grand estate, the story remained about a small-town girl from the sticks (Lora from Nowhere?) who made good by joining society's upper crust through matrimony. As radio serial marriages went, the Carvers' was pretty decent. (Theirs wasn't quite like the bliss of their nearby aristocratic neighbors, Sunday and Lord Henry Brinthrope, just down the road in Virginia. The Brinthropes exuded a mutual exclusivity, a trust and devotion to one another in spite of a multitude of evil third parties who were committed to destroying their alliance.)

Lora Lawton and *Our Gal Sunday* and most of the other serials visited at the start of this chapter were produced by Frank and Anne Hummert. Heroes and heroines of Hummert serials were subject to the usual string of half-crazed suitors who would stop at nothing to marry one or the other of the principals.

After her marriage, Lora continued to use her own name both professionally and privately. Was she, in the mid–1940s, living decades ahead of many other women of her time? Certainly if she had changed her name to Lora Carver, it would have presented an awkward dilemma for the network as well as for listeners. An established serial title existed; altering it might have been confusing for a while, at least.

What Lora did dispense with following her wedding was her housekeeping chores. Someone else was summoned to do the dirty work. Meanwhile, needing something else to do to fill up her time, Lora opened a dress shop. Having demonstrated some passion and flair for clothing design, she stocked some of her own creations for sale. Her success in the field was swift, and she gained widespread acceptance as a fashion designer.

Meanwhile, in true-to-Hummert form, the single and attached gals, both local and international, continued to pursue Peter as if Lora didn't exist. As in *Backstage Wife* and so many other formulaic, by-the-book Hummert dramas, when one would-be spousal substitute was dispatched, another would arrive. The new pursuer would attempt to replace one of the married parties, albeit under slightly altered conditions from the previous suitor.

In one late 1947 sequence, a young woman with less-than-honorable motives enticed Peter away from the safe confines of home. He followed her all the way to a lonely farmhouse on the coast of France, permitting her to put him under her spell and sway him with her wily charms.

Another time a beautiful and wealthy socialite, Helene Hudson, dug her clutches into the shipbuilding mogul. But her hopes, like others', were dashed. Carver would remain faithfully attached to his former housekeeper.

One of the man-chasers in *Lora Lawton* was Princess Erica Van Kiper — royalty of a "continental" country, though listeners were never absolutely sure which country. She debuted on the broadcast of March 4, 1947. Inviting the Carvers to tea at a Washington apartment they had rented to the princess through an agent, she first met Peter at his office. That afternoon at teatime, she welcomed Lora to the apartment.

> PRINCESS: Mrs. Carver, how very good of you to come — I'm
>   delighted to meet you!
> LORA: Thank you, princess. How nice of you to invite me.
> PRINCESS: Come by the fire.... You know, I did a wicked thing.
>   I've asked several people, but I told them all to come later,
>   hoping that you would be punctual and ... and I'd have a
>   chance to know you a little bit before they came.
> LORA: Well, I am punctual.
> PRINCESS: I hope your husband won't come too soon.
> LORA: (Surprised) Is Peter coming?
> PRINCESS: He said he would. I went to see him this morning.
>   He's divine! So handsome, and so charming.

LORA: (Laughing) I like him.
PRINCESS: And the apartment is wonderful—and you sound to
    me as if you were quite the most fascinating woman in
    Washington.... Tell me about your work.... Do you suppose
    you could make me look like anything?
LORA: There'd be very little effort required, princess.
PRINCESS: Howard Spalding told me you were terribly good
    looking, and he's so right. You enchanted him, and Howard
    Spalding is as blasé as they come, my dear.... Sit down here.
    Let's talk seriously before we're interrupted, shall we?

An organ bridge intervened, signaling the end of action for the episode. Over the music, announcer Ford Bond observed: "Lora finds herself coming under the princess' spell … as she sits down and listens to the enthusiastic chatter. And Peter, on his way, is wondering about the future, *his* future with … Lora Lawton."

Indeed, there was lots to fantasize about there. In fact, in the weeks and months ahead, Peter—and Lora too—would have their hands full of the continental princess, who was to become much more than simply another tenant in their apartment. Even though the ultimate outcome was always predictable, it was still absorbing stuff, leaving the audience wondering how this suitor would be eliminated.

Lora Lawton joined NBC's daytime lineup on May 31, 1943, and remained until it was replaced on January 6, 1950. Unfortunately, at no time did the series achieve lofty ratings. At least two factors may partially clarify the poor numbers.

The networks had learned, several years before *Lawton's* debut, that "block programming"—grouping similar shows in a type of mass scheduling approach—drew more listeners interested in the same kinds of programs than did placing like programs at scattered hours throughout the schedule. Thus, nighttime comedy shows were often preceded or followed by other comedies; mysteries were sometimes grouped with mysteries; quiz programs appeared with other quiz shows. (The same holds true of network TV today.) As a result, people looking for a certain type of amusement could scratch their itches in heavy doses. Audience research indicated that fans would remain tuned to a network or station longer if they could select from several related programs broadcast back-to-back.

The idea also worked well among daytime audiences as features and audience-participation shows were similarly aired. The concept really came into its own as housewives stood at their ironing boards and heard not one but several 15-minute soap operas in succession. But for whatever reason, this rule wasn't applied to *Lora Lawton* during most of its run. Instead, the serial was invariably scheduled before or after a 15-minute news segment, floundering apart from the traditional morning and afternoon soap opera blocks. Thus, the objective of involving large numbers of listeners in drama-by-installment through an unbroken pattern was imperiled by poor scheduling. When the series shifted to 11:45 a.m. in 1947, it was in total isolation, preceded by up to 45 minutes of musical programs and followed by news and other features. Ratings went down and remained down.

A second factor that undoubtedly diminished *Lora Lawton's* audience was its strong competition, particularly at 11:45. That was the hour CBS was just beginning its block of soap operas, extending past midafternoon. It was one of only four quarter-hour segments in which the two dominant networks, CBS and NBC, counterprogrammed serials during the 1948–49 season, for example. And CBS mounted its daily soap opera block with a powerhouse, *Rosemary,* which debuted in 1944 and grabbed a major share of the audience almost from its inception. *Rosemary* consistently won the time period two-to-one against *Lora Lawton.* Poor scheduling was once again a culprit.

Lawton was one of three serial dramas (*David Harum, Lora Lawton, Nona from Nowhere*) underwritten by B. T. Babbitt, Inc., a leading household-cleaning products manufacturer. Certainly not by coincidence, the announcer and product spokesperson for this trio of Babbitt shows was Ford Bond. His grandfatherly advice, delivered in vibrant tones lending authority to his sales pitches, obviously pleased Duane Jones, who packaged the programs for Babbitt.

For his part, Jones enthusiastically supported the idea of offering premiums to radio audiences. Perhaps more than anyone else in the industry, he diligently pursued the concept of supplying trinkets to listeners who mailed in coupons or box tops torn from a sponsor's product. For that, and ten cents, fans might receive a "lovely chain necklace just like the one designed and worn by Lora Lawton" or a packet of the same type of flower seeds planted by David Harum "in his very own garden."

While the *Harum* serial was reputed to have capitalized on the premium phenomenon more than any other single program, *Lawton* ran a close second. When a cast member nonchalantly referred to a batch of Christmas cards she would be sending one season, "just like the ones that brought Lora and Peter together again," Bond informed fans that they too could acquire those cards. Tens of thousands of requests poured in. It may have been an even better device than the rating services for demonstrating to sponsors how well their messages were being received.

Bond's staccato delivery barked similar lines day after day in opening and closing commercials for the Babbitt dramas. If listeners missed the message once, they often heard it somewhere else. Bond would deliver a sales pitch for Bab-O, the sponsor's flagship product, and invariably include the spelling of the product name, "B-A-B-O," with a deliberate pause between the "B" and "O." Often he concluded his missive with this line: "To save extra steps, get two cans — one for the bathroom, one for the kitchen."

His suggestion offers modern generations some insights on typical living conditions in households of that era. In the 1940s, most American homes had indoor plumbing. But most of the audiences that Bond hoped to reach still lived in dwellings with one bathroom. (Otherwise, he would have called for a can of Bab-O for every bathroom in the house. And the sales potential would have vastly increased had those multiple bathrooms existed!)

Before *Lawton* signed off each day, there was a hitchhike commercial for another Babbitt product. One of the more unusual sounding to generations today — but quite common then — was Lycons. A commercial for this product in the late 1940s went like this:

> Ladies, if you want to save money by making soap at home,
> discover Lycons. It's in modern flake form, so it pours freely,
> dissolves quickly. Try Lycons. See how the soap you make is
> splendid for heavy duty laundry, for white washes, too. Use
> recipe on the Lycons label or send for free book containing five
> tested soap recipes. Address: Lycons, L-Y-C-O-N-S, care of
> this station. Ask for free Lycons soap-making recipes.

In the *Lawton* story line, the title role was played by Joan Tompkins and Jan Miner. Tompkins is best recalled for her long association with another serial, *This Is Nora Drake*. And Miner will be forever remembered as the heroine of *Hilltop House*.

To complement them, the part of Peter Carver was played by two veteran actors. James Meighan, best recalled as the husband of Mary Noble in *Backstage Wife*, and Ned Wever, the perennial suitor in *Young Widder Brown*, took turns as the shipping tycoon.

Although *Lora Lawton* was formula soap opera to the letter and never achieved more than moderate success, it allowed its audience to fantasize about what it would be like to suddenly gain wealth and prestige. As listeners thought about the idea, they may have been impressed that this was, for sure, a world "where so few dreams come true."

13
Lorenzo Jones
(More Smiles Than Tears)

One of soap opera's few comedies, this Hummert drama centered on a would-be inventor whose intentions lacked logic and made him "a character to the town — but not to Belle, who loves him." Belle Jones, Lorenzo's faithful helpmate, stood by her man against the town fathers (and mothers) who frequently had reason to question his competency. Belle often wondered to herself about Lorenzo's dreams of instant fame and fortune. Such ill-fated ideas were seldom realistic. Lorenzo, an amateur detective, was also instrumental in capturing a crook now and then. But he usually realized little more for his efforts than the security of a job at Jim Barker's garage, where he toiled as an auto mechanic while daydreaming of future gizmos. To his credit, the impractical ideologue wasn't disheartened by his failures. Never a quitter, he believed that success was just around the corner. Such perseverance, and having a good woman at his side, allowed him to dream on. Even when the series took a melodramatic turn in its final three years, the character's fans were rewarded with a redeeming spirit of optimism that sometimes eluded the heroes and heroines of their other favorite serials. The net result was more smiles than tears.

Producers: Frank and Anne Hummert
Directors: Stephen Gross, Frank Hummert, Ernest Ricca
Writers: Theodore and Mathilde Ferro
Music: Ann Leaf, Rosa Rio
Sound Effects: Frank Loughrane, Manny Segal
Announcers: Don Lowe, George Putnam, Ken Roberts
Lorenzo Jones: Karl Swenson
Belle Jones: Betty Garde (1937–40), Lucille Wall (1940–55)
Others: Frank Behrens, John Brown, Art Carney, Louis Hector, Irene Hubbard, Joe Julian, Grace Keddy, Jean McCoy, Kermit Murdock, Ethel Owen, Elliott Reid, Ann Shepherd, Nancy Sheridan, Chester Stratton, Helen Walpole, Colleen Ward, Mary Wickes, Roland Winters, others

Theme: "Beyond the Blue Horizon"; "Funiculi Funicula" (Denza)

Sponsors: At inception, Blackett-Sample-Hummert governed for Sterling Drugs (including a long list of health-related products, often under the family names of Phillips, Bayer and Dr. Lyons). At the pinnacle of the show's popularity, Sterling bowed out and the quarter-hour was sold to Procter & Gamble (for Dreft dishwashing detergent and other cleansers), beginning on Dec. 12, 1949. Sponsorship went to rival manufacturer Colgate-Palmolive-Peet, Inc. (Colgate dental cream, Palmolive soap, Fab laundry detergent, others), in 1952 when Procter & Gamble relinquished it. Hazel Bishop participated in the commercials near the end of the run.

Ratings: Although the show's numbers never reached the knock-'em-dead variety, its median in 18-plus years was a healthy 6.1. The highest figure, 7.7, was achieved in 1939–40; it scored a 7.6 in three other years (1943–44, 1948–49, 1949–50). The series' lowest rating, 3.3, was recorded in 1951–52.

On the Air: April 26, 1937–1938, NBC, 4:00 p.m. ET; 1938–1939, NBC, 11:15 a.m.; 1939–June 29, 1951, NBC, 4:30 p.m.; July 2, 1951–March 26, 1954, NBC, 5:30 p.m.; March 29, 1954–Sept. 30, 1955, NBC, 5:15 p.m.

We all know couples like lovable, impractical Lorenzo Jones and his devoted wife, Belle. Lorenzo's inventions have made him a character to the town — but not to Belle, who loves him. Their struggle for security is anybody's story. But somehow with Lorenzo, it has more smiles than tears.
                                                    — Epigraph to *Lorenzo Jones*

For millions of homemakers during the late afternoons between the 1930s and mid–1950s, a funny thing happened on the way to preparing supper. Tuning their radios, they caught a diversion from the traditional matinee fare: a pursuit in trivia known as *Lorenzo Jones*. The show was a radical departure from almost anything they were accustomed to.

The gurus of daytime drama, Frank and Anne Hummert, dreamed up this little farce as an interruption in the usual melee of mayhem and social excess. Ostensibly a comedy serial, *Jones* arrived to a bouncing organ rendition of Denza's "Funiculi Funicula." The show favorably compared with radio's other attempts at serialized humor, most notably *Easy Aces, The Goldbergs* and *Vic and Sade*.

Promising "more smiles than tears," this dishpan drama centered on Jones, an irrepressible auto mechanic at Jim Barker's garage. Jones' idealistic schemes for producing all sorts of gadgets went well beyond the normal range of an obsessed fanatic. Frequently, in fact, his ideas bordered on sheer lunacy, like the time he developed a three-spouted teapot — including spouts for weak, medium and strong tea. He produced hair restorers that didn't work and bedwarmers that worked so well they ignited the beds! His sulfur-water pep tonic, contrived to get people moving again, accomplished that goal all right: one swallow and consumers were heaving frantically while hoping to keep anything down!

Poor Lorenzo: though he prided himself on being a law-abiding citizen, he nearly went to prison for dispensing such remedies without a license. Staying out of jail, in fact, became his most elusive quest, the result of frequent displays of imbecilic stupidity.

Despite this, some of his harebrained schemes actually worked. He created a ground-level wheel for walking canines in circles. He concocted a perpetual foot warmer that became a universal hit, then misplaced the proceeds from it. He had put his earnings in a piece of pottery on the living room mantel but discarded the container. He also invented an item that is in widespread use today, though he was nearly laughed out of town for it at the time — an outdoor vacuum cleaner. The trouble with Lorenzo's contraption was that it ate nearly everything it came in contact with, like topsoil, garden hoses, grass, etc.

Jones, the man, was a daytime version of the popular nighttime eccentric Fibber McGee, who aspired to invent numerous items that nobody wanted. (Aside from his myriad of misunderstood creations that neither impressed the folks of *his* town nor worked, McGee frequently attempted other ridiculous creations. He once wrote what he theorized would be an award-winning movie based on "The Typewriter.") Neither McGee nor Jones had much in the way of practical abilities for reasoning things out. Nevertheless, both were determined to pursue their idiotic concepts no matter what the cost and no matter that they became local laughingstocks.

Before the lilting "Funiculi Funicula" ushered the serial onto the air each afternoon, listeners were greeted with this promising epithet: "Now, smile awhile with Lorenzo Jones and his wife, Belle!"

An understanding Belle was as important to this series as Molly was to Fibber McGee. Belle Jones was the typical self-effacing spouse of that era who put her own hopes and dreams aside to support her mate in his preposterous quests. Even when Lorenzo's notions were too outlandish to share with anyone, Belle seldom argued against them. Instead, she preferred to murmur "Lorenzo, Lorenzo, I just don't know about that" in her own restrained fashion. But she never tolerated others who questioned her spouse's rationality. Belle was quick to defend her beloved Lorenzo when critics impugned his integrity or sanity.

Her favorite time of the day arrived when the couple reviewed the day's dilemmas while lying awake in their twin beds shortly before drifting off to sleep. Sometimes they quoted poetry to one another. In those quarter-hour glimpses into their lives, fans observed that there was more to Lorenzo than the often fanatical, hardheaded exterior he exhibited in public. Belle may have been perplexed by Lorenzo's incessant need to contrive the ridiculous, but she ended each day with thanksgiving for this man who cherished her above all else.

Lorenzo, who often fancied himself a detective as well as an inventor, got into some ticklish situations as a result. When aged Mrs. Carmichael asked him to move an ancestral portrait from above the mantelpiece of her colonial home, the amateur gumshoe uncovered a secret passageway. Legend had it that a treasure had been buried near the house; Lorenzo and Mrs. Carmichael were sure that the tunnel led to it.

A short time earlier Lorenzo had become friends with a smooth-talking Frenchman, Pierre Olivet, who purchased a neighborhood home for himself and an attractive female ward. Meanwhile, Belle was arranging for Lorenzo, Pierre and the sheriff to protect a million dollars in gems to be displayed during a charity-sponsored event. The cunning Frenchman successfully carried out his own agenda, however, stealing the diamonds and hiding them in a secret passageway from his home. *His* tunnel, listeners were not surprised to learn, connected with the one leading to the Carmichael estate.

Following the passageway, Lorenzo and Mrs. Carmichael naturally came upon the jewels and believed them to be the legend's hidden treasure. But when Pierre, brandishing a gun, confronted them, it looked like curtains for the amateur sleuths. Fortunately, Pierre had been followed by the police, and the sequence came to a happy end.

Lorenzo once had a not-so-pleasant encounter with a Parisian lass, the mysterious Fifi, who collaborated with him to build a "youth machine." Only after he borrowed enough to finance Fifi's return voyage to France did Lorenzo realize that she was a total phony. His trust in the common man (er, lass) was often misplaced.

When Jim Barker, Lorenzo's employer, could take no more of his off-the-wall day-dreaming, Jim fired the mechanic. Belle then took a job as a hairdresser at Madame Cunard's Beauty Salon, run by a Frenchwoman. (Has it occurred to anyone that this serial seemed preoccupied with the French?)

Lorenzo was soon hired as a foreman for Trapp and Sweeney, a building contractor, a field in which he had little experience. What he didn't know — but soon learned — was that Trapp and Sweeney were a couple of gangsters who used the business as a front for shady activities. They planned to draw Lorenzo into a tangled web. Gullible Lorenzo was their patsy until he exposed them after he lucked into learning their real intentions.

By the end of the 1940s Lorenzo idolized Marty Crandall, an old high school chum who returned to town touting success stories of his personal inventions. Belle too was impressed by Marty's tales of good fortune, and Lorenzo leased his workshop to his friend. Marty was working on a mysterious secret project, which he said he couldn't discuss even with Lorenzo. Poor Lorenzo didn't know whether to be jealous or suspicious of this man. Subsidized by a syndicate interested in his inventing skills, Marty's secret mission was finally revealed when Lorenzo pieced together a fantastic theory: Marty Crandall was actually constructing a counterfeiting machine in Lorenzo's workroom! When U.S. Treasury agents nabbed the racketeer, Lorenzo reveled in the local limelight as the town hero. (At one point he even fathomed the idea of turning his life story into a motion picture, *Lorenzo Jones, the Man!* Doesn't that sound like McGee?)

Like many of his peers in the more serious washboard weepers, Lorenzo was suspected of murder at least a half-dozen times. Given such circumstances, one might suppose that a guy's friends would avoid him. Not so in Lorenzo's case; his relatives, friends, neighbors, customers and acquaintances still beat a path to his door. Never once were their consciences bothered by the fact that Lorenzo, often suspected as a killer, continued to walk the streets as a free man. A man was truly innocent until proven guilty in their community!

Despite Lorenzo's many brushes with the law, for 15 years the serial remained light-hearted. Yet when the ratings cascaded to their lowest ebb, the Hummerts promptly took steps to correct the situation. The pair decided to inject a surprising twist into the story line, rivaling some of the turmoil in their other soap operas. (A historiographer suggested that since *Lorenzo Jones* immediately followed *Stella Dallas* on the air for most of its existence it was bound to acquire some of the melodrama so characteristic of *Dallas*, seeping across the 4:30 station break that separated the two serials.[1])

The plot revisions began to occur in mid–1952. Lorenzo was kidnapped and wounded by the accomplices of some gem thieves whom he had helped put away. Waking up in a clinic in New York City, he suddenly acquired a severe case of soap opera's classic malady, amnesia. But whereas everybody else's amnesia in daytime radio departed after only a few days, weeks or months, Lorenzo's remained. He was saddled with the affliction for nearly three years, in fact. He took odd jobs for a livelihood while his disorder left him wandering from place to place. Experiencing a total change in personality, ultimately he turned into a determined scientist, replete with romantic problems galore.

Listeners must have had some difficulty relating what they were then hearing to the show they had tuned in to during its earlier years. Had fate not intervened, in fact—in the form of the NBC brass, who canceled him—Lorenzo would likely have become soap opera's first bigamist. In the waning days of the serial's life he marched toward the altar with brilliant though predatory Gail Maddox. (Fortunately, that trip down the aisle was interrupted at an opportune moment too.)

The number of soap operas on the air was materially reduced by the networks in the 1950s. The programmers soon concluded that a comedy serial no longer held commanding interest for mass audiences. Thus, NBC decided to abruptly curtail Lorenzo's misery. It would also give the network's new behemoth magazine *Weekday*, then aired four and a half hours daily five days a week, an extra quarter-hour to do its thing.

So, just in time to bid good-by to his faithful listeners, Lorenzo was jerked back to reality. Though never recalling his marriage to Belle until then, he found his helpmate patiently awaiting the moment he would regain his memory. And listeners must have pondered many times how a series rooted in a formula of "more smiles than tears" could have arrived at such an awkward conclusion.

Not only was this serial set apart from most other daytime fare due to its humorous content, but *Lorenzo Jones* was just as unique from an acting standpoint. Only three people played its two leading roles over 18 years. Karl Swenson was Lorenzo while first Betty Garde and then Lucille Wall took on the duties as Belle. Even more unusual is that all three went on to prominent roles in TV soap operas after their radio careers ended.

Multitalented Karl Swenson was born in Brooklyn, New York, on July 23, 1908. The medical-student-turned-actor ventured onto the stage in 1930 in summer stock with the Berkshire Players. He appeared on Broadway in musical revues by Leonard Stillman and in *The Man Who Had All the Luck*, Arthur Miller's initial stage play. By 1935 Swenson debuted on radio's *The March of Time*. In this medium the full range of his versatile talents flourished, making him indispensable on many shows. In addition to Lorenzo Jones he was the male lead in *Our Gal Sunday*, sounding veddy veddy British as Sunday's husband, Lord Henry Brinthrope. He was "the man of many disguises," *Mr. Chameleon*, in that crime series' evening run. In that role, which some suggested the Hummerts created especially for him, Swenson readily assumed the dialect called for by his weekly disguise—Irish, Norwegian, German, Mexican, Yankee, Southerner, etc. His speaking abilities apparently knew no limit.

The busy actor found parts to his liking in these series, often playing title roles or masculine leads: *Father Brown, Joe Palooka, Lawyer Q, Linda's First Love, Mrs. Miniver, Rich Man's Darling, The Whisper Men, Cavalcade of America, World's Great Novels, Portia Faces Life, This Is Your FBI, Inner Sanctum Mysteries, Spy Secrets, Grand Central Station, There Was a Woman, The Mighty Show, Aunt Jenny's Real Life Stories, The Court of Missing Heirs* and *The Ford Theater*.

Moving to the small screen, he costarred with actress Fran Carlon as her husband, Walter Manning, on the televised version of *Portia Faces Life* (1954–55), a radio serial in which he had been cast several years earlier. He was a regular on *Little House on the Prairie* in the part of Mr. Hansen and turned up in supporting roles on several other TV series. Swenson appeared on the big screen in *The Birds* and *The Hanging Tree*. The actor was married to the actress Joan Tompkins, heroine of *This Is Nora Drake* and *Lora Lawton*. He died at Torrington, Connecticut, on October 8, 1978.

Betty Garde, who played Belle Jones during *Lorenzo Jones'* first three years, was equally adaptable. Born on September 19, 1905, at Philadelphia, she burst onto the stage as Aunt Eller in Rodgers and Hammerstein's original Broadway version of *Oklahoma!* in the 1940s. Earlier, she had been in several lesser-known theatrical productions. Garde played in numerous movies and is perhaps best remembered for *Call Northside 777*, a 1948 film.

Her radio credits, meanwhile, are legion: *The American School of the Air, The Big Story, Criminal Casebook, Front Page Farrell, Maudie's Diary, McGarry and His Mouse, Mrs. Wiggs of the Cabbage Patch, My Son and I, The Phil Silvers Show, Policewoman, Tish, We the Abbotts, Quaker Party with Tommy Riggs, The Aldrich Family, Theatre Guild on the Air, Cavalcade of America, America's Hour, The Henry Morgan Show, Jane Arden, Joe and Mabel, Mickey of the Circus, Perry Mason, Under Arrest, The Fat Man, Al Pearce and His Gang, The Columbia Workshop, Studio One, Gangbusters, Inner Sanctum Mysteries, World's Great Novels, Mr. and Mrs. North* and *The Thin Man*.

On television Garde appeared in 1954 as Mrs. Sweeney in *The World of Mr. Sweeney*. Two years later she turned up as Mattie Grimsley in TV's debuting thirty-minute soap opera *The Edge of Night*. She died on December 25, 1989, in Sherman Oaks, California.

The third member of the *Jones* trio, Lucille Wall, carried the part of Belle for most of the time, 1940–55. She also became the heroine of another radio soap opera, *Portia Faces Life* (see chapter 19 for more on Wall).

The small-town radio audiences of the 1930s, 1940s and early 1950s, who prided themselves on conformity, were comforted when Lorenzo Jones took his lumps over his failed ambitions. He was, after all, the ultimate nonconformist. And though these listeners may not have audibly expressed their feelings, millions must have chuckled to themselves — inwardly, "smiled a while" — as Lorenzo was soundly put in his place. Though his narrative was nonsensical, it must have had a certain ring of truth about it. As a result, the "character to the town" would surely have been recognized as such whether he lived in a fictional locale or among his most ardent fans.

14
Ma Perkins
(Mother of the Air)

An affable widow blessed with the wisdom of Solomon and situated in a rural, closely knit community marked by pathos and heartache were the parameters of this beloved drama. Such factors combined to distinguish it as one of the most enduring and heartwarming serials of radio's Golden Age. Ma's convivial spirit, her love for humanity and her concern that reason prevail and decency be practiced were hallmarks that endeared her to those in the drama and millions listening at home. As the unassuming conscience of Rushville Center (and possibly the nation), she was sought by citizens for her advice in solving moral and ethical mires. More often than not, the dilemmas involved her own little enclave — three children (including one who died in the war), their mates, her grandchildren and Ma's closest friend and business associate. Actress Virginia Payne, age 23 when she began the part, went all the way in the title role. Fans held her in the same exalted esteem they assigned to the character she played. The show's writers had the good fortune of being given 27 years to develop and interrelate the principal figures. Although all of it was purely make believe, of course, to those who welcomed it across the decades for a daily shot of adrenaline, this narrative seemed very real indeed. Their anguish, when the serial departed, may have been among the loudest cries that any audio network brass ever heard.

Creator: Robert Hardy Andrews
Producers: Frank and Anne Hummert, Lester Vail
Directors: Philip Bowman, George Fogle, Roy Winsor, Edwin Wolfe
Writers: Robert Hardy Andrews, Lee Gebhart, Lester Huntley, Natalie Johnson, Orin
  Tovrov (1939–60)
Music: Clark (Doc) Whipple
Sound Effects: Frank Blatter, Wes Conant, Jimmy Dwan, Russ Gainor, Bob Graham,
  Tommy Horan, John Katulik, John McCloskey, Vincent Ronca
Announcers: Jack Brinkley, Bob Brown, Dan Donaldson ("Charlie Warren"), Marvin
  Miller ("Charlie Warren"), Bob Pfeiffer, Dick Wells
Ma Perkins: Virginia Payne
Shuffle Shober: Charles Egleston (1933–58), Edwin Wolfe (1958–60)
Willie Fitz: Murray Forbes
Evey Perkins Fitz: Laurette Fillbrandt, Dora Johnson, Kay Campbell (1945–60)

Fay Perkins Henderson: Rita Ascot, Cheer Brentson, Margaret Draper, Laurette Fillbrandt, Marjorie Hannan
John Perkins: Gilbert Faust
Others: Casey Allen, Clare Baum, Rye Billsbury, Jack Brinkley, Herbert Butterfield, Fran Carlon, Maurice Copeland, Constance Crowder, Mary Frances Desmond, Nancy Douglass, Barry Drew, Patricia Dunlap, Bobby Ellis, Louise Fitch, Margaret Fuller, Don Gallagher, Rene Gekiere, Earl George, Stanley Gordon, Betty Hanna, Joe Helgeson, Wilms Herbert, Jonathan Hole, Fred Howard, Carl Kroenke, Ray Largay, John Larkin, Billy Lee, Sylvia Leigh, Forrest Lewis, Helen Lewis, Judith Lockser, DeWitt McBride, Stuart McIntosh, McKay Morris, Dolph Nelson, Marilou Neumayer, Angeline Orr, Jack Petruzzi, Glen Ransom, Mary Marren Rees, Curtis Roberts, Elmira Roessler, Billy Rose, Cecil Roy, Nanette Sargent, Ray Suber, Dan Sutter, Les Tremayne, Beryl Vaughn, Duke Watson, Stanley Waxman, Lillian White, Arthur Young, Beverly Younger, others

Theme: "Ma Perkins" (Larsen and Marcotte)

Sponsors: At inception, Blackett-Sample-Hummert governed for Procter & Gamble on behalf of Oxydol detergent. The long-running show was so clearly identified with the product that decades after P&G bowed out, on Nov. 30, 1956, fans still remembered the series as "Oxydol's own Ma Perkins." It was purportedly soap opera's best-established product identification. Later, when the series was sold to participating sponsors, it was carried by such firms as the Staley Corp. (Sta-Puf laundry products), Kellogg Company (cereals), CBS Records, Inc., and the Columbia Broadcasting System.

Ratings: High: 16.6 (1944–45, dual broadcasts); low: 4.5 (1955–56). (Figures based on records for the 1938–56 seasons.) The program consistently garnered high ratings, reaching into the double digits in ten of 18 seasons reported. In seven of those years it was broadcast twice daily; even when it was aired once, it stifled competition: 11.3 (1938–39), 10.4 (1939–40), 10.0 (1940–41), 9.2 (1949–50), 9.4 (1950–51). Over those 18 years the show's median rating was 10.7, about twice that of most of its contemporaries.

On the Air: Dec. 4, 1933–March 30, 1934, NBC, 3 p.m. ET; April 2, 1934–July 8, 1949, NBC, 3:15 p.m.; 1936–Feb. 5, 1937, MBS, 11:30 a.m.; Feb. 8, 1937–Dec. 31, 1937, NBC Blue; Jan. 3, 1938–May 27, 1938, CBS, 10:45 a.m.; May 30, 1938–Nov. 18, 1938, NBC Blue; Sept. 28, 1942–June 29, 1956, CBS, 1:15 p.m.; Oct. 8, 1956–Nov. 25, 1960, CBS, 1:15 p.m.

I give thanks that I've been given this gift of life, this gift of time to play my little part in it.
— Farewell monologue from Ma Perkins, November 25, 1960

The success of the *Ma Perkins* series was partially, yet inextricably, linked to the personal contributions of Virginia Payne, who singularly played the lead. The serial and its major character fed off the fortunes of each other. Much of that good luck could be attributed to their lengthy tenures together.

Only one other drama would air more episodes than *Ma Perkins*. *The Romance of Helen Trent* broadcast 7,222 chapters; *Ma Perkins* was heard 7,065 times. With regional broadcasts, *Trent* aired one month shy of 27 years and *Perkins* exceeded 27 years by three months. (*Perkins* was off the air briefly during that time, however.)

But Payne accomplished a feat that no other radio actress approached. For 27 years she portrayed the title character in radio's most revered soap opera, based on audience response. Although this exploit alone surpassed her contemporaries, she went further. In 27 years, Payne never missed a performance! Nobody, but nobody equaled that one!

The *Perkins* serial seemed to inspire longevity among members of its cast and crew. Murray Forbes, who played the role of Willie Fitz, Ma's hard-luck son-in-law, also remained with the series for 27 years — a feat perhaps unequaled by any other supporting player in the medium. And a third actor came very close to attaining that distinction. Charles Egleston, who appeared for a quarter-century in the part of Ma's closest friend and business partner, Shuffle Shober, died a couple of years before the program left the air. These three — Payne, Forbes and Egleston — combined their talents to play for seventy-nine years on one soap opera. That too was a record!

Others associated with the *Perkins* drama recorded significant tenures also. Writer Orin Tovrov penned the lines for more than two decades. Kay Campbell played the part of Ma's oldest daughter, Evey Perkins Fitz, in the series' final 15 years. Edwin Wolfe directed the program for many years, then added duties as actor Charles Egleston's replacement to the end of the run. And Margaret Draper played Ma's youngest daughter, Fay Perkins Henderson, for more than a decade.

Scholars studying radio drama coined phrases for *Ma Perkins,* more than adequately conveying the serial's and the heroine's places in soap opera history. One referred to her as the "mother of all soap opera," hardly a misnomer, while the program itself designated her as the "mother of the air."[1] Another observer labeled her the "den mom of our dreams," describing Ma Perkins as a "pie-baking Sherlock Holmes with an I.Q. of about one hundred and eighty."[2] Didn't Virginia Payne play her role with complete comprehension of that fantasy?

There were incessant comparisons to another homespun radio philosopher, Bill Davidson. One of radio's great commoners, Ma Perkins was referred to by one biographer as "a woman's answer to *Just Plain Bill.*"[3] Others were more colorful in their applications, calling her "*Just Plain Bill* in skirts."[4] The trade publication *Variety* classified her as "*Just Plain Bill* in drag."[5]

No matter. Just as Bill Davidson, the barber of Hartville, wasn't the protagonist of *his* drama, neither was Ma Perkins the central character of *hers.* The plot was instead largely concerned with the foibles and imbroglios in the lives of others. Bill and Ma were simple, down-to-earth folks who were widowed, had grown children and spent most of their time helping everybody else out of woe. (The fact Robert Hardy Andrews, the Hummerts' most fluent writer, authored the scripts for both series over several years may be sufficient enough to explain the infinite similarities between *Ma* and *Bill.*)

Ma, considered the wisest sage in her parts, was sought for counsel, advice and reflection. The basis of her technique was a trust in people and life itself. She lived by the Golden Rule. Her personal qualities included tough honesty combined with an instinctive understanding of the human spirit. In the Depression era from which she stemmed, people found a role model of strength and determination that inspired her listeners. Through her philosophy and successes as an arbitrator and problem-solver, Ma gave encouragement to the "little people" of Rushville Center, becoming the town's conscience. In addition to laundry soap, her sponsor Oxydol gently urged a logic of patience, benevolence and determination upon the nation — not wealth, image and prestige.

Ma's theory of forgiveness, just one of the moral bromides she sanctioned, would be typical of her philosophy. In a 1938 episode, she declared: "Anyone of this earth who's done wrong, and then goes so far as to try and right that wrong, I can tell you that they're well on their way to erasing the harm they did in the eyes of anyone decent."

Her wisdom didn't come from extensive formal education, for she was a bonafide homespun philosopher. We don't have to look beyond her grammatical constructions and enunciation patterns to verify it. "I ain't sure I understand it," she was fond of saying. In a 1950 episode she lamented: "I do know it is wrong to say something against a person without hearing from the person theirself." Equally atrocious was this epithet of that era: "He said so to Willie hisself." Finally: "In all these years we've knowed each other, I ain't never heard nothin' like this." You could say *that* again, Ma! It was a good thing that most of the nation's English teachers were in class at the time the serial was broadcast. They would have fainted dead away over the liberties that most Rushville Center townsfolk took with the mother tongue.

Ma was fond of prefacing her remarks with "Land," "Land sakes" or "Land o' Goshen." Listeners found this habit reproduced in Shuffle Shober. Although the repetitious "Land" wasn't part of his vocabulary, he steadily overworked the never-defined exclamation, "Tarnation!" Shuffle once used it five times in a brief conversation with Ma. "Tarnation, Ma!" he'd say. "I ain't never heard of such foolishness!"

Shuffle also maintained many of Ma's more flattering traits. He possessed tough honesty linked with an innate grasp of the human spirit. He wasn't as expressive as she, but he could often discern deceit before Ma. Her logic was that everyone was worthy of trust until proven otherwise. Shuffle, sometimes suspicious of those he didn't know well, formed opinions first and acquired facts later to support his impressions. And much of the time, his preconceived notions were absolutely correct.

Willie Fitz, who had a tremendous heart but also never professed to know proper English, continually offered dreadful phrases, such as, "I ain't seen Ma today." His wife, Evey, was the enigma of the family. Although her English wasn't so bad, she was a busybody whose demeanor often parted from the genteel ways of the others. As president of the Jolly Seventeen, a ladies' club perpetuating the local rumor mill, she was a heartache to her mother.

Finally, there was Fay, the young cosmopolitan who acquired an urbanese dialect. In contrast to the dialect of the rest of the clan, her quite proper vocabulary often allowed her to sound as if she had dropped in from a neighboring planet. There was seldom a metaphor out of place or a pronoun that didn't agree with its antecedent.

The imprint of Procter & Gamble (P&G) on the genre of what eventually came to be known as soap operas has been alluded to already. Before exploring the property that initiated it all, we should take note of the significance of P&G's contributions to the whole spectrum of daytime drama. More than any other firm, P&G paid the bills in developing an entertainment form that would influence millions of listeners and — in time — viewers around the globe. Its gifts are of no less import than those of Frank and Anne Hummert, Irna Phillips, Elaine Carrington and other innovators who, in their own way, left indelible impressions upon the serials.

P&G's history dates back to 1837, when it was founded by two successful business-men in Cincinnati—one who made candles, the other, soap. A year later, P&G was running small-print ads. By 1882 Harley T. Procter, son of one of the founders, was widely regarded for his marketing expertise. That year he persuaded his partners to fund a national adver-tising campaign. The story of P&G's practice of spending money to make money, princi-pally through advertising, is one of the most fascinating in the annals of marketing consumer package brands. In the early years of the twentieth century, P&G spent vast sums to keep its goods before American consumers. By the start of the Depression era it con-cluded that it must spend even more to retain and increase market share. But before doing so, the firm conducted an extensive program of market research.

Survey results told P&G that American women doing household chores at home dur-ing daylight hours wanted to be entertained by radio, not instructed as many series were then doing. Typical programs of the period included *Crisco Cooking Talks, Emily Post's* eti-quette chats, Helen Chase's *Beauty Forum, Washing Talks* and *Sisters of the Skillet*. P&G, performing independently of other firms, was on to something big. In 1932 it decided to exper-iment with dramatic programming aired in the daytime and targeting the distaff audience.

To test its theory, P&G turned to its local Cincinnati clear-channel powerhouse, WLW, with 50,000 watts of broadcast range. (Some actors appearing on the station claimed the call letters WLW stood for "World's Lowest Wages.") For its Oxydol granulated brand of laundry detergent, P&G's advertising agency purchased a serialized domestic comedy, *The Puddle Family*, akin to a comic-strip story. It aired on WLW starting in late 1932 and was far less than an instant success.

But early in 1933 the Oxydol trade was transferred to a different agency. An account executive, Larry Milligan, readily suggested a continuing narrative that would revolve around a "helping hand" character. He proposed the tale of a self-reliant widow whose family and friends leaned heavily upon her—*Ma Perkins,* it would be called. Oxydol's *own* Ma Perkins. The idea clicked with agency directors and P&G officials.

At the time all of this was going on, a lovely young blonde actress, Virginia Payne, then 23 years old, was portraying the title role in a WLW drama about a southern diva, *Honey Adams.* Jane Froman, who was destined to become one of the nation's most popular vocalists a few years later, supplied the singing on the show.

Unlike the homespun character for whom she would be recalled for the rest of her days, Payne was a highly cultured young woman. The daughter of a local physician, she was well educated, holding two master's degrees (one in literature) from the University of Cincinnati. A devout Roman Catholic, she held high principles that personified the every-day trust in human nature that Ma Perkins would embrace.

Payne was obviously in the right place at the right time. Despite her youthfulness, a certain tremolo in her versatile voice could make her sound as if she were considerably older. Thus, she was tapped for the role of Ma, never dreaming how far it would take her in years, miles and association.

A 16-week trial run was launched on WLW on August 14, 1933. Unlike its predecessor, *The Puddle Family,* this series was quickly adopted by its Cincinnati audience. P&G noted

The actress Virginia Payne appearing here as herself and not as her famous alter ego, *Ma Perkins*. Only 23 years old when she began her most recognizable role, she was a mere age 50 when it ended. Payne never missed a performance from the drama's inception in Cincinnati, moving with it to Chicago and finally New York. (Photofest)

too that grocers in the area were asking wholesale distributors for many more boxes of Oxydol than before, as listeners responded positively to the program's commercials. It was obvious that P&G's market research was correct: women wanted radio entertainment while working in the home.

With that kind of success in a local market, P&G was ready to send its fledgling series to a national audience. Under the soapmaker's watchful eye, the serial was entrusted to Frank and Anne Hummert of Chicago's Blackett-Sample-Hummert advertising agency. The Hummerts had already met with some success in *Judy and Jane; Betty and Bob; Marie, the Little French Princess; Easy Aces; Just Plain Bill;* and *The Romance of Helen Trent.* On December 4, 1933, at three o'clock Eastern Time, *Ma Perkins* debuted on the NBC network.

Throughout the run, *Perkins* would waft into kitchens and living rooms to a slight variation of "My Old Kentucky Home," played on the organ. It was an original melody written by Larry Larsen and Don Marcotte.

In its earliest days, *Perkins'* announcer would welcome listeners to the new series with this detailed inscription:

> And here's Oxydol's own Ma Perkins again. The true-life story of a woman whose life is the same, whose surroundings are the same, whose problems are the same as those of thousands of other women in the world today. A woman who has spent all her life taking care of her home — washing and cooking and cleaning and raising her family. And now her husband's death has pitched her head-foremost into being the head of her family as well as the mother. And we'll hear her true-life story every day at this time, except Saturday and Sunday.

It was a different Ma in those days — not the homey, soft-spoken, kindhearted matriarch that most listeners would fondly remember. She was originally envisioned as a harsh, gutless creature who barked orders and had a cynical outlook on life. On December 13, 1933, for instance, just eight broadcasts into the long run, listeners heard this exchange in the Perkins parlor between Ma and daughter Fay.

> FAY: Ma, Ma, what's happened? Where's Evey?
> MA: She ... she's gone, Fay.
> FAY: Gone? Ma, what did you say to her? I ... I heard her crying down here.
> MA: I wanted her to come back home with us.
> FAY: Oh, what are you talkin' about? You ... you surely don't want Willie Fitz and her and Junior here with us. There wouldn't be room for all of us.
> MA: I didn't want Willie Fitz. I just wanted her and Junior.
> FAY: What do you mean? You ... you wanted her to leave Willie Fitz? But he's her *husband*, Ma ... she couldn't do that.
> MA: And why not? That's what I'd like to know. It wouldn't be the first time a woman ever left her husband! And she'd be a lot better off with us than with that no-account scalawag!
> FAY: Oh Ma!

Oh Ma! is right. This surely *wasn't* the Ma Perkins with the compassionate heart who believed in everybody's dreams. And neither did Virginia Payne like her very much. Payne petitioned that the part be softened until Ma evolved into a warm, tolerant character at odds with only the small-minded residents of mythical Rushville Center. Fortunately, her request didn't fall on deaf ears. We'll see the results presently.

On making the change to a more accepting Ma, there was little further shift in her demeanors or in that of any of the other *Perkins* characters over the decades. Soap opera figures — in this serial and elsewhere — maintained a behavioral consistency that was dependable. Confronted with a crisis, heroes and heroines reacted precisely as they had done in the past and as listeners would expect them to in the future. It was comforting to know that values, traits and conditions ascribed to an individual wouldn't be altered.

Soap operas were fundamentally concerned with selling consumer goods while entertaining their audiences, although once in a while they dipped into topical subjects. This occurred more frequently in the early 1930s, with references to the Depression and situations resulting from it. Later, in 1938, perhaps the most definitive case of a serial character's tie to topical matters transpired. This happened during a crisis in the Soviet Union known as the Great Purge Trials.

In late spring of that year, *Ma Perkins'* plot line had her attempting to protect an anti–Stalinist couple, Gregor and Sonya Ivanoff. The pair was tracked to Rushville Center by Soviet secret agents, who kidnapped the Ivanoffs' son to hasten Gregor's surrender. While hiding in Ma's home, Gregor was fired on through a window by Russian officers. They missed him but inadvertently killed his beloved Sonya. It was a poignant example of how the soaps introduced reality into their sequences once in a while.

Notice that the Russians went to Rushville Center — not the other way around. Although Ma visited Washington, D.C., during the war, she seldom ventured far from home. Some of the characters in the narrative arrived from or traveled to New York City or other far-away places. Variety of locale simply wasn't required to tell this tale of down-home folks. Almost all the action occurred within a few miles of Rushville Center.

Measured by some of its peers, the *Perkins* serial was fairly free of grim and fateful moments. Though death was not a frequent visitor, when it did finally come, it removed major characters who were intertwined within every facet of the plot. Ma's youngest daughter, Fay, her pet, who "never done a wrong thing in her whole life," experienced the misfortune of marrying not one but *two* men who met untimely and tragic endings in life.

The first, Paul Henderson, was Fay's husband less than a year; he died in the early autumn of 1940. Paul left Fay with an estate that would eventually exceed $50,000 and become the object of some plotting relatives a decade later. Meanwhile, the couple's unborn child, whom Fay would call Paulette, would become *her* lifelong obsession.

Later, in the postwar era, Fay became one of radio's most emotionally abused heroines. In this period she simultaneously suffered psychosomatic paralysis and amnesia.

By the mid–1940s this lovely young sophisticate found herself looking for love once more. Torn between two swains — one poor, the other rich — she finally made up her mind to marry the wealthy playboy, Carl Michaels. But she became the focus of her whole family's concern for what appeared to be some nagging indecisiveness — even after choosing Michaels over his rival, Dr. Andrew White.

A month before their nuptials, with Michaels out of town, Fay received a phone call from White asking her to see him. With a spring in her step, she left home and went rushing to his side. Her older sister, Evey, who frequently amplified current action, watched. It didn't take Evey long to get to the Perkins Lumber Yard office. There, surrounded by Ma, Willie and Shuffle, she reported what she had seen, embellishing the story as she went along. After Evey's disclosure, the family mused thoughtfully over the situation.

> MA: Fay is Fay, the girl that all of us have brung up. Knowing Fay, how can we worry whether she's doing right or doing wrong? Fay never done a wrong thing in her whole life.
> EVEY: That's very true, Ma. But she *never* acted like *this* before.
> WILLIE: You know ... I'm gonna say something now which I ain't never said before.... The thing is ... does ... Fay love Carl...?
> MA: Fay's been in a funny frame o' mind. It started when I got sick. Fay got to feelin' all grown up all of a sudden. (Two-second pause) Oh, I ... I just can't bring myself to think that she'd marry Carl without no feeling for him, Willy....
> EVEY: All right, Ma. But how 'bout her feeling for Dr. Andrew White? I'm scared, Ma ... I'm scared!
> MA: (Starts out whispering) Oh Fay is Fay, the straightest girl that ever was. We just got to remember that. She's wearing Carl's ring ... she don't belong to nobody else.

One of the strokes of genius in writing *Ma Perkins* was the hook on which it left listeners hanging each day. Following the closing Oxydol commercial, announcer "Charlie Warren" submitted an epilogue. This was the epilogue on the day this dialogue was broadcast:

> And so, the whole family is deeply concerned about Fay. And though Ma expresses her deep faith in Fay, is Ma concerned too? Well, Fay *does* see Andrew White and ... Fay finds words on her tongue which surprise even Fay ... tomorrow.

Who could resist? Loyal listeners simply *had* to know what the darling of the family would say to Dr. White.

Eventually, Carl Michaels became history, and Fay would choose yet another suitor, a writer, Tom Wells. This husband would still be living when the series ended in 1960. There would also be ample evidence that Fay was expecting for the second time then, having given birth to Paulette two decades earlier.

Announcer Dan Donaldson—who often used the pseudonym "Charlie Warren," as had his predecessor Marvin Miller when the show broadcast from Chicago in its first thirteen years—promised listeners a great deal. He would introduce an episode by recapping previous action, then state something like the following: "Well, today we'll hear Ma express herself on this very important matter." His summary at the close of the previous day's episode would have told listeners the same thing, only in different words. Sometimes in those summaries he would get even bolder as he enticed the audience to stay with the show: "On Monday, Fay considers the proposal of marriage, while Shuffle wonders about those ulterior motives ... and there's that matter of the missing funds from the charity ball. We've got lots to listen for in the days just ahead."

Another frequent device used on this serial involved the announcer saying, "Let's turn the clock back." The listener would then hear what had transpired at another time: a snippet from a previous episode or some action never heard on the air before. Either way, this was an effective means of bringing listeners up to date with fresh detail or a development they could have missed.

Donaldson and Miller used the "Charlie Warren" name, incidentally, to avoid a conflict with other advertisers — presumably sponsors manufacturing laundry soaps. This allowed them to broadcast on other programs under their own names, not an assumed one.

There were at least two occasions in the life of *Ma Perkins*, the serial, when thousands of listeners abandoned all semblance of rationality. One — as might be expected — occurred when the series was canceled. That one will be examined later. The other happened more than 16 years earlier.

Although nearly 300,000 Americans died from the ravages of World War II, there was but one major soap opera personality who suffered fatal consequences — Ma Perkins' son, John. Killed in Europe, he was buried "somewhere in Germany in an unmarked grave." It was a very dark moment in the drama, and the audience reacted in shock, disbelief and outrage. The network was deluged with sympathy notes addressed simply to "Ma." The avalanche of complaints could hardly have been predicted. Callers and letter writers were rabid in their consternation. Many protested that mothers and wives of service personnel did not need such a vivid reminder of the dangers of battle.

Dancer-Fitzgerald-Sample advertising executive Roy Winsor was responsible for responding to the detractors. He supervised *Ma Perkins* for the agency. If radio was to be realistic, he answered, it could not ignore such a possibility. Ma Perkins, he said, confronted the same difficulty that thousands of American mothers, wives and girlfriends had to come to terms with. Winsor cited Ma's inner strength and suggested that she could be a comfort and encouragement to listeners facing this experience in real life. (Winsor, incidentally, was to go on to blaze trails in televised serials following radio. He either singly created or collaborated in developing *Search for Tomorrow, Love of Life, The Secret Storm, Another Life, Ben Jerrod* and *Hawkins Falls*. He was also head writer on *Somerset*.)

One of the things Winsor stated unequivocally was that the writers did "not intend to bring him [John] back" in subsequent episodes.[6] Even though John never reappeared, he was not soon forgotten. Perhaps to pacify the critics, though such was never admitted, a young man named Joseph was introduced into the plot to fill the void. The similarities between John and Joseph seemed too many to be coincidental.

Joseph, a young seminary student, arrived in Rushville Center in the company of his wife, Starr, and her father, Professor H. B. Bassett. Bassett would eventually be exposed by Ma Perkins as an unscrupulous charlatan. He sought local funding for Pleasant Haven, which he directed, "a refuge for the bereaved, the heart-sore, the world-weary." He was really siphoning off the town's cash for personal gain, however.

Before Bassett was run out of town on a rail, Gladys Pendleton, Fay Perkins' best friend and the restless daughter of banker Augustus Pendleton, brought Pleasant Haven to Fay's attention. On a tour Fay met Joseph, who looked enough like her late brother to pass for an identical twin. Even his speech, mannerisms and gait were duplicates. Of course, Fay insisted that the rest of the family go and meet him. Hesitant at first, Ma was the last to go. The resemblance was so strong that it took her breath away. Joseph even possessed John's characteristic gentleness of spirit, which deeply affected Ma.

Sometime after the trio of newcomers was forced to leave Rushville Center — even though Starr and Joseph were innocent of the charges brought against Professor Bassett — Starr, then pregnant, became ill and died. A distraught Joseph returned to Rushville Center, renouncing his studies for the ministry. At the Perkins home, which Ma shared with Fay and Paulette, Ma offered John's old room to Joseph. The young man took it and also accepted John's old job on a milk-delivery route. The number of "coincidences" was simply incredible.

Did Roy Winsor, the advertising executive, tell it like it was when he stated that John Perkins wouldn't return from the dead? Either way, it was difficult for longtime listeners to keep John and Joseph separate, given Joseph's sudden prominence and the parallels between the two.

By August 1949 Joseph was flirting with a New York magazine photographer, Anne Morrison. She and writer Alfred Sinclair had been sent to Rushville Center by a major national publication, *People USA*. Their assignment was prompted by the hamlet's designation as the "most typical town" in the nation. That limelight threw much of the community into a tizzy. Many of the locals put on airs. But Sinclair found that good-natured Ma Perkins could paint the little village simplistically. Through her eyes he discovered the true small-town ambiance that made Rushville Center a decent place to live and worthy of public recognition.

Joseph's pursuit of Anne Morrison (or was it the other way around?), meanwhile, set heads turning and tongues wagging. When Anne's spouse, an escapee from a mental asylum in Pittsburgh, arrived under cover of darkness, slipped and fell out of her hotel room to his death, Joseph was implicated. At last cleared in the incident, he lost interest in the lady shutterbug, who hadn't told him earlier that she was married. Joseph's disappointment in local citizens who had blamed him for the man's death hurt deeply. In time he packed his bags and left Rushville Center, never to return. Ma lost another son, albeit an "adopted" one. But listeners accepted Joseph's departure without castigating the show's producers through angry communications.

In December 1949 an old family friend — a Mr. Boswell — turned up to make Ma an offer that she would seriously consider. A prosperous lumberyard in the neighboring town of Middleboro had recently gone on the market. Boswell, a financier, was interested in buying it but needed someone to run it. He turned to Ma. While she saw possibilities, she wondered who could be spared to supervise the everyday operations. Not Shuffle; Willie and Evey had no interest in moving away from Rushville Center; and Joseph was, for the time being, content to drive a milk wagon.

Just when it appeared that no deal could be struck, the soap opera launched its most protracted and darkest sequence of its 27 years. Except for the loss of her son, this would be Ma's greatest ordeal for the entire run. For 12 months, millions of fans sat spellbound by their radios, the most faithful among them afraid to miss an episode. It was one of those situations where the audience knew what was happening and spent an interminable period wondering if Ma — who trusted *everybody*— could *ever* separate truth from fiction.

It began with a letter from the late Pa Perkins' cousin Bonita Hammacher. Ma had grown up with Bonita. At last report Bonita was homesteading in Alaska with her family: her husband, Ed, and her grown son, Sylvester. The Hammachers were of the country-bumpkin variety, poorly educated and lacking in sufficient means of support. The parents, in particular, seemed unable to cope with the minimal requirements of civilized society. They had not fared well in Alaska, another frustration in a string of ventures gone sour. Shuffle wondered aloud if the Hammachers were lethargic, unable to be successful anywhere. Seeking a new beginning, the Hammachers appealed to Ma. Did she have *anything* to recommend? Of course she did — the lumberyard in Middleboro!

The Hammachers arrived in Rushville Center on December 24, 1949, to spend Christmas with the Perkins clan. But not long after this happy occasion, a cruel stake was driven into the heart of this close-knit circle. Through some derision created by the male Hammachers, Ma's business partner and closest friend, Shuffle Shober, and her son-in-law, Willie Fitz, resigned their posts after 16 years as Perkins Lumber Yard employees. They were replaced by Ed and Sylvester Hammacher. Shuffle accepted the task of running the Middleboro lumberyard, moving away from Rushville Center. And Willie spent the next year looking for a job. It was a sad day for all of the drama's principals. The strong spirit of family ties was irretrievably broken. And it was to get much worse.

What the audience learned, and what Shuffle would come to suspect long before the others, was that the "cousins" — as they were collectively called in every episode — had fraudulent motives driving them to cheat anyone who could help them get ahead. They capitalized on Ma's empathy for their unfortunate plight. Because they were "family," she was vulnerable to their dishonesty, implicitly trusting their words and deeds. Only Shuffle, Ma's dearest friend, saw through their schemes from the start. He spent agonizing months without proof trying to convince everyone of what he suspected.

Bonita Hammacher was never a part of the scheming and was unaware of the dimensions of the deception. Ed and Sylvester, meanwhile, hatched a plan to capture some very large prizes. They would initially swindle the gullible Willie and Evey out of their life savings. Fay — already a widow for a second time — would be the next target. After they succeeded working over the Fitzes, Sylvester planned to pitch woo to Fay. (He and Fay weren't first cousins; Bonita and Pa Perkins had been first cousins, making Sylvester and Fay second cousins.)

Sylvester's strategy was to win himself a bride, but that was incidental to his ultimate goal. What he was really after was the $50,000 inheritance that Paul Henderson had left to Fay ten years earlier. Acquiring that, the Hammachers would then push Ma out of the family business and take absolute control of Perkins Lumber Yard. It was a vile plan, more fiendish than anything the show's listeners had ever heard. Could they drift from their radios before it concluded? Most of them could not.

As the tensions built, by late summer the Hammachers' strategy fell into place. They persuaded Evey and Willie to invest their life savings in some worthless mining stock, playing it up as if it were the most promising equity on the market. They also instructed the Fitzes not to talk about the investment "or everybody will want in on it and prices will fall." The Fitzes knew nothing about the stock market, of course, and thus had no way of knowing that the opposite is often true.

Shuffle, you remember, was slow to accept newcomers and quick to distrust anything he didn't comprehend. He wondered to himself, and then to others, if the Hammachers weren't scheming to take advantage of the family. He insisted that Ma question her older daughter and son-in-law to find out if Sylvester had lied when he had told Ma he had no business dealings with Evey and Willie. Ma dropped by their house, intending to do just that, on the morning of August 24, 1950, as the couple was finishing breakfast. And listeners were shocked by what they heard that day as Ma probed gently but intensely:

> MA: Here is an issue that, if we can tell once and for all where
> the truth is, once and for all the whole thing will be settled.
> Is Shuffle right or is Shuffle wrong? (Two-second pause)
> Willie ... Evey ... are you in some kind of business deal with
> Sylvester? (Two-second pause) Did Sylvester *lie* to me? *Lie*
> to Fay? Or is it simply more of Shuffle's — well, Shuffle's —
> mistaken feelings about our cousins? Please tell me.
> WILLIE: Gee, Ma ... look Evey, under the circumstances, don't
> you think we — maybe we...
> EVEY: (Cuts him off) No! No! I'm sick of Shuffle and his crazi-
> ness and his jealousies. And personally, I'm real fond of the
> cousins.
> MA: Evey, did cousin Sylvester tell me the truth? You did *not*
> turn over your savings to him?
> WILLIE: Listen Evey, I —
> EVEY: (Cuts him off) That's right, Ma. We did *not!*
> MA: (After two-second pause) All right, Evey. (Two-second
> pause) Thank you for telling me, Evey.

Oh, what a tangled web we weave, when first we practice to deceive! No, we wouldn't have believed it if we had not heard it with our own ears, for Ma's children were brought up to tell the truth. Announcer "Charlie Warren" mused over the dilemma before leaving the audience that day:

> And so, Evey does what Sylvester told her to do; she *lies* to Ma.
> What's going to happen now? Well, one thing I *do* know: We
> must *never* underestimate Ma's wise old eyes. Ma sees more
> than she lets on ... as we learn ... tomorrow.

And what those "wise old eyes" saw led her to attempt to corroborate what Evey had told her. When Ma was unable to do that, Shuffle had a stroke of genius. Cornering Willie out of earshot of his intimidating spouse, Shuffle enticed his chum to spill the beans about the business deal they had with the cousins. It was the first time the Hammachers had actually been caught in a lie.

The cousins hastily covered it by assuring Ma that they would return the Fitzes' investment in full. But Evey did not want the investment back, believing they were destined to reap phenomenal "profits" in the stock market. Willie, who came across many times as slow, acted responsibly this time. With no job and only eight dollars separating his family from starvation, he demanded the money be returned.

Sly Sylvester, however — always the cunning one — thought it through carefully. Then he explained some facts to his daddy, the terribly dumb one. The two were playing for much bigger fish than the $1,700 they had taken from the Fitzes, he told "Popsy" (his name for his dad). By returning the Fitzes' money in full, the Hammachers would vastly improve their credibility with the Perkins clan — and weaken the case Shuffle had been building against them. It took Popsy a few moments to take in all that his son was saying: to gain

Fay's $50,000, plus Ma's lumberyard, they'd have to show good faith by returning the paltry $1,700. Reluctantly, Popsy agreed to forfeit the smaller sum in order to get the higher stakes.

Sylvester had already spent what they had taken from Evey and Willie, buying a new automobile for himself. He conspired to stall and wreck the new car at a railroad crossing in order to gain insurance money to pay his debt to the Fitzes. But even his mother, Cousin Bonita, began to see through his deception. Threatening her, he instructed her to be quiet about what she perceived.

Later, a mining stock "official" appeared in Rushville Center to verify the authenticity of the original agreement. But the representative was found to be nothing more than a down-on-his-luck bum whom the Hammachers had paid to corroborate their scheme. Ma then faced down Cousin Ed with hard evidence.

While Fay stalled Sylvester in response to his proposal of marriage, something snapped in Sylvester. He attempted to kidnap Fay, intending to drive her to a justice of the peace so that a ceremony could be performed at once. Fortunately, she got away; as a result, his plans were permanently thwarted.

In December 1950, a year after the arrival of the Hammachers and the start of the family dissension and discord, the cousins *did* appear before a court official all right, a presiding judge. Accepting a plea bargain offered by Ma Perkins, the two men were required to refrain from certain practices and perform various tasks in order to remain out of jail. Bonita was assigned as their "keeper." She was to report to the court if either got out of line again, a responsibility she gladly accepted.

The Hammachers moved from Rushville Center to Middleboro to take over the lumberyard that Shuffle had been running — the business that had prompted their arrival in the first place — and weren't heard from again. Meanwhile, trust was restored in the little clan, forgiveness was extended and Shuffle and Willie were reemployed at Perkins Lumber Yard. The duo returned as happy as larks; the blessings of life, peace and harmony resumed in the Perkins household in manifold proportions. The separation of the past year, thankfully, would never be repeated.

A story line of this magnitude was almost sure to sustain high numbers in the audience over a prolonged period of time. When it ended, Fay was contemplating a Christmas visit by yet another beau, this one an advertising executive from New York, Spencer Grayson. But by mid–1951 Fay was again facing the dilemma she had encountered before her last marriage — two suitors! The other one was Tom Wells, a writer, whom she eventually married — but not before many anxious moments.

A topic that touched nearly all of the daytime dramas, including this one, was the pace at which the action moved. Critics who berated soap operas probably capitalized on this single factor more than any other, often having a field day with it.

For example, the actress Alice Reinheart, *Life Can Be Beautiful's* Chichi Conrad, disappeared into her bath one day and didn't resurface for a fortnight — miraculously coinciding with the actress's two-week vacation. Either she proved that soap and water could make *her* beautiful, or she preferred skin as wrinkled as a prune!

Fifteen episodes (three weeks) elapsed before the elevator in which *Pretty Kitty Kelly* was riding reached the floor of her destination. She was surely in the earth's tallest structure and the world's slowest elevator!

And the barber of Hartville in *Just Plain Bill* dispensed the royal treatment to one customer. He began giving the man a trim one week; nine days later he was still working on the same customer. Did Bill need to be put into a slower group?

Even beloved Ma Perkins gained at least one hardened detractor over the years. This person anonymously sent her an eerie-shaped parcel. Unaware that the bundle contained a deadly viper, Ma eyed it on her kitchen table for 11 episodes, debating whether she should examine its contents.

Such situations could compete for the title of "most offensive time lapses" in daytime drama. Of all that the critics had to lambaste the serials for, this was their favorite; it was so obvious. "I listened for two weeks and the woman never got out of the tub," they might say. "It took her three weeks to ride three floors in an elevator." "Let's face it, the guy simply doesn't know the art of cutting hair." "I thought she would stare at that box until her show got canceled!" The bottom line, they all could agree, was that "After so long a spell, nothing happened!"

But that wasn't totally true. Listeners couldn't be absolutely certain that a lightning bolt wouldn't strike Chichi's tub while she was in it … or that the elevator might not jam or fall with Kitty aboard … or that Bill might not have a heart attack, scissors in hand, while thinking about some poor soul's dismal plight in Hartville … or that granddaughter Paulette wouldn't open the strange-looking package on the kitchen table while Ma was in the hall answering the phone. Dozens of things *could* happen; the listener never knew for sure that they wouldn't.

Audience research would eventually reveal to serial producers and sponsors that the typical homemaker listened to favorite soap operas two or three times a week. Household duties some distance from the radio, interruptions by visitors and door-to-door salesmen, phone calls, errands, shopping, family needs and extraneous matters took priority among fans at other times. Thus, the leisurely pace of the serials was acceptable to most of them, for they found it impossible to tune in for every absorbing chapter. Only the professionals — media critics, researchers and other reviewers — invariably held the soap operas with disdain due to slow-moving story lines, seldom stopping to consider the audience and its unique requirements.

It was this leisurely gait at which *Ma Perkins* and her contemporary dramas ambled along that was one of their redeeming factors. Of all the forms of entertainment, only the soap opera granted enough time to include the minutiae of life. The three hours that a theatrical playwright might have to develop character and plot was no match for the opportunities afforded a radio serial writer. The latter was often given more than ten minutes of dialogue to fill five times a week for decades. The result? Numerous little details, forbidden by the press of time in other drama structures, could offer character insights that could never be attained elsewhere. This was the true beauty of the slow narrative. Working without preconceived limits, the serial writer could simply amplify a figure's peculiarities without very many constraints on time.

Robert Hardy Andrews notwithstanding, *Ma Perkins'* most prolific writer, Orin Tovrov, had the benefit of developing those familiar radio characters for more than two decades. This gave him an extraordinary and unprecedented affinity with the principals — Ma, Shuffle, Fay, Willie, Evey and the others — that few peers ever experienced. Tovrov was lauded for the quality of his work and may have been the best of his trade. In the early

1970s two radio historiographers stated that his serials were "as well written as any serious drama on television."[7] Another observer noted that this former newspaperman had an "inexhaustible" gift for stretching out drama.[8] Tovrov was elected by the Radio Writers Guild as its first president. In the 1930s he organized broadcasting's first strike. He wrote scripts for two other serials: *The Brighter Day*, for both radio and television, and TV's *The Doctors*. Tovrov died in Boston on August 16, 1980, at age 69. He was buried in Orleans, Massachusetts.

Although *Ma Perkins* and its peers received the critics' barbs for the slow narrative style in which they were written, there was one area in which the serials could never be seriously challenged: cost per listener. Minimal production costs attracted sponsors in the early days of soap opera. When the return on their investment translated into huge daytime audiences, advertisers bought even more time.

Production costs per rating point for *Kate Smith Speaks*, the highest-rated weekday program on the air in 1943, were $609.76. But the second-rated *When a Girl Marries* cost only $287.50 per ratings point. And *Ma Perkins*, boasting a rating very close to *Smith's*, cost $164.56 per point. While $5,000 was spent every week to produce *Smith's* quarter-hour, *Perkins* was produced for a scant $1,300. Costs were a factor that the critics of washboard weepers never substantially repudiated. The figures spoke for themselves, for they were almost always irrefutably impressive.

It can be noted further that *Ma Perkins'* audience size and influence also put most of its contemporaries to shame. In the heyday of radio, this serial had the good fortune to rack up dual broadcasts on all four networks over a period of nine seasons, seven of them consecutively. Not many dramas (or programs, for that matter) could boast such a feat. With ratings figures in the double digits in both dual- and single-broadcast years, *Perkins* was one of the most popular and compelling dramas ever on American radio. Listeners were so enthralled that in some communities door-to-door salesmen, who peddled consumer goods and services in that era, knew not to disturb homemakers during *Perkins'* quarter-hour segments.

The serial's recognition did not rest there. At its peak, *Ma Perkins* was carried on stations in Hawaii, Canada and Europe, the last through Radio Luxembourg. Dancer-Fitzgerald-Sample even attempted a TV pilot in the late 1940s, but it didn't work. Fans wouldn't accept it; they had created their own images of the citizens of Rushville Center and were satisfied, sight unseen.

Nevertheless, Procter & Gamble was pleased with its investment in the little radio epic. In early 1934 P&G decided to test the serial's success and find out how many people were actually hearing the program and where they lived. It offered listeners a packet of flower seeds in exchange for a dime and an Oxydol box top. To its surprise, responses soared past one million. The experiment told P&G how many replies were received per station broadcast zone and allowed it to compute a rough cost-per-thousand estimate for commercials. As a result, it became abundantly clear to P&G that a daytime drama directed at female homemakers was the most powerful advertising tool the company had ever employed.

Although P&G never allowed the premium to become the tail that wagged the dog on its serials — as was the case on *David Harum*, *Lora Lawton*, *Nona from Nowhere* and their ilk — it did resort to occasional mail-in efforts, called *mailhooks*, with great success. In the spring of 1940 four soap operas sponsored by other firms — *Ellen Randolph, Woman in White, Myrt and Marge* and *Aunt Jenny's Real Life Stories* — joined *Ma Perkins* in offering flower seeds. By then premiums had become valuable tools in measuring serial audiences. Libby glasses, recipe books and jewelry were all proffered in mailhook promotions on daytime serials that year.

Yet another measure of the popularity of these dramas could be illustrated by the motivational messages that became part of a program. When Ma Perkins — whose son, John, died in battle during World War II — asked American housewives to save used tinfoil or fat, millions could be expected to cooperate. To do less would seem like being a traitor to the nation. And although this didn't tell P&G how many were tuning in, such noble gestures helped America while very likely raising the perception of Oxydol and Procter & Gamble's other goods at the same time.

P&G virtually built daytime radio for the networks by becoming its leading sponsor measured by number of broadcast time periods. As women listened to *Ma Perkins* while they did their housework, they sometimes wept with emotion for the characters. And when they went to their markets to buy the week's groceries, they recalled what they had heard in P&G's commercial messages. As a result the wrapped-goods manufacturer's business boomed.

From 1933 to 1939, shipments of Oxydol increased nearly sevenfold. It became the nation's leading packaged soap virtually overnight. P&G was network radio's largest client on the globe by the close of 1935 and NBC's most valued client.[9] More than 85 percent of P&G's sponsored programs on NBC that year were aired in the daytime. That figure surpassed 90 percent a couple of years later, with P&G spending $4.5 million annually on radio.

There was a logical explanation: daytime advertising rates were half those of prime time, despite the fact that the size of the daytime audience had been woefully underestimated. By the end of the 1930s, P&G's radio staff had 21 programs vying for its attention. The firm was spending $8.8 million on this medium and only $4.8 million on newspapers and magazines combined.[10]

Eventually, the development of granulated soaps like Oxydol actually helped make washing machines popular. Conversely, the popularity of automatic washers stimulated sales of Oxydol and other granulated soaps. While *Ma Perkins* ran up $11 million in network time in its first two dozen years (to 1957), the program also helped P&G sell three million boxes of Oxydol.[11]

CBS claimed in 1957 that a single 15-minute serial broadcast five days weekly reached an audience of 6.4 million at a mere 49¢ cents per thousand listeners.[12] Despite this, a few months earlier, on November 30, 1956, P&G relinquished sole sponsorship of *Ma Perkins*. For 23 years the program had most commonly been introduced each day to radio audiences as "Oxydol's own Ma Perkins." The end of that association did not come about due to any lack of regard for the drama by P&G. The program continued to be loved by listeners and advertisers long after it was withdrawn from the air four years later. The decision by P&G to discontinue underwriting it was a reflection of the trend toward multiple sponsorship and away from sole participation. The washing powder and the Perkins serial were so closely intertwined in listeners' minds that the tie persisted for years after P&G bowed out.

In 1972 Virginia Payne recalled the camaraderie that the cast and crew experienced at rehearsals of the *Perkins* series. "We had fun but not at the expense of the characters we portrayed," she said. "For one thing, we had only ninety minutes to rehearse and put the show on the air; you couldn't afford to clown around very much."[13]

She spoke about the deep feelings that some listeners attached to the *Perkins* series. A baby girl was left on Ma's doorstep in one sequence, and the child became the subject of much dialogue on whether she should keep it. (Apparently there were no laws to prevent her from doing so if she chose to.) But a San Francisco admirer wrote that he and his wife could give the baby a comfortable home should Ma decide to give it up. He was retired, he explained, and lived in a house that overlooked the bay. As character references, he enclosed endorsements from his attorney, his minister and his physician. Obviously, he had convinced all of them that the serial was based on real life!

Payne said she maintained one recurring nightmare throughout the series' long run. Because of the significant difference between Eastern and Pacific time zones, broadcasts were performed live twice daily (at least until quality recording equipment came into vogue and a network ban against using it was lifted). Sometimes an actor would leave the studio and start for home not realizing the mistake until it was almost too late to return for the second show. (Actor Burgess Meredith, playing the title character in *Red Davis*, was fired when he missed the second show only once.) In Payne's hallucination, she saw herself as the only performer on hand for the latter broadcast. This never became reality, however.

In the early days of the series a note on an NBC file card cautioned that Payne's identity was never to be released to the public. This suggested that a certain perception might be destroyed if people knew who she really was — and, perhaps, how young she really was. With the passing of time, however — as Payne advanced in age — the rule was relaxed. In response to the demands of her fans, CBS wrapped the young blonde actress in a gray wig, steel-rimmed glasses, low-heeled Oxfords and dowdy dresses and sent her out to make public appearances. Local audiences loved it.

We've noted that only two actors in the *Perkins* series were with the broadcast from beginning to end: Virginia Payne and Murray Forbes (as Willie Fitz). The uniqueness of their record-setting is compounded further by the fact that they simultaneously played a married couple in two other series: *Lonely Women* (1942–43) and *Today's Children* (1943–50). Did their acting talents know no bounds? Imagine how many times they were on the air *together*, including West Coast repeats and dual *Perkins* broadcasts during that period! (They did the *Perkins* program live at 1:15 and 3:15 p.m. on CBS and NBC respectively, *Lonely Women* or *Today's Children* live in between those broadcasts on NBC, any running roles they may have shared throughout the day on other serials and, most likely, a second live performance for each show due to the West Coast time difference.) Payne and Forbes had to be fast friends to spend that much of their professional lives together for so many years!

Payne, born in Cincinnati on June 19, 1910, portrayed the feminine lead in *The Carters of Elm Street* and worked other serials, such as *The Brighter Day* and *The Light of the World*. She also frequently appeared on *The First Nighter* and *The Cavalcade of America*. By 1957 her income reached $50,000 per year, a tidy sum in that era, surpassing every other actress in daytime radio.

Active in the American Federation of Television and Radio Artists (AFTRA), she was president of local unions in Chicago and New York and eventually was AFTRA's national

With help from makeup, a hairdresser and a wardrobe stylist, Virginia Payne made public appearances as the feisty old broad she portrayed for 27 years, Ma Perkins. For a while the network had resisted releasing her name, perhaps fearing her youthfulness wouldn't be accepted by an adoring public. (Photofest)

president. Never married, Payne was an accomplished pianist who lived in a posh apartment on Manhattan's East Fifty-Fifth Street. She kept a summer home at Ogunquit, Maine.

She was only 50 years old when *Ma Perkins* left the air. Afterward, she recorded radio commercials and performed on stage. In 1964 Payne appeared with Carol Burnett in the Broadway musical comedy *Fade Out, Fade In*. At Houston's Alley Theatre she was a standing success. She toured the nation in the 1960s and 1970s in productions of *Becket, Carousel, Oklahoma!, Long Day's Journey into Night* and *Life with Father*. Not long before she died in Cincinnati on February 10, 1977, she appeared once more on radio in Himan Brown's *The CBS Radio Mystery Theater*.

Murray Forbes, meanwhile, who played Ma's son-in-law, also turned up on several other radio series — in addition to *Lonely Women* and *Today's Children*. These included: *Aunt Jenny's Real Life Stories, The Story of Mary Marlin, Knickerbocker Playhouse, Grand Hotel, Foxes of Flatbush, The First Nighter* and *Fu Manchu*. Born in Chicago in 1907, Forbes died on January 27, 1987.

Charles Egleston, who played Shuffle until his death in New York on October 31, 1958, was a native of Covington, Kentucky, a Cincinnati suburb. Born on July 16, 1882, he was a stage actor before entering radio in 1929. He too appeared on *The First Nighter* and *Grand Hotel*, as did some other *Perkins* regulars. He was also in the casts of *Uncle Ezra's Radio Station, Grand Marquee* and *Gateway to Hollywood*. His best-remembered recurring role outside the Shuffle character was probably as Humphrey Fuller on *Just Plain Bill*. Other running parts were in *Portia Faces Life* and *Backstage Wife*.

Kay Campbell, who played Evey for the last 15 years of the *Perkins* series, wasn't known for other radio roles. She died on May 27, 1985, at age 80. Earlier in the run, Evey was played by Dora Johnson and Laurette Fillbrandt. Johnson had no other memorable roles. Fillbrandt was Daisy Mae in *Li'l Abner* and appeared in *The Affairs of Anthony, The Chicago Theatre of the Air* and *Silver Eagle, Mountie*. She had running roles in numerous serials: *Bachelor's Children, Girl Alone, The Guiding Light, Lone Journey, Midstream, One Man's Family, A Tale of Today* and *Today's Children*.

The part of Fay was portrayed in the early years by Rita Ascot (also of *The Chicago Theatre of the Air*), Cheer Brentson (who sustained running roles in *Woman in White* and *Kitty Keene, Incorporated*), Laurette Fillbrandt and Marjorie Hannan. The latter two shared the feminine lead on *Bachelor's Children*, and Hannan also appeared in *The Story of Mary Marlin* and carried the title role in *Sally of the Talkies*. Margaret Draper, the last to play Fay, was the female lead — older sister Liz Dennis — on *The Brighter Day*.

Ma's son, John Perkins, who was killed during the war, was played by Gilbert Faust. Faust was one of the writers of the serial drama *Aunt Mary*, which ran for years on the NBC West regional network and appeared briefly on MBS in 1946.

In the 1950s, as television began to encroach on radio's heretofore unchallenged turf, long-running soap operas went on the chopping blocks in wholesale numbers. When General Foods announced the cancellation of three of its most successful series — *The Aldrich Family*, a nighttime comedy show, and two late-afternoon washboard weepers, *When a Girl Marries* and *Portia Faces Life*— Virginia Payne observed: "I feel as though the main pillars had been knocked out of the house." Colbee's Restaurant, where many heroes and heroines of daytime drama gathered socially, was "Forest Lawn without the flowers," according to one soap star.[14]

But that wasn't the end of *Ma Perkins*. The cast fought on bravely for a few more years, seemingly denying that a final episode would come, despite the fact that the serial's contemporaries were falling all around it. Network affiliates were demanding the release of time so that they could sell it more profitably locally. When CBS felt it could no longer stifle the pressure, the web at last set a date to clear its schedule of soap operas. By then there were only four open-ended stories left: *The Right to Happiness,* at one o'clock Eastern Time, *Ma Perkins,* at 1:15; *Young Doctor Malone,* at 1:30; and *The Second Mrs. Burton,* at 1:45. The day of demise was set for Friday, November 25, 1960, during the Thanksgiving weekend. Longtime listeners would see the irony, for they didn't feel grateful or blessed by the experience.

In the rush to tidy up all the loose ends of a drama that had continued for nearly 27 years, CBS issued this plot sequence to the media for *Ma Perkins'* final week on the air:

> Charlie Lindstrom has accepted a job in the East. He and Mary
> are taking leave of Ma Perkins and Rushville Center. On
> Thanksgiving Day, the entire family is gathered at Ma's house.
> Ma Perkins herself sees happiness ahead, primarily because
> Anushka and her grandson, Junior, will be married next
> month.

In the concluding episode, announcer Bob Pfeiffer suggested that listeners "turn back the clock" to the day before. The Perkins clan had gathered for its traditional Thanksgiving meal at Ma's house. As the turkey and dressing and cranberry relish were passed, over the babble of conversation the organist played a rendition of the hymn "Faith of Our Fathers." Ma turned to the microphone and softly reflected, to no one in particular:

> I look around the table at my loved ones and to me the table
> stretches on and on. Over beyond the other end past Shuffle I
> see faces somehow familiar and yet unborn, except in the mind
> of God....
>   Someday, Fay will be sitting here where I'm sitting, or Evey,
> or Paulette, or Jamie or Anushka's child. They'll move up into
> my place and I'll be gone, but I find right and peace in that
> knowledge....
>   I give thanks that I've been given this gift of life, this gift of
> time to play my little part in it.

The music went up and faded, and another commercial came on. Following it, the organist struck up the theme song one last time. Virginia Payne addressed her audience directly:

> Ma Perkins again. This was our broadcast 7,065. I first came to
> you on December 4, 1933. Thank you for all being so loyal to
> us these 27 years....
>   Ma Perkins has always been played by me, Virginia Payne.
> And if you'll write to me, Ma Perkins, at Orleans, Massachu-
> setts, I'll try to answer you.
>   Good-by, and may God bless you.

Pfeiffer reiterated: "And so, after more than 7,000 broadcasts — 27 years — we say 'good-by' to *Ma Perkins.* This is Bob Pfeiffer speaking." Then an unidentified announcer's voice broke in to laud CBS's daytime schedule changes: "Remember," he chortled, "Monday, CBS News goes double to ten minutes an hour weekdays on the hour on the CBS Radio Network." The expanded news concept wouldn't survive long. But the vain attempt to pump up an audience that was losing a friend who had visited in their homes daily for nearly three decades fell on deaf ears. Few saw the personal benefit to themselves in ten minutes of news in the face of pulling the plug on *Ma Perkins* and its peers.

So outraged were they, in fact, that the CBS switchboards lit up like Christmas trees. Angry callers and letter writers gave the network a piece of their minds, sparing no words in the process. Such offense had not been taken against this drama's producers and executives since the early 1940s. Only when Ma's son, John, was allowed to die on a lonely battlefield overseas did such abuse occur. Through tears of anguish, writers and callers vented their hostilities toward the network, some practically unable to write or speak due to extreme emotional states.

Deeply embedded in the very nature of the serials had been the implied trust that they would go on forever. On November 25, 1960, that trust eroded, resulting in pure myth. Rushville Center and its inhabitants were swept away without a vestige that they had ever existed in Radioland. The characters whom audiences had come to know so well disappeared, forgotten by the medium, never to be intersected again. It was too much for some of the faithful to comprehend; they had lost some of their very best and most dependable, albeit fictional, friends.

What happened that day—though it may have been the end of an era—was not the end of a genre. The radio serial died. In its place the successful medium, television, carried on a tradition that had begun in the 1930s and that continues today. A newspaper account totally misinterpreted the demise of the radio serials when it announced that they "along with their longsuffering relatives and friends were sent to the Valhalla of soap operas with the blessings of the network." It simply didn't happen.

Soaps would remain an enduring part of American popular culture for decades into the future. Radio had created an entertainment form that would not be dissolved—at least, not anytime soon.

15
One Man's Family

(Bewildering Offspring)

Unquestionably among the best literary series that radio produced, *One Man's Family* was a profound statement of life as it unfolded in an upper-middle-class American family. The serial debuted during the depths of the Great Depression and became a listening ritual in millions of households. Although the drama's central figures, the Barbours of San Francisco, had few financial worries, they were not without cares. Their concerns were universal — love, adolescence and a ceaseless amazement over the succeeding generations they nurtured. Unlike most other serials of the time, this one celebrated the positive aspects of living, abhorring stock formulas and devices (like amnesia) so typical elsewhere. More a novel than a soap, the drama's structure was built on "books" and "chapters" rather than typical subplot story lines. It was the crowning achievement of Carlton E. Morse, an adroit creative who wrote, directed and produced the program for most of its 27 years on the air. The series championed Morse's own philosophical disposition that the family was unparalleled in providing moral fiber for the nation. It was, to Morse, absolutely imperative that the family be honored and preserved for generations yet unborn. For 18 years, *One Man's Family* was broadcast as a weekly half-hour drama. Then it moved to a five-night-a-week format similar to that of the sudsy daytime washboard weepers. Even then its focus on daily life in one extended family's home remained, along with its literary and production superiority. The soap played out its final couple of years in a daytime quarter-hour. Failed attempts to see it succeed on both large and small screens never thwarted Morse and his associates; they routinely acquired virtually every prestigious award given for radio drama.

Producer: Carlton E. Morse
Directors: Charles Buck, George Fogle, Carlton E. Morse, Michael Raffetto, Clinton Twiss
Writers: Carlton E. Morse, Michael Raffetto (early episodes and 1949–55), Harlan Ware
    (1944–59)
Music: Paul Carson (April 29, 1932–May 11, 1951); Sybil Chism (May 14, 1951–March 26,
    1954); Martha Green (March 29, 1954–May 7, 1954); pretaped (May 10, 1954–May 8,
    1959)
Sound Effects: Ralph Amati, Floyd Caution, Fred Cole, Bob Grapperhaus
Announcers: William Andrews, Frank Barton, Ken Carpenter
Father Henry Barbour: J. Anthony Smythe

Mother Fanny Barbour: Minetta Ellen (April 29, 1932–July 8, 1955); Mary Adams (Feb. 13, 1956–May 8, 1959)

Paul Barbour: Michael Raffetto (April 29, 1932–July 8, 1955); Russell Thorson (July 28, 1955–May 8, 1959)

Hazel Barbour: Bernice Berwin

Claudia Barbour: Kathleen Wilson (April 29, 1932–Aug. 29, 1943); Floy Margaret Hughes (substitute for Kathleen Wilson during illness); Barbara Fuller (Oct. 14, 1945–May 8, 1959); Laurette Fillbrandt (summer substitute 1949)

Clifford Barbour: Barton Yarborough (April 29, 1932–Dec. 27, 1951)

Jack Barbour: Page Gilman

Others: Barbara Jo Allen, Robert Bailey, Edgar Barrier, Jeanne Bates, Dawn Bender, Tommy Bernard, Conrad Binyon, Henry Blair, Bill Bouchey, Francis X. Bushman, Herb Butterfield, Michael Chapin, Tom Collins, Hans Conreid, Frank Cooley, Lloyd Corrigan, Dick Crenna, Mary Jane Croft, Dix Davis, Rosemary De Camp, Ted de Corsia, Larry Dobkin, Sharon Douglas, Jack Edwards, Jr., Sam Edwards, Norman Fields, Eddie Firestone, Jr., David Frankham, Betty Lou Gerson, William Green, Virginia Gregg, Mary Lou Harrington, Bert Horton, Billy Idelson, Vivi Janniss, Cy Kendall, Jack Kruschen, Mary Lansing, Lyn Lauria, Leone Ledoux, Earl Lee, Jana Leff, Richard Legrand, Elliott Lewis, Forrest Lewis, Susan Luckey, Wally Maher, Maurice Manson, Charles McAllister, James McCallion, Mary McGovern, John McIntire, Howard McNear, Tyler McVey, Dickie Meyers, Marvin Miller (played 20 different roles), Helen Musselman, Jeanette Nolan, Jay Novello, Susan Odin, Dan O'Herlihy, Jill Oppenheim, Walter Paterson, Hal Peary, Victor Perrin, Ruth Perrott, Bill Peters, George Pirrone, Frank Provo, Cameron Prud'homme, George Rand, Isabel Randolph, Alice Reinheart, Jean Rouverol, Elizabeth Sharon, Ann Shelley, Marilyn Steiner, Naomi Stevens, Anne Stone, Gil Stratton, Jr., Richard Svihus, D. J. Thompson, Russell Thorson, Emerson Treacy, Les Tremayne, Lurene Tuttle, Luis Van Rooten, Theodore von Eltz, Janet Waldo, Anne Whitfield, Winifred Wolfe, Barbara Jean Wong, Ben Wright, more

Theme: 1932–41, "Destiny Waltz" (Barnes); 1941–59, "Patricia" (original theme by Carson)

Sponsors: While it was broadcast to a West Coast audience only, the program was a sustaining feature in its first three months, then sponsored by Wesson Oil (Aug. 3, 1932–May 10, 1933). It attracted its first national sponsor, Penn Tobacco Co. for Kentucky Winners cigarettes, on May 17, 1933. Listeners even in the early 1930s protested against the "linking of cigarettes with the clean-living Barbour family," according to Morse. Standard Brands, Inc., signed on, effective April 3, 1935, to advertise its food products (Tender Leaf tea, Royal gelatin and pudding, Fleischmann's yeast, Chase and Sanborn coffee, Snow Drift shortening, others). When it canceled 14 years later (Sept. 25, 1949), the program continued again as a sustaining feature (Oct. 2, 1949–June 4, 1950). In that time NBC asked listeners to write showing support for the program to help the web attract a new sponsor. Within three weeks 60,000 pieces of mail arrived. The show was sold to Miles Laboratories, Inc. (for Alka-Seltzer stomach-distress reliever, Bactine antiseptic, Tabcin heartburn antidote, One-A-Day multiple vitamins, Chooz antacid and Miles Nervine anxiety calmative), from June 5, 1950, to 1954. Then various sponsors backed the drama on a participating basis, including the Gillette Co. (for Toni home permanents and other hair-care products) and Radio Corporation of America (entertainment devices).

Ratings: The ratings exceeded those on all other serials because two-thirds of the show's airtime (in weekly format) was largely in prime evening hours when millions more listeners tuned in. Its greatest triumph, 26.7, came in 1939–40. Figures were in double digits during a dozen seasons (higher than all but a handful of daytime soap operas). In half those seasons, numbers topped 15.0. While the show broadcast as a daily (or nightly) serial instead of weekly, ratings fell to a more comparable 7.4 in 1950–51 and 3.2 in 1955–56.

On the Air: April 29, 1932–July 29, 1932, KGO (San Francisco) and NBC Red stations in Los Angeles and Seattle, Friday, 9:30 p.m.; Aug. 3, 1932–May 10, 1933, NBC West Coast stations, Wednesday; May 17, 1933, NBC (debut on full network), Wednesday; 1933–1934, NBC, Saturday, 11:00 p.m. ET; 1934–March 27, 1935, NBC, Wednesday, 10:30 p.m.; April 3, 1935–Sept. 27, 1939, NBC, Wednesday, 8:00 p.m.; Oct. 5, 1939–Dec. 28, 1939, NBC, Thursday, 8:00 p.m.; Jan. 7, 1940–July 8, 1945, NBC, Sunday, 8:30 p.m.; July 15, 1945–Sept. 25, 1949, NBC, Sunday, 3:30 p.m.; Oct. 2, 1949–June 4, 1950, NBC, Sunday, 3:00 p.m.; June 5, 1950–1957, NBC, Monday-Friday, 7:45 p.m.; 1957–May 8, 1959, NBC, Monday-Friday, 2:30 p.m.

One Man's Family, a Carlton E. Morse creation, is dedicated to the mothers and fathers of the younger generation and to their bewildering offspring.
— Epigraph to *One Man's Family*

There were seven members of the original Barbour family, who lived in the residential section of Seacliff overlooking San Francisco Bay when the series began. Each was introduced in the early chapters of the drama.

Father Henry Wilson Barbour, who was born in 1875, had worked his way from a grocery clerk to a stockbroker's aide by the time he started courting Fanny Martin. He would one day rise to full partnership in the brokerage house. Wasn't it a bold stroke for series creator Carlton E. Morse to cast Henry as the president of a bond concern at a time when bond salesmen were publicly esteemed about as poorly as bankers? Though set in his ways, and not an entirely sympathetic figure at the drama's start, Henry was also a deep thinker and possessed foresight, courage and the ability to reason solid answers for trifling situations. Although in later years he might have come across to listeners as a mindless, bumbling old codger ("Oh Fanny, Fanny, Fanny," he mumbled to himself), he remained an opinionated, driving force. Father Barbour never abdicated his role as the patriarch even though younger family members sought out the eldest son, Paul, for his insights when critical personal decisions had to be made. After troubled exchanges with any one of his children, Father Barbour would frequently retire to his gardening, there to grumble under his breath.

Radio's most prominent family drama, *One Man's Family,* was about the Barbours of San Francisco (*l–r*): Clifford (Barton Yarborough), Claudia (Kathleen Wilson), Henry (J. Anthony Smythe), Fanny (Minetta Ellen), Jack (Page Gilman), Hazel (Bernice Berwin) and Paul (Michael Raffetto). (Photofest)

Years before, as a suitor, Henry had steep competition for Fanny Martin's affections: Fred Thompson, a physician who made house calls via horse-and-buggy, and Glenn Hunter, an engaging young attorney. All three gave evidence of being able to provide a comfortable living, so that was never a serious factor in Fanny's deliberations.

The part of Henry was played by a single actor ("single" in more ways than one: oddly enough, the man who carried the role as head of the household for 27 years was a confirmed lifelong bachelor). J. Anthony Smythe, born in San Francisco on December 18, 1885, appeared in several Morse radio productions before being chosen for the part that would typecast him (and provide him with financial security) for the rest of his life.

The former University of San Francisco law student had performed in campus shows and regional theatre during and following his collegiate days. For two decades he portrayed the leads in stock-company productions that often featured Holbrook Blinn and Florence Reed. He tried radio in 1930, appearing in NBC's *Split Second Tales.* He also wrote, directed and took speaking parts in the network's *Carefree Carnival.* He was Father Barbour from 1932 to 1959. The distinguished actor died on March 20, 1966, in Los Angeles.

Mother Fanny Martin Barbour, born of New England stock in 1878, chose Henry as her lifelong companion in 1896. She said she turned down the doctor because he reeked of antiseptic and the lawyer because he constantly attracted a bevy of beauties and apparently did little to dissuade them. The rejected suitors continued as close friends of both Barbours, appearing intermittently in the story line.

Meanwhile, Fanny epitomized traditional female virtues, becoming a housewife and placidly raising five children of her own. She also influenced the formative years of several grandchildren and great-grandchildren. Morse labeled her "a staunch weather vane in a stormy climate, pointing always to the eventual triumph of fair weather."[1] Unlike Henry, she saw little to upset her about the comfortable, secure cocoon in which the Barbours resided.

Actress Minetta Ellen, who played Fanny and was never on a stage until after marrying and raising her own family, appeared in matronly roles in several shows staged by the University of California Berkeley Players. Born on January 17, 1875, in Cleveland, Ohio, she was 57 years old when she began the role of Fanny Barbour. She decided to retire from the serial at age 80, having missed only three performances (due to pneumonia) in 23 years! When the cast went to Hollywood to make a *One Man's Family* movie in 1937 and the deal fell through, she and the others voted to remain in Los Angeles instead of returning to San Francisco. Ellen died in Hollywood on July 2, 1965, at the age of 90, six years after the drama left the air.

In the series' final three years on radio, Ellen was replaced by actress Mary Adams, who had portrayed the same part of Fanny Barbour in a daily televised version. (Actors Bert Lytell and Theodore von Eltz played the role of Henry Barbour on the NBC-TV daytime series, which ran March 1, 1954–April 1, 1955. An earlier TV attempt, from November 4, 1949, to June 21, 1952, was on at night on NBC; neither televised version was considered an enormous success.)

Paul Barbour, the eldest son, was born in 1897. By the inception of the Barbours' radio tale in 1932 he was a disillusioned veteran of World War I. While stationed as a pilot in France in 1918, he married Elaine Hunter, an American Army nurse. Within a few weeks she died, the result of a fatal hospital meningitis epidemic. Thus, Paul — a widower, severely wounded in one leg during combat (he had to rely on a walking cane the rest of his life), and embittered — returned to San Francisco. Preferring solitude, he moved into an attic room in the Barbour mansion. There he practiced his craft of writing and for a while became a recluse. He verbally disagreed on many issues with his inflexible father while under that roof. As the drama's unofficial heartthrob, Paul had several girlfriends, although he never remarried.

In 1933 he adopted a foster daughter, Teddy, who predictably moved from one all-consuming passion to another. Long talks between the two became models of generational communications. As the years rolled by, Paul's hostility and anger over the cards that life had dealt him softened. In some ways he superseded his father as de facto master of the household. Others gradually turned to him for understanding and the benefit of his keen vision.

Michael Raffetto, associated with *One Man's Family* throughout the run, played the part of Paul during its first 23 years, "retiring" on the same day that Minetta Ellen gave up the role of Mother Barbour. (He suffered recurring bouts of tuberculosis, which had begun to noticeably affect his voice.) Raffetto didn't fully retire, however; the gifted artist had been helping to write many of the episodes and added directing to those duties. Earlier he played the leads on two other Morse series, *I Love a Mystery* and *I Love Adventure*, the latter a 1948 summer replacement. He also played the lead on the short-lived *Attorney for the Defense*.

Born on December 30, 1899, in Placerville, California, Raffetto appeared in University of California theatricals. Like J. Anthony Smythe (who played Father Barbour), he studied law and was actually practicing it while failing in an attempt to become accepted in such silent films as *Tillie's Punctured Romance*. He became a diction teacher and soon impressed NBC officials with his voice and a script he wrote in 1930 called *Arm of the Law*. Always looking for material, the network turned his script into a serial about a charming elderly attorney, engaging Raffetto as the lead. Raffetto became NBC's West Coast program director. In 1948 he had a bit part in a film starring Marlene Dietrich, *A Foreign Affair*. He acquired a similar role in a 1956 movie starring Bette Davis, *Storm Center*. The versatile actor died on May 31, 1990, in Berkeley, California.

His successor as Paul Barbour was the actor Russell Thorson, who had played the same part in the televised version of *One Man's Family*, which had just left the air. Thorson carried roles in three other Morse radio series: *I Love a Mystery*, *I Love Adventure* and *Adventures by Morse*, the last a 1944 syndicated program. He also played the male lead on an early soap opera, *Midstream*, and the title character on *Dr. Paul*, one of the last soaps introduced on radio. He also bore the title role of *Tom Mix*. Thorson's acting credits included a running part in *Road of Life* and stints on *Mystery in the Air*. He died on July 6, 1982, at age 75.

Hazel Barbour, the eldest daughter — and the one on whom Father Barbour unabashedly doted — was the second child, born in 1900. She was depicted as gentle of spirit, serene and evenhanded in bringing up three children. She married a dairy farmer, William Herbert, at the end of 1932. Although he was not accustomed to the financial privileges enjoyed by the Barbours, Herbert manifested a strength of character that harmonized completely with the Barbours' own ideals. He maintained a staunch friendship with Hazel's older brother, Paul, further ingratiating him to the family. Bill and Hazel had twins in 1934 — Henry Barbour Herbert, nicknamed Pinky, and William Martin Herbert, nicknamed Hank — and a daughter, Margaret, in 1936. Bill died unexpectedly four years later, leaving Hazel to raise the three youngsters. Her even temperament and levelheadedness paid off as she approached that formidable task. In 1945 Hazel remarried, to Daniel Murray, who was also well liked by the family. Thus, she was fortunate to select two husbands with whom she shared happy marriages.

For the full run of the show, the part of Hazel was played by Bernice Berwin. Except for the fact that Berwin returned to East Bay, California, near San Francisco to live after the radio series left the air, few details have been preserved about her.

Claudia Barbour, one of the twins born in 1912, was still a teenager when the radio series began. While none of the Barbours could be branded as arrogant, indolent or disrespectful, they were just as fallible as everybody else. This one certainly rippled the waters, a constant concern to her conventional father (and undoubtedly she lent credibility to the program's opening inscription about "bewildering offspring"). Impetuous and excitable, the high-spirited Claudia made snap judgments, challenging the traditional ideals of her conservative dad. At 18, while in college (before the radio drama began), she had eloped with Johnny Roberts, whom Mother Barbour termed "the most maddeningly handsome, most devil-may-care, most aristocratic-looking young man I ever knew."[2] He was also totally irresponsible, solely interested in new kicks. When he saw that marriage put more constraints on his happy-go-lucky lifestyle than he was willing to concede, just eight months into it he deserted Claudia, leaving her an expectant mother. (Joan was born in 1933.) Disappearing into China, Johnny was wounded while fighting with rebels. Returning home in good health, he suffered heart failure and died. In addition to Joan, Johnny also left Claudia with a quarter of a million dollars.

Despite this, Claudia was at loose ends and drifted into a state of despondency. She rejected her father's attempts to pull her out of it; instead she turned to her older brother, Paul, with whom she shared long talks. She also sought the solitude of long walks by the sea cliffs. Her father, however, continued to press her, arguing that it was not right for someone so young to have control of the large sum Claudia had inherited. As a result she took Joan and beat a hasty retreat to England, where — in 1935 — she met and married British Army Captain Nicholas (Nicky) Lacey. Three years later the couple had a daughter, whom they named Penny.

During World War II Nicky and Claudia were rescued from a ship that was torpedoed. For a couple of years, until the war ended, they were sequestered in a German concentration camp. Such influences, as well as Nicky's persistence, helped tame the rebel-rousing Claudia to the extent that her frequent and sudden outbursts were reduced to mere occasional storms. When the couple later moved to San Francisco, Nicky was prominently featured in the story line, more than any of the other Barbour in-laws.

The part of Claudia may have been played by more individuals than any other in the cast of *One Man's Family*, although only two people carried the role for substantial periods. The first, Kathleen Wilson, relinquished it in 1943 to become the wife of Lord Alastair Pilkington of London, changing her name to Lady Kathleen Pilkington. She had played in *I Love a Mystery*.

Barbara Fuller, who replaced Wilson as Claudia from 1945 to 1959, earlier had running roles in other serials: *Painted Dreams, Stepmother, Road of Life* and *Scattergood Baines*. She also appeared in *Madame Courageous, The Light of the World, Armstrong Theatre of Today, Manhattan at Midnight, Lux Radio Theatre* and *His Honor, the Barber*. Born on July 21, 1921, in Nahant, Massachusetts, Fuller played in films for Republic Pictures too. She assisted in developing and marketing inspirational audio tapes and radio talks of a prominent metaphysical instructor during the last three decades of the twentieth century.

Clifford Barbour, Claudia's twin, was a lot like his tempestuous sister. He was girl-crazy, though his advances weren't often welcomed. His elder brother, Paul, at last fell in love with one of his companions, the widow Beth Holly, and for years they were an item even though they never married. Cliff, meanwhile, married twice.

His first marriage, in 1937 to Ann Waite, was a mismatch. She had been warped by a dictatorial father, a professor at the university in Berkeley. Mother Barbour said that the day the professor and his daughter rented a small house from the Barbours was "the most tragic day in the history of the Barbour family."[3] Soon after their wedding, the couple split. The sex-hating, decidedly naive Ann moved into her father's new home in Berkeley.

Clifford never saw her alive again. He didn't know she was carrying his child, but later that year she gave birth to a son. Ann made such a determined attempt to leave the hospital to return to her father's home after the birth that she died while trying. Professor Waite didn't want the baby, and Clifford was so wrought over Ann's death that the senior Barbours went to the hospital to claim their grandson. Nearly a year passed before Cliff showed interest in his son, calling him only Skip or Skipper. The boy was almost eight, in fact, when Cliff and his father decided to name the child Andrew after his mother, Ann. Almost everyone called him Andy.

Clifford's second wife, Irene Franklin, whom he married in 1942, was a lovely, gracious person, the antithesis of his first wife. She died only four years later, in an automobile accident.

When the actor who played Clifford, Barton Yarborough, died unexpectedly late in 1951, the writers sent Cliff to Scotland to live rather than replacing him in the drama. From there he dispensed letters to the Barbours but never traveled home to San Francisco as long as the series remained on the air.

Yarborough had acted in student productions while attending the universities of Texas and California. Later he toured the nation and appeared in London in the play *Outward Bound*. He was Sergeant Joe Friday's original partner in *Dragnet* on radio and television. Born in Goldthwaite, Texas, in 1900, Yarborough died of a heart attack on December 19, 1951, in Hollywood. Between those years he appeared on *I Love a Mystery, I Love Adventure, Hashknife Hartley, Hawk Larabee, Today's Children, Tennessee Jed, The Adventures of Christopher London, Attorney for the Defense* and *The Halls of Ivy*. In 1942 he played in the Universal film *Ghost of Frankenstein,* which became a cult classic.

Jack Barbour, the baby of the original family, was born in 1919 and was only thirteen when the show began. In a sense, he fared better than his brothers for he appeared to have come closer to the ideals set by his father than they. After being drafted into the Korean War, he returned three years later to practice law in San Francisco. There never seemed to be any doubt that he would marry his childhood sweetheart, Betty Carter, although Father Barbour wouldn't offer his consent or blessing. Jack married Betty anyway, and in doing so, he achieved something none of his siblings was able to: he maintained a devoted, lifelong partnership with only one spouse. She bore him six daughters: Elizabeth Sharon Ann, in 1942; Janie, 1943; Mary Lou, 1944; and triplets, Abigail, Deborah and Constance, at the start of 1949. (With two sets of twins in this family already, multiple births didn't seem especially surprising.)

Jack and Betty's large family undoubtedly contributed to the occasional financial difficulties they experienced, the only money worries any Barbour ever had. But their resolve to confront their problems with boldness allowed the family to overcome such crises. In time, Jack's stability, self-reliance, sound thinking and age combined to suggest that he might ultimately succeed his father as the clan's next leader. After all, the eldest, Paul — the most likely candidate for that role and Jack's senior by 22 years — couldn't be counted on to guide the younger family members for an interminable length of time.

The part of Jack was still played at the end of the series by Page Gilman, who had originated it 27 years earlier at the age of 14. Only a break for army wartime service deterred him from the microphone during that span. Gilman was born on April 18, 1918, in San Francisco and launched his radio career in 1927 under the name Billy Page. He appeared during his high school and collegiate days at Stanford and UCLA on *Memory Lane* and *Ship of Joy*, NBC West Coast regional programs. In 1931 he was Penrod on *Penrod and Sam*. After military discharge, Gilman returned to radio, simultaneously operating a linotype machine, then becoming a daily newspaper's national advertising manager. He moved to Oregon to be a rancher in retirement.

Of thirteen Barbour grandchildren (including Paul's adopted daughter, Teddy), seven had already married once before the show left the air. And by late in the life of *One Man's Family*, the bewildering offsprings' offspring had started producing their own offspring. Paul John (Johnny) Farnsworth, son of Joan and Ross Farnsworth, was the Barbours' first great-grandchild, with promises of many more to come. Ross, incidentally, was a mixed-up mama's boy. Had the series lasted awhile longer, prospects weren't all that good that those parents would remain together. In all, the cast against which the principals danced and laughed and multiplied had grown so large that — by the show's demise — it included some 90 different actors and actresses.

Much of the success of *One Man's Family* rested with its inspired creator, Carlton E. Morse. A native of Jennings, Louisiana, he was born on June 4, 1901. At age five he moved with his family to a dairy and alfalfa ranch in Jackson County, Oregon. At 17 he moved with his family again, this time to Sacramento. Following two years of formal education at the University of California, young Morse gained employment with the *Sacramento Union*. Two years later he moved to the copy desk of the better known *San Francisco Chronicle*. Sometime later he transferred to the *Seattle Times*, where he gained notoriety by writing a human-interest feature. The San Francisco paper soon brought him back to produce a similar column while adding the police beat to his writing portfolio.

He left print journalism when he was only 28 to enter the exciting new medium of radio, then gaining enormous popularity. He pioneered in drama and action programs, learning what devices held the listening audience's interest. Morse discovered that younger radio fans preferred adventure and mystery, whereas female listeners enjoyed romance. Through experimentation, he learned that an audience existed for virtually every type of drama that was credible and well written. He claimed, "There is no medium that will ever attract the same kind of attention as radio — nothing will be as equal to the imagination."[4]

Morse was also distinguished from the pack of serial writers by the fact that he prepared his scripts with individual performers in mind. He did so even before adding new characters to his dramas. Undoubtedly this entered into his decision not to replace Barton Yarborough, the actor who played Clifford and who died during the long run of the series.

In *Family* he was able to turn long conversations into logical fragments of middle-class Americana. Underlying all of it was a spirit of warmth and optimism that even included subdued humor. Elsewhere, on most other daytime serials, such dialogue might have dwindled into nauseous exchanges.

In addition to *One Man's Family*, he created several other radio series, some more successful than others: *I Love a Mystery, I Love Adventure, Adventures by Morse, Family Skeleton, The Woman in My House* and *His Honor, the Barber*. After his radio series were gone, Morse wrote two well-received novels, *Killer at the Wheel* and *A Lavish of Sin*, both published in 1987 with intertwining family ties in their plots. He had earlier written another novel, *Stuff the Lady's Hatbox*, based on the series *I Love a Mystery*. Morse died on May 24, 1993, 11 days shy of his 92nd birthday.

The nighttime *Mystery* was his second-best-recognized radio achievement, but *The*

Woman in My House aired many more times. As one of radio's final entries among five-times-a-week daytime soap operas, it was given a home by NBC from March 26, 1951, until its cancellation in 1959, the year *One Man's Family* disappeared. Thus, *Woman* became the only serial to debut early in the 1950s and remain almost to the end of the decade (and genre).

This show bore out Morse's strong reverence for paternalism and family life too. Presenting a conservative image of family connections, it told the story of James and Jessie Carter of Miami and their relationships with their grown or nearly grown offspring. It was sponsored by Manhattan Soap Company for Sweetheart soap for three years and for another year by Procter & Gamble before Miles Laboratories, Inc. took it in 1955 just as Miles had accepted *One Man's Family* in 1950. Several members of the cast of *The Woman in My House* also appeared in *Family* (both series were broadcast from Hollywood).

The major difference between *Woman* and the epic story of the Barbours seemed to be that the Carters lived on the East Coast and the Barbours were on the West. (The former based their story on early scripts of the Barbour series, essentially changing the names and locales but not the situations.) Also, aside from the fact that *Woman* was performed for a daytime audience while *Family* was mostly a nighttime feature, the ideologies of Morse were gently woven throughout both dramas. Had *Woman* been introduced a decade earlier, during the heyday of the Golden Age of radio, the serial might have earned many of the same literary distinctions that its more noted sibling derived.

Those accolades included radio's highest honor, the distinguished Peabody Award. Only one other serial, *Against the Storm*, by Sandra Michael (author of *The Open Door* and *Lone Journey*), shared that prestigious designation. *Family* won more awards for its scholarly contributions to radio drama than any other serialized fiction about domestic life.

Other dimensions of notoriety surfaced while the long-running series was on the air. The "Barbour home" in the Seacliff district of San Francisco was added to the routes of sightseeing tour buses to accommodate the growing interest of visitors to the area. (The fictional family occasionally visited a nearby second home they called "Sky Ranch." In reality, their retreat was a King's Mountain hideaway occupied by Carlton E. Morse.)

On reaching the show's twentieth anniversary in 1952, the citizens of San Francisco marked the occasion by celebrating "*One Man's Family* Day." And when a member of the Barbour family was ill, the network learned to expect stacks of get-well wishes from devoted fans. As Christmas and birthday celebrations approached, the mail was always heavy with traditional greetings.

When premium offers were mentioned on the air — for cookbooks, flower seed packets, photographs, diaries, sheet music, record albums and scrapbook recollections of the family's past — hundreds of thousands of requests poured in. Offered in 1937, *Teddy's Diary*, purportedly in her own handwriting, drew more than a half-million requests. *Jack's Camera Scrapbook* was another popular giveaway. Father Barbour's printed legacy to each member of his family, *This I Give*, demonstrated the ongoing renown for premiums, even when television was taking listeners away. Tens of thousands of Bactine boxtops, each accompanied by a quarter, were received in Miles Lab's offices in Elkhart, Indiana. Father Barbour's 32-page booklet was initially promoted on the broadcast of March 23, 1953.

The characters and format of the series became so familiar to Americans that they lent themselves to parody. Comedians Bob and Ray obliged with recurrent sketches on their own radio series featuring "One Feller's Family, the Story of the Butchers." (Father Butcher's most repetitious line in those takeoffs was "Fanny, Fanny, Fanny.") The serial became accepted abroad too, playing for years in Canada and Russia. So revered was the program that its cast heard of numerous babies born to several generations who named their offspring after the Barbour children and grandchildren. Years after the radio series ended, a *Family* publication claimed that the Barbours were "the best-known and best-loved family in the United States from 1932 to 1960."[5]

If the best form of flattery is imitation, *One Man's Family* achieved that too. *Those We Love*, written by Agnes Ridgeway, copied the format of the successful Morse show, though it never became *Family's* equal. The story of the John Marshall family of Westbridge, Connecticut, *Love* also dealt with characterization and family relationships. Due to poor scheduling, however, the series was never strong enough to gain a solid footing with an audience segment to overcome its frequent changes in days, times and networks. It aired sporadically between 1937 and 1945.

A great deal of the subject matter of *One Man's Family* dealt with love affairs. In her teens, Joan Roberts Lacey, Claudia's daughter, fell in love with her Uncle Paul. But Paul's foster daughter, Teddy, had already expressed similar feelings for him. When Paul turned Teddy away, she looked in the direction of the distinguished and handsome Dan Murray, who was about to become her Aunt Hazel's second husband. Dan welcomed the teenager's infatuation, which sent Teddy to her foster father's unlicensed couch for counsel. Eventually, she retreated from this familial collection of attractive older males, became an army nurse and married a service dentist, Elwood Giddings. That marriage dissolved in a brief while. At last, in the 1950s she found fulfillment by caring for American servicemen hurt in Korea. She was based at a U.S. Army hospital in Japan at the time.

After Teddy departed, Joan figured she had Paul all to herself. Uncle Paul, however, never wavered. When she realized it wasn't going to work, she went after young Ross Farnsworth.

Hank and Pinky, Hazel's twin sons, received much of the drama's emphasis as it wound its way toward a final conclusion. Pinky was noted for getting into trouble. Hank was his opposite, preferring to live many of the ideals that Father Barbour had long attempted to instill in family members.

Several authorities have perpetuated the myth that *One Man's Family* was the longest-running drama in radio. That simply wasn't so, however, even though its record was substantial. From the time it went on the full network (May 17, 1933) to its final sign-off (May 8, 1959), the program lasted for nearly 26 years. Even tacking on another year for local and regional broadcasts doesn't exceed two other durable radio soap operas. Both *The Romance of Helen Trent* and *Ma Perkins* aired for 27 years. With local broadcasts added, the latter ran for an even longer time frame. And when the number of performances is compared, *Family's* 3,256 episodes pale alongside *Helen's* 7,222 and *Ma's* 7,065. Even *Pepper Young's Family*, with its historical lineage under three earlier titles, produced nearly 7,000 quarter-hours in more than 26 years on network radio.

The common theme in all soaps is family. Carlton E. Morse's views on the preeminence of the family were clearly and often stated on the programs he created. In 1938, for instance, Father Barbour admonished: "It's my opinion that the family is the source from whence comes the moral strength of a nation. And disintegration of any nation begins with the disintegration of the family. The family is the smallest unit in society. Millions and millions of these little units make a nation. And the standards of living set up by these family units indicate the high or low standards of a nation.... A well-disciplined, morally upright family is bound to turn out good citizens! Good citizens make a good nation."

Nine years later Morse had Father Barbour underscore his philosophy: "The American home is the backbone of this nation. The American family is the life blood of the American democracy, the seed of our way of life. If we let that seed die, if we kill the divine spark, then we've killed America.... Is it any wonder that we've made the home and the family our theme for 15 years...? We are dedicated to it and rededicated to it, world without end."

A month after the radio series left the air in 1959, Morse told a Los Angeles newspaper reporter: "My own sorrow is not so much in the cessation of the show as such as in the thought that one more happy, sober beacon to light the way has been put out. One more marker has been torn down.... The signposts for sound family life are now few, and I feel the loss of *One Man's Family* is just another abandoned lighthouse."

For a man who believed in the preeminence of the family, and for others like him, thinking otherwise would have been positively unconscionable.

16
Our Gal Sunday
(Can This Girl … Find Happiness?)

At the risk of sounding like a broken record, *Our Gal Sunday* pursued one of the great themes of soap opera — marrying a young female castaway into a male-ordered society of prominence and wealth. Despite its timeworn hypothesis, the show may have done this better than any other. Orphaned, raised by two old prospectors in a western mining encampment, a lass couldn't be expected to go far in life without the advantages that most others were exposed to. But out of such modest roots came Lady Brinthrope, the wife of one of the most dignified, prosperous, aristocratic Englishmen to settle on the East Coast. Lord Henry and Sunday's story wasn't largely one of marital discord, though there was an element of that. Instead, it popularized another of soap opera's celebrated precepts: introducing fiendish hussies who were determined to destroy the tranquillity of the heroine's life by vying for her mate's affections. (On rare occasions, the situation worked in reverse, with the wife becoming the object of an obsessive admirer's infatuation. More often than not, however, it was the husband who was the prize.) Some of these temptresses were rich snobs; others were your basic common vamp, the kind that could be imported from several other serials. Despite such shenanigans, Sunday and Henry genuinely loved each other, and their union stood as a bulwark against evil's forces. Listeners were comforted in knowing that no matter what was hurled against the couple,their marriage would last. Surviving more than two decades in a favored time period, the durable serial picked up listeners by the millions, many of them remaining with the rags-to-riches tale until the end.

Producers: Frank and Anne Hummert
Directors: Stephen Gross, Arthur Hanna, Anne Hummert, Frank Hummert
Writers: Helen Walpole, Jean Carroll (1945–59)
Sound Effects: Bill Brown, John McCloskey
Announcers: Ed Fleming, John Reed King, Art Millett, Bert Parks, Charles Stark, Warren Sweeney, John A. Wolfe
Sunday Brinthrope: Dorothy Lowell (1937–46), Vivian Smolen (1946–59)
Lord Henry Brinthrope: Karl Swenson, Alistair Duncan
Irene Galway: Fran Carlon
Peter Galway: Joseph Curtin
Others: Inge Adams, Charita Bauer, Spencer Bentley, Kaye Brinker, Delma Byron, Kather-

ine Emmet, Roy Fant, Ara Gerald, John Grinnell, Tom Gunn, Louis Hall, Van Heflin, Irene Hubbard, Venezuela Jones, Jay Jostyn, Elaine Kent, Alastair Kyle, Joe Latham, Charlotte Lawrence, Hugh Marlowe, John McGovern, John McQuade, Jay Meredith, James Monks, Louis Neistat, Clyde North, Santos Ortega, John Raby, Florence Robinson, Ruth Russell, Anne Seymour, Ann Shepherd, Robert Strauss, Joan Tompkins, Vicki Vola, Eustace Wyatt, Carleton Young, more

Theme: "Red River Valley"

Sponsors: For 16 years this program, governed by Blackett-Sample-Hummert, was offered by American Home Products Corp. (AHP) for its packaged-goods subsidiary, the Whitehall Pharmacal Co. (Anacin pain reliever, Freezone corn remover, Bi-So-Dol analgesic, Kolynos toothpaste and tooth powder dentifrice, Neet hair remover, Infrarub balm, Kriptin antihistamine, Heet liniment, Dristan and Primatene cold remedies, Preparation H hemorrhoidal medication, Sleep-Eze calmative and others). It also advertised wares from AHP's household products division, Boyle-Midway (Aerowax and Olde English floor cleaners, Easy-Off oven cleaner, Black Flag insect repellent, Wizard room deodorizer, Sani-Flush toilet cleanser and others). AHP, which carried the serial from its inception in 1937, relinquished sponsorship in 1942. The series was sold for one season to Standard Brands, Inc. (Tender Leaf tea, Royal gelatin and pudding, Fleischmann's yeast, Chase and Sanborn coffee, Snow Drift shortening and others). When Standard Brands departed, AHP returned, underwriting the show until 1950. Procter & Gamble entered for several of its consumer household commodities. When P&G bowed out a year later, AHP again picked up the tab, carrying the series through Aug. 26, 1955. From Aug. 29, 1955, the show was sold to participating sponsors. Toward the end of the run, it was largely carried as a sustaining feature by CBS Radio.

Ratings: Over the 16 seasons (1939–55) for which numbers were recorded, this serial's median was 7.8, an unusually strong posting. High: 9.9 (1949–50); low: 5.1 (1954–55). According to actress Mary Jane Higby, who played in several other long-running serials, this was the Hummerts' top-rated production.

On the Air: March 29, 1937–Jan. 2, 1959, CBS, 12:45 p.m. ET.

Once again, we present Our Gal Sunday, *the story of an orphan girl named Sunday from the little mining town of Silver Creek, Colorado, who in young womanhood married England's richest, most handsome lord, Lord Henry Brinthrope. The story that asks the question: Can this girl from the little mining town in the West find happiness as the wife of a wealthy and titled Englishman?*
— Epigraph to Our Gal Sunday

The capsuled thesis following the title, like the one announcing the arrival of *Our Gal Sunday* each midday, was supplied to acquaint the new listener with the premise of the story. A Hummert invention, the capsuled thesis soon spread to other parts of radio soap opera, becoming an integral part of dozens of serials. *Sunday's* critics called hers "the most famous cliché of old time radio."[1] Even though most listeners felt that happiness was possible, they also believed it would probably be painful to achieve.

Frank and Anne Hummert placed an unequivocal, incontestable emphasis on clarity of speech and proper enunciation in their dramas. Overlapping speeches could never happen — not *ever*. Without the slightest hesitation, the audience had to be able to tell precisely who was doing the talking *and* the listening in the dialogue on their shows. Excess sound and background music was minimized and even forbidden in a script. Clarity of speech was the essential overriding ingredient on every program.

Our Gal Sunday's scriptwriters understood their lessons at the Hummert school of elocution very well. Actually, they may have been better at their jobs than those who wrote for any of the vast complement of other Hummert serials. As each installment of *Our Gal Sunday* began, the strains of an organ rendition of the mournful "Red River Valley" filtered into homes across the land. But no announcer grappled with the organist to decide who could be heard above the other on *this* program. Only when the instrument finished playing, stopping altogether, did *Sunday's* longtime narrator, Ed Fleming, read the capsuled thesis noted above. Over the years, the words became so familiar to devoted fans that even though the speech was a long one, millions must have said it along with Fleming without missing a beat.

Following the thesis, the organist played a few more bars of "Red River Valley." When it was again Fleming's turn, he read the opening commercial. That done, the organist picked up a few notes from "Red River Valley" once more, thereby signaling the transition to the day's action.

When the music ended, Fleming would say: "And now ... *Our Gal Sunday*." After a two-second pause, he recapped some dramatic development from the previous episode. This was almost always followed by a fragment of dialogue from one of the principal characters, addressing no one in particular — a regression to the previous day's developments. A typical throwback on one day's broadcast went like this:

> ANNOUNCER: Last night, a chance remark made by Sunday's close friend, Irene Galway, gave Sunday a jolt. All night she has lain awake, one thought spinning through her mind.
> SUNDAY: Yesterday, Dr. Abbott told me I was all right ... that there's nothing wrong with me. Why, then, did Irene see Henry coming out of Dr. Abbott's office? And why didn't Henry tell me he was there? I *must* know, I *must* find out. Just what is Henry *keeping* from me?

At this point, Fleming set the stage for the current day's action. New dialogue ensued. After two or three scenes — at the close of each day's dramatic portion — Fleming posed several thoughtful questions for the listener to mull over. The last question invariably ended with the words *Our Gal Sunday*. For example: "Has Kevin made a serious mistake in being driven to Birchwood by *Our Gal Sunday*?" Or: "What was the special delivery letter, and is it to have a surprising importance for Lord Henry and *Our Gal Sunday*?" Or, "Is there, indeed, good cause for the fears of *Our Gal Sunday*?" A sharp organ sting and then a few notes of transitional music bridged the gap, leading to the next commercial message.

From there the program was a mishmash of elements offered by Fleming, separated by organ notes, and never at the same time. In the Hummert tradition, the prescription had been fine-tuned to perfection. Thus for years during its heyday, *Our Gal Sunday's* closing proceeded in the following manner:

> MUSIC: Pick up a few bright notes
> ANNOUNCER: This is Ed Fleming saying "good-by" until tomor-
> row at this same time.
> MUSIC: Pick up a few bright notes
> ANNOUNCER: Deliver hitchhike commercial message
> MUSIC: Pick up a few bright notes
> ANNOUNCER: *Our Gal Sunday* is based on the play *Sunday*. The
> radio sequel is originated by and produced under the super-
> vision of Frank and Anne Hummert. Dialogue by Jean Car-
> roll. Directed by Arthur Hanna. Vivian Smolen plays
> Sunday and Karl Swenson is Lord Henry. *Our Gal Sunday*
> will be on the air at this same time tomorrow.
> MUSIC: Pick up a few bright notes
> ANNOUNCER: This is CBS, the Columbia Broadcasting System.

Did you notice that — by this time — there was a scriptwriter who was earning credit for her talent? Jean Carroll obviously fell into favor with the Hummerts. For the last 14 years of the series' life, she wrote the dialogue and was recognized in the drama's latter days for her efforts. (Interestingly, she and Helen Walpole, who also wrote *Sunday*'s dialogue, penned scripts for another Hummert rags-to-riches tale, *Lora Lawton*.) The fact that Jean Carroll was identified on the air was a significant departure from an earlier Hummert prac-tice and was not duplicated on many of their shows.

On *Sunday*, the director and lead actors were also credited. The Hummerts allowed their director's name to be mentioned on several of their serials. He or she was the highest-ranking on-premises Hummert employee and was held accountable for everything that transpired on a show, while laboring within tightly controlled parameters. Names of mem-bers of the casts were seldom revealed, however. The exceptions may have resulted from a combination of factors including professional abilities, longevity and an occupational reward (perhaps in lieu of higher wages), to keep actors in their roles via public acknowl-edgment. Vivian Smolen and Karl Swenson were associated with *Sunday* over a long period of time, distinctly underscoring their contributions to the show.

Our Gal Sunday was a waif-to-prominence yarn that continued a theme popularized in serial dramas: women of lower social order marrying fortune or fame and moving into higher society (à la *Backstage Wife*, *Kitty Foyle*, *Lora Lawton* and others). The pattern was one of the more compelling Hummert creations. They would take a frail but determined heroine of humble origin and wed her into money and prestige. Then she would spend the rest of her life fending off jealous female competitors for the affections of her husband. These serials appealed to listeners' dreams of sudden wealth and social position.

In *Sunday*'s case, the story concerned an unwanted urchin who was abandoned at a Colorado mining camp. Raised by two old prospectors, Jackie and Lively, she was obviously exposed to the best they could offer in the way of education, despite their lack of sophisti-cation and means. The "radio sequel" was based on a Broadway play simply titled *Sunday*.

Ethel Barrymore, who starred in the original stage play shortly after the turn of the century, improvised a line at the drama's conclusion that summarized it all: "That's all there is, there isn't any more." But for the Hummerts, it was only the beginning. They took the story from where it ended onstage and carried it through Sunday's marriage to the "wealthy and titled Englishman" and far beyond.

Termed "radio's most appealing heroine" by one scholar,[2] Sunday confronted all of her difficulties in a kind of dreamlike fashion. She was able to make even the most demanding of her listeners comfortable with the fantasy. In fact, one was never quite sure whether he identified with Sunday or was actually in love with her.

Shortly after their marriage, a woman appeared to the Brinthropes claiming that Lord Henry was the father of her child. That sequence drew plenty of interest as Lord Henry went about proving that the woman's accusations had no basis. It was the kind of lunchtime bedevilment for which this serial would become widely acclaimed. In more than two decades, there would be many more confrontations of equal intensity.

Though critics of the program were quick to cite Lord Henry's "uncontrollable, unjustified jealousy," this author admits to recalling little of that. Instead, I recollect a couple supremely devoted to one another. The affirmations in their dialogue and particularly in Henry's speech — such as "darling," "sweetheart," "my sweet," "dear" and other praiseworthy expressions in reference to Sunday — were not misplaced. Each time such terms of endearment were applied, they came across as genuine.

Of course, there could be no doubt in the listener's mind that there was but one man in the whole world for the undeniably virtuous Sunday. That was a given. By the same token, even though Henry may have occasionally toyed with the idea of a dalliance with another woman — and heaven knows, he certainly had plenty of opportunities to experience it — he never strayed beyond the bounds of his commitment to Sunday. I believe that those who have written harshly of Lord Henry, suggesting he was a skirt-chaser and was insanely possessive, have overlooked his greater qualities. His fundamentally flawless devotion to his beloved Sunday would appear to be testimony enough to his impeccable character.

The pair had their moments of disagreement, of course, just as all couples do — even filthy rich ones. But together they came across as a mighty duo, formidable and impenetrable. Given the opportunity and time, they could vanquish any foe. Placing their intellect and determination to the test, the Brinthropes could triumph over even the most tenacious challengers. They would, together, rout the demons of evil pointed toward themselves, their friends and their neighbors in the affluent community surrounding Black Swan Hall.

Black Swan Hall, incidentally, was their "lovely Virginia estate" (Fleming's description) near the mythical town of Fairbrooke. Everybody lived on an "estate" in Fairbrooke; at least, everybody the Brinthropes dealt with had a home with a name on it. Their best friends, for instance, Irene and Peter Galway, resided at Bow Ridge, the manor adjacent to the Brinthropes' lavish plantation. Nearby, one of the town's meddling troublemakers, Elaine Cralle — who had it in for Sunday — owned a summer home at Birchwood, yet another estate. One got the impression that there simply weren't very many indigents living in and around Fairbrooke. The homeless, who weren't foremost in the public's mind in those days, obviously had to find other digs to hang out in.

Over the years Sunday would see her little boy, Davy, become crippled when a hit-and-run driver struck him. In time, she would cradle the head of her devoted dying friend,

Kevin Bromfield, after he took a bullet that was meant for her. Kevin, incidentally, had silently loved Sunday for years but kept it to himself, knowing he could never win her from Lord Henry. He suffered in anguish over a one-sided affair that he fought bravely to keep tucked within the recesses of his own soul.

And in 1946 Sunday suffered numerous indignities at the hand of Lord Henry's childhood friend Thelma Mayfield, who visited the Brinthropes at Black Swan Hall. Facing Lord Henry one morning across the breakfast table, Sunday informed him just how far things had gone:

> SUNDAY: She announced point blank that she's going to take you away from me! That everything that you have is going to be ... oh Henry, it's ... it's too preposterous to repeat.
> HENRY: Sunday, dear, you're joking. Thelma, why she couldn't have...
> SUNDAY: (After slight pause) Would I *joke* about anything like this...?
> HENRY: How could she *say* such things?
> SUNDAY: (Cuts in) She was angry ... she was in a violent temper and ... well, they were out before she stopped to think....
> HENRY: Oh, you poor darling. Well, it's perfectly ridiculous ... the whole thing is ... unreal!
> SUNDAY: As unreal as it seems, it happened. Thelma ... told me she intends to take my place, to get me out of the picture and become ... the second Lady Brinthrope.
> HENRY: She *must* be out of her mind.... Doesn't ... she know that nothing ... nothing in this *world* could separate us?
> SUNDAY: I know it Henry, and you do, but apparently Thelma...
> SFX: Chair sliding back from breakfast table
> SUNDAY: Where are you going?
> HENRY: To settle this once and for all ... and to settle it in the only way it can be settled. (Voice trails off) I'll see you later, dear.

It was a bitter pill for Sunday to swallow. But this incident with Thelma Mayfield was typical of the challenges Lady Brinthrope bore with dignity throughout her desperate search for that rather elusive bliss she sought, as listeners were reminded daily.

In a similar sequence, in 1950 the Brinthropes flew to England at the beckoning of Lord Percy, Henry's uncle. There they discovered that an old friend, Diane Caulfield, was possibly involved with an international ring of thieves. While Henry attempted to learn more about Diane's activities, Diane took more than a passing interest in Henry. Her overtures became obvious to Sunday: Diane intended to destroy the Brinthropes' marriage. Sound familiar?

By then thievery, forgery, smuggling and even worse debauchery had entered the plot lines of most of the radio serials in a conscious effort by producers and agencies to hold their audiences against the rising tide of television. In 1951 alone, there were two murders to be solved in *Our Gal Sunday*.

In one of them, the mistress of Black Swan Hall was relieved when she learned that

Keith Carlyle's death was caused by stab wounds. She had presupposed his death had occurred when she had accidentally hit him with her automobile, not knowing he was already dead. Left at that, of course, everything would have been too simple. Soap opera didn't handle things that way. Suspicion of Carlyle's murder ultimately fell on Lord Henry. It was believed Lord Henry had shut him up to keep him from telling about an earlier murder of a lawyer's son. Nothing could be tied into a neat little package if a serial was to hold an audience for a sustained period of time.

Lady Brinthrope had a turn at being accused of murder too, on the death of Tippy Rogers. Rogers was killed in the Brinthropes' summer house, and the murder weapon was eventually proven to be Lord Henry's revolver. The investigation dragged on interminably. After a while, with the Hummerts anxious to end the farce and tie up the loose ends so that another sequence could be launched, the following happened in a *single* episode: (a) Donald Berry voluntarily confessed to Rogers' murder, thereby avoiding a trial; and (b) the Brinthropes' New York bosom pal, lawyer Kevin Bromfield, alluded to a mysterious purpose that would hold him in Fairbrooke awhile longer. It sounded enormously foreboding to Sunday and Lord Henry. Their involvement in Kevin's secret mission would be the subject of the next dramatic entanglement.

In 1954 a magazine writer summarized the current plot line on *Our Gal Sunday*. Pointing out the obvious — that many alluring, temporal females had attempted to capture Lord Henry for themselves — the journalist observed that now Sunday found herself threatened by a woman "so ruthless that the specter of divorce looms over Black Swan Hall." Excuse us. Isn't this where we came in? It was a vicious cycle.

In between the murders and lesser atrocities, it was obvious that the bad women of this world weren't about to give up their attempts to put the bite on the somewhat vulnerable Lord Henry Brinthrope. He would be a genuine catch for most. Many more vixens would dedicate their passions and creative energies to snaring such a prize.

During World War II, radio stations and networks alike provided immeasurable service to the nation by offering special programs and series produced in conjunction with federal agencies. *Our Gal Sunday* was among a handful of soap operas cooperating with the Office of War Information (OWI) in the fall of 1942, helping explain the war to American radio listeners. Using characters within a story line to dramatize themes of wartime difficulties, the OWI provided an engaging, yet persuasive method of relating its messages. In a week in October that year, the cast of *Our Gal Sunday* highlighted the distress experienced by America's allies in their pursuit of the war.

Other soap operas devoting a week to similar emphases that fall included *Aunt Jenny's Real Life Stories, Big Sister, Life Can Be Beautiful, Ma Perkins, Portia Faces Life, Stella Dallas, We Love and Learn* and *Young Widder Brown*. Their combined effort was more than communicative and cooperative in nature. It had the added impetus of identifying the serials with reality, keeping them in touch with some larger issues going on in the world at that time. As a result, the characters and the stories themselves seemed more believable to audiences.

Let us briefly digress to consider the place that children occupied in daytime dramas. As a rule, both in *Sunday* and elsewhere in the serials, youngsters seldom filled their natural roles. Rather, they were most often presented within a story for the intention of adding difficulty to their parents' or guardians' lives. A very young child could be a cause for parental concern, a motive for maternal sacrifice, the object of a legal contest or an obstacle to marriage. Seldom were kids permitted to relate to others in commonly accepted ways for their ages. When their presence was immaterial to a currently evolving plot line, they seemed to be almost nonexistent.

Sunday and Lord Henry had three children: Lonnie, Davy and Caroline (the last two adopted). They were frequently referred to but seldom present. At breakfast one morning in a typical episode Lord Henry observed: "The children are late this morning." Sunday allowed: "I asked Kathy to serve their breakfast in the nursery ... I wanted to talk to you, Henry." Thus, fans knew the children were still living but only heard *about* their activities, not *from* them. On very rare occasions the offspring actually spoke lines of dialogue (usually through an adult child impersonator). But what they really contributed to that serial was the underscoring of an old adage: "Children should be seen and not heard." In *Sunday's* case, only in an infinitesimal portion of the program's life did they actually make appearances.

The same was true of *Young Widder Brown's* juvenile son and daughter. For nearly two decades the heroine's status "with two fatherless children to support" was cited on a daily basis in the soap opera's epigraph: "The story of the age-old conflict between a mother's duty and a woman's heart." In reality, however, matters of the heart almost always took precedence over interactions with that heroine's offspring. It was a constant reminder that although children might be important subjects for discussion, their presence wasn't required in serials to promote such deliberation.

The serial's focus question—"Can this girl from the little mining town in the West find happiness as the wife of a wealthy and titled Englishman?"—was first posed on March 29, 1937. It continued to be asked all the way to January 2, 1959, nearly 22 years later. Aside from its durability, the serial had another distinguishing characteristic. It entered the CBS daytime schedule at 12:45 p.m. Eastern Time in 1937. When it disappeared from the daytime program logs in 1959, it still occupied that *same* quarter-hour, having never held any other time slot. No other soap opera enjoyed that advantage for that long. (It could also probably be considered a godsend to be heard at the height of millions of Americans' lunch hour, when the potential for a greater audience was substantially increased.)

Two other serials lasting a decade or more occupied single time periods throughout their network tenures. *Stella Dallas* never left the security of its 4:15 p.m. quarter-hour at NBC in more than 17 and a half years. For obvious reasons, *Wendy Warren and the News,* with its midday headlines dispatch, was also a fixture in its broadcast slot. It aired at 12 o'clock noon for 11 years over CBS. But these serials fell shy of *Sunday's* impressive record of over two decades in a single time period.

Like with many of its long-running contemporaries, *Sunday* assembled a loyal cast of regulars who remained with it for many years. Its two leading roles were filled by only four actors and actresses.

Originated by Dorothy Lowell in Chicago, the part of Sunday was temporarily transferred in 1946 to Vivian Smolen while Lowell was on maternity leave. When Lowell died in childbirth, Smolen assumed the part on a permanent basis and carried it to the end of the run. Lowell was among those playing the lead on *The Man I Married*. She also worked in other serials—*Hilltop House, Lora Lawton* and *Trouble House.* Lowell was only 28 when she met her untimely death on July 1, 1946.

Smolen, a New York City native, appeared as one of three offspring on *Doc Barclay's Daughters* (1938–40). She is well remembered for the long-running role on *Stella Dallas* of Laurel Dallas Grosvenor (to Stella, "Lolly-Baby"), in which she soberly referred to Stella as "Mummy." (Her two-episode-a-week contract guarantee assured her of appearing there a minimum of twice weekly. Often she was in the story line five days a week.)

She was introduced to radio via the *NBC Children's Hour* on Sunday afternoons. Host Milton Cross labeled her "the girl with the sympathetic voice." Others apparently detected that too. Smolen was featured as Veronica Lodge, *Archie Andrews'* love interest, and had another recurring role on *Front Page Farrell*. She also took part in *Mr. Keen, Tracer of Lost Persons* on several occasions.

A scholar of the genre suggested that Smolen's portrayal of Sunday was "unforgettable." Smolen played Sunday with "a plaintive coolness and a dignity that made you feel that no man ... was really worthy of her."[3]

In the fall of 1958, Smolen reflected to this author on her years in the role of a soap opera heroine. Her comments provide some fascinating insights into the behind-the-scenes action:

> The show goes on the air at 12:45 p.m. The cast is called for rehearsal at 11:45 a.m. That is the first time I see the script. We spend a few minutes marking our scripts, discussing what we all did the night before, the events of the day, etc.
>
> Then we read the show for time. The director, Arthur Hanna, and the actors ask for changes in words or constructions they might find difficult. Sometimes we get the change and sometimes we just have to say it as written. Then there is more passing the time of day.
>
> At 12:15 we do a dress rehearsal. More cuts if necessary — until about five minutes till air time.
>
> I enjoy my work. I adore it. I work with a wonderful group of people and we laugh a good deal. We respect one another and like each other.
>
> I occasionally do other radio programs but there is not much work in New York right now.[4]

Smolen's words turned out to be prophetic. Six weeks later, *Our Gal Sunday* and three of its long-running peers —*Backstage Wife, Road of Life* and *This Is Nora Drake*— were off the air. (In April 1998 she recalled to this author that the way she learned of her show's fate was by reading it in the newspaper.) For many actors and actresses, the good times had come and gone. And regretfully, they would never return.

Smolen, who had just married in December 1958, went on to make radio commercials after her series departed. She is still married to the same man, and the couple resides in a Florida apartment.

The role of Lord Henry was carried initially by Karl Swenson and then by Alistair Duncan for the remainder of *Sunday's* long run. Aside from the part of Lord Henry, Swenson is best remembered for the title role of *Lorenzo Jones*, in which he starred for the 18 years of that series' run, 1937–55. Late in *Sunday's* run Duncan picked up where Swenson left off. With no other distinguishing radio credits, he was also the voice of Phineas Fogg on the NBC-TV cartoon series *Around the World in 80 Days* (1972–73).

For most of her radio career, Vivian Smolen played Lady Sunday Brinthrope, who sought happiness "as the wife of a wealthy and titled Englisman," Lord Henry Brinthorpe, on *Our Gal Sunday*. In real life Henry was the actor Karl Swenson. Swenson also appeared on *Lorenzo Jones* as the title character throughout that serial's long run. (Photofest)

Sunday and Lord Henry's best friends and nearest neighbors, Irene and Peter Galway, were portrayed by the prominent radio thespians Fran Carlon and Joseph Curtin. Carlon played the title role in the TV version of *Portia Faces Life* (1954–55), in which Karl Swenson was the masculine lead. She also appeared in TV's *As the World Turns* as Julia Burke (1968–75). She was Lorelei Kilbourne in radio's *Big Town*. For a time she carried the title role in the radio serial *Kitty Keene, Incorporated*. She had recurring parts in *Lora Lawton, Girl Alone, Ma Perkins, Today's Children, Attorney at Law, A Woman of America* and *The Story of Mary Marlin*. She worked other dramatic series too: *Joan and Kermit, The Chicago Theatre of the Air* and *Blackstone, the Magic Detective*. A native of Indianapolis, she died on October 4, 1993, at the age of 80.

Curtin, a native of Cambridge, Massachusetts, was born on July 29, 1910. He graduated from Yale University's School of Drama, then appeared in Shakespeare's *The Merchant of Venice* in an early 1930s Broadway production. A 1934 part in *Roses and Drums* was his initiation into radio. His most celebrated role would be as the male lead in the weekly lighthearted detective series *Mr. and Mrs. North* in the 1940s and 1950s. Curtin kept recurring parts in *Backstage Wife, David Harum, Myrt and Marge, Second Husband* (title role), *Hilltop House, The Thin Man* (in which he played the male lead for a time), *John's Other Wife* (playing the male lead for a while), *The Story of Bess Johnson, Stella Dallas, Young Widder Brown* and *Her Honor, Nancy James*. The prominent actor, whose distinctive voice was readily recognized by fans, died in Los Angeles on April 5, 1979.

The best remembered of *Sunday's* announcers, Ed Fleming, also narrated *The Light of the World* and *Mr. Keen, Tracer of Lost Persons*. Twice daily he was heard by audiences for the same sponsor, American Home Products. At 12:45 p.m. he narrated *Our Gal Sunday* on CBS. He returned to the microphone at 5:45 p.m. to announce NBC's *Front Page Farrell*.

Jean Carroll's success in writing *Our Gal Sunday* has been duly noted. Even before her turn, however, the program was earning accolades for its scripts. *Variety* referred to a Christmas 1941 episode in which Sunday read a fairy story to Caroline and Davy, her adopted children. It was "a memorable example of how impressive commercial drama can be, but rarely is," said the show business industry ledger.

Many wares were advertised on the drama over the years. Frequently the program carried a hitchhike plug for Kolynos toothpaste. But the most consistently advertised commodity, the one most closely identified with the program, was Anacin. This headache, neuritis and neuralgia remedy was often mentioned on multiple radio series for several decades. With little variation in advertising copy from show to show and year to year, listeners could say the words of Anacin's commercial messages right along with Ed Fleming and his contemporaries:

> Anacin is like a doctor's prescription ... that is, it contains a combination of medically proven active ingredients in easy-to-take tablet form....
>
> So many listening to me now have had an envelope containing Anacin tablets given them by their dentist or physician....
>
> I'll spell the name for you ... A-N-A-C-I-N. Anacin. At any drug store in handy boxes of twelve and thirty tablets and economical family-size bottles of fifty and one hundred....
>
> The first few tablets are guaranteed to give you the relief you seek or your money will be refunded in full.

It would have been difficult in those days to have tuned in regularly to *Mr. Keen, Tracer of Lost Persons* or *Front Page Farrell* or *Our Gal Sunday* or another American Home Products series without thinking of those words as Fleming read them. Thinking them — and even repeating them aloud in many cases — must have become habitual to some listeners. As a consequence, all that repetition undoubtedly reinforced the product's name when consumers appeared at the pharmacy counter for a pain killer — which was, of course, what the advertiser hoped would happen.

In the end, did Sunday find happiness as the result of her 22-year search for it? Did this pure, innocently faultless, utterly faithful spouse succeed in avoiding the situations that made her, on occasion, appear to be compromising to those whom she cherished most?

Our opinion is that as her decades-long pilgrimage drew to a close, Lady Brinthrope did discover that elusive ecstasy she had pursued for so long, if only for an instant. Though her reverie may have been short-lived, given the unstable characters that Fairbrooke bred, she found her moments of bliss as the wife of a wealthy and titled Englishman.

17
Pepper Young's Family
(The House That Camay Built)

It took three name changes for this compelling little drama to get up to speed before turning into the extraordinary tale of life in a typical post–Depression home. When it emerged at last, it turned into one of the best-loved stories of American fiction. And it brought to the forefront one of the most inventive talents that serialdom ever discovered. Elaine Sterne Carrington's attention to authenticity and detail and her obsession with making her narratives believable met with favorable public reaction. Of the major creators of soap operas, she alone claimed to have dictated every word of every script bearing her name. *Pepper Young's Family* and its predecessor titles aired for 27 years, rivaling other washboard weepers at the zenith of the longevity scale. Starting as a weekly nighttime frolic similar to *The Aldrich Family*, this lighthearted tale of a teenage youth and his kin evolved over time into a serious melodrama. With less pathos and heartache than its counterparts, the serial had its darker moments too. Eventually the central character grew to manhood, becoming a responsible member of society. His family's exploits were so popular that the program was broadcast three times daily, the only soap opera ever to attain such exalted status.

Directors: John Buckwalter, Chick Vincent, Edwin Wolfe
Writers: Bob Carrington, Elaine Sterne Carrington, Pat Carrington
Music: William Meeder
Sound Effects: Ross Martindale
Announcers: Martin Block, Alan Kent, Richard Stark
Larry (Pepper) Young: Curtis Arnall (1934–37), Lawson Zerbe (1937–45), Mason Adams (1945–59)
Peggy Young: Elizabeth Wragge
Mary Young: Marion Barney
Sam Young: Bill Adams, Thomas Chalmers, Jack Roseleigh
Linda Benton Young: Eunice Howard
Others: Grace Albert, Tony Barrett, Bert Brazier, Alan Bunce, Blaine Cordner, Michael Fitzmaurice, G. Swaye Gordon, Richard Gordon, Larry Haines, George Hall, Stacy Harris, Fred Herrick, Irene Hubbard, Leon Janney, John Kane, Virginia Kaye, James Krieger, Greta Kvalden, Ron Lackmann, Jean McCoy, Maureen McManus, Burgess

Meredith, Madeleine Pierce, Bob Pollock, Elliott Reid, Joanna Ross, Cecil Roy, Laddie Seaman, Annette Sorell, Jean Sothern, Katharine Stevens, Chester Stratton, Arthur Vinton, Charles Webster, Edwin R. Wolfe, more

Theme: "Au Matin"

Sponsors: From its inception until 1957, this was a Procter & Gamble (P&G) program, advertising Camay soap for most of its years. Product identification was very strong. In its early days the drama advertised P&G White Naptha soap and Duz detergent. Toward the end of P&G's association, sponsorship again diversified, plugging Fluffo shortening, Tide detergent and Joy dishwashing liquid. Like most of its contemporaries, the show was sold to participating sponsors after P&G withdrew.

Ratings: Throughout the 1940s and until the mid–1950s, the numbers never fell below 5.0. When the show was broadcast on more than one network, figures soared multiple times into double digits, reaching a high of 14.4 twice (1938–39, 1940–41). When broadcast singly, the series climbed to a lofty 9.4 (1949–50). Low: 3.1 (1955–56). (Note: figures are through 1956.)

On the Air: When this series moved to daytime, it occupied almost a dozen quarter-hour time periods on all four radio networks. For five seasons it was broadcast on dual networks. The drama attained the unthinkable in 1937–38, airing on *three* networks daily — NBC Blue at 11:15 a.m. ET, MBS at 1:30 p.m. and NBC at 3:00 p.m. — a feat no other regularly scheduled commercial series achieved. The soap opera's most enduring segment was at 3:30 p.m. on NBC (1938–56): as *Red Adams*, Oct. 2, 1932–1933, NBC Blue, Sunday, 10:30 p.m. ET (30-minute format); 1933, NBC Blue, Sunday, 8:30 p.m. (30-minute format); as *Red Davis*, 1933–34, NBC Blue, Monday-Wednesday-Friday, 8:45 p.m.; 1934–35, NBC Blue, Monday-Wednesday-Friday, 7:30 p.m.; 1935–36, NBC Blue, Monday-Wednesday-Friday, 8:00 p.m.; *Forever Young*, Jan. 13, 1936–June 26, 1936, NBC, 3:00 p.m.; *Pepper Young's Family*, June 29, 1936–May 27, 1938, NBC, 3:00 p.m.; 1937, NBC Blue, 10:30 a.m.; 1937–38, NBC Blue, 11:15 a.m., also MBS, 1:30 p.m.; May 30, 1938–Jan. 6, 1956, NBC, 3:30 p.m.; 1938–39, NBC Blue, 11:30 a.m.; 1939–40, NBC Blue, 11:00 a.m.; 1940–41, NBC Blue, 10:45 a.m.; April 6, 1942–Oct. 15, 1943, CBS, 2:45 p.m.; Jan. 9, 1956–April 13, 1956, NBC, 4:30 p.m.; April 16, 1956–Jan. 2, 1959, NBC, 3:45 p.m.

MUSIC: Piano-organ arrangement of "Au Matin"
ANNOUNCER: (Theme under) The Camay beauty soap program.... Camay, the mild beauty soap for a smoother, softer complexion, brings you *Pepper Young's Family*.
MUSIC: Theme up to conclusion
ANNOUNCER: Say, do you know what I'm absolutely positive of? I know a lot of women are going to have younger, lovelier-looking complexions just because they heard this song....
MUSIC: Piano roll

ANNOUNCER: Listen….
MALE VOCALIST: (Sings over piano accompaniment)
    Did you know that just one cake of Camay…
    Can mean a smoother, softer skin?
    Say, did you know that just one cake of Camay…
    Is the way you should begin?
    You ought to try it now,
    You'd better start today;
    The Camay mild soap diet is the lovely woman's way…
    For a softer and more glamorous complexion…
    Camay … Camay … Camay!
ANNOUNCER: Yes, you'll see a real improvement in your complexion if you'll change from incorrect skin care to regular, mild Camay care. Doctors' skin specialists tested Camay care. They had a whole group of women follow regular care with Camay. And those doctors reported … definitely smoother, lovelier complexions for most of those women. So, follow the Camay mild soap diet. Directions are on the wrapper. And I promise … with your very first cake of Camay … you'll have a lovelier-looking skin … yes, a softer, a smoother complexion.
MALE VOCALIST: (Sings over piano accompaniment)
        Just one cake the Camay way…
        Your very first cake, and you will say…
        Camay … Camay … Camay!
MUSIC: Pick up a few bright notes for transition
ANNOUNCER: (Music under) And now…
MUSIC: Pick up a couple of bright notes
ANNOUNCER: *Pepper Young's Family*, written by … Elaine Carrington.

As most announcers were fond of saying in days of yore, "We'll return to our story in a moment." But first … who *was* Elaine Carrington? And why did she receive top billing at the start of this drama? For answers to those questions, stay tuned. We *will* return to our story of Pepper Young … in a moment.

Following the incredible output of the radio soap opera factory headed by Frank and Anne Hummert and Irna Phillips' modified approach in fleshing out her scripts — in which she wrote part of it herself, notoriously producing copy on a manual typewriter, copy that was sometimes read within moments of its being written, by actors who were already on the air — the third-most-prolific creator of the genre was Elaine Sterne Carrington.

The major difference between her programs and the others was that Carrington didn't employ an assembly-line approach like they did — using staffers who took her plot sketches and filled in the dialogue. Not her. Nor did she bother with a typewriter. Instead she spoke *every word* of her characters' lines into dictating equipment while acting out each part. After the scripts were transcribed by clerical help, instead of delegating an editor to do it, she personally made the cuts and revisions.

At about ten o'clock every Monday morning she would stretch out on a large davenport at her home near the waters of Long Island Sound and begin dictating. Her weekly volume exceeded 38,000 words — more than two billion words annually! Working around the clock, she at times talked past midnight. Unless unusual circumstances prevailed, she finished a week's work by Thursday night and recuperated for three days, normally relaxing with her family.

Carrington didn't listen to playbacks of her dictation. Only rarely did she hear one of her own shows. Yet she loved to drop in on rehearsals unannounced. On those occasions, she defended her dialogue to the wall against any alterations a cast member or director might request.

Her most durable serials — *Pepper Young's Family, Rosemary* and *When a Girl Marries* — lasted more than a decade. *Pepper* and its three predecessors (*Red Adams, Red Davis* and *Forever Young*), out of which *Pepper's* story line grew, were on the air for 27 years.

Like Phillips and the Hummerts, Carrington also had some casualties among her dramas by installment. *Trouble House* appeared as an open-ended serial in an omnibus 1936–37 bag called *The Heinz Magazine of the Air*. It didn't make it beyond that year. Her other washboard weeper on radio, *Marriage for Two*, appeared briefly during the 1949–50 and 1951–52 seasons. The series simply never caught on with enough listeners.

Her single venture into televised serials failed too. *Follow Your Heart* (1953–54) was canceled by NBC after only five months on the air. Nonetheless, some observers believed Carrington's talent was equal to that of Phillips', perhaps exceeding it. Even though her one attempt at television ended and her serial volume was no match to that of Phillips, she certainly had the ability to influence drama on the small screen as much as Phillips ultimately did. Given a few more years of opportunity, she might have done just that.

Literary critics confirmed the superiority of her serials. One observer termed her "the most literate of all soap writers."[1] Another noted that when Carrington expanded the number of shows for which she was writing, the additions "did not appear to dilute the quality of her product."[2] Yet another classified her *Pepper Young's Family* as "one of the best scripted soaps."[3]

Perhaps as a result of the widely publicized experience of the indomitable Phillips — who lost an important, precedent-setting legal battle over the ownership of material she created — Carrington retained ownership of all her serials. Thus, she was credited on virtually every broadcast as a drama's writer. She became one of only a handful of daytime scribes whose name was well-known by the radio audience.

By the late 1940s, Carrington's annual earnings were estimated at nearly a quarter of a million dollars. This figure reportedly made her the highest paid serials author. Her celebrated status and wealth permitted her, as a founder of the Radio Writers Guild, to buttress the positions of writers whose work commanded less notoriety, influence and income.

Carrington's success allowed her to maintain three homes: a New York penthouse apartment, a waterfront estate on Long Island and another residence in Florida. Her high income, much of it from her efforts on Procter & Gamble shows (including *Pepper Young's Family* and *Rosemary*), entitled her to truthfully call her Bridgehampton waterfront retreat "the house that Camay built." For most of the years that *Family* was on the air, the program's commercials featured Camay, "the soap of beautiful women," as the sole P&G commodity. (Camay was the first P&G product advertised on network radio. In 1927 the firm's colored perfumed toilet soap sponsored a weekly Friday-morning NBC series called *Radio Beauty School*.)

A silver-haired, full-bosomed woman with a mischievous, gregarious personality, Carrington often dotted her writing with humor. Young characters routinely surfaced within her plots, another hallmark giving her a basis for sprinkling her dialogue with colloquialisms. Her ability to contrive, alter, improvise and overcome virtually anything was believed to have mesmerized, perplexed and sometimes incensed those with whom she worked. So relaxed was she that on some public occasions she showed up adorned in lace and old tennis shoes. She chain-smoked cigarettes, enjoyed risqué tales and appeared oblivious to what anybody thought. She even slipped double entendres into her scripts to see if she could get away with them.

It wasn't unusual for the infamous author to unhesitatingly brush past studio warning signs flashing the cautious "On the Air" message. To no one in particular she would bellow: "Are you all on the air?" Mary Jane Higby, heroine of Carrington's long-running *When a Girl Marries*, observed, "She just didn't give a damn!"

Although Carrington was required by her advertising agency to submit a proposed annual story outline, conveniently or otherwise she was usually unable to abide by her submissions. She preferred to see her characters grow in unrestrained ways from the positions in which they found themselves, without pressure from preconceived notions.

She prided herself on her romantic scenes and adamantly refused to allow them to be altered. They often contained such effusive lines as, "I'd like to give you the whole world as a bauble to swing at your wrist."

After Carrington's death on May 4, 1958, at the age of 66, the writing of *Pepper Young's Family*— her only serial still on the air (which survived her by eight months)— passed to her grown children, Bob and Patricia.

A native New Yorker, Carrington could be deemed a success by every measure. Well-educated, married to an attorney and the mother of two, she earned a noteworthy reputation as a magazine writer of obvious merit. Initially accumulating a sizable number of rejection slips for her short stories, when she finally experienced a breakthrough with publishers she was able to sell her articles to many slick magazines: *Collier's, Good Housekeeping, Harper's, Ladies' Home Journal, Pictorial Review, Redbook, Saturday Evening Post* and *Woman's Home Companion*. Furthermore, she wrote a successful Broadway play, *Nightstick*, which enjoyed a fair run. The production was twice turned into screenplays, each time under the title *Alibi*.

Her foray into serial writing at age 40 was something of a fluke, however. In 1932, driven by a rainstorm into the NBC building in New York, she waited for a break in the weather. There she struck up a conversation with the network's head of program continuity. He encouraged her to try writing a radio play. Carrington returned a short time later with a sketch for a family drama. She later recalled:

> I stopped in one day at the National Broadcasting Company with a one-act play of mine.... It was called "Five Minutes from the Station." They read it at NBC and liked the dialogue and sent for me and asked me if I would care to tackle a serial. The idea appalled me. I didn't feel I could keep any idea going for any length of time, as my true medium was the short story. However, they prevailed upon me to prepare two audition scripts, which I did, and these were the scripts that became *Red Adams*.

> I should have said, when they asked me to do a serial, that I
> had no idea what to write about. I should have said, frankly,
> that all I knew about was an American family, such as I was
> trying to raise myself, and that, if this idea appealed to them,
> I'd take a fling at it.
>
> Thus, *Pepper Young* was born. It was then, and still is, the
> story of an average American family doing their darndest to
> give every advantage to a son and daughter, to understand
> them and encourage them and correct their faults. It seemed to
> me that in this time of flux, the only thing stable was Ameri-
> can family life itself. And that is what I built the story
> around — the very best family life I could possibly offer my
> public.[4]

Red Adams, a forerunner of *Pepper Young's Family*, first appeared on October 2, 1932, on the NBC Blue network as a half-hour sustaining feature. The *New York Times* carried this announcement on its radio page the day before the debut:

> "Red Adams" Appears — Elaine Sterne Carrington, whose sto-
> ries have hitherto found their way between magazine covers
> and into celluloid, now turns to a new medium, the micro-
> phone. Beginning tomorrow, her sketch, "Red Adams," will be
> presented for WJZ's audience at 10:30 p.m.

Red Adams was the story of a typical middle-class, happy-go-lucky teenager (who *did* have red hair) and his family. The Adamses, including mother, father and Red's younger, often obnoxious sister, lived in the small fictitious hamlet of Oak Park.

A popular fan magazine of that day, *Radioland*, specified that the straits in which Adams found himself resulted in "a riot of laughs and dramatic episodes." Sometimes the plot merely concerned Red's need to borrow the family automobile and his mother would intervene with Red's dad. Often Red would be tangled in scrapes with the opposite gender, usually older women, with whom he fathomed himself in love. For one reason or another his one-sided fantasies never worked out. Conveniently, the loose ends would be tied up by the end of the program.

After a short interval, the 30-minute show was moved two hours earlier, to 8:30 p.m. Eastern Time, still airing on the Blue network. Within 90 days of its inception, the series attracted a sponsor, bringing yet another change. *Red Adams*, with a rather insatiable quest for its identity, was known for the next three years as *Red Davis*.

Its new sponsor, Beech-Nut gum, had prevailed on its advertising agency, the net-work and Elaine Carrington to alter the title. One of Beech-Nut's major competitors was the Adams Gum Company. In no way was Beech-Nut about to give even tacit approval of Adams by sponsoring a series with a rival's name in the title. Without explanation, then, the Adams family became the Davises.

The show was destined for further changes. In its second season, 1933–34, it became a three-times-a-week 15-minute series aired at 8:45 p.m. on NBC Blue. That format carried for two years at varying evening hours.

The program reverted to a sustaining basis in 1935. On January 13, 1936, it moved to the daytime, joining the NBC network. At that juncture, for both creative and pragmatic reasons, the serial's name was altered once again, this time to *Forever Young*. It joined another popular feature, *The Goldbergs*, which also shifted to daytime. The dual dramas followed a path opened by *The O'Neills*, which had successfully jumped from nighttime to the sunshine three months earlier. (Not all night-to-day transfers enjoyed a satisfactory outcome: *Myrt and Marge* experienced a rough time when it moved to the daylight hours, with a diminishing audience and the unforeseen sudden death of the actress playing Marge.)

    Forever Young, *The Goldbergs* and *The O'Neills* were quick to capture the market for family epics. (Several prewar introductions never seriously caught on with listeners. Included were *Those Happy Gilmans*, *Your Family and Mine*, *The Carters of Elm Street*, *The Andersons*, *The Bartons*, *The Johnson Family* and *We, the Abbotts*. Regarding *The Andersons*, the trade paper *Variety* stingingly criticized it as "a first class example of a vacuum wedded to static." That particular venture, in the spring of 1942, lasted a mere 14 weeks.)

    The protagonist in *Forever Young* was Larry Young; he too sported locks of red hair, a holdover from earlier days. Other figures in the soap opera adopted a new nickname for Larry, soon calling him "Pepper." Only a few months down the road, on June 29, 1936, the show's title made yet one more turn, emerging as *Pepper Young's Family*. Procter & Gamble acquired sole sponsorship. In less than four years, the series had outgrown three monikers — more name changes than any other dishpan drama would ever experience.

    In addition to Pepper, the Young family included his father, Sam, his mother, Mary, and his sister, Peggy. They weren't quite as prosperous as their predecessors, the Davises and the Adamses. But they were still considered middle-class Americans. They spoke less of educating their son at Yale and didn't maintain a room in their home known as the library, as the Davises had.

    They lived in the fictitious town of Elmwood, somewhere in the Midwest, a region where so many of the characters in serial dramas resided. Sam, a man of simple likes and ambitions, was a banker by trade; Mary was a typical housewife. (Most women of that era didn't work outside the home.) Pepper aspired to a career as a writer. He grew up to be a newspaper journalist for the *Free Press*, the town mayor and a public relations specialist for an oil company.

    Peggy fell in love with dashing young Carter Trent of Chicago, who came from what would probably now be classified as a dysfunctional family. He moved to Elmwood and proposed to her in 1941, telling her how splendid their lives would be if only he could find an occupation paying him seven dollars a day. "I love you, darling, and I expect to go on loving you more every time I see you," he told her. "Every time I'm near you, it's … well … it's just going to mount and mount until I don't know where it'll end. I guess nobody will ever have loved anybody as much as I love you." It was one of those tender, romantic moments that Elaine Carrington prided herself for having written.

    Red Adams/Davis' escapades, so reminiscent of those encountered by radio's illustrious Henry Aldrich, faded under Pepper Young. Instead, the plights of the other family members were pushed to the forefront. The early comedic diversions of the series dissipated, and the drama settled into middle age as a full-fledged daytime serial with some of the trials and tribulations that typically beset most characters of the genre.

    Mrs. Carrington's perception of soap opera advanced from her demonstrated skills in pulp fiction. While the writing habits of some of her contemporaries had developed along the lines of domestic novels, her frame of reference was a little more mature. The Youngs faced trials, but the audience could assume that their problems were plausible in almost any American family. The characters could actually have been real people. Listeners worried with the Young family over the simplest things — going on dates, attending social events and merely paying the bills in the Depression. The Youngs were called "your friends," and it must have appeared that way to the millions who heard them each day. This made for a much more believable soap opera than most of the others on the air. And it helped acquire large audiences and keep them satisfied for years.

The program's popularity remained strong well into the 1950s. Radio comedians Bob Elliott and Ray Goulding frequently parodied the series in that decade on their own network show. Sometimes they would offer a play-by-play description of a mythical baseball game between figures in two favored NBC serials, *One Man's Family* and "Pepper Young's group." Not only were the principals from the dramas activated in playing the various positions on the field, but Bob and Ray often "borrowed" talent from other serials to fill out their fantasies. While Fannie Barbour might be coming to bat for *One Man's Family*, Pepper Young might be pitching, with Ivy Trent stationed at first base and Mary Young out in left field. Meanwhile, "Lolly-Baby" (Stella Dallas's appellation for her daughter, Laurel) would be playing shortstop and Lord Henry Brinthrope, husband of *Our Gal Sunday*, was catching for Pepper's "group." It was a riotously hilarious farce and served to reinforce the esteem with which the soap operas were held by their fans.

During the drama's long association with Procter & Gamble, in the mid–1950s it also advertised Fluffo shortening, Tide detergent and Joy dishwashing liquid. Even revered sportscaster Red Barber was brought on to deliver the Fluffo commercials, although listeners may have questioned the idyllic connection he supposedly maintained with millions of housewives. In one commercial he gushed over a homemaker's prize-winning cake recipe made with Fluffo. He added to her "amazing results" description with such epithets as "that's the stomp-down truth," designed to reassure listeners of its authenticity. At best, it seemed dauntingly unbelievable.

Larry "Pepper" Young, the title character, was an easygoing, sometimes whimsical male who contradicted the melodramatic breeds found in most other washboard weepers. Moral, innocent, even peculiar at times, he often mixed solemnity and amusement. He was a wholesome, affable adolescent who emerged into a laid-back, naive adult.

His sister, Peggy, did marry the invincible Carter Trent and thereby hung the cue for many a chapter to follow. It wasn't that Trent himself was such an extraordinary character. But his mother, who frequently paid long visits to Elmwood, had plenty of peculiarities to suffer over.

Ivy Trent was a wealthy, self-serving, domineering mother-in-law who considered it her duty to maintain vigilance over the affairs of her son and his bride. In one sequence, she intervened in a developing relationship between her secretary, Miss Taylor, and Jerry Feldman, a pilot friend of Pepper's. Ultimately she drove them apart, something that utterly inverted Mary Young, who had been watching from the sidelines.

Later, Mrs. Trent paid a Chicago ruffian and his wife to go to Elmwood and be available to carry out anything she needed to have done. Listeners weren't exactly sure what she had in mind. Complications arose for Mrs. Trent when her thug imported his extramarital Chicago girlfriend. If it hadn't been obvious before, steady listeners had a clearer picture that Ivy Trent, accustomed to having things her way, was a tad unbalanced. Within a year, suspicions about her hysterical mental state were impartially confirmed.

Pepper's childhood sweetheart was Linda Benton, a lovely girl who in adolescence encouraged him to pursue his dream of becoming a writer. Somewhere along the way a young coworker of Pepper's, Diana, displaced Linda as his prospective bride. Listeners overheard some revealing thoughts on the situation on a warm summer day in 1945. Mrs. Young, an expectant Peggy Trent and the Youngs' housekeeper, Hattie, were sipping freshly made lemonade. Mrs. Young had been reading aloud from a letter just received from her husband, Sam, who was away on a fishing expedition.

> MARY: Oh, there's a note in your father's letter I didn't see. Let's see ... Hank says he can't get over his disappointment that Pepper's wife isn't to be Linda, but someone else. He says that Pepper and Linda belong together from way back.... And that, as Hank puts it, "Some folks is meant for each other. You can spot 'em a mile away. And Pepper and Linda are those kind of folks...."
>
> PEGGY: Oh mama, I honestly think that Diana is much better for Pepper than Linda *ever* was.
>
> MARY: Well, Pegs, darling, I can't go that far ... but I know that Pepper's going to marry Diana, and I do think she's a darling girl. There's nothing I can do about it.
>
> PEGGY: But mama, why should you *want* to do anything about it? Diana's so *right* for Pepper.... She'll make him a *wonderful* wife.
>
> MARY: I'm *sure* she will, but ... I'm not sure there isn't something in what Hank says.... I'm not sure that I won't *always* have the feeling, as Hank does, that Pepper and Linda are the two that belong together — that they were *meant* for each other.

In *The Sheltered Life*, Ellen Glasgow put it this way: "Women like to sit down with trouble as if it were knitting."

So whom did Pepper marry? Linda. She was an important part of the plot during the entire run. In much of the decade of the 1950s, for instance, she was preoccupied with depression and shame, unable to bear another child to replace one who was lost in a hospital fire.

In the late 1940s there was a prolonged sequence involving young Edie Hoyt, a girl whom the Youngs had adopted. She was living in the Youngs' home following the disappearance of her husband, Andy, "somewhere in South America" after his airplane crashed. (Radio seldom pinpointed a specific city, mountainous range, body of water or country where such events transpired. By taking in all of "South America," listeners couldn't develop an emotional reaction, favorable or unfavorable, to a particular segment of earth's inhabitants. In the audience's collective mind, this nebulous place was merely somewhere "South of the border.")

Edie maintained that Andy was still alive, even though more than a year had passed since the plane disaster. Eventually, the Youngs and Edie learned that a man was seen "deep in South America" who *might* be Edie's missing husband. (This was a rather large territory to spot one man in.) Sometime later it was confirmed that Andy was alive, "very ill in South America," recovering from his ordeal.

When, in 1951, Andy found his way home, a new set of anxieties developed, acutely disturbing to Pepper. Linda had been caring for Andy and Edie's baby, Edith. With the parents reunited, Linda no longer felt needed. In time, Pepper and Linda would become parents of Button. Carter and Peggy presented the elder Youngs with their first grandchild, Hal, in the mid–1940s. (On several serials, including this one, child impersonator Madeleine Pierce was called on for "goo-goo" and other cooing sounds at appropriate intervals.)

By 1950 the Youngs were coping with troubles closer to home than the reaches of far-flung South America. The Elmwood Bank, where Sam was employed, was robbed, and violence occurred during the heist. A security officer implicated Sam. Despite the highly respected position he had held for years in the community, Sam felt bound to resign his post. Incensed that anyone might think his dad was guilty, Pepper launched his own investigation to clear the tarnished Young name.

There were even darker days ahead for this soap opera. By 1953 Pepper and Linda moved into a new home on farmland owned by Sam. But their solitude was shaken when oil was discovered on the property. Could Sam have been justified in mortgaging his entire financial position to take advantage of such an unexpected windfall? Was he, as Mary insisted, misguided by a delusion that could only lead to tragedy?

The oil wells did erupt into heartache and tragedy. There was a fire at the site, destroying about half of Elmwood. Two people died, including Sam Young's best friend and business partner, Curt Bradley. Blaming himself for the disaster, Carter Trent, asleep at the site when the inferno erupted, wandered far from home. Unable to meet his accusers, for more than a year Carter lived the life of a nomad, traipsing hither and yon. In the end, he finally took his own life, never realizing that Sid Grayson had been convicted of starting the blaze. Carter's suicide left Peggy a widow and his children fatherless, and it had a devastating effect on his mother, Ivy Trent, who had already shown serious mental lapse.

It was a sad period in the lives of the Young family. Their drama purported to chronicle the events of a typical middle-class family. More than 15 years after Carter entered the story line, longtime listeners felt a sense of remorse in his tragic end. Mrs. Young's gloomy premonition about the disastrous consequences of the oil discovery was ultimately fulfilled.

The inner goodness of certain soap opera figures was not always subtly blended into their personalities. In numerous instances, audiences found their abiding, upright ideals blatantly moralizing. Mother Young was among those with an uncanny ability to articulate precisely how the majority of the radio audience felt on any given subject. Her disturbing revelation about Linda while Pepper was betrothed to Diana may have expressed the listeners' collective mind. In the same way, on Christmas day 1945, with her family gathered about her, she offered a petition resolutely expressing the gratefulness of a nation that was victorious in battle. Her words could have been echoed by millions who heard them:

> I'd like to say a little prayer just now at this minute ... a little
> prayer for all the families of those boys who gave their lives, so
> that we may continue our lives in the way those boys wanted
> us to do. And pray that God will fill their families' hearts with

love and pride ... for the courage those boys had, to make the supreme sacrifice so that we may be here today. So that we may have a world which they would have come back to with so much happiness in their hearts. By making their supreme sacrifice worthwhile ... by making the American way of life continue ... for letting our homes remain standing ... and for granting us an opportunity to make this a better world for everyone to live in ... so that there need never again be a war ... so that there need never again be the terrible loss of life ... that's what they've done for us — made all this possible. Bless them! And bless their memories, all! Amen.

On Christmas Day six years earlier — when her family surprised her by leaving their home on Harvey Street to return to the little house they had previously occupied on Union Street, a house that Mary Young had always loved most — she offered another prayer. It reflected a kinder, gentler age in which the supreme Deity was often paid honor in American homes. Although such thoughts might never get on the air in a dramatic series broadcast today, perhaps not even an eyebrow was raised as her petition was offered in 1939.

A prominent name associated with the stage and screen in later years, Burgess Meredith, initiated the roles of *Red Adams* and *Red Davis*. For three weekly quarter-hour broadcasts, plus repeat performances on those same nights for West Coast audiences (due to the three-hour time difference) of *Red Davis*, Meredith was paid a handsome Depression-defying sum of $350 per week. One night in 1934 he inadvertently missed the second show's performance. The director stepped in and attempted to imitate his voice. But the sponsor, Beech-Nut, was not impressed. Meredith was promptly fired.

In a short while the thespian, born on November 16, 1909, in Cleveland, Ohio, and educated at Amherst College, moved on to other roles. He appeared as an actor and host on radio's *Spirit of '41, The Cavalcade of America, Lincoln Highway* and *Inner Sanctum Mysteries*. He also worked on *The Pursuit of Happiness* and *We, the People*. In 1933 he appeared on the legitimate stage with a New York acting company. Following radio, Meredith eventually played on the big screen as a crusty trainer in *Rocky* and waddled as the Penguin on TV's *Batman*. His film credits included *Of Mice and Men, The Story of G. I. Joe, Magnificent Doll, Advise and Consent, McKenna's Gold, Grumpy Old Men, Grumpier Old Men* and *Tom, Dick and Harry*. The distinguished actor died on September 9, 1997, in Malibu, California.

Following Meredith's abrupt disappearance from the *Red Davis* cast, radio actor Curtis Arnall was tapped to succeed him. Arnall not only played the leads in *Red Davis* and *Forever Young* but also initiated the role of the infinitely more famous Pepper Young (1934–37 inclusive). Arnall was born on October 1, 1898, at Cheyenne, Wyoming. He was playing the title role of *Buck Rogers in the Twenty-Fifth Century* when he followed Meredith.

Arnall was active in radio from 1932 to 1942 with running parts on *The Adventures of Dick Tracy, Just Plain Bill, One Man's Family* and several other serials. Before and after that decade, he was employed as a broker, cowpuncher, fisherman and telegrapher. Before his radio experience, he performed in local theater and repertory companies. Arnall died on September 24, 1964, in Washington, D.C.

Veteran actor Lawson Zerbe followed as the next Pepper Young (1937–45). Zerbe's radio credits are legion. They include stints on *Against the Storm, Big Town, Counterspy, The Adventures of Frank Merriwell, Lora Lawton, Married for Life, Murder at Midnight, The*

Mysterious Traveler, The O'Neills, Road of Life, Rogue's Gallery, Valiant Lady and *Yours Truly, Johnny Dollar*. He died on August 18, 1992, at age 78.

Despite the impressive talents of the three thespians who preceded him, the role of Pepper Young belongs to Mason Adams. He carried it for 14 years, starting in 1945 and continuing until the end of the run. His voice, well identified across the 1980s and 1990s as the spokesman for Smucker's jams, jellies and preserves and other commercial ventures, is best recalled as the no-longer-adolescent hero of *Pepper Young's Family*.

Born in New York City on February 26, 1919, this versatile actor with the high-pitched, squeaky brogue was heard all over the radio dial. A few of Mason's recurring parts were in *Big Sister, Big Town, Gasoline Alley, Hearthstone of the Death Squad* and *Road of Life*. He had just been discharged from the U.S. Army when he signed for the role of Pepper Young, turning down a Chicago stage production of *Dear Ruth* because radio paid more.

Before the war, he acted in community theater, college and stock productions. He was introduced on Broadway in Saroyan's *Go Away Old Man*. He was spokesperson on scores of radio and television commercials after radio's Golden Age. Adams acted in the 1970s television series *Lou Grant* as newspaper managing editor Charlie Hume. American Tobacco, Ford and U.S. Steel also frequently cast him in their dramatic TV presentations.

Adams lauded radio for its "variety, spontaneity and quick-silvery quality," confirming that it "provided those of us who were lucky enough to do it well with much joy." Radio acting, he said, gave him "great pleasure and a comfortable living," even as it allowed him to strive for his "first love," the theater.[5]

Surprisingly, three major figures in the cast of *Pepper Young's Family* were never replaced, remaining with the series all the years it aired: Peggy Young Trent, Pepper's sister, portrayed by the actress Betty Wragge; their mother, Mary Young, played by Marion Barney; and Pepper's childhood sweetheart and then wife, Linda Benton Young, a role awarded to the actress Eunice Howard.

Betty Wragge, a native New Yorker born on September 22, 1918, began her alliance with *Red Davis* in 1933, missing *Red Adams* but moving to *Forever Young* and subsequently to the final series. She was relieved of duty — though never replaced — while in a conflicting Broadway production for two years. Wragge appeared in what is purported to have been the first commercial radio series employing child actors, *Gold Spot Pals*. It aired in 1927 on NBC when she was nine. She acted on several other NBC children's features, including a weekly nighttime children's anthology show, *Mary and Bob's True Stories* (1928–32). Following radio, she toured in musicals, dubbed Italian films into English, made TV commercials and surfaced in industrial and training videos.

Marion Barney landed matriarchal parts on *all* of Elaine Carrington's durable dramas! In Young, she was Mary. Filling out her day, she was Mother Davis on *When a Girl Marries* and Mother Dawson on *Rosemary*. In each, her soft-spoken words of wisdom and genteel spirit yielded the near-perfect mom and mother-in-law. She was there for *Red Adams, Red Davis* (in which she played *another* Mother Davis!) and *Forever Young*. She also appeared in the title role of a 1932 summer radio run, *Tish*.

Eunice Howard, as Pepper's wife, Linda, gained experience in the title role of the short-lived *Hello, Peggy* serial in 1937–38. She had recurring roles in a situation comedy, *The Grummits*, in *Pages of Romance*, another short-lived serial, and in one much better known, *The Story of Mary Marlin*.

Completing the family of Pepper Young, the part of Sam, the father, was portrayed by three actors: Jack Roseleigh, Bill Adams and Thomas Chalmers. Jack Roseleigh made his mark in radio on such series as *Buck Rogers in the Twenty-Fifth Century, Circus Days, Hilltop House, Road of Life* and *Roses and Drums*. The actor died at an untimely age 54 on January 5, 1940. Bill Adams, probably best remembered as Uncle Bill of *Let's Pretend* (1943–54), announced *The Peggy Lee Show*. Other radio credits were *Abie's Irish Rose, The Adventures of Mr. Meek, Big Town, The Cavalcade of America, The Collier Hour, The Eternal Light, The Gibson Family, The Light of the World, Ma Perkins, The March of Time, Rosemary, The Story of Mary Marlin* and *Your Family and Mine*. Born in Tiffin, Ohio in 1887, he died in New York on September 29, 1972. Chalmers' history in radio was limited. His only recorded contribution beyond *Pepper Young's Family* was as narrator for *The Cavalcade of America*. His death occurred on June 12, 1966, at age 82.

Two daytime dramas—*Ma Perkins* and *The Romance of Helen Trent*—exceeded 7,000 performances over approximately 27 years. But combined, *Red Adams, Red Davis, Forever Young* and *Pepper Young's Family* broadcast for a similar period, offering nearly 7,000 episodes before leaving the air in 1959.

Although dramas-by-installment could seldom be classified as literary masterpieces, *Pepper Young's Family* is one of the few to have come close. It realistically recounted a story that could be both understood and appreciated by mainstream middle-class Americans in the first half of the twentieth century. But for two factors, all of the serials birthed and nourished by Elaine Carrington might have attracted more caring authors to the field— writers whose contributions could have substantially lifted the quality of daytime programming: (1) A stampede developed to get as many serials on the air as quickly as possible in the latter years of the 1930s. (2) A single soap opera assembly line, with mass-production methods and little concern for creativity, dominated the genre while disregarding most of the potential merits of the end products.[6] That combination was enough to scare anybody who might have been duly concerned about his or her literary creation—wondering how it might be altered in the hands of ad agencies, sponsors, producers, directors and networks.

For her part, Carrington set lofty parameters. She took the time to dictate every single word while acting out all the parts, then clucked over her brood like a mother hen. Had her formula been taken in large doses, it might have strikingly raised the quality of daytime drama while offering critics a lot less to censure.

18
Perry Mason
(Murder and Mayhem in the Afternoon)

In the trilogy of formats (pulp fiction, radio, television) used to portray the best-recalled fictional attorney of all time, the populace seems to least remember the radio drama. Perhaps because *Perry Mason* was heard mostly by a few million homemakers, there is a tendency to ignore the fact that the great supersleuth was ever on radio. Yet for a dozen years he carried the tradition of an earlier print hero, becoming a forerunner of the "defender of human rights" admired on TV by people of both genders and still seen internationally in cablevision reruns. *Mason*, for sheer intrigue, was never more faithfully portrayed than through gripping moments in the theater of the mind. The drama was intense, often holding fans spellbound for weeks as Mason sought to trap a deranged demon before the rogue caught up to an intended victim. Unlike the TV series, on radio the criminal's identity was almost always known by the audience. The craftiness of the pursuer, hell-bent on destroying the pursued, would in time be overwhelmed by the mental dexterity of the brilliant lawyer. In the meantime, innocent lives were put in harm's way. Conceived by respected attorney-turned-author Erle Stanley Gardner, *Mason* was masterfully perfected on radio by the pen of Irving Vendig and the authoritative enunciation of the actor John Larkin. The series offered a diversion from the typical fare of most dishpan dramas. While it lasted, it gave fans mayhem aplenty as housewives conjured up images of unspeakable crimes provoked by some of radio's most dastardly rapscallions.

Producers: Tom McDermott, Leslie Harris
Directors: Hoyt Allen, Carlo De Angelo, Ralph Butler, Carl Eastman, Arthur Hanna
Writers: Ruth Borden, Erle Stanley Gardner, Dan Shuffman, Irving Vendig, Eugene Wang
Music: Paul Taubman, William Meeder
Sound Effects: Jimmy Lynch
Announcers: Bob Dixon, Alan Kent, Richard Stark
Perry Mason: Donald Briggs, Santos Ortega, Bartlett Robinson, John Larkin (1947–55)
Della Street: Joan Alexander, Jan Miner, Gertrude Warner
Paul Drake: Matt Crowley, Charles Webster
Lieutenant Tragg: Frank Dane, Mandel Kramer
Others: Maurice Franklin, Betty Garde, Mary Jane Higby, Arthur Vinton, more

Theme: Original melody

Sponsors: From its inception, the drama was governed by Pedlar and Ryan advertising
agency for Procter & Gamble (P&G), which plugged Camay soap in the early years. For
most of the run the show solely promoted Tide detergent, however.

Ratings: High: 8.6 (1949–50); low: 3.6 (1944–45). In ten of 12 seasons, figures remained
above 5.0. Median: 5.8.

On the Air: Oct. 18, 1943–March 31, 1944, CBS, 2:45 p.m. ET; April 3, 1944–March 23,
1945, CBS, 2:30 p.m.; March 26, 1945–Dec. 30, 1955, CBS, 2:15 p.m.

Perry Mason — the famous character created by Erle Stanley Gardner ... dramatized by Irving Vendig.
Perry Mason — defender of human rights ... champion of all those who seek justice.
                                        — Epigraph to *Perry Mason*

Does intrigue in the sunshine offer as much aura and mystique as tales shrouded under the
ominous clouds of impending darkness? One of radio's most chilling melodramas was
played out, surprisingly, every weekday afternoon for a dozen years to a fiercely loyal band
of listeners. Few people under the age of 50 can remember that television's most famous
attorney of all time, *Perry Mason*—who solved murder cases in closing witness-stand
sequences and kept audiences guessing the identities of culprits for nearly an hour each
week — was catapulted into that series by a successful radio soap opera.

    Nor will most know that the concept for one of television's most enduring and sus-
penseful early daytime dramas, *The Edge of Night*, was born out of sequences that the
famous lawyer-detective confronted in the *Mason* radio series. *Edge,* in fact, was a thinly
veiled version of *Mason.* Protagonist Mike Karr — initially a detective, later an attorney —
was Perry Mason, only under another name in that five-times-a-week drama. John Larkin,
the actor identified with the part of Perry Mason on radio, became *Edge's* original Karr.
(Procter & Gamble and CBS agreed in 1955 to transfer *Mason* from radio to TV as a thirty-
minute daytime serial. But *Mason* creator Erle Stanley Gardner wouldn't hear of it.
Undaunted, head radio writer Irving Vendig tinkered with the concept, hired Larkin and
put *Edge* on the air on April 2, 1956. When Gardner gave his blessing at last, the nighttime
Mason series debuted the following year.)

    By the time *Mason* reached CBS's fifteen-minute soap opera lineup on October 18,
1943, the character had already become familiar to millions of mystery-novel fans. In the
late 1920s Gardner, himself a southern California attorney, tried writing as a diversion.
Creating an imaginary alter ego whom he called Perry Mason, Gardner was successful in
turning his sideline craft into something more lucrative than a mere pastime. By the early
1930s, he had earned widespread public acclaim for a series of *Mason* mystery novels that
attracted large reading audiences.

    But the unanswered question remained: could a collection of avid crime readers and
simple homemakers be persuaded to transfer their loyalties from pulp fiction to a daytime

soap opera exploiting the escapades of the lawyer-turned-supersleuth? The advertising agency and network programmers were optimistic, believing a little daytime intrigue would offer fans an attractive alternative to the normal audio misery fare. For a dozen years, the serial became one of CBS's well-received daytime ventures.

The term "soap opera" was probably instigated in the entertainment trade press of the late 1930s, a few years before *Mason* arrived on radio. *Variety*, a bible of the industry, may have coined the term. By 1939 *Newsweek* and other national publications were referring to the "daytime dramatic serial" with easier-to-understand handles. Journalists preferred simpler names like "soap opera" and "washboard weeper." "Soap" in the term "soap opera" was derived from the fact that manufacturers of household and personal cleaning products took great interest in sponsoring serialized dramas. Foremost among these were Procter & Gamble, Lever Brothers, Colgate-Palmolive-Peet, B. T. Babbitt and Manhattan Soap.

Camay was the very first P&G product advertised on network radio, in 1927. The perfumed toilet soap, to be closely associated later with *Pepper Young's Family*, was selected by P&G to sponsor its new *Mason* series in 1943. Another brand—P&G's "new washday miracle"—would be linked with *Mason* in the minds of true devotees long after the series ended. A sprightly female vocalist sang daily to a bouncing melody: "Tide's in, dirt's out, T-I-D-E, Tide!"

And when the announcer exploited the virtues of Tide as a laundry detergent, reminding listeners, "Nothing else will wash as clean as Tide … yet is *so* mild," the vocalist belted out more of the liltingly buoyant tune, accompanied by the studio Wurlitzer:

> VOCALIST: Tide gets clothes cleaner than any soap…
> ANNOUNCER: (Inquiring) *Any* soap?
> VOCALIST: Yes, *any* soap! Tide gets clothes cleaner than any
>   soap … T-I-D-E. Tide!

The results of those commercials were phenomenal. Introduced in 1946, Tide became the most popular brand-name laundry product in history.[1] By 1949 it was the best selling washday commodity in the United States, a preeminence it held for nearly five decades. Although all of the credit for Tide's success can't be assigned to a single quarter-hour soap opera, this compelling drama contributed solidly to the product's launch.

At *Mason's* inception, Erle Stanley Gardner penned the scripts. The show's format at that juncture may have more closely paralleled what the TV version would become than at any other time. The first radio sequence was labeled "The Case of the Unwanted Wife," typifying action marked by a beginning and a conclusion (closed-ending).

The idea of a titled case was soon abandoned, however, perhaps at about the time Gardner grew weary of the rigors of churning out five daily installments of dialogue per week. He relinquished that duty to others, including the writer for whom *Mason's* authorship would become most laudably identified, Irving Vendig.

Under Vendig, the series flourished, reaching its stride by the late 1940s. He developed the central character into one whose prolonged yet absorbing action-packed exigencies caught the fancy of millions. As America's housewives attended to their ironing boards, dishpans and diapers, murder and mayhem in the afternoon must have been a welcome diversion.

Even though *The Guiding Light* may have injected more organ stings into soap opera than any other serial, an award for their appropriateness and effectiveness should go to *Mason's* keyboard virtuosos. Vendig's writing excelled in the way he used those sharp, disquieting chords at the most tactical moments. The musical director, Paul Taubman, and the instrumentalist William Meeder introduced them with a flourish. Convincingly, the unexpected stings held listeners at rapt attention as they awaited the next piece of defining monologue issued by announcer Richard Stark.

Meeder, an accomplished artist on several instruments, adroitly offered simultaneous organ and piano renditions of *Mason's* familiar theme as the program arrived and left the airwaves daily. (The theme was created especially for the program. Its first notes were later adapted to the opening of the familiar TV series theme by the same name. Of the durable radio serials, only two—*Mason* and *Pepper Young's Family*— adopted arrangements of their respective themes played on organ and piano together.)

Fans who followed one of TV's earliest and most abiding serials, *Search for Tomorrow,* in the 1950s witnessed numerous similarities between it and the *Mason* radio version. In its earliest years, *Search* was heavily flavored with large doses of intrigue accompanied by dramatic organ stings. There can be little wonder why: Vendig wrote this P&G-sponsored series too.

When Gardner's fictionalized stories made the jump from the printed page to the sound stage, all of the characters long familiar to avid readers went along as well. A full complement of helpers with whom Mason could dialogue included his trusted Girl Friday and right-hand confidante Della Street; the private detective Paul Drake, who did much of the important legwork on his cases; the police homicide detective Lieutenant Tragg, sometimes Mason's foil, at other times his peer; and Gertie Lade, his receptionist, adept at funneling important messages to Della and Perry at innocuous moments. But it was Mason—the dashingly handsome, virile, proper young lawyer-turned-detective—who made it work.

Mason was one of a handful of male professionals to receive top billing on a daytime serial. In three decades, the small number of serials exclusively bearing masculine designations included *Barry Cameron: The Soldier Who Came Home, David Harum, Dear John, Doctor Paul, Five Star Jones, Front Page Farrell, Just Plain Bill, Lorenzo Jones, Michael Flagg, M.D., Terry Regan: Attorney-at-Law* and *Young Doctor Malone.* (Even *Arnold Grimm's Daughter, Dan Harding's Wife, Doc Barclay's Daughters, John's Other Wife* and *Pepper Young's Family* don't qualify by this definition.)

Despite the popular image that most men on radio soap operas were mere weaklings, Mason and a few of his masculine peers dispelled—or, for a while, subdued—that old wives' tale. The supersleuth was brilliant—cool, calculating, a good match for even the most formidable foe who challenged good with evil. The situations in which Mason landed were guaranteed to fascinate fans, enrapturing them almost into a trance. Daily, not just occasionally, they clung to every word ... to every sound ... to every sting.

Listeners must have typically been on the edge of their seats on May 2, 1950. Announcer Dick Stark poignantly inquired in his articulate, decisive style:

> ANNOUNCER: At the moment, in Perry Mason's own hotel, a
> tragedy is being played out. And what do we know? We

> know this: on a bed in an apartment next to Perry Mason's,
> a young woman sobs her heart out.... And then, driven by
> her overwhelming despair and unreasoning emotions, she
> rises from that bed, walks to her dresser, opens the
> drawer....
> SFX: Phone rings over and over
> ANNOUNCER: (Phone ringing under) The telephone in her
> room blares an urgent summons, but Kay Clement, if she
> hears it, pays no attention.... Her mind is too full of her
> own bitter thoughts, with the seeming collapse of her own
> personal world....
> SFX: Clock ticks loudly
> ANNOUNCER: (Clock ticking under) Minutes pass. Kay's bitter
> sobbing grows less. And then.....
> SFX: Glass shatters as shots are fired, followed by...
> MUSIC: Sharp organ sting

Meanwhile, listeners learned that Mason and his secretary, Della Street, had interrupted their busy work schedule for a little sustenance. Downstairs, the pair was finishing an early dinner in the hotel dining room. Taking the elevator up to Mason's suite to resume working, they saw the door standing open to the Clement apartment. Calling out and receiving no answer, they stepped inside and discovered four smashed clocks on the floor and — at the end of the hall — Kay Clement. She was lying under a window, hardly breathing, wearing a watch, its face also smashed.

"What do you make of it, chief?" Della asked Mason.

"I'm not gonna try," he countered.

As they moved the young girl to Mason's residential quarters, a blue envelope dropped from Kay's hand.

"What do we do now? Call a doctor?" Della inquired, as the organ stingingly rose and faded to the episode's final commercial.

Following the Tide pitch, Stark's gripping monologue, delivered over a disruptive and disjointed organ backdrop, struck fear in the hearts of listeners. His words, as usual, were deliberately chosen, coolly calculated to retain the fans for subsequent mayhem:

> ANNOUNCER: As Perry Mason stands looking at the small,
> pathetic figure of Kay Clement, unconscious on his
> couch...[and] wonders what caused these strange events ...
> he has no idea that the key lies in the blue envelope Della
> saw drop from Kay's hand ... the blue envelope which is to
> lead to so much intrigue, excitement and heartbreak.
> MUSIC: Sharp organ sting
> ANNOUNCER: Won't you join us ... tomorrow?
> MUSIC: Theme begins

Six weeks later, in the episode of June 13, 1950, Mason and Street were still involved in the Clement sequence. By then a man named Gonzalez, identified as a drug pusher and "probably a killer," had vowed that his next mission was to locate and silence Clement. Clement, meanwhile, had eluded the protective police custody that was volunteered by Lieutenant Tragg. She was then hiding out in fear for her life. Who would reach her first —

Gonzalez or Mason? And who among those following that suspenseful action in Radioland could turn off their sets and fail to rejoin such captivating exploits again? Not many.

Some five years after the Clement sequence, Mason found himself involved with a determined, cunning, heinously immoral man named Sid Kenyon. Kenyon's penchant for becoming wealthy, and erasing from the face of the earth anyone who threatened his ends, was obvious. To him, an infant-switching ploy to further his goal was — no pun intended — "child's play." Kenyon had bigger quests in mind, like dispensing with an elderly well-to-do gentleman who was already in poor health. In so doing, he could gain a fortune. Kenyon arranged for a woman with obligations to himself to slowly poison the old man while Kenyon plotted to pin the crime on a third party whom they both despised. Would Mason catch on to Kenyon's diabolical scheme in time to save the old man?

In another sequence, a year earlier, Mason befriended Kate Beekman, at 19 one of the youngest unfortunates he ever encountered. Beekman was spun into the web of the tyrannical underworld figure Gordy Webber. Webber gave Beekman a job as a dancer in a nightclub that he owned and that fronted for organized crime. Pretending to fall in love with Beekman, Webber used her to get to her father. Ex-con Ed Beekman was sought by Webber's crime boss, known only as "The Big Fellow," for further evil intent. Meanwhile, Toni Fascina, a temperamental beauty who played the piano at Webber's club, fancied herself in love with Webber. She became enraged by his display of affection toward Kate Beekman. How could Mason extract this naive young damsel from a sinister plot that threatened to pull her into an abyss of despair and perhaps murder — her own or someone else's?

In another sequence, Gertie Lade, Mason's receptionist, was found beside the corpse of blackmailer Wilfred Palmer. Listeners knew that the flamboyant Allyn Whitlock had plunged a letter-opener into Palmer's heart. Seeking the identity of the mastermind behind an empire of crime spreading its tentacles across the region, Mason sent decoy Helen Henderson on a probe under the guise of a newspaper reporter. Henderson met Whitlock, not knowing that she had committed one murder already. Nor did Henderson know that Whitlock was the girlfriend of crime lord Walter Bodt, whom Mason sought. Henderson and Mason played a dangerous game; the slightest mistake could have been their last.

Radio's *Mason* and the courtroom lawyer who advanced to TV were in some ways worlds apart. As a start, different actors portrayed the roles of Perry, Della, Paul and Tragg in the two mediums. Ruggedly handsome actor John Larkin, the last to play Perry on radio, was reportedly disappointed when he wasn't chosen for the TV role. In the video version, who could forget the imposing figure of the burly actor tapped for it, Raymond Burr? Or his competent ally, Miss Street, played on TV by the demure Barbara Hale?

Did a cigarette ever cross Miss Street's lips? Not on TV. But in the radio drama, Mason and Street could be construed as nicotine addicts. Lighting up in no way diminished their abilities to pursue dangerous criminals. It was a part of the accepted lifestyle in the era in which they lived.

The witness-stand revelation of the real killer on the televised version was a dramatic departure from the radio drama. On radio, the audience usually knew who the bad guy (or gal) was quite early and what the villain's next move would be long before Mason discovered it. The mystique was often in the uncertainties lurking nearby. If Mason didn't make the moves the audience knew that he must make, what then? Bad things would happen to good people.

Bartlett Robinson (hero in *Portia Faces Life*) originated the role of Perry Mason, soon turning it over to Santos Ortega. Ortega is best recalled for a long stint as Grandpa Hughes on TV's *As the World Turns* (1956–76). He was featured in many radio title roles: *The Adventures of Ellery Queen, The Adventures of Nero Wolfe, The Affairs of Peter Salem, Bulldog Drummond, Charlie Chan* and *Hannibal Cobb*. In *City Hospital* and *Who Dun It?* he was the lead. He narrated *Green Valley, USA* and had running roles in *The Shadow, Myrt and Marge* and *The Man I Married*. He frequently appeared in *Boston Blackie, Criminal Casebook, The Light of the World* and *Dimension X*. Born in New York City, this versatile actor could play roles with many dialects. He died on April 10, 1976, at age 70 at Fort Lauderdale, Florida.

As Mason, he was succeeded by Donald Briggs, who had running parts in *Dick Daring's Adventures, Girl Alone, Betty and Bob, David Harum, Hilltop House, Portia Faces Life, The Story of Bess Johnson* and *Welcome Valley*. Briggs announced the *What's My Line?* radio series (1952–53), carried title roles in *Death Valley Sheriff* and *The First Nighter* and appeared in the dramatic company of *Grand Hotel*. He played the lead on *City Desk* and the male lead in *The Adventures of the Abbotts*. He died on February 3, 1986, at age 75.

But doubtlessly, John Larkin is the man all radio listeners remember as Mason. He entered the role on March 31, 1947, and played Mason to the end of the run on December 30, 1955. For almost three-fourths of the radio span, Larkin breathed life into Gardner's defender of innocence. Helping to make Vendig's and others' scripts sparkle, Larkin offered a fascinatingly quick-tempered interpretation of the attorney.

A Kansas City, Missouri, native, Larkin was a graduate of the University of Missouri and married the radio actress Teri Keane. Only a station break separated the pair for years. Keane immediately preceded Larkin at two o'clock on CBS when she played the heroine of another popular serial, *The Second Mrs. Burton*, which was followed by *Mason* at 2:15. In 1956, a few months after *Mason's* cancellation, the *Burton* drama inherited *Mason's* old time slot. Larkin soon launched the role of Mike Karr as *The Edge of Night* debuted on CBS-TV, carrying it until illness forced his retirement at the end of 1961. The 52-year-old actor met an early death on January 29, 1965. The year before, Teri Keane had joined the cast of Larkin's old serial, *Edge of Night*, in the major role of Martha Marceau. She continued with the part until 1975.

Larkin's radio accomplishments included casting as leads in *Buck Rogers in the Twenty-Fifth Century* and *Mark Trail*, plus masculine leads in *A Tree Grows in Brooklyn* and *Helpmate*. He was often cast in a principal part in *Radio City Playhouse*. In addition, he held running roles on *Backstage Wife, Lone Journey, Ma Perkins, Portia Faces Life, The Right to Happiness, Road of Life, The Romance of Helen Trent* and *Stepmother*. Few actors rivaled him in gaining so many desirable roles. His distinctively deep voice and gifted talent allowed him to work almost everywhere during the Golden Age of radio drama.

The part of Della Street was played at varying times by three of radio's most respected actresses. Veterans Gertrude Warner (heroine of *Young Doctor Malone*), Jan Miner (*Hilltop House*) and Joan Alexander appeared, in that order, in the role of Mason's Girl Friday. Alexander, who had the memorable run as the last and most durable of the trio, appeared opposite Larkin. She is credited with the part of Lois Lane in radio's *Superman* and played recurring characters on *Rosemary, This Is Nora Drake, Young Doctor Malone, Woman of Courage, Leave It to Mike, The Open Door, Philo Vance, Against the Storm,*

Dashingly handsome John Larkin portrayed the title role of *Perry Mason* and was aided by Della Street, played by Joan Alexander. Mason's crusades against evil were a warm-up for the role that Larkin would play as attorney Mike Karr on *The Edge of Night*, a televised serial growing out of the radio drama. (Photofest)

Bright Horizon, David Harum, Lone Journey and *The Man from G-2.* She also turned up in dramatic casts on *The Light of the World, Quick as a Flash, Dimension X* and *Columbia Presents Corwin.* Born in 1916 at St. Paul, Minnesota, Alexander pursued a modeling career and stage roles before moving to radio in 1940. From 1966 to 1969 she reprised her part as Lois Lane, supplying the voice for a weekly CBS-TV *Superman* cartoon series.

Whereas Camay and Tide were the official sponsors of *Perry Mason* on radio, at the pinnacle of the serial's popularity certain daytime dramas were targeted for public-service messages. Announcer Dick Stark once concluded a *Mason* broadcast with this admonition:

> Today, the world looks to the United States for leadership. So
> that word "united" has got to mean what it says. We can't have
> prejudice dividing us. We must refuse to listen to or spread
> rumors about any race or religion. Let's keep prejudice out and
> keep America really united.

Widespread recognition of differences in treatment of Americans was gaining momentum. Civil rights would be a prominent topic in the years to follow.

On another day, Stark offered this endorsement:

> Remember this, friends: millions of people overseas have for-
> gotten the meaning of a square meal — they need gift food
> packages. The safe, sure way to send them is through Care.
> Care is an approved, nonprofit agency. Send more for your
> money; send your gift food packages through Care ... C-A-R-E
> ... Care ... New York.

Such appeals implied that radio and its advertisers understood their obligations to listeners. By making time available to charitable bequests, broadcasters demonstrated a responsible attitude toward their privilege of serving vast audiences.

Perry Mason, the show, dispelled any lingering doubts that some fans might have entertained that the only way for a radio soap opera to become successful was to feature a female lead, the preferred protagonist in the overwhelming majority of serials, or a philosophizing or senile male, or a male in a contrived story where the lead was flanked by an ambitious woman. In *Mason,* listeners found a bright young masculine professional admired by women of all ages — and whose exploits for righteousness and civility while defending the innocent and unfortunate carried those same housewives far from the mundane of their often simple existences. Even though it was all pure fantasy, big doses of the formula became addictive to a fault.

19
Portia Faces Life
(Courage, Spirit, Integrity)

Without Walter Manning, this could have been a feminine version of *Perry Mason*. For Portia, the most successful woman lawyer among radio soap heroines, had the ability and brains to dazzle the prosecution, defending her clients with masterful strokes of legal strategy. She was a woman whom men desired outside the hall of justice and feared inside it. Her serial might have been an altogether intriguing tale of courtroom drama had it not been for the mail. Listeners preferred melodrama, they indicated in overwhelming numbers. Left with a small son to raise after the accidental death of her husband, the feminine barrister was often preoccupied with domestic matters rather than issues pertaining to her career. A lot of turned-on males, including Walter Manning, found her charms totally captivating. From the day of Walter's arrival in the plot it appeared that his lone function was to create problems for Portia to solve. Despite frequent, lengthy unexplained lapses in time, during which he was gone for weeks and months — once for over a year — Portia, a woman of brains, courage and skill, still married him. Walter suffered constant physical, mental and emotional setbacks and even called on his wife to defend him on at least two occasions — once for treason, another time for murder. Their union produced a daughter, and in their household Portia's son, Dickie, grew up. The men with the roving eyes never relinquished their desire for Portia. And in the end she too faced life — or part of it — behind bars for a crime she didn't commit.

Producers: Don Cope, Tom McDermott
Directors: Hoyt Allen, Mark Goodson (the TV game show mogul), Paul Knight, Beverly Smith
Writers: Hector Chevigny, Mona Kent
Sound Effects: Wes Conant
Announcers: George Putnam, Ron Rawson
Portia Blake Manning: Lucille Wall, Anne Seymour (four months in 1948)
Walter Manning: Myron McCormick, Bartlett (Bart) Robinson
Dickie Blake: Edwin Bruce, Skip Homeier, Raymond Ives, Alastair Kyle, Larry Robinson
Others: Marjorie Anderson, Joan Banks, Luise Barclay, Donald Briggs, Peter Capell, Les Damon, Nancy Douglass, Rosaline Greene, Ethel Intropidi, Bill Johnstone, Ginger Jones, Richard Kendrick, John Larkin, Ken Lynch, Santos Ortega, Esther Ralston,

Elizabeth Reller, Doris Rich, Selena Royle, Alison Skipworth, Cora B. Smith, Lyle Sudrow, Barry Sullivan, Karl Swenson, Henrietta Tedro, James Van Dyke, Walter Vaughn, Carleton Young, more

Theme: "Kerry Dance" (Molloy)

Sponsors: Benton and Bowles brought this serial to radio for General Foods largely as a commercial vehicle for Post Raisin Bran and Post 40% Bran Flakes cereals ("Life is swell when you keep well"). It also advertised Gaines dog food, Jell-O desserts, Maxwell House coffee and other cereals and kitchen staples. The serial was never sponsored by any other concern.

Ratings: This late-afternoon "drive time" drama consistently garnered some of the best numbers of all the serials. For a decade, 1941–51, *Portia* never fell below 6.5, a high ranking. For three years it achieved figures above 8.0, including a lofty 8.7 in 1943–44. The numbers exceeded 7.5 for 60 percent of that decade. Low: 3.5 (1940–41). The ratings suggest that as suppertime in millions of homes approached, homemakers were listening more faithfully to soap operas or men were listening en route home from work, and probably both.

On the Air: Oct. 7, 1940–April 25, 1941, CBS, 4:00 p.m. ET; April 28, 1941–March 31, 1944, NBC, 5:15 p.m.; April 3, 1944–Sept. 29, 1944, CBS, 2:00 p.m.; Oct. 2, 1944–June 29, 1951, NBC, 5:15 p.m.

Portia Blake Manning may not have been facing life as her series departed the airwaves on June 29, 1951, but she was headed for the slammer just the same.

To this author's knowledge, no other soap opera ever left the air like this one. To have the central figure in the series, whom legions of fans had doted on for more than a decade, headed for prison after being sentenced for a crime she didn't commit — with no visible means of correcting such a serious miscarriage of justice — was incredible. And yet … would you believe? … the producers wanted it precisely that way.

There was a motive in their madness. Those connected with the show were hopeful, perhaps even convinced, that there would be such an outpouring of sympathy by the fans that the network (and maybe the series' only sponsor) would have no alternative but to reinstate the long-running drama. They probably figured that, if for no other reason than to right the travesty that had been done in this instance, listeners would demand that their heroine be restored to her proper place. Eventually, all would go on as before.

But whoever believed that was due a reality check. It didn't happen. Either the audience didn't protest nearly or severely enough or — more likely — the protests fell on deaf ears. Whatever the reason, the serial didn't return, and poor Portia was left to rot in her cell. It was a heartless way to say good-by to a heroine who had been greatly admired for so long.

Sending an upstanding citizen to the pokey on the theory she'd soon be free would never happen again in radio soap opera as a ploy to "Save Our Show." From that experience, others learned not to sacrifice good people for that motive. The best intentions go awry. To the contrary, some producers took precautions to make *sure* their dramas were intact should a series ever be called to make a comeback.

Rather than allowing Anthony Loring and Ellen Brown to get hitched while on the air, ending an 18-year premise around which *Young Widder Brown* was constructed, the pair rode off to obtain a marriage license in their final episode. Hoping the series might return, the producers weren't about to let them tie that infernal knot and evaporate nearly two decades of obstacles that had kept them from the altar.

Portia faced a lifetime of misery in her decade-plus on the air before her final miscarriage of justice. Her dashingly handsome lawyer-husband Richard Blake was killed in an automobile accident while seeking to put a major crime czar out of business—leaving her with a young son, Dickie, to raise. That transpired in the very first episode. The indomitable Portia, named after the heroine in playwright William Shakespeare's *The Merchant of Venice*, was a force to be reckoned with, however. Brilliant as an attorney in her own right, Portia took over her late husband's law practice and finished the job of nailing the local crime boss for corruption in their fine upstanding community of Parkerstown. Her extraordinary forensic skills habitually devastated the poor male-chauvinist barristers who attempted to match her.

Creator Mona Kent preferred to distinguish her serial from the melodramatic moments so typical of its counterparts. The soap opera was introduced each day as "a story reflecting the courage, spirit and integrity of American women everywhere." Its writer (followed by Hector Chevigny, author of *The Second Mrs. Burton*) took pains to personify her characters, but with negligible results. Every time Kent tarried too long in that direction, the fans responded with angry protests. (Producers must have wondered later: where were those irate scribes when the show went off the air?) Audiences were accustomed to a steady diet of run-of-the-mill action, having heard it all day long. They saw little reason for Portia to escape the trivialities of domestic crises afflicting other serial heroines. A professional simply couldn't be absolved of the mundane due to position.

Into that environment, Walter Manning was introduced. Looking back from this vantage point, we see his purpose was obviously to give Portia something to constantly fret over. And fret she did. When he was there, he brought new problems into their lives; when he wasn't (which was a great deal of the time, since he kept disappearing on lengthy sabbaticals), she wondered where he was and whether he was still alive.

Portia, like many another soap opera heroine, was too much for even a strong male. She needn't have worried, of course; strong males didn't appear very often in the serials. Although soap opera males were fairly promising in business and professional life, they generally lagged their women in force of personality. Heroines were essentially perfect; on the other hand, men really weren't heroes, for they were most often devoid of some virtue or desirable trait. Frequently, they were unduly attracted to other women, indecisive, unstable, jealous or a combination of any of the four requisites. Masculine weakness and feminine superiority were likely the resultant perception. That certainly applied in Walter Manning's case; at times he put all four of these undesirable characteristics to the test.

Manning was a journalist by trade. A roving newspaperman, he later became editor of the local paper, the *Parkerstown Herald*. Portia, as attractive to men outside the hall of justice as she was their undoing inside it, was the object of many a man's affections. One of them, Christopher Manning, was Walter's brother, with whom she dallied for a time.

After Walter injured the snooty Arline Harrison in an automobile accident (let's face it — Portia may have had a knack for choosing fabulous lovers, but behind the wheel of a car, they weren't worth a dime!), Walter suffered colossal guilt. To assuage his feelings, he married Arline. (An idea didn't have to be logical to make its way into melodrama. And the fans, remember, *loved* this!) Later, he and Portia dumped their current relationships to become engaged to each other.

Walter was to experience many tough months in Germany during World War II before returning to the warm embrace of his fiancée. While working for U.S. Army Intelligence, he was falsely accused of spying for the Germans. Resigning his commission and becoming a foreign correspondent, he was captured and tortured by the Nazis, who sought to obtain his military secrets. Eventually, he was rescued and flown home. There he faced accusations of being a Nazi sympathizer and sharing proprietary information with the German high command. When he landed in court, Portia successfully defended him against those charges. His future remained uncertain, for he required intense psychiatric rehabilitation provided by yet another man who was in love with Portia, adding to his humiliation.

In addition to her interest in other men, Portia also became involved in more espionage cases. When her drama shifted from NBC back to CBS in 1944, she continued to pursue enemy agents with a vengeance, despite an ultimatum from CBS banning network broadcasts of spy stories. This violation may have contributed to the serial's rather brief tenure at CBS its second time around. Within six months it returned to NBC, where it stayed for the remainder of an 11-year run.

Portia and Walter at last overcame their immediate obstacles to marriage and finally made it down the aisle. But all was not well in the little house they shared on Peach Street. While on another overseas foray, Walter developed some mysterious malady that left him nearly dead and left Portia believing that he *was* dead. He was gone for more than a year. By then she had given him up, accepting the proposal of Dr. Norman Byron, a fellow professional.

The following day Walter resurfaced at Dr. Byron's clinic in New York City using an alias supplied by the government. Only the good doctor's assistant, Kathy, an old friend of Walter and Portia's, realized his true identity. He was anxious for a clean bill of health so he could continue his journey to Portia, then engaged to Kathy's boss. "For a little while at least," said announcer George Putnam, "these three are completely at her mercy." Such convoluted plot lines surfaced in bucketloads after the fan mail arrived at Mona Kent's writing studio.

The pair met other obstacles to a happy life. Clint Morley, the town's district attorney, set loose tongues wagging when he took more than a passing interest in Portia and she reciprocated. Portia was obviously pregnant in the autumn of 1948, at a time when Walter had once again disappeared for a long spell. The townsfolk believed the lady barrister had been unfaithful to her spouse. No one in Parkerstown knew that at that moment, Walter — who was the *real* father-to-be — lay gravely ill in a run-down hotel in Ankara, Turkey.

A physician informed him that he had a fatal disease that would capture his sight before taking his life. Together with his longtime friend Eric Watson, Walter — already blind — waited for the end, determined that Portia would not have to care for an invalid in his last days. Suddenly a plan to save him developed. One man was capable of reversing Walter's debilitating condition, ending the fatal threat to his body. Eric Watson sent for Dr. Peter Steinhart, who flew to Ankara to do just that.

Portia gave birth to their daughter, named Sheila, whom Walter was not even aware of until he returned home. Portia hoped to give up the practice of law and devote full time to raising this baby. But for a second time she was forced to undertake her husband's defense — for the murder of Joan Ward. District Attorney Morley, who had never gotten Portia out of his system, fought tenaciously to have Walter put away. Accomplishing that, he would then have his way with Portia.

During the trial, Portia's son, Dickie, was brought to the witness stand to provide incriminating testimony against his stepfather. He did so reluctantly — in fact, Dickie ran away from home when he knew he would be called to testify. But Portia's friend, waitress Connie Abbott, worked grimly to intervene on Walter's behalf, hoping to get Nick Evans to testify. She knew that his testimony could break the alibi of Steve Ward, the murdered woman's husband. Once again, Portia's brilliant legal maneuvering was enough to get her husband acquitted and the killer exposed.

In the final months before the series left the air, Walter was again believed dead — by everybody but Portia. (She had been down this road so many times that she seemed to have reason to be skeptical.) Walter had been in a near-fatal accident but was still alive, suffering (what else?) amnesia. Paul and Beauty Ingersoll, a malevolent couple of conspirators who saw a glorious opportunity to capitalize on Walter's memory loss, convinced him that his name was Stewart Prescott. As a part of their grand scheme, they had him committed to a mental hospital. He eventually escaped and found his way back to Parkerstown and Portia's waiting arms.

By then the clock was running out on the series, and there was just enough time to set up some unjust charges against Portia. Having saved nearly everybody else and Walter, perhaps more times than she should have, Portia quietly went off to incarceration. What a tease!

Even though this was the finale of the radio version, Portia did face life, if only briefly, as a TV heroine some three years later. With veteran radio actress Fran Carlon in the title role, CBS added *Portia Faces Life* to its live 15-minute stable of soap operas in 1954. Almost in the blink of an eye, however, it was gone, whisked away with another radio retread that CBS-TV had programmed at about the same time, *Road of Life*. (There were a couple of interesting footnotes to the TV series. For one, Walter became jealous of his wife's professional success, creating a source of tension at home. In the TV version he strongly advocated that Portia's place was in the home. If she had followed his suggestion, of course, the show's original premise would have evaporated. Second, for some unidentified reason, in the final few months of its 15-month run the show was retitled *The Inner Flame* on TV. This still wasn't enough to save it from cancellation.)

For years actress Lucille Wall pulled off a rather surprising feat that other radio actresses could only dream of. On one network, in the interval of an hour — five days a week for more than a decade — she was the heroine on *two* soap operas. For most of that era both programs were broadcast live also, thus she had to shuffle back and forth between dramas to accommodate rehearsals scheduled shortly before each day's performances.

At 4:30 p.m. Eastern Time, she appeared before the NBC microphones as Belle, the faithful spouse of *Lorenzo Jones*, a part she played from 1940 until the series was canceled in 1955. At 5:15 p.m., only thirty minutes after that show left the air, Wall broadcast from another NBC studio in the title role on *Portia Faces Life*. If listeners noted the similarity in the two heroines' voices, they were loath to admit it. *Portia* departed for the last time on

Friday, June 29, 1951. The following Monday, *Lorenzo Jones* shifted to 5:30 p.m. The change in *Jones'* airtime, if it had come sooner, would likely have made it impossible for Wall to continue on both serials due to an even more intense rehearsal conflict.

Lucille Wall portrayed Portia for the entire run. While the actress recovered from a fall in 1948, she was replaced for four months by veteran actress Anne Seymour. Born on January 18, 1899, in Chicago, Wall broke into radio in 1927 at WJZ. She played the "Collier Love Story" girl under an assumed name of Polly Preston opposite actor Frederick March on the *Collier's Hour* broadcasts. Later she signed for many radio roles under her own name, including the female lead in *Your Family and Mine* and parts in *Pretty Kitty Kelly, Island Boat Club, Sherlock Holmes, True Confessions, The First Nighter* and *A Tale of Today*.

Although she wasn't selected for the title role in the brief stint of *Portia Faces Life* on TV, she later acquired a much more durable part — nurse Lucille March on TV's *General Hospital*. For about 14 years (1963–76 and again in 1982), longer than any of her radio characterizations, she played nurse March. Wall died on July 11, 1986, in Reno, Nevada.

Two seasoned radio actors played the part of Walter Manning. Bartlett (Bart) Robinson, the first, could be described as a serial fanatic. He firmly entrenched himself in radio soap operas on *Perry Mason, Pretty Kitty Kelly, Valiant Lady, Backstage Wife, Ellen Randolph, The Romance of Helen Trent, The Second Mrs. Burton, A Woman of America* and *Young Doctor Malone*. His counterpart, Myron McCormick, had equally impressive references, although he mixed his. McCormick appeared on *The Adventures of Christopher Wells, Buck Private, Central City, A Crime Letter from Dan Dodge, Helpmate, Passport for Adams, Listening Post, The Man Behind the Gun, The March of Time Quiz* and *Joyce Jordan, Girl Interne*.

Despite the fact that *Portia Faces Life* consistently harvested high numbers among daytime ratings, it left the air almost without a whimper. By then another barrister, *Perry Mason*, had established a radio law practice, following in the line of earlier colleagues *Terry Regan, Attorney at Law* and *Her Honor, Nancy James*. Mason's virility was perhaps even more persuasive to daytime listeners than the time-honored devices at Portia's command. One could be sure that with Mason on a case, an unwavering deportment both inside and outside the hall of justice would be maintained. *Portia* was simply a "housewife version of *Perry Mason*," one longtime radio biographer advanced.[1]

Portia represented her clients with impressive credentials and integrity but faltered in her ability to stabilize her personal life. The network, and obviously the public, decided to let her cool her heels for a while. She would have lots of time on her hands to weigh how she might have done it all differently.

20
The Right to Happiness

(Ivory Soap's *Own* Story)

Rooted in *The Guiding Light,* which began in 1937, *The Right to Happiness* gained a separate berth on NBC Blue on Oct. 16, 1939. Creator Irna Phillips transplanted the popular character of Rose Kransky from *Light* into her own series. A short while later, the focus shifted to the more appealing Carolyn Allen, whose destiny seemed preordained by an unsavory past that was certified in her series' initiation. Single, Allen would give new meaning to the term *woman's suffrage* while her endurance was tested with four husbands — three of whom were in general terms inflexible, contentious and headstrong — and a recalcitrant teenager whose unruly behavior made her life at times a living hell. The melodrama was so absorbing to millions, however, that it maintained a lock on its favored NBC quarter-hour for 13 years. Procter & Gamble retained sole sponsorship for 17 years. Outliving all but three of its contemporaries, *Happiness* was among a final quartet of soap operas canceled by CBS on "the day radio drama died," Nov. 25, 1960.

Producers: Fayette Krum, Kathleen Lane, Paul Martin, Carl Wester, Bruno Zirato, Jr.
Directors: Gil Gibbons, Arthur Hanna, Frank Papp, Charles Urquhart, Bruno Zirato, Jr.
Writers: Irna Phillips (1939–42), John M. Young (1942–60)
Music: William Meeder
Sound Effects: Frank Loughrane, Manny Segal
Announcers: Hugh Conover, Michael Fitzmaurice, Hugh James, Ron Rawson
Rose Kransky: Ruth Bailey
Carolyn Allen Walker Kramer Nelson MacDonald: Eloise Kummer (1939–42), Claudia Morgan (1942–60)
Bill Walker: Reese Taylor
Dwight Kramer: Frank Behrens, David Gothard, Ed Prentiss, Dick Wells
Miles Nelson: John Larkin, Gary Merrill
Others: Daniel Arco, Luise Barclay, Charita Bauer, Joseph Bell, Peter Capell, Staats Cotsworth, Constance Crowder, Les Damon, Jimmy Dobson, Robert Dryden, Helene Dumas, Peter Fernandez, Maurice Franklin, Sarah Fussell, Lee Graham, Walter Greaza, Larry Haines, Violet Heming, Irene Hubbard, Ginger Jones, Carlton KaDell, Art Kohl, Elizabeth Lawrence, Bill Lipton, Sunda Love, Jerry Macy, Ian Martin, Marvin Miller, Julian Noa, Ethel Owen, Mary Patton, Bill Quinn, Billy Redfield, Rosemary Rice, Selena

Royle, Anne Sargent, Mignon Schreiber, J. Ernest Scott, Alexander Scourby, Anne Sterrett, Hugh Studebaker, Reese Taylor, Lenora Thatcher, Gertrude Warner, Charles Webster, Sarajane Wells, Seymour Young, Alice Yourman, more

Theme: "Song of the Soul" (Breil)

Sponsors: Procter & Gamble (1939–56) for Cheer detergent, Crisco shortening, Ivory soap, Spic 'n' Span cleanser, other household products; Columbia phonographs and records; CBS Radio; sustaining.

Ratings: Above 6.0 every year from 1940 to 1953 (Median: 7.4); high: 9.9 (1949–50); low: 2.2 (1939–40).

On the Air: Oct. 16, 1939–Jan. 19, 1940, NBC Blue, 10:15 a.m. ET; Jan. 22, 1940–Dec. 26, 1941, CBS, 1:30 p.m.; Dec. 29, 1941–1942, NBC Red, 11:15 a.m.; 1942–July 1, 1955, NBC, 3:45 p.m.; July 4, 1955–June 29, 1956, NBC, 4:00 p.m.; July 2, 1956–1957, CBS, 2:00 p.m.; 1957–Jan. 2, 1959, CBS, 2:05 p.m.; Jan. 5, 1959–Nov. 25, 1960, CBS, 1:00 p.m.

Carolyn Allen Walker Kramer Nelson MacDonald was the most married heroine in radio, living at a time when multiple marriages weren't in vogue. She killed one husband, divorced another, outlived a third and was wedded to a fourth when — alas! — her series came to an enigmatic end. Had her story continued, she might have tied the knot with her fifth, sixth, seventh and eighth prospects and even more. For as long as the writer could have squeezed out enough pathos and heartache, in fact, the tale would almost certainly have perpetuated itself. New suitors could have been imported for successive trysts that were as enthralling as those she had already experienced.

But those were just *some* of her troubles. While seldom enjoying connubial bliss, Carolyn experienced even more difficulties while trying to raise a rebellious son. Surely this most-married mom was to earn rewards beyond her present station for attempting to cope — sometimes as a single parent — in crises instigated by her hard-to-discipline teen, Skip Kramer. Without her fortitude, a lesser mother would have given in to his demands.

But her long suffering would not go unrewarded. Strict reliance on time-honored principles eventually saw her troublesome Skip turn into a decent, self-respecting young man. He became her greatest source of agony and elation. As a by-product, her perseverance likely inspired thousands of *real* mothers coping with similar foibles in their own family circles.

Although Carolyn's oft-married record stood unchallenged on radio, the precedent that she set in the first half of the twentieth century was to be superseded by another serial mom in the second half. On TV, the long-running daytime soap opera *Search for Tomorrow* focused on a character who would surpass Carolyn's feat. By the time *Tomorrow* breathed its last on December 26, 1986, heroine Joanne Gardner Barron Tate Reynolds Vincente Tourneur had exceeded Carolyn's number of trips down the aisle by one. (Her first four husbands died; she divorced the fifth.) But by then, the idea of multiple marriages had gained a measure of respect in polite society. Carolyn, for sure, lived a life more typical of a 1970s woman than one of the 1940s.

The Right to Happiness, which seems like a whimsical title for a serial predicated on relentless misery, found its origins in another highly successful Irna Phillips venture. For two years Phillips carefully crafted the characters in what would ultimately result as her most durable soap opera, *The Guiding Light*. (As this is written, it is still on the air via television, currently in its seventh decade.) Phillips decided to transfer one of *Light*'s figures, Rose Kransky, to a separate, newly created series. The serial was one of broadcasting's earliest program spin-offs.

The move convincingly swayed skeptics with lingering misgivings that Phillips might misunderstand what American homemakers wanted to hear as they went about their chores. It was soon obvious to most critics that anything with the name Irna Phillips attached to it was almost sure to be successful. By that time she had achieved widespread acclaim with *Painted Dreams, Today's Children, The Guiding Light, Road of Life* and *Woman in White*. In her future were other entries into daytime radio such as *Lonely Women, Masquerade* and *The Brighter Day*. The visual medium, of course, was to loom even larger on her horizon, where she would be personified as "the single most important influence on television soaps."[1] But that was later.

For two decades, her forte was radio. In it she knew no creative equal — despite the fact that Frank and Anne Hummert turned out far more serials than she. The Hummerts' fame resulted from their production volume; they earned it largely by employing assembly-line techniques. And even though the writing quality of Elaine Carrington's dramas is generally regarded as superior to those of most other authors — she wrote or dictated every word of every show — she didn't create as many soap operas as Irna Phillips.

A short time into the spin-off series, Phillips decided to reduce the role of her central character, Rose Kransky. On *The Guiding Light,* Kransky lived with her Jewish parents in a small-town apartment building. There she was best friends with the local Protestant minister's daughter, Mary Rutledge. But Kransky's liaison with an employer resulted in his scandalous divorce before she pursued her quest in *The Right to Happiness*. While Kransky was a rational young woman and possessed a heart of gold, Phillips determined that the more engaging personality of Carolyn Allen was better suited to what her listeners wanted to hear.

Allen, a magazine editor's daughter, also thrived on the problematic outside of marriage. She too had indulged in questionable dalliances before her first walk down the aisle. Phillips had to clean up Allen's act a bit before allowing her to inherit the mantle of protagonist.

Carolyn's search for her "God-given right to happiness" began with unfilled promise during her first marriage, to Bill Walker. Walker was a self-centered, ill-tempered husband who branded himself "capable of anything." Their relationship soon soured, a pattern to be repeated in Carolyn's subsequent unions. In a mishap that authorities labeled a homicide, she accidentally shot her spouse to death. Coming perilously close to spending the rest of her days behind bars, Carolyn weathered several months of interrogation, prosecution and trial before beating the rap by the skin of her teeth.

 In the meantime, while incarcerated, she gave birth to Skippy. The baby's father, Dwight Kramer, who was to become Carolyn's second husband, offered early indication that he was as erratic as she. This condemned any chance of a lasting covenant for the pair. By the end of the 1940s they were divorced, and Carolyn was fighting Dwight in a nasty court battle to regain custody of Skippy, who had been awarded to his father. Complicating matters, her close friend Constance Wakefield became the new Mrs. Kramer, creating a rift between the women. Fortunately for Carolyn, Dr. Dick Campbell, one of her ardent admirers, hung close, providing a shoulder for her to lean on in her loneliest hours.

For her legal contest she turned to a brilliant, dashing young attorney, Miles Nelson. Wasting no time, Carolyn engaged his services not only as her lawyer but also as her third husband. The couple's home was in a make-believe town called Meridian. Some listeners undoubtedly assumed that this referred to a city by that less-than-common name in Mississippi. In the theater of the mind, the audience was free to paint any image it wished and locate the action wherever it chose. If the fans' assumptions were correct, then the "state capital" so often referred to in the drama was Jackson. And Nelson's political ambitions led him to the highest elective office in the Magnolia State. This is conjecture, of course, but who's to say it wasn't what the writer had in mind?

In the hall of justice, Nelson eloquently pled before an impartial judge to overturn the earlier custody decision. But his courtroom acumen briefly faltered when he was summoned by his political party to the state capital to tackle a thorny crisis of some import. While pursuing his own political ambitions, Nelson temporarily relinquished the custody case to a partner, Harlow Sloan, who possessed crude skills. Carolyn watched as the inept Sloan defectively sparred with Dwight Kramer's clever but unprincipled attorney, Arnold Kirk. All the while she felt Nelson had let her down at a most inopportune moment.

On Nelson's return from the capital, another diversion distracted him from the case. The powerfully influential newspaper magnate Annette Thorpe — whose paper supported Nelson's gubernatorial candidacy — obviously had more than his political intentions on her mind. Witnessing the two from the sidelines, Carolyn hatched her own plan to regain custody of her son: she would simply grab Skippy and flee the court's jurisdiction. Before she could act on her ill-conceived plan, other factors surfaced that worked to her advantage.

Constance Kramer, Carolyn's former friend, failed to sympathize with her husband's attempts to discredit Carolyn in order to retain custody of Skippy. Convinced that Skippy preferred living with his mother and was miserable in their household, she inquired of Dwight how he could be so insensitive. The tide was beginning to turn. In the end, a dejected Dwight Kramer reluctantly gave in, releasing the boy to Carolyn.

The addition of Miles Nelson, who went on to win the governorship, introduced political intrigue into the story line. It also led to physical and emotional destruction. Nelson was a handsome man, pursued by the ladies, popular with the electorate and (as sometimes happens with politicians) surrounded by an unsavory contingent. He appeared, at least in the beginning, capable of thwarting those undesirable influences. Yet in time Carolyn was left inquiring if her husband had not really changed in a fundamental way. She felt betrayed, left to face moral dilemmas as a result of his own ethical breaches. But before that surfaced, when attempts by some of Nelson's detractors failed to place him in their pockets, they took a more direct approach — one of physical violence.

Under Carolyn's watchful care, and despite a bullet that had lodged near his heart and couldn't be removed, Governor Miles Nelson stubbornly discharged his official duties. The year was 1951. His newspaper benefactress continued to heavily intrude into his daily activities. A year later, the habitually plucky Carolyn found herself wondering if her husband might not have been better off to have lost the election for governor. His health was still guarded; it frequently limited him from performing his duties. And he had to mount a campaign refuting some strong character assassination that was leveled against him.

Under the guise of being an inmate, Carolyn revisited one of her old haunts, a women's prison, in an effort to save her man from destruction. He neither understood nor appreciated her methods. Despite her sacrifice, when Carolyn's resolve thawed, she absently wondered aloud if the couple's struggle to withstand the forces of evil wouldn't ultimately be for naught.

By late 1953, having courageously won the battle at last, Carolyn questioned whether the power of high office hadn't corrupted her mate. Miles was giving mixed signals that he might be in league with sinister forces. With Annette Thorpe influencing him in one direction and dishonest politicians in another, Carolyn wondered if there was any viable middle ground left.

Eventually, Miles' deteriorating physical condition took its toll. Following his death, Carolyn — by then a wealthy woman — was sought by various causes hoping for a piece of the action, a stake in her financial fortune. Some needs were legitimate. Others used questionable means to accomplish desired ends. Her philanthropy once led her to write a $50,000 check to the DeWitt Home for Children in Bridgeton. Unknown to her, however, a $40,000 "finder's fee" was paid out of the proceeds to Jack Townsend, an unscrupulous scoundrel who negotiated her gift. His subsequent scheming led him to try to "take" the affluent dowager for every dime she had.

Meanwhile, Carolyn continued her lifetime pursuit of the opposite gender, picking up a lover here and there. At one point in the mid–1950s she and a Mr. Chalmers seemed destined for the altar. But somehow he got away. In the latter part of 1957, the same could be said of Victor Moore, a whimsical artist. Was Carolyn's technique in frequently tying the knot beginning to unravel?

At this crossroads her son, Skippy (who by then was referred to as Skip), became the principal focus of her attention and of the drama's as well. Having at last reached adolescence, he would unequivocally create for this single parent something of an existing netherworld.

By himself, Skip wasn't a bad kid. He had been privileged to live in the governor's mansion. And he had been the irrefutable object of his mother's affection during her custody battle with his biological father. In another environment he might not have been difficult to handle. But given the circumstances of no stable father figure in his life, coupled with his mom's penchant for entertaining gentlemen, Skip got into trouble. Actively seeking the approval of some questionable peers, he was drawn into group-induced snares. While Skip required more expertise than she could supply, Carolyn tried to reassure him that he was the pivotal axis of her life. But the defiant teenager was not convinced. Given his mother's history, why should he be?

In autumn 1955 Skip was trying to adjust to a new high school. Hoping to gain favor with coed Molly Jarvis, he also sought to score points with a gang of juvenile hoodlums. Trying to impress his new friends, he carried out some petty acts of vandalism. But Skip was caught and punished by the school principal, Mr. Blair. As a result, Carolyn soon became a frequent caller at Blair's office as she diligently sought to "straighten out" her fractious son's unruly behavior.

Undaunted by his failure to win the gang's respect, Skip decided to make another try. In January 1956 he mused over the consequences of destroying the interior of Mr. Blair's automobile while recalling an admonition from his mother: "I've leaned over backwards trying to play according to your rules, Skip. I've made allowances. I've even given in to you.

And where has it gotten me? You'll follow my rules now. You'll do what you're told. I will not have you getting in more trouble, Skip. We'll work this out together, dear. But meantime, you're going to do what I say."

Carolyn meant every word of it. She was absolutely determined to keep her offspring on the straight and narrow path. Any housewife in the listening audience faced with similar anguish might have openly cheered her resolve.

Skip lamented: "The gang says all I've gotta do is slash up the front seat ... then get in the back and carve that up.... It's a terrible thing to do; I don't wanna.... Mother would be disappointed in me if she knew. But she's gonna marry Mr. Chalmers some day 'cause I heard 'em say so. And she told me she wasn't.... Rod says Mr. Blair's fed up with Jefferson — he'll go somewhere else, leave the school. He'll get outta my hair.... It's all *his* fault — he's the one — and this is *his* car. And I'm gonna do it; I've *got* to — there isn't any other way out."

Despite such action, his mother would eventually see Skip outgrow his hostility and become a contributing member of society. When Carolyn married her fourth husband, Lee MacDonald, another profoundly handsome, middle-aged lawyer, Skip demonstrated his maturity. In a concluding sequence for the long-running soap opera, Skip showed respect for his new father, frequently calling him "dad" while asking for his advice on several weighty matters. By then a college student, Skip also had a new love, one whom he expected to ask to be his wife in the not-too-distant future.

Only four open-ended soap operas remained on network radio then, all on CBS. The "survival of the fittest" was a compliment to the four: *The Right to Happiness, Ma Perkins, Young Doctor Malone* and *The Second Mrs. Burton*. CBS pulled the plug on the quartet on November 25, 1960. (One reviewer implied that traditional radio programming died that day.)[2]

Carolyn and Lee MacDonald used their last few on-air moments to muse over some of the definitions of happiness that she had been collecting for decades. In the study of their rambling home, the lovebirds philosophized: "We are all born with a right to happiness, yet happiness depends on the thoughts we think ... on the things we do ... on how generously we live." Admitting one's mistakes, profiting by them and attempting to make up for them leads an individual a long way in a search for that elusive right to happiness, they surmised. But if there was a simple answer to happiness, Carolyn injected, this definition came closest: "Happiness depends upon our relationship with those we love." Having endured endless miseries at the hands of four husbands and a troubled son, she'd had more than two decades to practice living that one.

Over the serial's long run, the commodity best identified with *The Right to Happiness* was Ivory soap. In the 1940s and early 1950s, announcer Ron Rawson introduced the serial with this couplet.

> Your fav'rite soap since baby days;
> It's got those gentle baby ways.

Following the familiar tag line "Ivory soap — 99 and 44/100ths percent pure" — Rawson (and later Michael Fitzmaurice) added: "Now, Ivory soap's *own* story ... *The Right to Happiness.*"

Listeners were beckoned with this lofty epithet: "Considering only oneself is not the way to true contentment. We should think carefully in seeking our own happiness, lest we endanger the happiness of others."

In the program's final year under the Procter & Gamble umbrella (1955–56), the commercial emphasis was altered. By then narrator Hugh James welcomed listeners with these lines: "Spic 'n' Span, the wonderful once over cleaner for walls, woodwork and linoleum, and new blue Cheer, the only suds with the blue magic whitener, present ... *The Right to Happiness.*"

Happiness also adopted a seldom-used format among soap operas. Instead of inject-ing the traditional product commercial before the opening scene, as most of its peers did, the serial instantly launched into the plot after James' introduction and the familiar theme song. The first advertising plug was delayed four or five minutes into the quarter-hour. After six or seven minutes of subsequent dialogue, dual commercials aired. These were separated by the announcer's pitch enticing listeners to catch the next episode. *Happiness* used this innovative format during the program's latter days at NBC. The technique was virtually a novelty in 1955, but it caught on. Decades later, the bulk of daytime and nighttime TV series featuring continuing characters, including serious drama and comedy, employed it.

In 1942, production of *Happiness* transferred from Chicago to New York. A short time later, Irna Phillips sold *The Right to Happiness* along with two other serials, *Road of Life* and *The Guiding Light*. New owners Procter & Gamble launched a writing competition to determine the series' new author. John M. Young got the nod. The experienced radio writer had been — or would be — a dialoguer for *Bright Horizon, Road of Life, The Second Mrs. Burton, Gunsmoke* and *Yours Truly, Johnny Dollar.* Over the next 18 years Young was to be responsible for churning out more than 4,500 scripts for *Happiness.*

Not only was there a shift in the scripting, but the lead role was also reassigned. Until then, veteran Chicago actress Eloise Kummer played the central character of Carolyn Allen. Kummer earned her stripes on important daytime series like *Betty and Bob, Lone Journey* (in which she played the feminine lead), *The Guiding Light, Road of Life, The Story of Mary Marlin* and *Backstage Wife.* For a while she was the lead on *Hot Copy* and appeared in the dramatic casts of *Dear Mom* and *Silver Eagle, Mountie.* Kummer also narrated *Ameri-can Women.* She landed in two of NBC-TV's earliest short-lived serials. The first, in early 1949, Irna Phillips' *These Are My Children,* lasted only four weeks. *The Bennetts,* in which Kummer played the feminine lead, was around but a few weeks longer in 1953–54.

The hands-down winner to replace Kummer when the serial moved to New York was Claudia Morgan, hailing from a family of renowned thespians; her father, Ralph Morgan, and her uncle, Frank Morgan, were professional theatrical actors. She too would be success-ful on Broadway and later in touring companies as Maggie Cutler in *The Man Who Came to Dinner.* Born in Brooklyn on November 12, 1911, she appeared at 17 in her first stage play with her famous father.

This soon-to-be workaholic, whose name is linked with *The Right to Happiness* more than anyone else's, simultaneously combined many radio and theatrical roles. Smooth and poised, Claudia Morgan studied drama at Yale and, in 1938, wed an architect. The follow-ing year she landed a continuing role in daytime radio's *Against the Storm.* Ironically, that soap opera — broadcast from New York — debuted the very same day (October 16, 1939) as *Happiness,* airing from Chicago with Eloise Kummer as Carolyn Allen.

Morgan won parts in *David Harum, Dimension X* (a.k.a. *X Minus One*), *Lone Journey,*

The Adventures of the Abbotts and *Quiet, Please.* She appeared infrequently in *Radio City Playhouse* and *The Falcon.* She is recalled by fans as the audacious Nora Charles in *The Adventures of the Thin Man.* Morgan and Les Damon were selected for the roles of Nora and Nick Charles in the radio detective series (1941–50) on the theory that they sounded like William Powell and Myrna Loy, who had been cast as leads in an earlier movie by that title. Morgan took the part of Nora so seriously, in fact, that she was fired from a theatrical job because of it. When her radio role delayed the start of the stage play *Ten Little Indians* every Friday night, she lost her part in the play to honor her broadcast contract.

In early 1955 the actress had a brief stint on an NBC-TV dramatic anthology series, *Way of the World.* Morgan appeared infrequently in the early 1970s in Himan Brown's *The CBS Mystery Theater.* She died in New York City on September 17, 1974.

Ruth Bailey, who played the original protagonist, Rose Kransky, on *Happiness*— as she had done earlier on *The Guiding Light*— acquired recurring roles on three other serials: *Bachelor's Children, Arnold Grimm's Daughter* and *Woman in White.* She died on September 20, 1989, at age 84.

Reese Taylor (with continuing roles in the serials *Amanda of Honeymoon Hill, Archie Andrews, Lone Journey, Lonely Women, Road of Life* and *The Romance of Helen Trent*) was Carolyn's first husband, Bill Walker. Dwight Kramer, her second mate, was played at various times by four actors: Frank Behrens, Ed Prentiss, David Gothard and Dick Wells. Behrens (also of *Arnold Grimm's Daughter, The Guiding Light, Joyce Jordan, Lorenzo Jones, Road of Life, Woman in White, Caroline's Golden Store* and *Jack Armstrong, The All American Boy*) died on December 15, 1986 at age 67. Prentiss (*Arnold Grimm's Daughter, Painted Dreams, The Barton Family, Captain Midnight, The Guiding Light, The Romance of Helen Trent, Woman in White* and *Today's Children*) was a Chicagoan, born on September 9, 1909. He was the narrator of Irna Phillips' innovative *General Mills Hour* featuring three of her popular soap operas. Prentiss left radio to act in several TV series: he narrated a sitcom lasting three months in 1949, *That's O'Toole*; he was a banker on *Bonanza*; and he had stints in two serials, *Morning Star* (1965–66) and *Days of Our Lives* (1966). He died on March 18, 1992. Gothard is best recalled as long-time suitor Gil Whitney in *The Romance of Helen Trent.* Wells appeared in running roles in *Kitty Keene, Incorporated* and *Ma Perkins.*

The part of husband number three, Governor Miles Nelson, was played by both Gary Merrill and John Larkin. Merrill, who was featured in *The March of Time Quiz, The Second Mrs. Burton* and *Superman*, also played the title role in the short-lived *Dr. Standish, Medical Examiner.* The actor died on March 5, 1990, at age 74. Larkin is best remembered as radio's *Perry Mason.*

The actor serving a brief tenure as Carolyn's fourth spouse, Lee MacDonald, hasn't been identified by audio historians.

The Right to Happiness perhaps appealed to the baser instincts of America's housewives. While Carolyn Allen Walker Kramer Nelson MacDonald may have been living ahead of her time, the beleaguered heroine offered her fans welcome relief from the adversities of marriage gone sour. In these homemakers' fantasy worlds, they may have seen a ray of promise in Carolyn — an opportunity to escape the entrapment of their own miserable circumstances. For a few minutes each weekday, they might have imagined how it would be to walk on the wild side for even a little while. No one would be the wiser. After all, in the theater of the mind, a listener could be anything she wanted to be.

21
Road of Life

(The Duz Program)

"A most important soap opera," as one radio historian characterized it, *Road of Life* was broadcast on dual networks for two-fifths of its existence, considerably widening its audience appeal beyond the normal reach of typical washboard weepers. The program became a long-standing tradition in many homes, showing up at numerous points on the radio dial at a variety of hours. With more than one hundred performers in its cast, the drama focused on a small town physician, Dr. Jim Brent, and the foibles impinging on his life and those he loved. While most of it avoided the eccentric stuff found on other serials, it encountered a few tragic moments along the way. The show was rooted in creator Irna Phillips' strong bent toward characterization. Across two decades there was ample opportunity for listeners to examine the gifts and perils in the lives of major figures. While Brent's career provided substance for the narrative, his interaction with two wives — one good, one not-so-good — also contributed heavily to the evolving plot. Carried out in the inimitable Phillips tradition in which realism played a dynamic part, *Road* became a daytime staple, the first of a long string of serials in which medics became the subjects around which the action transpired.

Producers: Fayette Krum, Kay Lane
Directors: Stanley Davis, Gil Gibbons, Walter Gorman, Charles Schenck, Charles Urquhart
Writers: William Morwood, Irna Phillips, Howard Teichmann, John M. Young
Music: Charles Paul
Sound Effects: Russ Gainor, Jerry McCarty, Manny Segal
Announcers: George Bryan, Nelson Case, Clayton (Bud) Collyer, Ron Rawson
Dr. Jim Brent: Matt Crowley, David Ellis, Ken Griffin, Don MacLaughlin, Howard Teichmann
Carol Evans Brent: Louise Fitch, Marion Shockley, Lesley Woods
Jocelyn McLeod Brent: Barbara Becker, Virginia Dwyer
John ("Butch") Brent: Roland Butterfield, David Ellis, Donald Kraatz, Bill Lipton, Lawson Zerbe
Francie Brent: Elizabeth Lawrence
Others: Peggy Allenby, John Anthony, Betty Arnold, Bob Bailey, Frank Behrens, Viola Berwick, Jack Bivens, Sidney Breese, Muriel Bremner, John Briggs, Dale Burch, Ralph

Camargo, Angel Casey, Frank Dane, Charles Dingle, Jeannette Dowling, Robert Duane, Harry Elders, Ethel Everett, Dick Foster, Dorothy Francis, Vivian Fridell, Barbara Fuller, Betty Lou Gerson, Stanley Gordon, Robert Griffin, Bill Griffis, Gladys Heen, Percy Hemus, Arthur Hern, Dick Holland, Carlton KaDell, Arthur Kohl, Eloise Kummer, John Larkin, Joe Latham, Grace Lenard, Abby Lewis, Helen Lewis, Janet Logan, Charlotte Manson, Mary Mareen, Doris Mead, Marvin Miller, Bret Morrison, Angeline Orr, Effie Palmer, Eileen Palmer, Olive Parker, Eva Parnell, Mary Patton, Cornelius Peeples, Jack Petruzzi, Dick Post, Terry Rice, Doris Rich, Jack Roseleigh, Dorothy Sands, Nanette Sargent, Guy Sorel, Leslie Spears, Julie Stevens, Hugh Studebaker, Ray Suber, Lyle Sudrow, Hope Summers, Reese Taylor, Russell Thorson, Hellen Van Tuyl, Evelyn Varden, Beryl Vaughn, Vicki Vola, Sam Wanamaker, Willard Waterman, Sarajane Wells, Lillian White, Ethel Wilson, Joan Winters, Lee Young, Lois Zarley, more

Theme: First Movement of Tchaikovsky's Sixth Symphony, "Pathetique" (Breil)

Sponsors: Compton Advertising brought this drama to radio for Procter & Gamble (P&G) primarily to advertise Chipso detergent. But in the early 1940s the show became a commercial vehicle for P&G's Duz detergent and acquired the designation "The Duz Program." Its tie with that laundry product was one of soap opera's strongest. By 1953 it diversified to other P&G commodities, notably Ivory soap. When P&G bowed out in 1955, the series was sold to multiple participants, including Hazel Bishop lipsticks.

Ratings: High (single broadcasts): 9.9 (1949–50); low: 4.1 (1955–56); high (dual broadcasts): 16.8 (1941–42). From 1937 to 1956, the program's ratings reached double digits in six seasons, all in dual-broadcast years. Median: 9.1 (1937–56).

On the Air: Sept. 13, 1937–May 27, 1938, CBS, 9:30 a.m. ET; Sept. 13, 1937–May 27, 1938, NBC, 4:45 p.m.; May 30, 1938–1939, CBS, 1:30 p.m.; May 30, 1938–1939, NBC, 11:45 a.m.; 1939–1942, CBS, 1:45 p.m.; 1939–1940, NBC, 11:15 a.m.; 1940–Dec. 26, 1941, NBC, 11:30 a.m.; Dec. 29, 1941–1942, NBC, 10:45 a.m.; 1942–June 1, 1945, NBC, 11:00 a.m.; April 2, 1945–May 30, 1947, CBS, 1:45 p.m.; June 4, 1945–July 8, 1949, NBC, 10:30 a.m.; July 11, 1949–June 25, 1954, NBC, 3:15 p.m.; Dec. 29, 1952–June 29, 1956, CBS, 1:00 p.m.; July 2, 1956–Jan. 2, 1959, CBS, 1:45 p.m.

SFX: Washing machine agitator churning water to a rhythmic
  beat, followed by woman's voice humming first line to the beat
FEMALE VOCALIST: (Sings)

> D-U-Z, D-U-Z,
> Put Duz in my washing machine...
> See the clothes come out so clean;
> When I Duz my wash, I sing,
> D-U-Z does everything!

SFX: Churning water fades
MUSIC: Organ notes signal end of melody
ANNOUNCER: Yes, it's the Duz program, *Road of Life*!

At this point the familiar strains of the first movement of Tchaikovsky's Sixth Symphony, "Pathetique"—more simply recalled by housewives as "music for the Duz program"—filtered into millions of living rooms across the land, played by the organist, Charles Paul. Another "absorbing episode" of the serial that gave rise to a new breed of character, the professional, was on the air.

Named for its creator's premise that the pathway of a physician is the road of life, this enduring soap opera was destined to become an instant success with daytime audiences. *Road's* early emphasis on doctors and nurses, the skilled artisans here, would signify it as a forerunner of medical-related soap operas on radio and television.

The program was the handiwork of Irna Phillips. Radio (and later, TV) actor Don MacLaughlin, whose span as a "star" of Phillips' melodramas would possibly continue longer than anyone else's, observed: "Soap opera is basically character, not story. It's the people in it who make it work…. It's like the cave men telling a little story every night by the fire and then gathering the next night to hear a little more of it."[1]

That grasp of what people wanted to hear on the installment plan allowed Phillips to earn the reputation of "reigning queen of soaps."[2] And on her way to that title, she became a master of her craft.

Phillips' strong accent on character development opposed story fantasy or "common heroes"—concepts that other writers had already established in their serials. Phillips' stories had unique qualities in which strong personalities were placed within credible situations. The essential distinctions (and strengths) of her plots were in how those mortals acted—and reacted—in their environments. More often than not, the plausibility factor in her serials was high and was rooted in Phillips' realistic dialogue and her subjects' literal common sense. Their conduct and speech were often a cut above that of characters prevailing in most other serials; together with strong acting, her shows offered an unbeatable combination.

The protagonist in *Road of Life* was Dr. Jim Brent. In true Phillips tradition, he would age as the show aged. While Brent's adventures were often based on domestic crises in his own home, some plights embracing hospital staff and patients intermittently spilled over into his personal life. Criminal activity, murder and wickedness of lesser sorts didn't control this serial. Yet an air of mystery and deceptive activity habitually frequented *Road's* story line.

As the drama began on September 13, 1937, broadcast from the air theater of station WBBM in Chicago, Jim Brent was a medical intern whose sweetheart had died only a short time earlier. The tragic turn of events left him deeply bruised, unable to cope with the thought of marriage—*ever*. Instead, he threw himself into an almost relentless passion for becoming a physician. In so doing, the promising young intern rebuffed many attractive debutantes whose subtle—and not so subtle—advances could have led him to the altar.

In the mythical town of Merrimac, presumably situated somewhere in Illinois, Brent's achievements as a City Hospital intern brought him to the attention of Dr. Reginald Parsons, chief of staff. Down the road, Brent would one day succeed Parsons. But this wouldn't happen overnight, nor before a clandestine side of Parsons emerged. Parsons embarked on a self-destructive course against family and friends. Brent was called to comfort Parsons' ex-wife, faced with the chief's emotional unevenness. It was an early hint of a role that Brent would play many times in the years ahead.

Even at a youthful age, Brent took on a signature characteristic that faithful listeners came to anticipate. Brent was to become a kind of all-knowing, omnipresent "father confessor" to a procession of troubled individuals filing by him over the decades. And as he matured, the depth of his wisdom increased.

Though Brent was single, early in *Road*'s story line he adopted a young orphan, naming him John Brent. He also gave the lad the nickname "Butch." Years later Butch became a pediatrician at City Hospital, where his father practiced. Eventually, the younger Brent married a San Francisco girl whom he had met during World War II. His wife, Francie, neither educated nor refined, was soon beset by overwhelming self-doubts about her ability to meet Butch's requirements. Sharing her insecurities with her father-in-law, she offered to divorce Butch so that he might pursue his career unencumbered by someone lacking culture. Jim Brent would have none of it. Thoughtfully, he counseled Francie to stay and work out her troubles, encouraging her to accept her rightful status as Butch's wife.

Long before Francie entered the drama a single young woman, Carol Evans, arrived in Merrimac and immediately saw husband material in Jim Brent. Some genuine concern on her part for Butch's welfare resulted in the desirable by-product (from her point of view) of eliminating Dr. Brent's resolve against marriage. In time, he wed Carol. But from the start it was a bond characterized by anything but bliss.

A daughter, Janie, was born to the couple early in their marriage. Yet Janie was shuffled aside many times as the headstrong Carol put her own career ahead of duties as a wife and mother. As an employee of the White Orchid Cosmetics Company, Carol became a frequent international traveler, gone from home for lengthy periods. Although she didn't have to work for economic security, Carol made a conscious choice to do so. That resulted in many stormy outbursts in the Brent home.

In the mid–1940s Jim made a career decision to abandon his general surgical practice and concentrate in neuropsychiatry. Leaving City Hospital, he accepted the post of chief of staff at Theodore Wheelock Memorial Sanitarium in Merrimac.

Carol soon became spitefully jealous of a young associate in Jim's new field, an attractive heiress named Carson McVicker. Listeners learned that Dr. McVicker could be ruthless in meeting her own objectives, frequently resorting to deceptive practices to achieve desired ends. McVicker eventually suffered a nervous breakdown, forcing her to resign from the sanitarium. Carol, who more than once boasted that she herself could wrap Jim around her little finger, breathed a sigh of relief.

In the late 1940s Carol persuaded Jim to offer a position as research chemist to Alec Ransom, a nephew of Carol's employer. Arriving in Merrimac, Ransom was invited into the Brent home as a guest while he sought a permanent place to live. Subsequently, fans learned — along with Carol, to her dismay — that young Ransom had an undisputed reputation in previous locales as a ladies' man. An acquaintance reported that Ransom had, in fact, been engaged to four different women in a single year!

Carol, who until then had been enjoying the almost unbridled attention of the charming younger man, suffered a mild setback. His history was forgiven in short order, however. It was obvious that the distraction offered by the dapper young house guest played to her heartstrings. Yet even Carol was surprised when one evening — after dinner, with Jim returning to his laboratory and Ransom and Carol alone in the parlor of the Brent home — Ransom passionately kissed her.

A short while later, Carol sat alone in her bedroom doing some sewing while trying to compose herself, awaiting Jim's return. Jim had already begun to have doubts about Ransom's unrestrained ambitions. As he entered the room, the couple exchanged pleasantries. Then Jim reported that, downstairs, he had encountered their daughter-in-law, Francie. Francie and Butch were living under that roof at the time, too. Francie was quite shaken by advances she alleged that Ransom had made toward her, and she pled with Jim to order Ransom out of the house.

The exchange between Carol and Jim on the broadcast of November 14, 1947, went like this:

> JIM: Alec Ransom seems to me to be a person without too
>   many scruples.
> CAROL: You're wrong, Jim. And it's unfair to misjudge Alec like
>   that. I know him better than any of you, and I tell you that
>   he's a very fine and a very respectable person.
> JIM: Well, I suppose I could be mistaken, but—
> CAROL: (Cuts him off) You are, Jim, believe me. Alec Ransom
>   isn't the sort of man who makes improper advances in a
>   house that he's visiting. And he certainly wouldn't approach
>   a married woman, Jim.
> JIM: Hummm.
> CAROL: After all, Butch is living under the same roof with him,
>   and—even if Alec was attracted to Francie ... aw—it's just
>   too ridiculous to consider even for a moment.

The two continued in that vein for a little while. And then, laying her mending aside, Carol remarked: "There, look at the pile of socks I've darned!"

"You've done a good evening's work," Jim replied.

The scene concluded with Carol's statement: "Hummm ... that's true ... I *have* done a good evening's work."

Over an organ bridge, announcer Clayton (Bud) Collyer intoned: "As far as she is concerned, the episode is closed."

Less than a week later, with Jim out of town on business, Alec borrowed Jim's car to take Carol to dinner at a restaurant many miles from Merrimac. En route home, despite mild protests from Carol, he stopped to kiss her. Back at the house he kissed her again. By then, if listeners hadn't realized it before, they could confirm that Alec wasn't the only one "without too many scruples," as Jim had observed only a few nights earlier.

The plot took a bizarre twist not many months later. On one of her overseas trips, Carol's plane reportedly went down in a fiery crash. Her body was never recovered. Despite the unexpected shock and loss, Dr. Brent at last appeared to have an opportunity to gain sustained happiness. He had worked for a while alongside an attractive lab assistant, Maggie Lowell. The pair fell deeply in love. After a period of mourning, they set a wedding date. But it was not to be: the very day of their nuptials, who should show up but long-lost Carol!

Actually it wasn't Carol at all but an actress, Beth Lambert, down on her luck. Employed by a ring of thieves, Lambert had been sent to steal top-secret data that Jim was acquiring from some government experiments he was conducting. With some coaching and plastic surgery, she was able to convince almost everyone of her veracity, including Jim. (This was radio, remember, where virtually anything could be contrived into acceptance within a listener's ability to comprehend and reason.)

There was one unconvinced skeptic, however. A hungry newspaper reporter, Frank Dana, whose duty it was to be objective, wasn't buying Beth Lambert's story. While Dana sent a detective to Europe to check out her account of "Carol's" disappearance during the past year, things began to unravel at home. Lambert didn't anticipate falling in love with her "daughter," Janie, and with Jim. That complicated everything. As a consequence, Lambert made a conscious decision to stall her employers from gaining the information they sought.

It didn't take the gang long to realize that she had had a change of heart and was no longer cooperating. Risking exposure on the one hand and retaliation on the other, she played the odds for as long as she could. Finally identified, she faced trial with charges of treason. The group's leader was determined to sway the jury by blaming the hoax on Lambert. But Jim Brent, the primary victim of her deception, came to her defense. Testifying for her, he saw to it that the conspiratorial masterminds were sent to their long and just rewards.

Following the trial, Jim concentrated on restoring a young Jocelyn McLeod, his patient, to full mental health. She had been the victim of years of unmerciful mental abuse at the hands of her family. In time, even though Jim was several years Jocelyn's senior, the two were romantically attracted to one another. In a recovered Jocelyn, he saw an opportunity for true and sustained love. By the early 1950s she saw it too. At last, after what seemed like a lifetime of heartache, he wed Jocelyn, settling into a union secured by long-lasting happiness, mutual respect and contentment — all of which he had previously missed. While Jim would be embroiled in crises of one kind or another until the show was canceled, he faced them confidently with a partner who offered reassurance. The series closed on a note of optimism that the years ahead would be better than those that had gone before.

Road of Life literally drew an audience from all over the daytime schedule. Unlike most other soap operas that fell into a comfortable spot and were left to idle for years, *Road* moved in and out of more than a dozen time periods, ranging from 9:30 a.m. to five o'clock p.m. on two networks, CBS and NBC.

It wasn't uncommon for more than one network to air the same dishpan drama on the same day, albeit at different hours. *Road* became the premier soap opera in dual broadcasts, appearing on both CBS and NBC at different hours in nine of its 21 full seasons.

The program was also carried for fifteen minutes daily on CBS-TV from December 13, 1954, to July 1, 1955. (An appreciable number of affiliates failed to clear the time to make the drama feasible, so it was dropped.) Don MacLaughlin and Virginia Dwyer, from the radio series, played the TV roles of Jim and Jocelyn Brent. Bill Lipton and Elizabeth Lawrence reprised their roles as Butch and Francie Brent.

The radio show was sold as a package to the networks with commercial spots already included. In the 1930s, sponsor Procter & Gamble promoted its Chipso detergent there. But *Road of Life* is surely best remembered for another P&G laundry product, Duz. Duz became so synonymous with the drama that announcer Clayton (Bud) Collyer, who extolled its virtues daily for years, exclaimed as he introduced the serial: "Yes, it's the Duz program, *Road of Life!*" Over and over Collyer told listeners: "It's the *soap* in Duz that does it!" At the conclusion of every commercial, he stressed: "Duz does *everything!*" And as he signed off each day, Collyer bade farewell to his audience with the phrase: "Good day, and good Duzing!"

The little ditty that was quoted at the start of this chapter — and that opened the show for many years — was also sung during those same years on a Duz-sponsored audience-participation comedy-quiz show, *Truth or Consequences*. For several seasons *Truth* was an enormously popular national phenomenon on NBC's Saturday-night lineup. Bud Collyer delivered the Duz commercials there too. Master of ceremonies Ralph Edwards—who invariably screamed as he put a prank over on a contestant, "Aren't we devils?"—sang along every week to a female vocalist's rendition of what he called "the washday song." The studio audience roared, and the show was a ratings smash.

Together, the two programs (*Truth or Consequences* and *Road of Life*) provided a blockbuster marketing combination for Duz. Billions of boxes of detergent were sold throughout the 1940s to happy homemakers living in every state of the union as a result of the campaign's potency. Anyone wondering why the term *soap opera* was applied to serialized drama need look no further. The Duz program's success was why washboard weepers were inexorably associated with the cleansing product manufacturers.

In the fall of 1952, cancellation was announced for another popular long-running soap opera, *Big Sister*. For years it had aired in a quarter-hour that P&G traditionally reserved for its Ivory soap brand—one o'clock on CBS. (*Road of Life* was then being heard at 3:15 p.m. on NBC.) Because *Road* commanded a strong following, P&G decided to run it twice daily, as it had in several earlier years. The show was assigned the time period being vacated by *Big Sister*.

Collyer, whose voice was clearly tied to Duz, departed to other pastures. Now the series was narrated by the gentle, soft-spoken, earthy tones of veteran announcer Nelson Case. Whereas Collyer had emphatically barked "Road of Life!" when he introduced the series each day, for the first time the definite article was added to the title. Case preceded the serial's familiar theme with an unpretentious, matter-of-fact billboard. "*The Road of Life*, compliments of Ivory Soap," he would gently announce before the Tchaikovsky music rolled. It sounded an awful lot like CBS's adroit, philosophical commentator Charles Osgood, who would deliver humorous rhyming couplets years later.

In *Road's* earliest days, yet another device ushered in the serial. Collyer barked the program's name, and then—a few bars into the theme—actress Angel Casey or Jeannette Dowling paged: "Dr. Brent, call sur-ger-eee! Dr. Brent, call sur-ger-eee!" For years he got that same message every day.

The lead role of Jim Brent went to five actors: Ken Griffin (*Backstage Wife*), Matt Crowley (*Perry Mason*), David Ellis (stints in *Adventures by Morse* and *Richard Diamond, Private Detective*), Howard Teichmann (no other prominent roles but the only actor to write the scripts *and* play the lead) and Don MacLaughlin. MacLaughlin is most notably associated with the Brent role and may have carried it longer than the others. He brought depth of resonance to the part, turning the physician into a warm, authoritative figure. Born on November 24, 1906, at Webster, Iowa, he earned a degree as a speech and English major at the University of Iowa. After teaching and coaching, in 1933 he decided to try his luck in New York as an actor.

He appeared in Broadway productions of *South Pacific* and *Fifth Column*, before landing in radio, where he would make a significant mark over two decades. MacLaughlin gained leading roles in four other series: *Chaplain Jim, U.S.A.; David Harding, Counterspy; Tennessee Jed;* and *The Zane Grey Theater*. He appeared sporadically in *Ethel and Albert, Gangbusters, Superman* and *The Witch's Tale*. And he acquired ongoing parts in more soap operas: *The Story of Mary Marlin, Young Widder Brown, The Romance of Helen Trent, Lora Lawton* and *We Love and Learn*.

The skilled thespian didn't retire when the Golden Age of radio ended. Unlike some of his peers, he handily made the leap to TV. First appearing as Dr. Brent in the short-lived *Road of Life* TV series, MacLaughlin won the masculine lead of Chris Hughes in a serial that debuted on April 2, 1956: *As the World Turns*. He carried the part until his death at age 79 three decades later, on May 28, 1986, in Goshen, Connecticut.

Three actresses appeared as Dr. Brent's first wife, Carol, on radio's *Road of Life*: Lesley Woods, Louise Fitch and Marion Shockley. All were veterans of other series.

Woods was the girlfriend-confidante-accomplice of a trio of radio sleuths: *Boston Blackie*, *The Shadow* and *Casey, Crime Photographer*. She also had recurring roles in 15 other serials. On radio she played in *Backstage Wife*, *Bright Horizon*, *The Guiding Light*, *The Romance of Helen Trent*, *Rosemary*, *This Is Nora Drake*, *We Love and Learn*, *Woman in White* and *Joyce Jordan, Girl Interne*. Moving to television, between 1958 and 1989 she gained ongoing parts on serials in this order: *Young Doctor Malone*, *The Edge of Night*, *Search for Tomorrow*, *Bright Promise*, *Return to Peyton Place* and *The Bold and the Beautiful*.

Fitch had running roles in three humorous series: *That Brewster Boy*, *Mortimer Gooch* and *Scattergood Baines*. From time to time she appeared in *The Light of the World*. She had leads in two serials—*Two on a Clue* and *We Love and Learn*—and worked regularly in several more: *Arnold Grimm's Daughter*, *Backstage Wife*, *Big Sister*, *Kitty Keene*, *Ma Perkins*, *Woman in White* and *Joyce Jordan, Girl Interne*. The actress died on September 11, 1996.

Shockley, who in the late 1940s married *Road of Life* announcer Bud Collyer, hailed from Kansas City, Missouri. In the 1930s she played in Broadway's *Dear Old Darling* opposite George M. Cohan. After subsequent theatrical attempts led nowhere, she launched an audio career in a Kate Smith show. Regular assignments surfaced on *Mystery Theatre*. She won recurring parts on *The Adventures of Ellery Queen* and *Abie's Irish Rose*.

Actresses Virginia Dwyer (*Front Page Farrell*) and Barbara Becker were featured as Jocelyn McLeod Brent on *Road of Life*. Becker had no other prominent radio credits. She was in the *Road of Life* TV series and later carried a running role in *The Guiding Light* on TV (1961–63).

Historiographers of the genre called *Road* "a most important soap opera."[3] Without stretching the point, it was a phenomenal success. When the impact that this serial made on those that followed is taken into account—through early emphasis on medical professionals, realism, character development, durability, extraordinary sponsor identification, vast audience potential with 40 percent of its run airing on dual networks, plus influence on TV serials via a trial run and the fact that its creator, lead actor, sponsor, network and others in front of and behind the microphones converged for *As the World Turns*—its legacy is remarkable and likely unsurpassed. Like Duz, this one really seemed able to do *everything*!

22
The Romance of Helen Trent
(The Goddess of Goodness)

She may have been the most guarded, most virtuous heroine of all the serials, this long-standing temptress among legions of weak males. Helen Trent was a tease who could wait forever if need be for true love to prove itself beyond her slightest anxiety. Better, it seemed, to be utterly certain about a man's devotion than learn decades later that he hadn't quite meant "till death do us part." So, though middle-aged, and beyond, poor Helen rebuffed suitor after suitor on her way toward a hoped-for commitment that would transcend time. As it turned out, the noblest swain of all, Gil Whitney, stood by, awaiting confirmation for over two decades while Helen dillydallied without making a decision. Meanwhile, some of the most repulsive sweet-talkers in radio theatrics attempted to lure her into their lairs. It was all in a day's work for the unblemished Helen, who never had a decadent thought — and who never lived in a real world. Listeners loved her anyway, keeping her at the top of the weekday ratings (even beating *Arthur Godfrey Time* for first place) much of the time. Her struggles lasted 27 years, more episodes than any other soap opera. When it ended, the ageless beauty was still unwed, still dutifully searching for the man who could turn her dreams into reality. The problem was that by then, she would have been well past three-score in years. If she didn't quit dreaming and start doing, all she would have left to fantasize about was what she had missed.

Producers: Frank and Anne Hummert
Producer-Director: Stanley Davis
Directors: Richard Leonard, Les Mitchel, Ernest Ricca, Blair Walliser
Writers: Martha Alexander, Marie Banner, Ruth Borden, Margo Brooks, Ronald Dawson
Music: Stanley Davis, Lawrence Salerno
Sound Effects: James Lynch, Romeo Quantro
Announcers: Pierre Andre, Don Hancock, Fielden Farrington (1944–60)
Helen Trent: Virginia Clark (1933–43), Betty Ruth Smith (1943–44), Julie Stevens (1944–60)
Gil Whitney: Marvin Miller, William Green, David Gothard (1936–37, 1944–60)
Jeff Brady: Ken Daigneau
Cynthia Carter Swanson Whitney: Mary Jane Higby
Others: Jay Barney, Bill Bouchey, Sarah Burton, Whitfield Connor, Cathleen Cordell, Mary

Frances Desmond, Helene Dumas, Patricia Dunlap, Katherine Emmet, Marilyn Er-
skine, Vivian Fridell, Lauren Gilbert, Lucy Gilman, Alice Goodkin, Mitzi Gould, Hilda
Graham, Alan Hewitt, Alice Hill, John Hodiak, Leon Janney, Ginger Jones, Carlton
KaDell, Louis Krugman, John Larkin, Ed Latimer, Janet Logan, Don MacLaughlin,
Charlotte Manson, Bernice Martin, Bess McCammon, Audrey McGrath, James
Meighan, Les Mitchel, Bret Morrison, Marie Nelson, Patsy O'Shea, Loretta Poynton, Ed
Prentiss, Donna Reade, Linda Reid, Doris Rich, Grant Richards, Bartlett Robinson, Flo-
rence Robinson, Selena Royle, Klock Ryder, Nanette Sargent, Bernice Silverman, Cora
B. Smith, Olan Soule, Amzie Strickland, Hope Summers, Reese Taylor, William Thornton,
Les Tremayne, Peggy Wall, John Walsh, George Ward, Karl Weber, Lesley Woods, more

Theme: "Juanita" (hummed and strummed on ukulele)

Sponsors: Blackett-Sample-Hummert governed this show in its early years for Edna W.
Hopper (Hopper's White Clay Pack facial mask) and in 1955–56 for Pharmaco, Inc., for
Feen-A-Mint laxative chewing gum and other products. After that, the show was sold
to participating sponsors. For 16 seasons it was the property of American Home Products (AHP) Corp. AHP rotated goods advertised on its serials. From Boyle-Midway, the
sponsor's household products division, it plugged Black Flag and Fly-Ded insect repel-
lents, Aerowax and Olde English floor cleaners, Wizard Wick room deodorizer, Sani-
Flush toilet cleanser, Easy-Off oven cleaner and other brands. From the Whitehall
Pharmacal Co., AHP's packaged drug division, the sponsor advertised Kolynos toothpaste and tooth powder dentifrice, Anacin pain reliever, Kriptin antihistamine, Bi-So-
Dol analgesic, Freezone corn remover, Heet liniment, Dristan and Primatene cold
remedies, Preparation H hemorrhoid medication, Neet hair remover, Infrarub balm,
Sleep-Eze calmative and more. In a memorable campaign, announcer Fielden Farrington was concerned about a malady the commercial gurus had labeled "American Stomach." For months Farrington pushed a product designed to correct that debilitating
condition.

Ratings: Records are available for the years 1938–56 inclusive. High: 11.0 (1949–50); Low:
4.7 (1955–56); Median: 7.7. Of the serials airing single episodes daily, this one often led
the charts, beating all other competition on weekday radio. During the last hurrah of
radio's Golden Age, in the 1949–50 season before ratings began a steady slide to TV,
nine of the top ten weekday shows were serials: (1) *The Romance of Helen Trent*, 11.0;
(2) *Arthur Godfrey Time*, 10.5; (3) *Wendy Warren and the News*, 10.2; (4) *Aunt Jenny's
Real Life Stories*, 10.1; (5) (triple tie) *Our Gal Sunday, The Right to Happiness, Road of
Life*, 9.9; (8) *Pepper Young's Family*, 9.4; (9) *Big Sister*, 9.3; (10) *Ma Perkins*, 9.2. Seven
were then CBS features; half were sponsored by Procter & Gamble; three began under
the Hummerts' watchful eye, two were Irna Phillips products and one each was from
Elaine Carrington and three other creators; all aired between 11:00 a.m. and 4:00 p.m.
ET; eight had been on the air a decade or longer.

On the Air: Oct. 30, 1933–May 10, 1935, CBS, 2:15 p.m. ET; 1935–1936, CBS, 11:15 a.m.;
1936–June 24, 1960, CBS, 12:30 p.m.

And now The Romance of Helen Trent, *the real-life drama of Helen Trent who, when life mocks her, breaks her hopes, dashes her against the rocks of despair, fights back bravely, successfully, to prove what so many women long to prove in their own lives: That because a woman is 35, or more, romance in life need not be over; that the romance of youth can extend into middle life, and even beyond.*
— Epigraph to *The Romance of Helen Trent*

Radio's grand old daytime dame Helen Trent (who would have been 62 years old by the time the show left the air, assuming she was 35 when it began) brought millions in advertising revenues to CBS. "And," noted one magazine reviewer writing the durable serial's obituary in 1960, Helen probably "interfered with more housework than any other serial queen on the air."[1]

The Romance of Helen Trent was the relentless struggle between Good and Evil. It was a kind of audio simmering pot of primitive emotion heavily seasoned with unrequited love. Along with it came heavy doses of the bizarre in the form of insane killers, jealous lovers, would-be rapists and the usual sort of despicable perverts who characteristically pursued lovely damsels in distress — even middle aged ones.

Helen was the kind of girl that listeners either identified with or misunderstood altogether; they adored her or they loathed her. Circumspect in every way, her only excess was in wearing the glamorous gowns that she designed for a living. If her followers appreciated a squeaky-clean deportment, they could be subjects for life.

Conversely, Helen also had her detractors, who were perhaps more vocal than anyone else's critics in daytime radio. And their appraisals were almost universally negative:

• The series may well have been "the most maligned program to survive on either radio or television," one conceded.[2]

• Another labeled it, "a wretched melodrama."[3]

• The program was decried as "perhaps the most backward of all serials."[4]

• Still another critic suggested that the drama was "the ultimate in high camp."[5]

• Helen Trent herself was proclaimed "the most colorless serial heroine ever devised."[6]

• One critic claimed Helen was endowed with "the dullest personality the Creator could muster."[7]

• Even an actress who played the part found her to be "a pretty boring lady."[8]

Despite the pronounced negativism, Helen was utterly loved by her fans, having few if any equals. In her heyday *she* — not the actresses portraying her — received more than a thousand letters *per week* from her legions of admirers. From them she acquired free advice and gifts and was remembered on anniversaries, holidays and other special occasions. On a typical midday, four million women tuned in to her exploits carried on more than two hundred CBS network stations.

This "indisputable queen of the soaps,"[9] depicted even more generously as "the goddess of all radio,"[10] outlasted almost all of her contemporaries — and arguably aired on more episodes than any other serial hero or heroine. If she was as awful as her detractors alleged, how did she achieve an unsurpassed record of 7,222 broadcasts? And how did she consistently appear in the top tier of all weekday radio programs for so many years? There may be a very rational explanation.

The environment of *The Romance of Helen Trent* (locally, at first, in Chicago) was a far cry from what American life has become. Men were, virtually everywhere, undisputed masters of their households. As a direct consequence, most women suffered in silence, living difficult lives. Time-saving appliances weren't yet available to them: midcentury would arrive before automatic washers, dryers, dishwashers and other conveniences began offering some relief in most homes.

Homemakers devoted entire mornings or afternoons to rubbing large bars of soap across washboards, lifting heavy scalding-hot irons and cooking budget meals made from scratch. In addition, they often cared for too many children. Many women suffered emotional, mental and physical abuses too. Meanwhile, the prevailing attitude in polite society was that divorce could be neither tolerated nor afforded.

Given this climate, is it any wonder that so many of these women devoutly turned to Helen Trent? Here was a heroine who, in their imaginary worlds, lived an existence that they would love to experience. To them she seemed very real, charming and glamorous. Helen had everything any downtrodden woman might dream of—freedom, enchanting acquaintances, a successful career, modest resources and a seemingly endless procession of impassioned lovers. Under different circumstances, they could aspire to her achievements themselves. And they could fantasize about it right then.

Some of Helen's harshest judges suggested that her attractive romantic situation, most unusual for a woman of her age, was the link to the program's popularity. Romantically inclined women of 35 or more could promptly identify with her. CBS explained that this age had been selected because it was old enough for her to have acquired emotional security but still young enough for her to pursue passion and vocation simultaneously. And if personality was the basis for Helen's magnetic draw of multiple swains, most of her listeners who themselves possessed little or no compelling character could certainly resonate as her equals. Her most persistent suitor, Gil Whitney, for instance, observed that the frenzied romantic beehive of activity surrounding Helen—who drew 30 suitors in her lifetime—existed simply "for no damn good reason at all."

Helen, who never made it down the aisle in 27 years, avoided marriage for a very simple reason: the whole premise of the show would have evaporated had she tied the knot! Instead, she became the hopelessly pursued. And whether her audience realized it or not, this could never be otherwise.

The altar apparently eluded only one other of radio's popular daytime heroines who possessed sustaining abilities similar to Helen's. On her final broadcast *Young Widder Brown*—for 18 years stalked by lecherous gents with liabilities remarkably similar to those held by the men pursuing Helen—was also short of matrimony. For about two decades each of these women led a singularly devoted male on a merry chase. Both women chose professionals as their most faithful beaus: Ellen's was a physician; Helen's was a lawyer. Coincidentally (or perhaps not), Ms. Brown was named Ellen while Ms. Trent was named Helen. The similarities in the two shows were uncanny—so great that even the heroines' names sounded alike!

And it should come as little surprise that both these enduring dramas, bearing the same precise theme, were churned out in a single shop by scriptwriters who worked on both shows. No puzzle there: each was a product of the Hummert production factory.

Helen's entourage included a strange assortment of men: a psychotic, a gangster, a movie star, a millionaire, a fascist and a hypnotist. Of the 30 who chased her over those years, two dozen got near enough to propose marriage. But none got any closer.

Usually they were tainted by some sort of villainy or avarice that Helen was invariably the last to detect. Though she was pure and noble, she seemed magnetically drawn toward men who were up to no good, who never looked on her as a sister. Her lovers often suffered misfortunes like dying or disappearing. Invariably, those with evil intents were rewarded in appropriate ways: fatal falls from cliffs, airplane tragedies or exile to faraway places.

Her admirers fell into four categories:

• A few were simply a little shy of a full load of bricks. Though these were basically decent sorts, they were never convincingly equal to Helen's IQ. Gil Whitney and her final suitor, senatorial candidate John Cole, could be assigned to this division.

• A second group included the bad boys who, when rebuffed, determined that if they couldn't have Helen for themselves, by golly nobody else would either. Several tried to do away with her — shooting her, pushing her off a precipice or drugging her. At least one vowed his intention to rape her. Others framed her for every imaginable crime, including murder. Kurt Bonine made Helen's twenty-third year on the air especially memorable by trapping her in a tower. He was finally imprisoned a couple of years later for shooting Gil Whitney.

• Third, there were those who merely destroyed themselves when Helen turned thumbs down. Oilman Dwight Swanson deliberately crashed his plane into a mountain. The millionaire Texan Brett Chapman disappeared to South America for the rest of his natural life. And Dr. Reginald Travers, who pleaded for Helen's hand three times a week, selected Vienna as his place of exile when his hopes were dashed.

• Finally, there was a host of individuals whose situations were so unique that they just didn't fit into any other category. Helen told most of them to buzz off, except for one: an artist who at last won her hand simply died of a heart attack the night before their wedding! When she became sweet on a gangster, her audience was so incensed that he was quickly written out of the plot via a volley of bullets.

Still, Helen's ardent admirers in real life knew that, for most of her show's life, there was but one true love for her — the gallantly handsome attorney Gil Whitney. From his introduction into the plot in 1936 until he finally gave up and said "I do" to somebody else in 1958, his love never wavered. For nearly all of the show's run, Gil pursued his infatuation while Helen indulged him. The only thing that could ultimately prevent their life together, as it turned out, was Frank and Anne Hummert. Hordes of obstacles would come between the pair as the Hummerts alone decreed that Gil would never have his way with Helen. If he had, a premise that dated from 1933 would have evaporated; and with no premise, there would be no show.

In the mid–1940s, when war wounds confined Gil to a wheelchair, Helen — having experienced a momentary change of heart while Gil was incapacitated — insisted they must marry "this very month of June or never." While a distraught Gil listened, Helen paced back and forth:

> HELEN: Gil, I'm ready to reach out and take what belongs to us
>   and deal with the hindrances afterward. If you aren't ready,
>   say so and ... we'll let the whole thing drop.
> GIL: How long do I have to decide on the answer?
> HELEN: No time, not any ... I want the answer right now....
> GIL: I'm a *man*! To me you're the most beautiful and desirable

> creature on earth … and I … I long for you with all I'm
> made of…. I loathe everything that's ever happened to keep
> us apart. I'd like to marry you, and get away from every-
> thing and everybody and … have you for myself for years,
> not months. I love you more than you'll ever know,
> Helen…. And yet, here I am … too helpless even to walk
> over to where you stand. What can I give you when I'm this
> way? Suppose something happens and I stay this way for
> years?
> HELEN: Don't say that again! You won't be an invalid for
> long….
> GIL: Oh great scot, it'd be so easy for me to say "yes," so hard
> to say "no." I'm so sick … and weary of waiting….

Homer, the Greek epic poet, once observed: "His speech flowed from his tongue sweeter than honey."

Of course, Gil was right. Something *always* intervened when those two started talking wedding plans. Their postponements actually became one of radio's longest-running gags.

One of the oddities about Helen, apart from the fact that she couldn't marry, was her unapproachable virtue, which gave her a superiority not enjoyed by any other serial heroine. What possessed Helen to become such a master of moral strength and courage? About her past, listeners knew little. Even her writers didn't know much of her history. It was established that sometime earlier, she had been married to a man about whom her fans were told almost nothing. He disappeared at sea and remained Helen's secret forever, for she chose not to talk about him. But married to her, he must have been a fantastically lucky man.

Helen was typical of her contemporaries. When a soap opera heroine was single, listeners could assume almost without exception that she was a widow. It would have been practically unthinkable for one to have been divorced or never married. The hardest thing to reconcile with the virtuous notions of such heroines was their previous liaison with at least one gentleman.

Actions were at cross-purposes here. On the one hand, biologically speaking, the virginal heroine was seldom found in daytime dramas. On the other hand, behaviorally speaking, she was always present. Although such leading ladies had once been married, their actions never hinted that they had even been kissed. Displaying the innocence of an untouched flower was ridiculous, of course, but several gave that impression as if totally above a degrading thought.

The Hummerts' interpretation of sex in their soap operas was patently naive. Helen Trent was an excellent example of such purity beyond relief. When a fiancé (Helen had several) asked to hold her hand on one occasion, she reminded him that a mere engagement ring did not buy such privileges. Helen and her kind had a way of making a peck on the cheek appear to be sexual excess.

As late as 1957, when villain Kurt Bonine had Helen right where he wanted her—snared in an abandoned house—he proceeded lustfully toward her. "Kurt, you're mad!" she screamed. Her life, and her reputation, were spared for another 60 seconds as a commercial interrupted. But he would have his way with her, and he pursued his revenge immediately following the ad. As the day's episode drew to a close, Kurt informed his quarry: "When I'm through with you…." And Helen, her back to the wall, cut him off with the injunction that Hummert heroines always relied on when placed in a corner by an advancing villain: "Kurt, Kurt, you wouldn't!" (What sounded like attempted rape in these programs sometimes resulted in something less heinous by Hummert standards, something like attempted murder, maybe.)

Certainly it wasn't that Kurt *wouldn't*. Given the time and opportunity, the audience knew without a doubt that he very well *would*. But loyal listeners also knew that Bonine and his counterparts *didn't*. Someone or something would invariably interrupt, postpone or abandon those evil intentions.

Yet Helen — this very same Helen who was so far above reproach — had her "moments," though not very many or very stimulating. On one occasion on a pleasure cruise, she ventured off course and into the stateroom of a male passenger. Because of her sterling image, faithful listeners were outraged, and CBS censors got an earful. Another time, in 1954 when she obviously wasn't in her right mind, she threw caution to the wind and asked Gil to press his face close to hers. To avoid a deluge of protests from fans, she quickly asked him to marry her, right then. What else could a good girl of 35 or more do to maintain her honor? Gil, ablaze after waiting for this invitation since 1936, blurted out, "You betcha!" Pointless to add, it didn't happen.

Helen seldom showed any temper; she never smoked and never drank alcohol. For all of those years she remained chaste. Nobly selfless, she refused to stoop to the maneuvers of the lunatic fringe about her. By contrast, gossip columnist Daisy Parker, who frequently resorted to smear tactics in order to taint Helen's reputation, smoked, drank and dipped into all sorts of skullduggery. Yet housewives who themselves smoked three packs a day were probably convinced that any woman who smoked or drank on *The Romance of Helen Trent* had low ethics and loose morals.

The continuing plot was a mishmash of stuff that often wound up in a romantic triangle. There was usually one good guy (frequently Gil Whitney) that the fans were pulling for and an evil one in Helen's pursuit. Sometimes the evil one turned out to be a woman. Fay Granville pretended to be alone and penniless, charming Gil into giving her a job as his secretary. Feeling sorry for her, he took her out to dinner. But the conniving Fay claimed he proposed to her, then threatened a scandal if he didn't marry her.

Behind this facade was Gil's wife, Cynthia Carter Swanson Whitney, whom he had married in a misguided moment. (Anthony Loring did the same thing on *Young Widder Brown*, the drama with the similar premise.) Cynthia, whose sole ambition was to ruin Helen's life, refused to grant Gil a divorce. But she was willing to step aside for Fay to marry him; in fact, she masterminded a plan to fly to Mexico to get a quick divorce. Then Fay could marry Gil, and Helen would be destroyed. Gil's reaction was to offer Fay a million dollars to get out of his life; he would go into debt for the rest of his days to rid himself of her.

In the late 1940s Helen was accused of murder after discovering the body of Rex Carroll. Stumbling onto the murder scene, with Helen standing over the body, was columnist Daisy Parker. Lawyer Gil Whitney pulled out all the stops to keep his lady friend out of the gas chamber, but he nearly lost her. A sinister mentalist, Carl Dorn, who was willing to let Helen take the rap for him, was finally put away for the crime.

A year later producer Jeff Brady, who owned the Hollywood motion picture studio where Helen designed clothes, helped her buy Gil's house when Gil left town. Jeff then assisted Helen in reselling the house to Cynthia Swanson. He gave Helen a bank book showing she had made a handsome profit on the sale. But the book fell into the hands of Jeff's jealous wife, Lydia, who naturally assumed — given Helen's uncompromising reputation — the very worst about Jeff and Helen. Gossip columnist Daisy Parker, who seemed to have it in for Helen, had a field day with that tabloid topic.

Helen's romantic chase continued until June 24, 1960. This was a big year for endings, you will recall. When word came down that it was all about to end, the cast and crew thought up several scenarios that they deemed appropriate for the series' demise. One ending would have had *Ma Perkins* chuckling over a poisoned turkey dinner she had fed to Helen and her suitors. *Perkins* survived the June 24 CBS massacre and would be around until its own collapse five months later. Perhaps in deference to the heroine's eternal modesty, or her age, *Trent* was permitted to slip from the lineup before the final blow came to the few soap operas still on the air.

The most intriguing projected final sequence was probably the one suggested by actor Leon Janney, then playing Helen's last swain. He proposed that during each of the last five episodes, one of the main characters be polished off in some brutal way — perhaps a landslide, an amnesia attack, a lightning bolt or a plane crash. For the finale, Helen would get hers. While she was standing on a balcony overlooking a deep ravine, the balcony would give way and she would literally become history. In the final moments of the episode, there would come a knock on her door, followed by several more urgent knocks. Then a most familiar voice would plead: "Helen! Helen! It's Gil." Sanity prevailed, however.

There were three Helens in the serial's long run. Virginia Clark, twice divorced in real life (in sharp contrast to the character she portrayed), originated the role when the serial was broadcast from Chicago. Relinquishing the part a decade later, she moved to Puerto Rico as a recreation director. Clark was credited with no other major radio roles.

The actress who succeeded her, shortly before the series moved to New York, was Betty Ruth Smith. By then Smith had been a heroine on three other soap operas —*Judy and Jane, Lone Journey* and *Woman in White*— and a regular on *Backstage Wife*.

The most famous of all the Helens, however, was Julie Stevens, who lived in New York. In the summer of 1944 the Hummerts decided to originate the show from the Big Apple, leaving behind the Windy City. Auditions were scheduled on the final broadcast day of the serial *Kitty Foyle*. Stevens had played the title role on that series during the two years it had been on the air. She recalled dashing across the street to CBS in a torrential downpour after her final performance as Kitty to participate in the *Trent* competition. Soaked to the skin from the rain, she was met by another actress who had already auditioned.

"Why on earth would you be interested in this part, Julie?" quipped the woman. "You're much too young to play it." Stevens was in her mid–20s and felt a little dejected by those words. But the producers never detected it. Stevens' crisp, velvet tones readily persuaded them, and she was signed for the lead. That same year Stevens married steel executive Charles Underhill. While playing Helen over the next 16 years, in private life she became the mother of two daughters, Sarah and Nancy.

In an interview after the series ended, Stevens recalled that the cast used to take potshots at Helen's straitlaced ways. Ernest Ricca, the show's director for many years, let the cast members clown around and scream with laughter during rehearsals. By airtime it was out of their systems, and they were dead serious about the dialogue.

Stevens envisioned Helen as a tall, striking brunette, whereas, she herself was short and blonde. She played the title role with a soft, lolling voice, claiming she was instructed to be "salaciously breathy."

Born in St. Louis in about 1917, Stevens launched her acting career in *The Male Animal* on Broadway. In the 1940s she was featured in radio's *Abie's Irish Rose, Ethel and Albert, Road of Life, Stella Dallas, The Light of the World, Quick as a Flash, The Adventures of the Abbotts* (in which she played the female lead) and most other crime, mystery and dramatic anthology programs. After radio, she appeared in video commercials and TV's *Big Story* adventure series. Retiring to her New England home for more family time, she cohosted a local radio program, "Ted and Julie," with Ted Bell on WVLC in Orleans, Massachusetts. Stevens also continued her stage career, accepting occasional parts in the Cape Cod community theater. She died on August 26, 1984.

In addition to the trio of actresses who played Helen (two of them for over a decade each), there was an occasional substitute in the role. But a *New York Times* reporter, writing in 1956 about the long-running series, dismissed them as no more than "Helen Trentlets."

Just as there were three Helens, a like number of actors filled the role of Gil Whitney, her long-suffering suitor who gave up in 1958 to marry somebody else. Marvin Miller, who played in virtually every dramatic program on the air, was the first. Born in St. Louis on July 18, 1913, he developed an interest in radio while a student at Washington University. At his hometown's station, KMOX, he launched a professional career, soon becoming a freelance announcer. Before he was 30 years old, he was appearing on 40 radio shows weekly originating in Chicago. Later moving to the West Coast, he was the personal secretary, Michael Anthony, on TV's *The Millionaire* starting in 1955. In the fictional series, he delivered million-dollar cashier's checks from John Beresford Tipton to surprised recipients. He did voice-overs for television's *The F.B.I.* and a trio of cartoon shows: *Aquaman, Mr. Magoo* and *Fantastic Voyage*. He also played the part of numerous oriental figures in film and on TV. Miller was still active at age 71, recording a five-minute syndicated show called *Almanac* as a lead-in to local weather reports. He died at Santa Monica, California, on February 8, 1985.

Eventually successful in movies and television, Miller may have been unparalleled by anyone else as a radio announcer and actor. His documented credits include *The Affairs of Anthony, The Andrews Sisters Eight-to-the-Bar Ranch, Armchair Adventures, Aunt Jemima, Aunt Mary, Backstage Wife, Beat the Band, Beulah, The Bickersons, The Billie Burke Show, The Buster Brown Gang, Captain Midnight, The Chicago Theatre of the Air, The Cisco Kid, Coronet Storyteller, The Danny Thomas Show, A Date with Judy, Dear Mom, The Don Ameche Show, Dreft Star Playhouse, Duffy's Tavern, The Family Theater, Father Knows Best, The First Nighter, The Gay Mrs. Featherstone, Great Gunns, The Guiding Light, Harold Teen, Irene Rich Dramas, Jack Armstrong the All-American Boy, Jeff Regan, Judy and Jane, Knicker-bocker Playhouse, Lassie, Lonely Women, Louella Parsons, Maisie, Ma Perkins, The Martin and Lewis Show, Midstream, Moon Dreams, Name the Movie, The Old Gold Show, One Man's Family* (Miller played 20 roles in this series), *Peter Quill, Play Broadcast, Press Club, The Railroad Hour, The Red Skelton Show, The Right to Happiness, Road of Life, The Romance of Helen Trent, Roy Rogers, The Rudy Vallee Show, Scattergood Baines, Songs by Sinatra, Space Patrol, Stars Over Hollywood, Stepmother, Stop That Villain, Strange Wills, Tell It Again, That Brewster Boy, This Is Life, Today's Children, Treat Time, Uncle Walter's Dog House, The Whistler, Woman from Nowhere* and *Woman in White*.

The most persistent swain on *The Romance of Helen Trent*, Gil Whitney, was played by David Gothard for all but a decade of the show's 27-year run. During the last 16 years on the air, Julie Stevens was Helen, attempting to prove that "because a woman is 35, or more, romance in life need not be over." (Photofest)

A second Gil Whitney, the actor William Green, turned up in *Jack Armstrong, the All-American Boy* and *His Honor, the Barber*. He also played the masculine lead in *Stepmother*.

The part of Gil Whitney, however, is most notably associated with David Gothard, the actor who played it for most of the run, in both the Chicago and the New York casts. A native of Beardstown, Illinois, Gothard was born on January 14, 1911, and attended high school in Los Angeles. In his initial try at acting, he appeared with local theater groups. But intrigued by radio, he hitchhiked to Chicago, where in 1932 he was offered an announcing job. This led him to dramatic roles across the breadth of radio's Golden Age: *Bachelor's Children, Big Sister, Hilltop House, The O'Neills, The Right to Happiness, The Adventures of the Thin Man* (he played the lead) and *Woman in White*. Gothard died on August 2, 1977.

In her book *Tune in Tomorrow*, Mary Jane Higby, who played Cynthia Swanson Whitney in the *Trent* cast, recalled a fan who identified her and Julie Stevens one day by their voices. Between broadcasts, the actresses had gone to a spa. Hoping to gain their autographs, the female fan followed the pair from gym to showers to hot room to steam room to showers again — while totally nude!

While most radio soap operas were introduced by live organ music, a few relied on pianos (notably *Pepper Young's Family, Perry Mason* and *Backstage Wife* in its early days) for their themes. A handful required something still more distinctive (a harmonica, for instance, played *Just Plain Bill's* overture, and a xylophone prefaced *Hilltop House*).

Stanley Davis was perhaps the most gifted, versatile and nonconventional radio theme artist of all. On *John's Other Wife* he sang, whistled and accompanied himself on the guitar to the tune of "The Sweetest Story Ever Told." He strummed the guitar while humming "Sunbonnet Sue" to open and close the *David Harum* series. And for decades, each day he would launch *The Romance of Helen Trent* with a ukulele or guitar. As he played, he hummed the long-running soap opera's theme, "Juanita" so familiar to fans. The multitalented artist doubled as *Trent's* producer-director for many years, although the Hummerts were its executive producers. Lawrence Salerno supplanted Stanley when he was no longer available to hum for Helen.

Although several writers authored the *Trent* series, Mary Jane Higby claimed that Martha Alexander (who also wrote *The Second Mrs. Burton*) was the best of the lot. "When she took over the scripts," said Higby, "the dialogue instantly brightened."

The writer of one *Trent* obituary recalled that in her final episode, Helen "gazed into the sunset with the last of her panting Romeos," senatorial candidate John Cole, "in a frothy climax bathed in rose petal cologne." It would be her final triumph: John asked her to marry him — not then, but in six months. Why rush into these things? By then she would be a half year older, but — we can probably rest assured — no wiser. "Oh yes, I'll wait six months. Darling, I'll wait," came her answer. John interrupted: "Not *forever*, Helen. Not unless you're sure." He listened closely for her final vow: "I'm sure now, John ... very sure."

From somewhere in the studio a rendition of "Love, Here Is My Heart" came up full volume, then was turned down for the message that Fielden Farrington had been standing by to read from network executives: "With this broadcast, we bring to an end the present series in *The Romance of Helen Trent. The Couple Next Door* will be heard every weekday, Monday through Friday, at this same time."

Then she was gone, her series never to resume. It was gut-wrenching for her millions of loyal listeners. To swiftly replace nearly three decades of *Helen Trent's* anguish and pathos with the contrived antics of Peg Lynch and Alan Bunce, minus a laugh track, was a bitter pill for Helen's entourage to swallow.

CBS had disillusioned millions of unsuspecting housewives everywhere by forcing them to abruptly join the real world of the 1960s. At the time, all they really wanted was to bask in the reverie that the goddess of goodness, Helen Trent, had faithfully given them for so long. Now they would have only Carolyn MacDonald (*The Right to Happiness*), *Ma Perkins*, *Young Doctor Malone* and *The Second Mrs. Burton* to cogitate over for a little while longer, until radio soaps were gone forever.

Many turned off their radios that day in protest, pledging not to turn them on again until their anger, frustration, hurt and bitterness subsided. For so many, a lifelong friend had rudely departed without good cause. After they had spent decades expectantly waiting for her midday visits, things simply couldn't be the same again.

23
Rosemary

(This Is You)

A better subtitle for this serial might have been: "Shall We Move to New York or Not?" If any question begged answering here, perhaps it was that one. Rosemary and Bill Roberts spent so much time shifting their residence back and forth between the small town of Springdale and New York City that the IRS, the people who hook up and disengage utilities and their creditors must have wondered what type of con game this couple had going on. Actually, Bill was the one who did most of the traveling; Rosemary stayed put much of the time. Although Bill, a practicing journalist, had good intentions, he was shiftless, unable to put down roots for very long anywhere. Like many a serial hero (although that term seems inappropriate in representing him), he had a roving eye that kept him in touch with a pretty skirt. Meanwhile, Rosemary was the stabilizing force in his life; her feet were planted securely on terra firma. Her goals and ideals and virtues were intact, and she deserved better than she got. Occasionally, though understandably, she showed a weakness for jealousy. Her fans empathized with her nonetheless, some probably hoping she'd wash that man right outta her hair. She never did—he brought her pain and sorrow, yet she sustained an abiding faith in him. In the end Bill Roberts proved his mettle, choosing Rosemary over all other women. A unique postscript could be added. The principals on this show did something that most other heroes and heroines never did: they married each other in real life. Surely their own situation was a far cry from that of the wretched pair they portrayed on a daily basis.

Producer: Tom McDermott
Directors: Hoyt Allen, Ralph Butler, Carl Eastman, Charles Fisher, Leslie Harris, Theodora Yates
Writer: Elaine Sterne Carrington
Music: Paul Taubman
Sound Effects: Ralph Curtiss, Jerry Sullivan
Announcers: Fran Barber, Harry Clark, Bob Dixon, Gil Herbert, Ed Herlihy, Joe O'Brien
Rosemary Dawson Roberts: Betty Winkler, Virginia Kaye
Bill Roberts: George Keane, Robert Readick
Mother Dawson: Marion Barney
Audrey Roberts: Joan Alexander, Lesley Woods

Others: Bill Adams, Jone Allison, Patsy Campbell, Helen Choate, Marie De Wolfe, Elspeth Eric, Michael Fitzmaurice, John Gibson, Larry Haines, Mary Jane Higby, Jackie Kelk, Ed Latimer, Joan Lazer, Woody Parker, Charles Penman, Guy Repp, Sidney Smith, James Van Dyk, Ethel Wilson, more

Theme: Original composition

Sponsors: It took three advertising agencies to oversee this show for Procter & Gamble, its only sponsor for the entire run: Compton, Pedlar and Ryan, Benton and Bowles. The serial was largely a commercial vehicle for Ivory Snow dishwashing formula but also advertised Dash and Tide detergents, Camay soap and Prell shampoo.

Ratings: High: 8.0 (1949–50); low: 2.9 (1945–46); median: 5.5. Numbers reached 6.0 or higher in five of 11 seasons.

On the Air: Oct. 2, 1944–March 23, 1945, NBC, 11:15 a.m. ET; March 26, 1945–June 21, 1946, CBS, 2:30 p.m.; June 24, 1946–July 1, 1955, CBS, 11:45 a.m.

Rosemary, written by Elaine Carrington, author of Pepper Young's Family *and* When a Girl Marries, *is dedicated to all the women of today. Yes,* Rosemary *is your story — this is you.*
                                        — Epigraph to Rosemary *(early episodes)*

Rosemary was Elaine Carrington's third major drama, although she created more than three. To soap operas, just as Irna Phillips had done, she bequeathed an emphasis on character development. Her situations were often plausible, and her audiences were held at rapt attention by the responses those figures made to the environment in which they were placed.

The story of Rosemary Dawson began as the 20-year-old secretary struggled to provide sole financial support for her mother and her teenage sister, Patti. The Dawson home was just outside Springdale, thought to be about midway between New York City and Chicago. The Dawsons lived in a little Cape Cod cottage on Newtown Road, a place Rosemary purchased for her mother, though listeners were never sure how she did so on a meager clerical salary. (Such was radio drama: the action moved along and the fans didn't have a lot of time to devote to such wondering.)

Lewis Dawson, the family patriarch, had disappeared years before without a trace. Mrs. Dawson resisted any hint that would have had her husband declared legally dead so that she could begin looking for another man. A few months into the plot, a Mr. Dennis, a stranger presented only as "the man from Nowhere" (Did he know Nona from there?), told the Dawsons that Lewis was indeed alive and seriously ill in New York. For a large sum of money, he would take Mrs. Dawson to see Lewis.

Skeptical at first, Mother Dawson was soon persuaded to follow Mr. Dennis. Unknown to Rosemary and Patti, she mortgaged their house, sewed the proceeds into the lining of her tattered coat and accompanied the stranger to New York. Her hopes were soon dashed, however, and she returned to Patti and Rosemary a sadder, poorer but wiser mother. Perhaps she accepted the fact that Lewis was never coming back, yet she decided not to displace his memory through remarriage.

The serial's emphasis then shifted almost entirely to Rosemary. She would clearly be its protagonist from that day forward. There was some prospect that this eldest daughter might become engaged to a highly visible local intellect, the handsome attorney Peter Harvey. But Rosemary ultimately chose differently, preferring her boss, newsman Bill Roberts, to the promising young lawyer. Despite her supreme devotion to the one she selected, she surely must have wondered to herself many times, "What if?"

Roberts was a shell-shocked World War II lieutenant who soon developed a severe and prolonged case of amnesia. He had been previously married, and his ex — Audrey Roberts — had brought him much grief. Their union had produced a child, Jessica, whom he dearly loved. During his amnesia experience he could, unfortunately, recall Audrey and Jessica but not Rosemary.

On the broadcast of July 12, 1946, Bill — then in the full throes of amnesia — had a vision of a nurse who visited him. The audience, of course, knew her to be Rosemary, but Bill didn't recognize her.

> BILL: You remind me of something ... something I want to remember ... something I feel such a ... a longing for ... some part of my life that meant a great deal to me, and yet I ... I don't know what it is.
> ROSEMARY: Oh, Bill, my dearest....
> BILL: (Reflecting) It seems strange not to remember you. And yet, I ... I *do* seem to remember you ... and I'm ... I'm awfully glad you're here....
> ROSEMARY: I'll be here for as long as you want me, Bill ... just like everyone else who lo- ... who's so fond of you.
> BILL: Oh, that makes me feel still better, your saying that. Knowing that I'm ... I'm not quite alone.
> ROSEMARY: No, you're not alone. Never think for one minute that you're alone. You have people around you who ... who think the *world* of you.
> BILL: You know, I ... I wish you'd tell me who they are some time. Not ... not ... not now, but someday, I wish you'd say their names over to me ... slowly. Perhaps ... perhaps I'll remember them. I ... I ... I know *your* name. It's a ... It's a *lovely* name. It's ... it's the name of a *flower*, isn't it? *Rosemary!*
> MUSIC: Music up and out

While Bill spent a long time confined to a hospital, Rosemary undertook several dangerous missions on his behalf. She traced his little Jessica, who had disappeared with her mother. She risked her own life among some sinister underworld forces who abducted her and threatened to kill her while Bill — in a complete reversal of the male-female stereotype — awaited her return.

When Bill was at last freed from his four-year bout with amnesia, he and Rosemary faced the usual run of typical maladies besieging soap opera characters: lies, deception, jealousy, marital discord and a murder trial (in which Bill, the accused, was eventually found innocent). Just about every serial had one or more deaths in which a leading character, falsely accused, faced the prospect of dire consequences. A year before that, the pair had been swept up in a near-fatal typhoid epidemic. Add to this Bill's instability — including his difficulty in making firm decisions about job and home — and Rosemary's role became even more crucial. She wore the pants; with Bill an emotional cripple, it was good that she was able to pick up the pieces and make any sense of them.

Bill's ex-wife, Audrey, provided a thorn in the flesh to both Robertses for much of the run. Jealousy frequently lurked in the background, and sometimes in the foreground, on *Rosemary*. Rosemary inquired of a close friend how a woman could be sure that a man would not suddenly change in his feelings for her. Seemingly satisfied in her marriage to that point, she began having misgivings the moment Bill hired a young female research assistant, even before she met the assistant.

To make matters worse, Rosemary remained in Springdale while Bill went to work in New York City accompanied by Jane Springham, the new assistant. Gossip, and her own intuition, convinced Rosemary that Jane was in love with Bill. But when Jane admitted this very fact to Bill in New York, he suggested she return to Springdale. On her arrival there she informed Rosemary that she planned to take her husband away from her. (Could Elaine Carrington have been frittering away her coffee breaks listening to the Hummert melodramas?)

Convincing herself that Bill's love for her would never be swayed, Rosemary went to New York to join him. He had accepted a promising position at an advertising firm in the Big Apple. But the trip turned out all wrong. Bill, having only recently dispatched Jane Springham, had fallen head over heels for Blanche Weatherby, the attractive daughter of his new boss. Rosemary made a quick exit and returned to Springdale, devastated by the unexpected turn of events.

While out for a walk one day, Bill had to be hit by a truck to bring him to his senses. (Soap opera folks never found it easy when tough choices had to be made.) During his convalescence he realized that it was Rosemary he truly loved, not Blanche. He returned to Springdale, and all went well for a while. Then Bill quit his job, telling Rosemary he was returning to New York to try again to reconnect career-wise. He would send for her when he found a job and a place to live. Based on his past indiscretions, Rosemary couldn't help wondering how much latitude she should allow him.

A consumer magazine of that day, *Radio and Television Mirror*, published a writing competition in 1951 based on her moral dilemma. It posed two questions: How much faith should a woman have in her husband? And once a man has made a mistake, is he forever after unworthy of trust?

An accompanying article recounted Bill Roberts' dalliance with the beguiling Blanche Weatherby. It noted subsequent actions within the story line, culminating with Bill's desire to return to New York alone. The magazine offered to purchase answers to its questions. In the opinion of the editors, the writer of the "best answer" would be awarded $25, a sizable prize for a contest at that time. Those submitting the five "next-best" answers would receive $5 each. Writers were to state their views in a letter of not more than one hundred words. It was a popular readership-building feature of fan magazines of that era.

Rosemary waited at home for a reunion with Bill — who had returned to New York by himself — when a new complication arose: following a confrontation between Bill and Blanche, someone shot Blanche. Could Bill convince Rosemary he hadn't attempted to kill Blanche? Soap opera figures really didn't have it easy!

Eventually proven innocent, Bill decided to permanently cast his lot in Springdale. Soon he was tapped by publisher Van Vleck as editor of the *Springdale Banner*, the newspaper for which he had earlier been a reporter. His crusading editorials allowed the journal to take partial credit for cleaning up the town, until then overrun by a political boss and some strong-willed punks. With the assistance of $5,000 from Van Vleck and other donations from local business people, a boys' club was formed. A gymnasium would be built to assist troubled young men in refocusing their lives on longer-term goals rather than hanging around pool halls all day.

Bill and Rosemary encountered yet another personal crisis. They lost a baby they had hoped for many years to have. In due time, their sadness was partially offset when they adopted two young siblings, Anna and Lonny Cisare. The children were to bring them both joy and sorrow in the years to follow.

Anna, who gave them joy, married the assistant editor at the *Springdale Banner*. Well in the future, her husband would buy out Van Vleck as the paper's publisher. Teenager Lonny, on the other hand, could be bane or blessing. Headstrong and bent on making his own decisions about everything, he got involved with a girl from "the wrong side of the tracks." Monica, a few years his senior, persuaded him — as treasurer of the new Springdale Boys' Club — to withdraw bank funds given for the gymnasium. She asked him to marry her and run away to Florida. But Lonny, doing some soul-searching en route, realized his mistake and — without telling Monica — mailed the misappropriated funds back to the bank. In the middle of the night, as Monica slept, he turned the car around and headed for Springdale to face the music. When Monica awoke and realized what he had done, she grabbed the steering wheel and the car slid into a telephone pole. Her injuries proved fatal. Lonny recovered, however, and was forgiven and restored to his place in the family. (There was no hint of jail time or community service for his "misdemeanor," it should be noted — only in a fictitious series!)

In time Lonny met a "proper" girl, Betty Gray, a neighbor living across the street from the Robertses. After a courtship, the pair married at Rosemary and Bill's home, with a reception at the Grays' home. Not much else was heard from them; presumably the couple lived in a state of marital bliss forever.

Meanwhile, a new and provocatively mysterious arrival in the neighborhood, Diane Thompson, gained Bill's and Rosemary's immediate attention. They became so spellbound by this attractive woman, in fact, that when she suggested the three take a week's vacation in New York together, they were quick to accept. (Today we would say this sounds a tad kinky; back then, it was viewed as rational behavior, at least on radio.) While in New York, initial clues arrived that not all was quite what it appeared to be in Diane's life.

She didn't answer the telephone when Rosemary called her hotel room, although they knew she was in. When a thug recognized Diane in front of the Robertses, he called her "Goldie" and accosted her. She received telegrams that caused her to turn pale. On their final day in New York, Bill and Rosemary found Diane sobbing uncontrollably in her room. She insisted that they return to Springdale without her.

During that week Bill was approached by an old journalism crony who asked him to write several investigative articles for a national magazine. The series was to be an expose of the narcotics industry and its influence on American youth. Although it would be a dangerous assignment, it would also be lucrative and would raise Bill's visibility while offering him a new challenge. He readily agreed. On their return to Springdale, not surprisingly, Bill encountered some very serious threats.

The investigation required several fact-finding trips to New York City and Chicago. A lovely young research assistant, Mercy Ainsworth, accompanied him. (Whatever happened to reporters who pursued their *own* stories? Bill Roberts *always* had a helper, invariably an attractive young woman.) Naturally, this arrangement prompted lingering doubts for Rosemary. Their mission was so secretive that even Rosemary wasn't to be told about their findings. Of course, that did nothing to allay her fears that not all of it was totally aboveboard.

Meanwhile, Rosemary became increasingly involved with the mysterious Diane Thompson. When Diane's brother, Ray, arrived in Springdale with his five-year-old daughter, Betsy, to visit his sister, Rosemary offered to baby-sit Betsy while Diane worked and Ray looked for work. Listeners, however, overheard a phone call that Ray made to New York, revealing he was in Springdale to spy on Bill Roberts on behalf of syndicate drug forces.

Bill soon arrived at the conclusion that Springdale was too small a place to absorb his talents. He wanted to dedicate the remainder of his career to bigger things, perhaps tied to writing, narcotics and — who knows? — possibly Mercy Ainsworth. How was Rosemary to deal with this latest craze in the life of her unstable spouse?

Bill's son-in-law bought the newspaper from Van Vleck just then, planning to manage it with Bill's son, Lonny. (No explanation was given as to where this pair came into that kind of money.) While Rosemary was showing their Springdale home to prospective buyers, Bill displayed his immaturity. He claimed he was being pushed out of both job and home and resented it. Balking, he did an about-face, deciding to remain in Springdale.

But Mercy, the sultry temptress, attempted to get him to change his mind and go with her to New York. In the end — with the series about to depart the airwaves forever — Bill confronted reality. "I can't go to New York with you," he told the cunning villainess. "Being Rosemary's husband is the most important thing in my life. I'll take no chances with that."

Before the final switch was thrown, Rosemary — not Bill — asked the newspaper's new owners to give Bill his old job back as editor. She got more than she asked: Bill was offered an equal partnership in the *Banner*. In their haste to depart, the loose ends were neatly tied together, except for unresolved questions about gangsters who threatened to kill Rosemary and whether friendly Diane was a heroin addict with a sinister past. And if Ray was Diane's husband — not her brother — then little Betsy was Diane's own child. But those questions seemed incidental; at least for a little while, the Robertses could live happily, until Bill took a notion to hit the road again.

In those days, public-service announcements crept into the closing credits for each day's episode, just as they did on many other serials. "Don't relax on saving used fat," *Rosemary* announcer Harry Clark often admonished listeners. "It's urgently needed to prevent soap shortages. You help yourself when you save used fats." It all seemed such a contradiction to the commercials for the sponsor's product, Ivory Snow dishwashing powder. But industry sentiment was that there were some larger concepts the country must collectively support, even beyond the call to economic duty. Such messages, in existence since the outbreak of World War II, continued even after the war ended.

A more direct appeal, at the start of one episode during the war, came from Rosemary herself:

I am speaking to you ... all of you ... my friends out there, listening to *Rosemary*. I am speaking to the mothers and wives and sweethearts of our men who are fighting to bring this war to a close—to make this a free world, the kind of world you want to live in, the kind of world we Dawsons want to live in.... If you will do something for me, I'll do something for you. If you'll buy a war bond—because I, Rosemary Dawson, ask you to—and send me the receipt showing me you have purchased it, I shall return that receipt with a personal letter from me. I am doing this because I want so much to make the Seventh War Loan Drive the biggest drive we have ever had. And so will you, my dear friends, who have listened to and enjoyed this program — who have laughed with us and cried with us — buy a war bond? Or as many bonds as you can. And send your receipt to Rosemary Dawson, care of Rosemary, to this station. And you will receive a letter from me and my thanks.

Betty Winkler was born on April 19, 1914, at Berwick, Pennsylvania. Having studied acting at Cleveland Playhouse, she became an NBC radio actress in Chicago and played on most dramatic series originating there. She was fortunate in gaining title or leading parts on *Abie's Irish Rose, Girl Alone, The Man I Married* and *Joyce Jordan, Girl Interne*. She had recurring parts on *Attorney-at-Law, Betty and Bob, The O'Neills, This Life Is Mine, Welcome Valley, Just Plain Bill, Grand Hotel* and *Don Winslow of the Navy*. She also appeared in *Fibber McGee and Molly* and in dramatic ensembles on *The Chicago Theatre of the Air, Curtain Time, Knickerbocker Playhouse, Inner Sanctum Mysteries* and *Lights Out*. In retirement she taught sensory awareness at the New School of Social Research in Manhattan. She wrote the book *Sensing: Letting Yourself Live*.

Winkler played the part of Rosemary Dawson Roberts for most of the run. She was succeeded by a lesser known actress, Virginia Kaye, who had one other credit on her radio vita, a recurring role on *Pepper Young's Family*. She also later earned a berth on television's *The Edge of Night* (1973–79).

Bill Dawson, meanwhile, was played for most of the run by a little-recognized actor. George Keane had no other known radio or television acting credits. Keane was succeeded by the better-connected Robert Readick (*Let's Pretend, The Second Mrs. Burton, This Is Nora Drake, Aunt Jenny's Real Life Stories, Whispering Streets* and *Yours Truly, Johnny Dollar*). Readick was the son of radio actor Frank Readick (*The Shadow* and multiple other roles).

The two long-running leads in the show, Winkler and Keane, first met at the studio. Developing a real-life romance behind the microphones, the pair became husband and wife, a novelty among soap opera leads on the same serial. When illness forced George to relinquish his role as Bill Dawson, Betty gave up her part too, and the couple moved to seclusion in Europe.

Marion Barney, meanwhile, who gained something of a reputation in long-running matriarchal roles on Elaine Carrington dramas—"Mother Young" on *Pepper Young's Family* and "Mother Davis" on *When a Girl Marries*—turned up on *Rosemary* as "Mother Dawson." By the early 1950s, she spent her days offering motherly advice on three networks!

The part of Audrey Roberts, Bill's first wife, went to veteran actresses Lesley Woods and Joan Alexander. Woods made a career out of playing mean-spirited first wives — she was Peg Martinson on *This Is Nora Drake* and Carol Evans Brent on *Road of Life*. Alexander also played Peg Martinson in *This Is Nora Drake* and a kinder, gentler Della Street on *Perry Mason*.

Critics of the genre have often pointed out that most soap opera men were weaklings. That was on purpose, of course, and in that arena Bill Roberts qualified as Exhibit A. His lack of backbone and direction in virtually every decision branded him as inept. Still, through it all, the love of his woman never faltered.

Rosemary was a genuine love story, although much of the time it was a one-sided affair. Despite that, Bill Roberts could ultimately be counted on to make the right call — to discover in Rosemary an unswerving devotion, to sense what his life would be like without her to share it. When it really mattered, he *knew* her value. In that sense, he answered the most important question they both faced.

24
The Second Mrs. Burton
(Second Wife)

The premise behind the catchy title of this little family-oriented drama was that the *second* Mrs. Burton was the *first* one's daughter-in-law! Clever, right? Actually, only partially right. The protagonist here was Terry Burton, whose husband, Stan, *had* been married earlier, to a woman named Marian. Marian was quite prominent in the story line at the series' inception. But over time she was virtually written out to the point that some memories about her faded. Stan's mom ("Mother Burton"), however, took a more active role in the plot, becoming the stereotypical, overbearing boor that gives mothers-in-law a bad name. This Mrs. Burton was meddling, wealthy and lacking in modesty about her good deeds, yet likable in a strained sort of way. To her credit, easygoing Terry rolled with the punches, humoring the aging widow and turning what could have been trying situations into warm, good-natured experiences. Stan, meanwhile, was habitually agitated with his mother and showed it. This serial had the peculiar aspect of occupying a trio of authors who — when it was their turn to write — took the show in contrasting directions, each placing an indelible stamp upon it. Listeners who missed some episodes during scripting changes may have wondered what happened to the drama they had been hearing. The serial also had the arguable glory of being the very last one to be broadcast on network radio — definitely the worst of times.

Producer: Jack Hurdle, Lindsay MacHarrie
Producer-Director: Ira Ashley
Directors: Stuart Buchanan, Viola Burns, Beverly Smith
Writers: Martha Alexander, Hector Chevigny, Johanna Johnston, Priscilla Kent, John M. Young
Music: Chet Kingsbury, Richard Leibert
Sound Effects: Jimmy Dwan
Announcers: Harry Clark, Hugh James, Warren Sweeney
Terry Burton: Sharon Douglas, Claire Niesen, Patsy Campbell, Teri Keane
Stan Burton: Dwight Weist
Mother Burton: Charme Allen, Ethel Owen, Evelyn Varden
Marcia Burton Archer: Arline Blackburn, Alice Frost
Lew Archer: Larry Haines

Others: Joan Alexander, Betty Caine, King Calder, Ben Cooper, Cathleen Cordell, Staats Cotsworth, Helen Coule, Dix Davis, Elspeth Eric, Gale Gordon, Rod Hendrickson, Lois Holmes, Madaline Lee, Craig McDonnell, Jane Morgan, Robert Readick, Doris Rich, Bartlett Robinson, Larry Robinson, Janet Russell, Alexander Scourby, Anne Stone, Les Tremayne, Karl Weber, more

Theme: Original melody

Sponsors: Young and Rubicam governed this serial for General Foods, Inc., from Jan. 7, 1946, to Sept. 17, 1954. It advertised Satina laundry starch, LaFrance bleach, Postum instant beverage, Swans Down cake mixes, Post cereals, Maxwell House coffee and Jell-O puddings and pie fillings. From Sept. 20, 1954, to June 17, 1955, Armor Packing underwrote the series for a variety of meat products. The drama was under multiple sponsorship from June 20, 1955, to Nov. 25, 1960, with commercials for wares such as Dial soap and shampoo, Columbia phonographs and Chase and Sanborn coffee.

Ratings: Figures are based on the years 1945–56. High: 8.0 (1949–50); low: 2.8 (1945–46); median: 5.2.

On the Air: Jan. 7, 1946–June 29, 1956, CBS, 2:00 p.m. ET; July 2, 1956–Jan. 2, 1959, CBS, 2:15 p.m.; Jan. 5, 1959–Nov. 25, 1960, CBS, 1:45 p.m.

The story of a modern marriage.

— Epigraph to *The Second Mrs. Burton*

An analysis of *The Second Mrs. Burton* must be influenced by the writing styles of its three most prominent authors: Martha Alexander, John M. Young and Hector Chevigny. To explore the serial in any other light would be a disservice to the significant contributions of this writing triumvirate, each of whose forms varied sharply from the others. As a result, their characters and story lines reached near-metamorphosis proportions when each writer was replaced.

As this engaging serial matured, the talents of these wordsmiths became obvious to the continuing audience. All had the ability to blend radically different techniques into harmony so that the listener was never lost. In so doing, they offered a smooth transition from a previous set of influences and circumstances.

Alexander was the first of *Burton's* three most influential scribes. She left the writing of one of radio's preeminent daytime dramas, *The Romance of Helen Trent*, to join the program. On *Burton*, Alexander penned skillful and intelligent dialogue for Terry and Stan Burton and their cohorts. The Burtons lived in the small town of Dickston, where Stan operated a retail emporium. Their story was launched with Terry's search for happiness as his second wife. An earlier version, which had aired on CBS's West Coast stations between May 4, 1942, and December 25, 1942, was in fact titled *Second Wife*.

In those days *Burton* was one of the few authentic "family" serials, in the tradition of *One Man's Family*, *Pepper Young's Family* and, later, *The Woman in My House*. Each of these explored character more than traditional elements of plot and melodrama. In the lives of the principals, there were few difficulties over which they had little control. External forces were simply seldom overbearing.

Martha Alexander's abrupt departure from *Burton* in 1947, a little more than a year into the run, had a profound effect on the series. Her early exit resulted from some philosophical differences encountered with Young and Rubicam, the advertising agency producing the show. As an example, she requested that the Burtons say an open-mouthed "ah" instead of a puckered "prunes" in a kissing scene. That was simply too depraved for radio's "prissy" standards, and she and the show went separate ways.

Burton then became a strictly formulaic serial under the hand of its next creative genius, John M. Young. As it evolved into a true dishpan drama, it could hardly be distinguished from nearly three dozen other soap operas pursuing similar themes — amnesia, backbiting, discord, jealousy and tyranny of many sorts. Young, a polished radio veteran who was already credited with scripting *The Right to Happiness*, applied all the pathos and turmoil in his arsenal to create misery for *Burton's* heroine and hero. Within a brief period, plot conflicts of major proportions had arrived like a hurricane force. A brief introduction of the characters in Young's initial sequence offers some clues to where this tale of woe was headed.

• Terry Burton, the *second* Mrs. Burton, found herself in the sometimes awkward position of being adored by her husband, Stan, and by Brad, the son from his first marriage, while mustering the grace, charm and intelligence to tactfully handle Stan's ex-wife, Marian. Although Marian remained a family friend, her ability to stick her nose where it didn't belong created tremendous strain for everyone, requiring gentle but tough diplomacy on the part of Terry.

• Stan Burton, deeply in love with his second wife, felt insecure with Marian's interference in their lives. She further intimidated him by trying to influence his business decisions.

• Brad Burton, Stan and Marian's son, was shuttled between the homes of his parents. In his teen years, this lack of permanency sowed seeds of discord, encouraging him to experiment on troubled paths.

• Marian Sullivan, divorced from Stan Burton, found no happiness in a second marriage. An intensely possessive woman, she used every device at her disposal to remain a disruptive factor in Stan's life, at times succeeding.

• Mrs. Miller, the Burtons' elderly neighbor, had a big heart and a ready ear. Friendly, calm and wise, over many cups of coffee she eased turbulent hours while cautioning a less experienced Terry against many pitfalls.

• Lillian Anderson was one of Marian's few remaining friends. For the sake of the years they had known one another, Lillian attempted, without success, to help Marian let go of the past and relinquish her hold over Stan.

• Jim Anderson, Lillian's husband, loved his wife and had a happy home and a successful business. Content with life, he was surprised by people like Marian who made such a mess of their lives.

• Greg Martin was a new toy Marian wanted because he was a successful playwright and a most attractive man. The sophisticated Greg, however, was more than a match for Marian. He recognized — and skillfully eluded — her attempts to make a possession of him.

During *Burton's* years of strife, Young wrote a sequence involving a woman named

Barbara Wright from "far-off Wisconsin" who was moving to Dickston. Terry's father, who lived in the same town as Barbara, received an invitation from Terry and Stan for the newcomer to board in their home until permanent living arrangements could be made.

En route to Dickston by train, Barbara met up with an unscrupulous traveling companion, Helen Green. Barbara unwittingly told Helen about the Burtons, whom neither had met. In a subsequent train disaster, Helen came out unscathed but Barbara fell victim to—what else?—amnesia. She was abandoned in a strange city, many miles from her destination.

The fortune-hunting Helen, meanwhile, equipped with information that Barbara had given her, assumed her identity and moved into the Burton home. From the beginning, the guest behaved strangely. In a brief time some of Terry's jewelry and other small objects were missing. Terry was unaware that Helen had pilfered through her possessions. Helen disposed of items through a partner, Grimes, who ran a junk shop specializing in fencing stolen goods. She also picked up merchandise in Stan's store for resale through the junk shop. Soon fancying herself in love with Stan, Helen launched a gossip campaign against Terry in an effort to discredit her and break up their marriage.

Just as all seemed lost, Barbara — who had been wandering in the distant city without her memory — found in her coat pocket a slip of paper bearing the Burton address. Impulsively, she went there seeking her identity. When she saw Helen, she began to remember. Helen, realizing that jail was possible if Barbara succeeded in regaining her memory, plotted to kill Barbara. Kidnapping Barbara from the Burton home, she was followed by Stan and Terry, whose suspicions had been aroused. Fortunately, they arrived in time to rescue Barbara before Helen could complete her heinous plan.

By then Stan and Terry had become parents of a little girl, Wendy. But the danger of neglecting a teen was brought home when Wendy fell seriously ill and her parents focused attention on her to the exclusion of Brad.

Feeling grown up, lonely and unwanted, Brad joined what he believed to be a boys' social club. He soon learned that most of the club's activities were illegal rather than social, however. Under the instruction of an unsavory adult, this gang of youths was being groomed for a life of crime. Brad could easily have proceeded down that road as a juvenile delinquent. But he realized the intentions of his young friends and abandoned them, choosing the ideals instilled in him earlier by his father and stepmother.

By 1951 the green-eyed monster of jealousy visited the *Burton* plot. Stan hired the beautiful Amy Westlake to manage the Burton store in Dickston. Though Terry tried hard to trust and accept the voluptuous Amy, she was soon forced to admit that she really didn't like Amy at all.

A year later Stan himself was coping with amnesia. So debilitating were the consequences that Terry was forced to bow to economic necessity and move into Mother Burton's house. She did it for the sake of her family, albeit reluctantly, convinced that her mother-in-law would undermine her marriage while she was living there. At about that time, in 1952 Hector Chevigny became the third of *Burton's* most influential writers. He plotted an entirely new direction for the serial. The strong imprint he made wasn't apparent overnight, however. He took time to transform the situations and characters into a lighter, genuinely homespun soap opera. Within a few months he was writing what he considered his most successful sequence: the courtship of Stan's sister, Marcia, by Lew Archer. For years Marcia had struggled to escape the domination of her mother's personality and money. Stan and Terry recognized that handsome Lew was the answer to her prayers. But the ensuing conflict with Mother Burton was a foretaste of where this serial would dwell for the remainder of the run.

Gradually, Chevigny returned the story line to its earlier themes. But he went even further than Martha Alexander had. Instead of being preoccupied by the fact that the second Mrs. Burton was the second *wife*, Chevigny strengthened the character of Mother Burton.

Regrettably, a few well-intentioned radio soap opera historiographers missed or discounted the action in the pre–Chevigny era. Said one: "The *first* Mrs. Burton referred to Terry's meddlesome mother-in-law."[1] Another concurred: "This was the story of Terry Burton and her husband Stan. They lived in a small town with Stan's domineering mother, who was the 'First Mrs. Burton.'"[2] Still another noted: "The first Mrs. Burton was in reality, the second Mrs. Burton's mother-in-law!"[3] Finally one added: "The 'first Mrs. Burton' was the 'second Mrs. Burton's' mother-in-law."[4] The fact that Alexander and Young had strongly involved Stan's *first wife*, Marian, in the early years of the story line was ignored. Omitting references to her existence eliminated a major focal point in the serial's legacy.

In late 1954 CBS Radio assumed control of *Burton* from the advertising agency. At that juncture, Chevigny was offered an answer to an author's prayer: He was essentially given a blank check to write the program in any manner he chose. Consequently, the serial evolved into an easygoing drama with comedic relief, nearly 180 degrees opposite the formula it had followed since 1947.

Among Chevigny's most daring adventures, in late 1957 he included in the story line a seven-part enactment of Oscar Wilde's dramatic classic *The Importance of Being Earnest*. The serial's characters formed a little theater group, and the Wilde play was one of its productions. This was perhaps the only case in radio serials where a renowned drama of such magnitude was aired. And the show's ratings perked up during the sequence.

In 1958 Chevigny claimed that his principal characters, Terry and Stan, were "well married, sexually satisfied ... not preoccupied with sexual misadventures."[5] His assessment was that most people hope for strong marital ties even if they have never experienced them. As a result, he contended, Mother Burton and her incessant efforts to manage the lives of her children invariably failed. After all, she was no match when pitted against the security of her son's and daughter's unions to stable personalities.

Chevigny admitted that in his years of scripting the show, much was borrowed from the tradition of comedy writing. At least two of the principals during those years — Ethel Owen, who played Mother Burton, and Alice Frost, as Marcia — were comediennes in their own rights. Teri Keane and Dwight Weist, who portrayed Terry and Stan Burton, could readily adapt to lighter moments too. Chevigny attempted to write for the personalities who played the parts in his program rather than writing roles into which any performer could be cast. (Carlton E. Morse had done the same thing on his award-winning drama *One Man's Family*.)

Aside from Alexander, Young and Chevigny, at least two other writers — Priscilla Kent and Johanna Johnston — penned the *Burton* series. Johnston was writing at the time it left the air.

The Second Mrs. Burton contained some other unique features over its long run. At midcentury, Wednesdays were designated as "Family Counselor Day." Special guests were invited into the studio to talk about subjects of interest to listeners. On one broadcast a

Reverend Smith, pastor of Roxbury Methodist Church in Stamford, Connecticut, answered the question put to him by Terry Burton: "What is faith?" On a Christmas show, Mrs. L. V. Douglas visited. As a little girl, she had written a letter 52 years earlier inquiring, "Is there a Santa Claus?" The famed answer began: "Yes, Virginia, there is a Santa Claus." These weekly vignettes were often written in article form and published in a consumer fan magazine.

At the close of daily installments during *Burton*'s early years, announcer Hugh James offered a household hint of the day. The concept was reminiscent of *Aunt Jenny*'s daily cooking tips to homemakers hearing her long-running show. On the program of September 25, 1947, James gave this advice for what to do when cod-liver oil is spilled on a baby's bibs and dresses: "Remove the stain as soon as possible with carbon tetrachloride or similar fluid; boiling or washing tends to set the stain."

How many American homemakers knew if they had carbon tetrachloride lying around the house? Or even what it was? (It is a nonflammable, colorless, poisonous liquid used in fire extinguishers as a solvent for fats.) Would most homes in which there was a baby have such a fluid exposed outside a fire extinguisher? If a degree in chemical engineering was a prerequisite for applying James' daily homemaking tips, some of his suggestions probably fell on deaf ears despite their worthy intentions.

One idea the announcer interjected at the end of each program seemed inspired. Before leaving the air, James asked listeners to invite neighbors to gather with them around their radios at the same time the following day to catch the next exciting chapter of the *Burton* story. It was a capital idea, but one that *Burton*'s peer dramas disregarded.

The part of Terry Burton was played by four actresses, in order: Sharon Douglas, Claire Niesen, Patsy Campbell and Teri Keane. Douglas gained running parts in a half-dozen other series, most of them lighter fare: *A Day in the Life of Dennis Day, Janie's Tea Room, Village Store, The Life of Riley, The Judy Canova Show* and *One Man's Family*. Niesen is best remembered for her portrayal of Mary Noble, *Backstage Wife*. Campbell also played in a half-dozen other series, in three of them as the feminine lead: *House in the Country, Joe and Ethel Turp* and *McGarry and His Mouse*. She had running roles in *Big Sister* and *Rosemary* and was often cast in *Under Arrest*.

Keane is perhaps more prominently associated with the role of Terry Burton than the others. She was in the part for much of the run and was with it when the series left the air. A native of New York City, she was born on October 24, 1925. Her theatrical credits included *The Vagabond King* and *What a Life*, both on Broadway. On radio's *Life Can Be Beautiful*, she was feminine lead Chichi Conrad for several years and also played the feminine lead on *Marriage for Two*. Recurring roles turned up in *Big Sister, Just Plain Bill* and *Road of Life*. She participated in dramatic ensembles on *The Cavalcade of America, Inner Sanctum Mysteries, Gangbusters, Show Boat* and *The CBS Mystery Theatre*. Married to the actor John Larkin, hero of radio's *Perry Mason* and the first lead actor on TV's *The Edge of Night*, Keane transferred to television too. She gained running roles on four serials: *The Guiding Light* (1957), *The Edge of Night* (1964–75), *One Life to Live* (1976–77) and *Loving* (1983–84).

Versatile actor Dwight Weist carried the part of Stan Burton throughout the 15-year run of *The Second Mrs. Burton*. Born on January 16, 1910, at Palo Alto, California, he wrote for a local radio station and took a job as a staff announcer while attending Ohio Wesleyan College. Before moving to New York City he performed at the Cleveland Playhouse. He founded the Weist-Barron School of Television and Commercial Acting and taught for 35

Rehearsing an early episode of *The Second Mrs. Burton* are (*clockwise, l–r*) engineer Carl Campbell, Jane Morgan, Sharon Douglas, Janet Russell, sound technician Don Creed (standing), Gale Gordon, CBS rep Gene English and producer Jack Hurdle (back to camera). (*Courtesy of Dan Haefele*)

years. When Weist entered radio, his ability to imitate a wide range of ages and accents came to the forefront. He acquired the designation "man of 1,000 voices" within the industry. He worked dramatic roles in *Buck Rogers in the Twenty-Fifth Century, The March of Time Quiz, The Texaco Star Theater, The Theatre Guild on the Air* and *We, the People*. Weist had running parts in *Big Town, Valiant Lady* and *The Shadow*; he played the title role of *Mr. District Attorney*; and he assisted Irene Beasley on the daytime giveaway show *Grand Slam*. The busy performer was announcer for *The Aldrich Family, By Kathleen Norris* and *Inner Sanctum Mysteries*. For many years he announced television's *Search for Tomorrow*. Weist did voice-overs for commercials as well as Pathé newsreels shown in motion-picture theaters. He appeared in two movies, *Radio Days* (1986) and *The Name of the Rose* (1989). He died at Block Island, New York, on July 16, 1991.

The part of Mother Burton was portrayed by three actresses: Evelyn Varden, Charme Allen and Ethel Owen. Varden, who appeared on Broadway in *Our Town*, was tapped for running parts in several serials: *Big Sister, Front Page Farrell, Marriage for Two, Road of Life* and *Young Doctor Malone*. Allen was perhaps best known for her role as Aunt Polly in the *David Harum* series. Owen, born on March 30, 1892, at Racine, Wisconsin, attended Northwestern University. She began a radio career in dramatic and musical shows at Milwaukee's WTMJ. Moving to Chicago and eventually New York, she appeared on *Fibber McGee and Molly, The Callahans, Gangbusters, Listening Post, The First Nighter, City Desk* and *The Creightons*. She gained berths on more than a dozen soap operas: *Backstage Wife, Betty and Bob, The Romance of Helen Trent, Life Can Be Beautiful, Lorenzo Jones, The Man I Married, The Right to Happiness, Stepmother, A Tale of Today, Today's Children, Valiant Lady, When a Girl Marries, Helpmate, Houseboat Hannah* and *Joyce Jordan, Girl Interne*. Owen played on Broadway in the 1940s, appearing in *Show Boat* and *Three's a Family*. The actress died on December 28, 1990.

Alice Frost, who was Marcia Burton Archer for most of the *Burton* run, played the lead in *Big Sister*. Arline Blackburn, who succeeded her as Marcia, carried title roles in *Linda's First Love* and *Pretty Kitty Kelly* and had running parts in *Young Widder Brown* and *The O'Neills*.

Actor Larry Haines was Lew Archer. A native of Mount Vernon, New York, where he was born on August 3, 1917, Haines studied at the Westchester branch of City College of New York and was offered a drama scholarship. He decided to forgo it, however, to enter the profession at once, working at New York's WWRL. Haines later recalled auditioning for "everything," claiming he eventually worked 15,000 shows. "I love radio because it allows the audience to paint its own sets," he said. His radio credits included many of the drama and mystery series originating in New York: *Dimension X, Gangbusters, The Man Behind the Gun, The FBI in Peace and War, Big Town, Now Hear This, Mr. District Attorney, The CBS Mystery Theatre* and *David Harding, Counterspy*. He played in serials too: *Pepper Young's Family, Rosemary, Young Doctor Malone, David Harum* and *Joyce Jordan, Girl Interne*. He had a running role on *The Falcon*, the title role on *That Hammer Guy* and a leading role on *Manhunt*.

Despite numerous radio appearances, his longest-running role, for which he won three Emmys, was as Stu Bergman on TV's *Search for Tomorrow* (1951–1986). In her autobiography *Both of Me*, that series' star, the actress Mary Stuart, termed him "genuine and wonderful." Stuart wrote, "All the delicious bits of business he had worked out in high school with his friend Art Carney slid into the character ever so subtly and Larry's own inventiveness added more each day." In 1995 Haines had a bit part in the TV serial *Loving*. He played on Broadway in *A Thousand Clowns, Generation* and *Promises, Promises*, earning Tony nominations for the latter two. He also won supporting roles in a pair of movies, *The Odd Couple* and *The Seven-Ups*.

Because *The Second Mrs. Burton* completed the hour in which the last of four daily closed-ended soaps aired in 1960, it holds the dubious honor of being the final serial broadcast on a national radio network. (The other three departing on November 25, 1960, were *The Right to Happiness, Ma Perkins* and *Young Doctor Malone*.) At the conclusion of *Burton's* final performance, Teri Keane, Dwight Weist, Ethel Owen, Larry Haines and Arline Blackburn spoke personal farewells to the audience. It was clearly the passing of an era.

25
Stella Dallas

(Nothin' but Trouble)

Its origins embedded in a popular turn-of-the-century novel, *Stella Dallas* was an NBC staple at 4:15 p.m. ET for 17 years. This story of "mother love" saw seamstress Stella, a divorcée lacking in proper dialect and social graces, temporarily sacrifice her relationship with her daughter, Laurel, when the girl married above her station. Reentering Laurel's life despite her lack of education, Stella proved her mettle in numerous ways: she stood firmly on precepts of righteousness, becoming the champion of many an underdog; she tracked and subdued evildoers of widely diverse sorts; and she exhibited an uncanny ability to suspect those with debauchery on their minds long before it became obvious to everyone else. In a long-running feud with Mrs. Grosvenor, Laurel's widowed mother-in-law, Stella became a thorn in the side of the grandame of Boston's elite. But Dick Grosvenor, Laurel's husband, who ardently admired his mother-in-law, was often caught in the cross fire between the two matriarchs. On this show, the audience never knew what mischief might require the attention of a lowly tailor to counteract the effect. Though the serial's action was grossly exaggerated, Stella became the dramatic heroine for millions of late-afternoon listeners who followed her relentless pursuits for decency at home and abroad.

Producers: Frank and Anne Hummert
Directors: Richard Leonard, Ernest Ricca, Norman Sweetser
Writers: Frank and Anne Hummert, Helen Walpole
Music: Richard Leibert
Sound Effects: John Glennon, Agnew Horine
Announcers: Ford Bond, Howard Claney, Jack Costello, Frank Gallop, Roger Krupp, Jimmy Wallington
Stella Dallas: Anne Elstner
Laurel Dallas Grosvenor: Joy Hathaway, Vivian Smolen
Dick Grosvenor: Jim Backus, Spencer Bentley, MacDonald Carey, Bert Cowlau, Michael Fitzmaurice, George Lambert, Carleton Young
Mrs. Grosvenor: Jane Houston
Minnie Grady: Grace Valentine
Ada Dexter: Helen Claire
Stephen Dallas: Arthur Hughes, Neil Malley, Leo McCabe, Frederick Tozere

Others: Albert Aley, Barbara Barton, Ed Begley, Julie Benell, Raymond Bramley, John Brewster, Warren Bryan, Helene Carew, Kenneth Daigneau, Peter Donald, Ethel Everett, Ara Gerald, Richard Gordon, Mary Jane Higby, Raymond Edward Johnson, Elaine Kent, Walter Kinsella, Mandel Kramer, Joan Lorring, Frank Lovejoy, Elizabeth Morgan, Henry M. Neeley, Paul Potter, William Quinn, Luis Van Rooten, Dorothy Sands, Nancy Sheridan, Bill Smith, Hal Studer, Tom Tully, Harold Vermilyea, Arthur Vinton, more

Theme: "Memories" (6 weeks); "How Can I Leave Thee?"

Sponsors: From its inception, Blackett-Sample-Hummert governed the serial for Sterling Drugs, which underwrote the program for 16 years. Sterling brand names included the following: Astring-O-Sol mouthwash; Bayer aspirin; Campho-Phenique canker sore medication; Double Danderine shampoo; Energine cleaning fluid and Energine Shoe-White polish; Fletcher's Castoria laxative; Haley's M-O mineral emulsion oil laxative; Ironized Yeast vitamin supplement tablets; Lyons' toothpaste and Dr. Lyons' tooth powder; Mulsified Coconut Oil shampoo; Phillips' Milk of Magnesia laxative, antacid tablets, toothpaste, tooth powder and face creams; ZBT baby powder; and other remedies. In 1954 the serial was sold to participating sponsors. Near the end of the run, it was offered by NBC on a sustaining basis.

Ratings: In 17 years, only once did the audience fall below a highly respectable 5.0 (in 1946–47, at 4.7). In its peak year, 1939–40, it reached 9.6. Other high ratings included 8.8 in 1949–50 and 8.0 in both 1942–43 and 1943–44. The series made a strong finish at 5.1 in 1954–55.

On the Air: June 6, 1938–Jan. 6, 1956, NBC, 4:15 p.m. ET.

We give you now— Stella Dallas!— a continuation on the air of the true-to-life story of mother love and sacrifice in which Stella Dallas saw her beloved daughter Laurel marry into wealth and society and, realizing the difference in their tastes and worlds, went out of Laurel's life. These episodes in the later life of Stella Dallas are based on the famous novel of that name by Olive Higgins Prouty and are written by Anne Hummert.

— Epigraph to *Stella Dallas*

If Stella had actually followed that declaration and stayed out of her prized Laurel's affairs (Stella nicknamed her "Lolly-Baby"), there would have been no story, and everybody would have been out of work. Fortunately for all concerned, this mother hen clucked over her offspring for nearly two decades, daring anyone to come between them. The enormously popular late-afternoon series was based on a veritable social chasm — leaving the child to fend for herself, but by implication only.

The addlepated Lolly-Baby was only 25 when she married into "wealth and society," and she never seemed to grow any older, either chronologically or emotionally. With a mom like Stella, obsessed with her every move — protecting her from lecherous sheiks while capturing sundry kidnappers who doted on Laurel ad nauseam — this deficient girl never really had much room to grow. It's true that inept, befuddled Lolly-Baby may have been the most rattlebrained female in radio soap opera. While making what was arguably the best decision of her life by choosing to marry wealthy young banker Dick Grosvenor (the "s" is silent) — a man who was "madly infatuated" with her — this helpless boob never would have gotten through it without her mother's surveillance.

Poor Laurel had a nasty way of stimulating the male juices, inspiring wild seduction schemes in many a man. To shield Lolly-Baby was her mother's highest calling. Yet despite the affection she bestowed on her offspring, thankless Stella received nothing more than a trio of lousy handkerchiefs one Christmas as an expression of Laurel's gratitude for her abiding care. (This must have reduced her fans to tears.)

Stella Dallas was one of a new breed of washboard weepers, developed in the late 1930s, that placed a courageous woman either by herself or without benefit of strong companionship against the adversities of life. Such were the premises of *Girl Alone* (first heard by a national audience in 1936) and *Stepmother* and *Valiant Lady* (which premiered in 1938). At about the same time, *Dallas* was introduced alongside a group of daytime heroines who were drawn by duty or held captive by unique circumstances. Among these series were *Hilltop House* (1937), *Houseboat Hannah* (1938), *Woman of Courage* (1939) and *Mother o' Mine* (1940). Of the five, only *Dallas* was successful in giving its audience nearly 18 uninterrupted years to observe the responses of a protagonist facing the crises of life. Over time her fans developed a warm, affectionate regard for Stella, positively affecting the program's outcome.

In a radio interview several years after the show's cancellation, Anne Elstner — the actress who portrayed Stella — recalled missing only one performance during an 18-year run on local and network radio. Elstner's husky dialect is etched forever in the minds of millions of the drama's faithful. Some claimed her tones marked her as the most distinctive character on daytime radio. One compared her voice to the distinguished, earthy brogues of Tex Ritter and Tallulah Bankhead.[1]

Elstner herself was convinced that she won the part over two dozen other Stella aspirants because she sounded more like Barbara Stanwyck than her rivals. Stanwyck played the role of Stella in a 1937 film, which was based on a turn-of-the-century novel by Olive Higgins Prouty. (In an earlier movie, Belle Bennett and Ronald Colman had starred as Stella and her divorced mate, Stephen.) Although the radio sequel purportedly picked up where the celluloid versions left off, the indomitable Ms. Prouty found little to her liking in the series produced by Frank and Anne Hummert.

Prouty's novel focused on a crude but benevolent mother who felt she must suppress her attachment with her daughter for the child to realize fulfillment. Bowing gently before her unkind fate while in print, in radio she became a tough old bird who wouldn't have bowed before a sultan. As heard on the air — where sex triangles involving philandering husbands, willing secretaries and aggrieved wives eventually waned, taking a back seat to more formidable fare like exposing miscreants of diverse persuasions — Stella Dallas soon became a supersleuth. After the series ended, Elstner confessed that the most notable line she uttered during the long run was: "Lolly-Baby, I ain't got no time for nothin' but trouble!"

Ostensibly, Stella — the attractive daughter of an indigent farm hand — earned a living as a seamstress and never went hungry. Still, in the quarter-hour peeks that radio allowed into her world, she depended on a needle and thread to maintain her sustenance about as often as rancher Sky King drove a herd of cattle to the railhead. Is it any wonder that Ms. Prouty, at the ripe old age of 92, may have gone to her grave in March 1974 rejecting most of what she had heard on a series whose billboard paid homage to her every single day? (Let's face it, the story in pulp fiction without the fantasy supplied by the broadcast medium would never have spawned such a loyal following. After a while it would have been Dullsville with a capital D.)

That billboard also credited Anne Hummert with the writing of *Stella Dallas*. By now the reader knows that the dialogue of *all* the Hummert shows was provided by a myriad of nameless scribes whose efforts were part of the Hummert syndrome: Frank or Anne would set down the rough action of a show's plot, then leave the fleshing out of conversations to others — subject to the Hummerts' ultimate approval. With rare exceptions, on-air credit was omitted for these faceless wordsmiths. Most understood their roles and performed a service for which they were compensated; any who balked could be summarily dismissed and replaced by other hungry journalists hoping for a crack at network radio.

In the case of *Stella Dallas*, something unusual was done, something not commonly observed among the several dozen other Hummert serials. From its earliest years, the billboard for *Dallas* credited either both Hummerts or Anne Hummert alone as the scriptwriter — not once but *twice* on *every* broadcast. In the 1940s and 1950s, immediately following a reference to Prouty's novel, listeners could expect to hear an added notation that these episodes were "written by Anne Hummert." (The reference is present in the epigraph quoted at the start of this chapter.) The credit was repeated at the end of the quarter-hour. The following words, broadcast in the waning days of the run, were typical at the conclusion of each show:

> This chapter in the later life of Stella Dallas is written by Anne
> Hummert, and is based on the famous character created by
> Olive Higgins Prouty in her great novel. Today's episode of
> *Stella Dallas* was brought to you by the National Broadcasting
> Company. *Stella Dallas* will be on the air at this same time
> tomorrow. This is Howard Claney speaking.

Whereas the Hummerts' acclaim was often subdued on some of their nighttime crime thrillers (*Mr. Keen, Tracer of Lost Persons; Mr. Chameleon; Mystery Theatre* and similar series), normally arriving at the end of a broadcast if then, and was missing altogether from some of their other daytime features, on *Stella Dallas* their names were read right up front. Yet in this author's memory, on no other soap opera — and certainly on none as prominent or as durable as this one — was the Hummert alliance spelled out in the opening lines.

The discerning reader may ask, "Why?" What was so peculiar about *Stella Dallas* that caused Anne Hummert to link her name with it alone, given all the choices she could have made from her vast empire? Did she herself genuinely aspire to write a serial and thus credited her own name for this one as if she had fulfilled a dream? Would she have had the spare time to actually turn out a 15-minute plot five days a week? Hardly. To this writer's knowledge, such inquiries have never been answered. Perhaps they have never been asked. Anne Hummert died on July 5, 1996, preceded in death on March 12, 1966 by her beloved Frank. The pair left others to ask the unanswered questions and to speculate on their thinking.

Dick Grosvenor, the man whom Laurel Dallas would marry, hailed from a well-to-do conservative Back Bay family in Boston, the city where Stella ran a little sewing shop on Beacon Street. By himself, Grosvenor would have been the near-perfect spouse for the inept but unmistakably stunning Laurel. He was handsome, personable, rich and successful as an investment broker. To his credit, there never seemed to be any doubt that he was deeply in love with Laurel. Together they had a daughter, named Stella Louise after you-can-guess-whom.

Dick was also the near-perfect son-in-law, for he had both the ability and the desire to be kind and compassionate to Stella. He was so impressed with her insights that he repeatedly sought her counsel. If he had been limited to frequent bouts of soap opera's malady of choice, amnesia, and occasional attacks of tropical fever, he could have been considered a pretty swell guy. But Dick was handicapped by the baggage he brought to his marriage in the form of his own mother.

Mrs. Grosvenor, a bitter, intolerant, unpleasant society matron looked on any association with Stella as tarnishing the Grosvenor name. It did not matter that Stella's intuitive perception about people helped the socialite thwart various malcontents from sharing in the fortune left by her late husband. The affluent dowager simply never could separate Stella's unselfish acts from the fact that her benefactress was born on the wrong side of the tracks (er, bay).

Among her faults, Stella had a penchant for liberally lacing her speech with "ain't." She embraced the double negative while regularly clipping the "g" off any word ending in "ing." It was all too much for the boorish Mrs. Grosvenor to bear, either in private or certainly in public conversation. She used every means at her disposal to distance herself and her family from Stella—even seeking to drive her son and his wife apart—to end the humiliation Stella caused her. This mean-spirited woman must have lain awake at night plotting legal means of ridding herself of Stella. Therefore, she couldn't contribute much to charity causes where her time and efforts and dollars could have made a difference; she was busy pursuing her all-consuming passion of abolishing Stella from their lives. It was a rotten way to live, and it kept the plot simmering.

At least three other characters routinely appeared in the *Dallas* story line. Stephen Dallas, an adventurer-entrepreneur, gained high office as a foreign diplomat. He too was a far cry from the uneducated Stella. In a moment of passion, perhaps, he decided to marry her. Though she loved him dearly and gave evidence of doing so long after they were separated, their union was doomed from the start. Stephen was the father of Laurel, but that was not enough to hold her parents together. The dapper young man was on the way up and had worlds to conquer. He wouldn't be hampered by such a clumsy encumbrance with an infant daughter. Stephen went out of both Stella's and Laurel's lives for years—Laurel was grown, in fact, the next time she saw him. By then he had remarried.

Following Stella's long absence from Laurel's life, Stephen was already there when she reentered it. He was considerate of Stella, and a strong friendship renewed between them. Stephen encouraged Laurel and Stella to reunite permanently and found ways to help make it happen. When his second wife died, Stella stood by his side and supported him through his grieving.

At long last, as the series drew to a close, Stephen demonstrated an about-face from his earlier ambitious nature: his top priority became the welfare of Stella. At their marriage he had transferred ownership of some apparently worthless South American mining properties to Stella's name for safekeeping. Those projects later developed into some valuable pieces of real estate. Only then did a bloodthirsty business associate, Raymond Wylie, sur-face. Wylie had made millions in Brazilian diamonds, coffee, rubber and other commodi-ties. In league with Stephen he had purchased the now-profitable holdings that Stephen had presented to Stella years before. Wylie vowed to his wife, Mildred, that he would kill Stephen and claim the property for himself. But on learning that the titles had been trans-ferred to Stella, he altered his intentions, telling Mildred he would kill Stephen *and* Stella.

In the meantime, Stephen asked Stella to forgive him for his past indiscretions. He determined to ask her to remarry him. As Wylie's plans were exposed, and on the prospect of Stella and Stephen's remarriage, the series played out its final dramatic scenario, leaving the air and probably an unsatisfied audience forever.

Minnie Grady, another recurring character in the long-running series, operated a Boston rooming house. When Stephen Dallas split, she became not only Stella's landlord but also her close confidante. Her distinctive, gravelly voice (that of actress Grace Valen-tine) was likened to that of Mrs. Davis, the comical landlady in another famous radio series, *Our Miss Brooks*. Though Minnie Grady was often deadly serious, she offered soli-tude to which Stella could retreat from the rigors of crisis. In her reverie alongside a kin-dred spirit, Stella found temporary solace.

Finally, as if one misguided old bat were not enough for a soap opera, this one had *two*. The second was Ada Dexter, whom the announcer commonly designated as "Mad Ada" Dexter. Possessed with an abundance of both anger and wealth, just as Mrs. Grosvenor was, Mad Ada bore an additional trait: she was literally insane. Adding tense elements to a farce that was already stretched to the average listener's limits, Mad Ada seemed like an intrusion into the plot, offering weird humor. If she had been around dur-ing the kingdoms of the Middle Ages, she might have found work as a court jester. Even though her contributions to *Dallas* bordered on the macabre, her diversions injected a calming effect on the tensions created by the more serious exigencies that Stella faced: stolen artifacts, lecherous sheiks and running battles with Mrs. Grosvenor.

A typical example of Mad Ada's menace should suffice. Stella once learned that this deranged woman and Rolfe, her chauffeur, were headed for the golf course at the local country club. Gunning for Dick Grosvenor, Mad Ada intended to drop her unsuspecting victim with the aid of an elephant gun. Almost too late, Stella arrived at the golf links, hop-ing to head off Mad Ada. Unable to locate her son-in-law to warn him of his impending danger, the quick-witted Stella hired a sound truck. Merrily she rolled over the greens, shouting through its public address system: "Dick Grosvenor, take cover! Dick Grosvenor, take cover! Dick Grosvenor, take cover!" The warning got to him in the nick of time. Such tense moments in the narrative seemed to disintegrate, at least from this distant vantage point, into pure comic relief.

The plots of the *Dallas* series were often thin and almost always exaggerated. In one trial, the clever Ms. Dallas found herself trapped in a skyscraper by unruly sorts who had kidnapped Laurel for what fans might assume were less-than-wholesome intents. How could the invincible old broad escape her towering cubicle and save Lolly-Baby from who knows what? Never-vexed Stella merely seized a roll of darning thread from her handbag (she was a seamstress, recall). Unraveling it, she allowed it to dangle dozens of floors below until it was noticed by pedestrians strolling along the sidewalk. Another time — while seek-ing rare orchids in the African wilds — she miraculously broke free of chains that had bound her to a mighty tree. Admit it: no restraint existed that could confine a determined Stella Dallas against her will for very long!

Continuing her adventures, at the end of the 1940s Stella crossed paths with a pair of unprincipled siblings, Gordon and Mercedes Crale. Suspecting them as no-goods from the start, she soon learned that they intended to destroy Laurel's marriage en route to gaining control of the Grosvenor fortune. To accomplish it, Gordon wooed the widowed matriarch and nearly got her to the altar. But Stella's intuitive distrust of the smooth-talking gentleman exposed the pair's intentions at an opportune moment. Although the elder Mrs. Grosvenor was humiliated, she would have been an even bigger fool had Stella not intervened.

At midcentury there was a sequence in which Stella herself nearly got to the altar with a man other than Stephen Dallas. For several years she had witnessed many admirable traits in Phil Baxter, who became something of a colleague in her crusades. On one occasion, she applied his technological expertise to trap an evildoer on the spot. Together they made a rather formidable team, confronting situations that involved several stubborn foes. When Phil finally got up enough nerve to ask Stella to marry him, she consented.

But forces intervened to prevent their nuptials. Clark Marshall and Maxine Booth, with agendas of their own, committed themselves to the notion that this wedding must never take place. An equally determined Mrs. Grosvenor fought tenaciously to destroy any chance for Stella's happiness. The erstwhile happy couple soon began receiving threatening messages. In the end, they never made it down the aisle. The Hummerts and their writing staff would have been severely handicapped if they had. After all, a female supersleuth who put dragons to rest by herself for so many years would be limited in subsequent pursuits with a spouse hanging on. Just how many husbands allow their wives to go sheik-hunting in the Sahara, for instance?

Which brings us to what is arguably the most frequently recalled sequence of the series' long run — at least, by those who have published accounts of the *Dallas* drama. What do you do if one of those salacious sheiks takes your precious Lolly-Baby, out for a stroll on the desert, to his harem? You go after him with a vengeance, of course, with everything you can muster. Actually, the culprit that Stella faced was merely a wolf in sheik's clothing.

Arabian Sheik Ahmead Ben Akbar, who controlled an unidentified Middle Eastern empire, was a very good sheik. He ruled fairly and was apparently loved by his subjects. But the sheik had a twin brother, Sheik Rahshed, who plotted to overthrow his sibling and acquire home rule. Impersonating his brother, Rahshed naturally began his quest by stealing a precious artifact, an Egyptian mummy, from the home of Mrs. Grosvenor. She had intended to impress some uppercrusts with it by having the relic on display during a party at her estate. When the mummy was pilfered, Mrs. Grosvenor pinned its disappearance on Stella Dallas, suggesting that she had taken it to embarrass the dowager before her friends. What neither party knew at the time was that Stella's old friend Ed Munn, blackmailed by the false sheik, had filched the curio on behalf of the impostor.

Lolly-Baby and Stella reviewed their options when it seemed that Mrs. Grosvenor would press charges that might land Stella in the slammer. Laurel, who always referred to her doting mother as "Mummy," injected this engaging, though confusing, line into their dialogue: "Mummy, anybody who knows you knows you could never steal an Egyptian mummy!" The words would become puzzling to nearly everybody soon enough, when — in an effort to clear Stella's name — Lolly-Baby made a jaunt to the Middle East to regain the stolen mummy. Isn't that the course that anyone who was falsely accused under similar circumstances would have pursued?

While there, Laurel met her match with Rahshed the lecherous, became a part of his harem and, as a result, saw him incur the wrath of Stella Dallas. (The program's long-standing theme song was the haunting and invariably apropos "How Can I Leave Thee?") In hot pursuit of both offspring and artifact while Dick Grosvenor valiantly sought wife, her mummy and *the* mummy, Stella saved a lot of folks from a train wreck while en route to Rahshed's native land. Her trek included a submarine cruise through the Suez Canal. Then, crossing the Sahara, she braved sandstorms and survived nonpassionate attacks by bands of desert nomads.

Finally tracking the unscrupulous Rahshed to his seraglio, Stella learned that Lolly-Baby had held her captor at bay — for three solid weeks, yet — while the real mummy sought his lair. Stella absconded with both Lolly-Baby and the mummy *and* restored the rightful Sheik Ahmead to his throne. Was she Supermom or what? On the following day's broadcast, Stella opened the dialogue with this line: "Golly, Minnie, it sure is good to be back in Boston." It took her a while to navigate the Suez and cross the desert, but her return to Minnie Grady's rooming house was faster than a speeding bullet.

This whole bit of nonsense provided the serial's sponsors with a golden opportunity to introduce a premium offer tied to the plot development. An "exact copy" of a necklace worn by Egypt's Queen Sit-Hat-Nor-U-Net could be any listener's prized possession for only two bits. But just as the premium was about to be announced on the air, the tiny plant that had contracted to make the trinkets temporarily shut down. During the three weeks that Laurel held the impostor at bay, a writer was left holding the bag; the writer strung out the dialogue in measured words, without any mention of the queen's precious bauble, awaiting the opportune moment to introduce it. If the dialogue had proceeded at the normal pace, the sequence would have ended with Stella returning to Boston long before the costume jewelry rolled off the assembly line. When its manufacture began at last, Stella tore into the harem, the narrator offered the premium for a quarter and the perspiring writer resigned from the show. It wasn't the radio premium's finest hour.

Even though Stella's exploits were often too much to be believed, the source of her moral fiber was obviously placed in a higher power. A conversation with Phil Baxter in the summer of 1945 illustrates:

> STELLA: I feel so strong, Phil, that ... good is always stronger
> than evil. Sometimes folks think it's not. Sometimes it seems
> like there's nothin' but trouble in our lives. But underneath
> everything, there *is* a plan — a plan that can only be — God's
> plan.... We human bein's aren't always good judges of
> what's best. But there is a *perfect* judge. And we're *all* in —
> *His* hands.
> PHIL: You've certainly followed the teachings of the Church,
> Stella. *Always.*
> STELLA: Well, I try my best to. Anyway, I most certainly do
> have faith that ... God is helpin' us show Neil that Harriet is
> disruptin' his home.

Ever the champion of worthwhile causes, Stella did her part during the World War II by laboring in a factory that made products for the defense lines. Her service may have had more than fictional impact on the nation's behalf: she may have implanted an idea in the hearts and minds of women in the listening audience who had time to spare for authentic volunteer efforts while their men were away.

Originating locally at 12:30 p.m. on October 25, 1937, for Tetley tea on NBC's flagship affiliate, New York's WEAF, *Stella Dallas* went to the full network beginning on June 6, 1938. Airing at 4:15 p.m., the program never left that quarter-hour until its cancellation more than 17 years later.

Time ran out for *Dallas* at the start of 1956 as a result of a decision NBC made in 1955 to reorient its daytime programming. By abolishing several of its most prestigious and durable soap operas, the network hoped to stave off TV awhile longer. Its appeal to listeners was to offer an innovative multihour magazine called *Weekday,* which would hopefully do for daytime what NBC's highly successful *Monitor* was doing for weekends. Like *Monitor,* the new marathon series was to include popular hosts, intriguing guests, news and information, interviews, advice, music, drama, comedy and other features.

To reach its objective, the network decided to banish *Backstage Wife* and *Joyce Jordan, M.D.* on July 1, 1955. (Fans were elated when *Wife* was granted a reprieve as rival CBS picked it up and continued it until early 1959.) Meanwhile, NBC soon increased its commitment to *Weekday* and axed *Just Plain Bill* and *Lorenzo Jones* (both on September 30, 1955). A little more than three months later — on January 6, 1956 —*Stella Dallas* finally bit the dust.

The network had broadcast eleven daytime serials just a scant half-year earlier. By the early part of 1956, only a half-dozen washboard weepers remained: *Hotel for Pets* (at 3:30 p.m.), *The Doctor's Wife* (3:45), *The Right to Happiness* (4:00), *Young Widder Brown* (4:15), *Pepper Young's Family* (4:30) and *The Woman in My House* (4:45). Half of these —*Hotel for Pets, The Doctor's Wife* and *The Woman in My House*— had been created in the 1950s and thus were unable to add longevity in attracting fans over sustained periods. Without such ties, their numbers were at a disadvantage.

The NBC brass quickly realized that pinning its hopes on *Weekday* —by then filling four and three-quarter hours of the web's daily schedule — had been a tragic mistake. Though never admitting it publicly, management must have seen that tampering with listening patterns that had worked for decades contributed heavily to a dwindling audience. By then it was too late, however. A trust with the fans had been irretrievably broken. Radio audiences were leaking like a sieve and this would soon turn into a flood.

The Right to Happiness and *Young Widder Brown* disappeared from NBC by the summer of 1956. (*Happiness* was lucky enough to be granted a stay of execution by shifting to CBS.) This left NBC in mid–1956 with only a single soap opera with a continuous and appreciable tenure on its daytime roster, *Pepper Young's Family.*

To that point, NBC had lost or abandoned a score or more of its durable daytime dramas. While its programmers struggled to reacquire a fading audience (a plight that was hitting *all* the networks), a few new serials and self-contained dramas were added at NBC. Yet the momentum had passed; only a fraction of the faithful who had listened in the pre–1955 years were still tuning in.

The demise of the *Dallas* series was a bitter pill for loyal fans like Lady Mendl (Elsie de Wolfe, 1920s and 1930s socialite, well-known interior decorator and international hostess), singer Elsa Maxwell and composer Cole Porter, as well as millions of less notables. When word leaked out about the fate of their favorite series, this trio organized a letter-writing campaign. Though the outcome was unchanged, the flood of protests that NBC received may have opened some eyes to the impact of tampering with long-established listening habits.

The woman who played Stella for the entire *Dallas* run, Anne Elstner, was born in Lake Charles, Louisiana, on January 22, 1899. Moving north early in life, she met and married FBI agent Jack Mathews. In the pre–Depression era, the couple lived on his Maryland tobacco plantation. Eventually, they became outspoken right-wingers, crusading against communism and championing the American way. But that was several years later.

When the nation's economic picture worsened, the pair went to New York to find work. Elstner had made her living in acting, including appearing on the Broadway stage, before her marriage. She decided to pursue it again. Radio beckoned with unlimited opportunities in 1930 — without requiring a great deal of effort. She auditioned and soon found herself in the role of Cracker Gaddis in a debuting series, *Moonshine and Honeysuckle,* carried for three years on NBC on Sunday afternoons. It was one of soap opera's precursor series.

Soon afterward other parts began to arrive regularly. Elstner's radio credits included roles on *Cindy and Sam, Trouble House* (a dramatic vignette of *The Heinz Magazine of the Air*), *Tish, Wilderness Road, The Gibson Family, Just Plain Bill, Maverick Jim, Brenda Curtis* and *Heartthrobs of the Hills.* She acted on *The Fat Man, Great Plays, Pages of Romance, The March of Time* and *Mr. Keen, Tracer of Lost Persons.* At one time she was playing roles on ten different shows daily!

But the part with which she identified most and took very, very seriously was Stella Dallas, which became an extension of herself. A colleague remarked that Elstner was so personally caught up in the role that she had difficulty separating the two. Her friend intimated that the actress nearly believed at times that she *was* Stella herself! There is little doubt that the role offered her dimensions that most radio heroines likely never experienced. It became a consuming passion that undoubtedly contributed to her missing only a single performance. That happened when a train delay prevented her from reaching the studio on time from her home in Stockton, New Jersey.

Even after the series ended, Elstner continued to bask in the years she spent as Stella. One of her favorite pastimes became guesting on celebrity talk shows. In 1970 she and two impostors appeared before the panel of TV's *To Tell the Truth.* Panelists attempted to discern which of the three was radio's *real* Stella Dallas. She chortled gleefully when the experts couldn't identify her, which suggested that the impostors had been coached very well.

During the serial's final years on the air, Elstner and her husband purchased a swanky restaurant. Located at nearby Lambertville, New Jersey, it overlooked the Delaware River opposite New Hope, Pennsylvania. Elstner would arrive at the restaurant at 7:00 a.m. to write out the daily menu. Then she'd go to New York for her broadcast (and sometimes several additional shows). By 6:00 p.m. she was back at the restaurant, where she stayed until the midnight closing.

Given permission to apply her serial's moniker to the enterprise, she renamed it Stella Dallas' Rivers Edge Restaurant. Advertising signs were strategically placed along area highways to announce that Stella herself was the proprietress. During the years Elstner and her husband owned the restaurant, patrons would greet the renowned actress and beg her to thrill them once more with some original Dallas monologue — a request she was happy to honor. The actress died on January 29, 1981, at Doylestown, Pennsylvania, a week following her 82nd birthday.

Anne Elstner (*l*) was the omnipresent title character in the 18-year run of *Stella Dallas*. Her beloved "Lolly-Baby" was played by Vivian Smolen. Elstner was so wrapped up in her role that she had trouble separating it from life, even opening a restaurant and naming it for the character she played. (Photofest)

Joy Hathaway, who carried the title role in the serial *Amanda of Honeymoon Hill*, was Laurel Dallas Grosvenor in the earliest days of the *Dallas* run. She also had running roles in *Second Husband* and *Young Widder Brown*. Her date of death was November 4, 1954. But this part is more familiarly associated with Vivian Smolen — radio's *Our Gal Sunday*— who played the featherbrained Lolly-Baby for most of the *Dallas* show's run.

Seven actors, several of them well-known beyond their radio work, portrayed Lolly's husband, Dick Grosvenor. They, and some of their on-air credits, included the following:

• Jim Backus, who once jokingly acknowledged that "they fired you to see if you were paying attention" (*Gaslight Gayeties, The Alan Young Show, The Bob Burns Show, The Jim Backus Show, The Penny Singleton Show, The Big Talent Hunt, Columbia Workshop, Kate Smith Hour, The Danny Kaye Show, The Edgar Bergen and Charlie McCarthy Show, Lum and Abner, The Mel Blanc Show, The Sad Sack*; TV's *Gilligan's Island*)

• Spencer Bentley (*Barry Cameron, Betty and Bob, Hilltop House, Jane Arden, The Man I Married, Our Gal Sunday, The Romance of Helen Trent*)

• MacDonald Carey (*The First Nighter, Heartbeat Theatre, Jason and the Golden Fleece, Woman in White, Young Hickory, Ellen Randolph, The Family Theater, John's Other Wife, Just Plain Bill;* TV's *Days of Our Lives*)

• Bert Cowlau (no other known radio credits)

• Michael Fitzmaurice (*The Right to Happiness, The Adventures of Superman, Brenda Curtis, Highway Patrol, Land of the Lost, Nick Carter Master Detective, The Quiz of Two Cities, The Sparrow and the Hawk, Tales of Fatima, This Life Is Mine, Her Honor Nancy James, Joyce Jordan, M.D., Myrt and Marge, Pepper Young's Family, Rosemary, When a Girl Marries*)

• George Lambert (*Amanda of Honeymoon Hill*)

• Carleton Young (*Front Page Farrell* and many more)

The actress who played Mrs. Grosvenor for the run of the show, Jane Houston, was also a radio veteran. She appeared in *Mr. and Mrs., The Open Door, Amanda of Honeymoon Hill, Second Husband, Seth Parker* and *Young Widder Brown.* She died on September 27, 1979 at age 88.

Grace Valentine, appearing as Stella's landlady Minnie Grady, was also heard on *Lone Journey.*

Helen Claire ("Mad Ada" Dexter) routinely turned up on *The O'Neills, Echoes of New York, Backstage Wife, Death Valley Days, Great Plays, Dr. Christian, The Strange Romance of Evelyn Winters, Roses and Drums, The Sheriff, Stories of the Black Chamber, The Twin Stars Show* and *David Harding, Counterspy.* She was the only heroine to die on the air in childbirth, on *The O'Neills.* She appeared on Broadway and with touring companies. From 1937 to 1949 she was a fashion commentator for Fox Movietone News. Born on October 18, 1911, at Union Springs, Alabama, Claire died on January 12, 1974, at Birmingham, Alabama.

Of four actors heard as Stephen Dallas — Arthur Hughes, Neil Malley, Leo McCabe and Frederick Tozere — only Hughes is credited with other series. For 23 years he was hero Bill Davidson of *Just Plain Bill.*

The Hummerts seemed almost amused with the theme of taking a woman from the boondocks and having her marry above her station in life. The soap opera innovators did it so often that they earned a reputation for mixing the rich and the poor as protagonists in a high percentage of their serials. In most of them, whatever destiny brought a couple together normally bound them forever. But *Stella Dallas* was different. Based on a widely read novel and two screenplays in which the heroine became a divorcée, this series demanded that the Hummerts tinker with their concept. In the 1930s divorce was neither widely practiced nor widely accepted by the masses of American people. Had the Prouty tale not been the basis for the radio drama, the Hummerts might have failed with this one. But maybe because the subject was so innovative — a departure from the adopted norm — it worked well.

Was it the attachment of the Prouty acclaim or possibly the novelty of the divorced heroine that intrigued Anne Hummert into adding her own name to the show's credits? Perhaps (but only perhaps) she too had tired of the same old propositions that were literally earning her a fortune.

26
This Is Nora Drake

(A Modern Story)

There never seemed to be enough unattached men to go around in soap operas. The heroines who were single, virginal and looking for a mate seemed incessantly drawn to experienced suitors who had been married at least once. Some of those gentlemen still were attached. If that situation didn't prevail at the inception of a serial, in due time it frequently occurred. Such was the case of Nora Drake, a career-oriented professional who could have had her pick of many eligible bachelors. She had the misfortune to fall in love with Dr. Ken Martinson, who—in a moment of haste—put her aside to marry nurse Peggy King. Peggy turned his life into misery maximized. Nora pined for Ken to obtain the divorce that Peggy told him he'd get only over her dead body, setting in motion a waiting game; fans were sure the outcome would one day arrive. On the way there, the serial gave new meaning to the old adage: Hell hath no fury like a woman scorned. Peggy Martinson acted as did so many other serial troublemakers faced with similar prospects, believing her lot on earth was to dish out as much agony for "the other woman" as she could. Her target would seldom have a moment's rest. Only when nurse Nora went after some other men did Peggy let up. When those pursuits didn't pan out, the pressure resumed. In the end Peggy got hers, falling victim to an assassin's intent. Though it took five years, it was only a question of time. Getting there was what made it all so compelling.

Producer: Foote, Cone and Belding advertising agency
Directors: Dee Engelbach, Arthur Hanna, Charles Irving
Writers: Julian Funt, Milton Lewis
Music: Charles Paul
Sound Effects: Ross Martindale, Jerry Sullivan
Announcers: Bill Cullen, Ken Roberts
Nora Drake: Charlotte Holland (1947–49), Joan Tompkins (1949–57), Mary Jane Higby (1957–59)
Ken Martinson: Alan Hewitt
Peggy Martinson: Joan Alexander, Mercedes McCambridge, Lesley Woods
Arthur Drake: Ralph Bell, Everett Sloane
Charles Dobbs: Grant Richards

Others: Lester Damon, Roger DeKoven, Elspeth Eric, Larry Haines, Irene Hubbard, Leon Janney, Joan Lorring, Charlotte Manson, Doug Parkhirst, Robert Readick, Arnold Robertson, Lucille Wall, more

Theme: Original melody

Sponsors: Foote, Cone and Belding governed this show on behalf of the Gillette Co. for its Toni hair care products division (home permanents, shampoo, rinse and other commodities). In 1952 the serial became one of the first sold to multiple sponsors. It gained another sole sponsor, Bristol-Myers, Inc. (for Sal-Hepatica stomach distress reliever, Ipana toothpaste and other health aids), in 1953. The show reverted to Toni in 1954 and again to Bristol-Myers in 1955. For the remainder of the run it was sold on a participating basis.

Ratings: High (single broadcast): 7.0 (1949–50); low: 3.2 (1947–48); high (dual broadcasts, 1948–49): 8.1; median: 5.9 (based on 1947–56 inclusive).

On the Air: Oct. 27, 1947–Nov. 18, 1949, NBC, 11:00 a.m. ET; 1948–June 29, 1956, CBS, 2:30 p.m.; July 2, 1956–Jan. 2, 1959, CBS, 1:00 p.m.

MUSIC: Trio of organ notes
FEMALE VOCALIST: (Sings to organ accompaniment)
      For ... soft wa-a-ter shampooing,
      Use Toni Creme Shampoo;
      Even in the hardest water...
      Toni Creme Shampoo.
      T-O-N-I ... Toni!
ANNOUNCER: Yes, even in the hardest water, Toni Creme Shampoo gives soft water shampooing that rinses away dandruff instantly. Leaves hair so soft ... so smooth ... so shining clean. Today, bring out the sparkling beauty of your hair with soft water shampooing. Get the handy tube or jar of Toni Creme Shampoo. It's new!
MUSIC: Pick up a few bright notes, hold under
ANNOUNCER: Toni...
MUSIC: Dual notes, hold under
ANNOUNCER: Toni...
MUSIC: Dual notes, hold under
ANNOUNCER: Toni Home Permanent presents...
MUSIC: Dual notes, halt abruptly
NORA: *This is Nora Drake.*
MUSIC: Theme song
ANNOUNCER: (Theme under) *This is Nora Drake*, a modern story seen through the window of a woman's heart.

Thus, in the late 1940s, the second of a trio of successful late-morning postwar soap operas flowed into kitchens and living rooms across America. (The others were *Wendy Warren and the News* and *The Brighter Day*.) Arriving for the first time on October 27, 1947, *This Is Nora Drake* exploited the issue of a woman's career clashing with her personal happiness. Whereas this drama's heroine was a nurse, she maintained plenty of company in other serials in a struggle to balance her own desires with restraints imposed by vocation.

In this story, like others, the fact that the central characters were employed sometimes appeared to exist only as a kind of scaffolding, surrounding them for the action that transpired outside of work. Is this a contradiction? Not in the least. The fact that they had jobs insulated some against the harsh realities linked with producing an income. For the most part, soap opera figures could roam freely, returning to work sites when not required elsewhere — or when needed to produce action enhancing the current story line.

The mere mention of an occupation in the life of a professional was often enough to allow that figure to live on borrowed time, to go about the aberrations that intruded into his or her existence without a lot of thought as to how a salary was sustained. That isn't to say that Nora and the other medics didn't work for their livelihoods occasionally — intertwining personal dilemmas within the context of the workplace — but gainful employment simply wasn't a priority for most. (To substantiate that, try watching a TV soap opera for a while. Observe how little importance is attached to showing up for work on a regular basis and focusing on the job as if it mattered.) If a serial character had a job, that might be sufficient, whether he or she practiced it frequently or not. In many cases, that fact made for more interesting predicaments in their lives than if they dutifully reported for daily labor.

Nora's work environment was the mental health clinic at Page Memorial Hospital. The medical profession has always achieved a degree of public trust and esteem that has eluded some other occupations. The nature of Nora's calling allowed her a certain measure of recognition, status and acceptance not enjoyed by some others. Consequently, she could rather easily move about in society, dipping into other peoples' lives as she saw fit while maintaining a high level of respect by almost everybody.

The series opened with Nora believing herself to be an orphan. She soon landed in the middle of a romantic triangle that was destined to plague her for much of the run. As ill luck would have it, she fell in love with one of her colleagues, physician Ken Martinson. Their ongoing affair, seldom offering a flicker of prolonged optimism, gave evidence it was heading nowhere while taking a long time getting there. Despite the fact that love held Ken and Nora permanent hostages, they struggled on in a kind of vain persistence, hoping one day to arrive at the altar.

The endless array of entanglements Nora was to meet would have confounded a lesser woman. She possessed remarkable stamina, defying the odds. Nora remained true to Ken when evil forces intervened. Her resolve helped turn away more than one admirer seeking her for his wife. Delays of one kind or another made it seem like Ken would forever be off-limits. Still, patience prevailed; she would wait for him forever if necessary. *That* is a long time to wait for another woman's husband!

While Ken also loved Nora without inhibitions, in a moment of haste he did something foolish that was to haunt him for the rest of his days. Another nurse, Peggy King, an unruly daughter of a local millionaire, convinced him things would never work out with Nora. Professing to love him, she persuaded him to marry her, rushing him down the aisle before Nora had time to know what was going on.

Not long after their nuptials, Ken regained his senses and realized how deeply he loved Nora. Faced with the consequences of his haste, he did the only thing an honorable man could do: he approached Peg with a petition for divorce. But the cold-hearted Peg responded to the young Romeo in no uncertain terms. It wasn't to be — not then, not ever. The turn of events resulted in years of agony for him and his lady friend, Nora Drake. In fact, Peg's sole preoccupation in life became the destruction of Nora's happiness.

For her part, Nora was definitely the other woman. But she carried it off with dignity. Perhaps because of her vocation as a nurse, she remained insulated from tongue-wagging about loose living and man-chasing, the gossip that was the bane of others in similar straits. Thus, she exalted her charms without acting out her fantasies. This kept her circumspect, maintaining her virtue throughout years of quiet anguish. While not giving up hope that she would one day become Mrs. Ken Martinson, Nora accepted her fate and went about life, relegating the stormy outbursts to Peg and Ken.

After refusing Ken's request for a divorce, Peggy appeared before Nora, lashing out at her and warning her that she would never have Ken. With that, Peg got into her automobile in a rage and drove off at high speed. As luck would have it, she caused an accident that rendered her a cripple for the rest of her life.

Ken, ever the considerate man, could think of but one solution to the new circumstances: he would set aside any hopes and dreams he might have harbored for his and Nora's contentment. Instead, he would do the decent thing and devote the rest of his life to caring for his invalid wife. His decision, of course, meant that he committed all three of them to hopelessly miserable existences. The radio audience would share that anguish as well.

But these were the crises on which successful serials were contrived. Here was a situation that could be plucked forth at appropriate intervals for as long as the show lasted. It would give Peg absolute license to heap all the distress she possibly could upon poor Nora's wretched existence while creating a natural sympathy for Nora among legions of fans.

As the story progressed, Nora learned she was not an orphan after all. Arthur Drake, her long-lost father, resurfaced, proving himself a man of strong emotions but weak mind (a typical male in serialdom). Shortly after making peace with Nora about his years of absence, Drake introduced his daughter to an old crony, the notorious gambler Fred Molina. A little while later Drake accidentally shot Molina.

In an effort to protect Drake, Ken jeopardized his career by failing to report the incident to police. Instead he went to Molina's suite to remove a bullet lodged near the victim's heart. Hoping to keep all of this from Nora, Ken urged Peggy — who assisted him in the operation — to remain silent.

On the broadcast of September 13, 1948, Nora, at home in her apartment, received a telephone call from her father. He inquired if there had been any messages for him. Nora told him she had had a call from Ken. Arthur Drake then became quite anxious, wanting to know what was said. Unaware of the shooting and subsequent surgery, Nora told her father there was nothing out of the ordinary to the call.

Drake ended their conversation abruptly, raising Nora's level of curiosity. Yet when she picked up the phone to dial Molina's suite, she was ill-prepared for the greeting she got. At Ken's direction, Peggy, posing as Molina's secretary, answered. Molina was drifting in and out of a coma and at times was totally incoherent. Nora asked to speak to Molina and — in a kind of subconscious stupor — Molina took the phone from Peggy's hand.

MOLINA: Hello, Nora…
NORA: (On filter) Hello, Mr. Molina. I … I just called to let
    you know that dad came home … very late last night.
MOLINA: Why … I told you he would, Nora.
NORA: (On filter) Yes, I wanted to thank you for…
MOLINA: (Moans)
NORA: (On filter) Molina, what's wrong?
MOLINA: (Agonizingly) Nothing, Nora. It's just…
KEN: (Whispers, commanding) Peggy, pick up that phone!
PEGGY: Hello, Miss Drake…
NORA: (On filter) Hello, where's Mr. Molina?
PEGGY: He's … He's been called away from the phone.
NORA: (On filter) Called away?
PEGGY: Yes.
NORA: (On filter) But I thought I heard … I … I want to talk
    to Mr. Molina again.
PEGGY: I … I'm afraid you won't be able to … for just a while,
    Miss Drake.
NORA: (On filter) Then will you give him a message, please?
PEGGY: What is it?
NORA: (On filter) Tell him that I'm coming up to see him in
    just a few minutes. Good-by.
MUSIC: Sharp sting followed by transition notes

After the concluding commercial for that episode, announcer Bill Cullen offered this enticement for the following day's installment: "Nora had no idea of the strange surprise that awaited her in Fred Molina's suite. And Ken Martinson, becoming more and more involved in a dangerous situation, wondered how he could avoid seeing Nora. Peggy, of course, smiled to herself when she saw the consternation on Ken's face. She wasn't worried about Nora coming there because … that was just what she wanted."

In the end the good doctor's efforts were exonerated. But poor Arthur Drake was carted off to prison. Nora had only recently located her father, and in a brief time, she lost him again. Another tragedy was added to the dilemmas of her life.

In a later sequence, with Ken apparently forever attached to Peggy, Nora fell in love with a bright young attorney, Charles Dobbs. Dobbs had gained some notoriety for his achievements as an assistant district attorney. In fact, he was up for an appointment by the governor as a special prosecutor. But he also came with excess baggage that could wipe out the possibility of the nomination.

His brother, George Stewart, was *his* albatross, his political liability. (The two men were half brothers, thus the difference in their last names.) George was a deadbeat whose personal lifestyle typified the very kinds of people special prosecutors often sought. In reality, he lived a fine line between legal and illegal activities and had never kept this a secret.

Conversely, Charles was a gentle man, one of principle and compassion. On numerous occasions he had rescued his brother from tough situations while hoping George would reform. George didn't, of course, and that created the dilemma in which Charles found himself at the time of his ballyhooed appointment by the governor.

George was again in need of immediate cash to pay gambling debts. To collect, he sent his charming and attractive young wife, Dorothy, to call on Charles. Having been down that road before, Charles anticipated the nature of Dorothy's visit. This time George needed $10,000, an enormous sum by 1950s standards. Not having that kind of dough available, Charles — who couldn't refuse his brother — knew of only one source he could readily tap for a sum that size. He would go to one of the most corrupt crime bosses in the city, a man known to be capable of murder, Big John Morley. (Of course, any thinking listener might have deduced that bank loans were still available to rising young lawyers. But in the world of soap opera, that was summarily dismissed without mention; it simply wouldn't have been interesting or enhancing to the plot.)

Meanwhile, the honorable assistant district attorney detected an ethical and moral dilemma: how could he possibly make a deal with the devil himself, then rise to the office of special prosecutor? He was too above reproach to do it. He would accomplish his mission another way.

When Charles approached Big John Morley for the $10,000, he wasn't surprised that Morley wrote him a check. But he was unprepared when Morley told him he didn't expect to be repaid. Unaccustomed to doing business that way, Charles told Morley he would pay him in full with interest. He handed the crime boss a letter to the governor declining the special prosecutor's appointment, asking Morley to mail it. Morley tore the letter in two and put it in the wastebasket. Charles laid the $10,000 check on Morley's desk, thanked him for his generosity and left.

At last Charles had to face George and Dorothy. When he admitted he didn't have the money, Dorothy placed an envelope containing $10,000 in it before the two brothers. Believing Charles wouldn't compromise his convictions, she had sold the precious jewelry George had given her early in their marriage.

Sometime during all of this, Nora began to fall out of love with Charles, even though he was a man of extraordinary integrity. Though she had not admitted it to him, or even completely to herself, she was having a change of heart.

The connection with Big John Morley was not yet over, however. It was to become far more sinister in the weeks ahead. This tie provided so many opportunities for intrigue that it couldn't be readily dispatched. Morley had a son, Tom, a recent college graduate, whom the gangster doted on. The lad was blind to the illegal activities and public outcry against his dad. There was even a hint that Tom might want to follow in his father's footsteps.

By this time Charles Dobbs had received the governor's designation as special prosecutor. His first mission was to build a strong case against — who else? — Big John Morley. To gather sufficient data that could result in putting such a well-known criminal behind bars was a formidable and dangerous assignment. No agent before Charles had lived to carry out similar efforts.

Tom Morley was convinced that all of Charles's accusations were contrived and the charges to be brought against his father were false. But as he was about to go to trial, Big John Morley drowned in a boating accident. Nora suggested that it might have been no accident but suicide, so that Tom "would have a better chance in life."

Tom wouldn't believe it. He blamed his dad's death on Charles, for pursuing what he contended was a misguided effort, and on Nora, for being with Charles when Big John raced off in his boat. Together, he reasoned, they had driven his father to suicide. He vowed to avenge his father's death.

When young Morley located a forged check supposedly signed by Charles's brother,

George Stewart, he felt he had Charles and Nora right where he wanted them. Tom planned to use the check to force Charles' resignation as special prosecutor. That provided many agonizing moments for Charles, Nora and George. However, Nora recalled a brown manila envelope filled with evidence that Charles had gathered on Big John for the trial. It contained details, dates, names, places — reports of misdeeds, murder included, which the senior Morley had committed in his grasp for power. If she could persuade Tom to read it, Nora believed he would rethink his misplaced loyalty and the destructive course he intended to follow.

With George's forgery trial about to begin, Tom had to learn the truth or an innocent man would be sent to prison for a crime he didn't commit. Charles, who was also innocent of wrongdoing, would have to resign as special prosecutor. Eventually the truth came out: Nora was at last able to persuade Tom to read the file, even after he had earlier refused. Three days later, under oath, Tom admitted he had known all along that the check was a forgery plotted by his father — that his dad had wanted to trap George Stewart by using the check so that Charles would be forced to resign as special prosecutor. At last he realized his father had hurt many people. When the trial ended, George went free, and Charles continued as special prosecutor.

As the Dobbs sequence concluded, Nora knew she no longer loved Charles. She resolved to break her engagement and look elsewhere for romance. But her decision didn't leave only Charles disillusioned. Peggy Martinson, having long hoped that someone else would sweep Nora off her feet, had been delighted by Nora's engagement to Charles. With their breakup, her ambitions were thwarted. She retaliated with renewed vigor, employing daring tactics to keep the pressure on and deny Nora any repose.

Nora later became infatuated with yet another medic, a psychiatrist, Dr. Robert Sergeant. There was another woman in his life too, his ex-wife, Vivian. Like Peggy Martinson, Vivian demonstrated deviant behavior. She intended to strengthen her hold over her ex by destroying the life of their young daughter, Grace. But Robert was equally strong-willed and up to the challenge. No matter what the cost, he would intercede on Grace's behalf — even if it meant losing Nora Drake.

By 1952 Peggy Martinson's career as a maker of mayhem came to an end when she died at the hands of an assassin. Suspicion fell on her chauffeur, Spencer. Nora, believing Spencer's plea of innocence, asked Ken to go with her to see Irene, Spencer's wife. Irene pulled a gun on them, forcing Nora and Ken to accompany her to her girlfriend Gloria's apartment. There they found a seriously wounded Spencer and Gloria in a semihysterical state. With Spencer's life hanging in the balance, Irene — gun in hand — forced Ken to operate on the semiconscious Spencer, removing a bullet while Nora assisted. Irene wouldn't permit anyone to call the authorities.

Did any of this sound vaguely familiar? (It had held listeners at rapt attention before; the producers figured it would work just as well a second time around.) Longtime fans perhaps thought they were living in the twilight zone. They must have also wondered how Ken Martinson continued to hold a valid medical license while avoiding prosecution and malpractice suits!

Charlotte Holland initiated the role of Nora Drake. She had running roles in several other Chicago-based serial dramas: *Against the Storm, Big Sister, Lone Journey, The Open Door* and *Joyce Jordan, Girl Interne*.

Surrounded by some of Bellevue Hospital's younger patients, Joan Tompkins (in character) maintains an enchanted audience. The actress played the title role in *This Is Nora Drake* for about eight of the serial's eleven years. She is reading to the children from a Nora Drake doll-cutout book. (Photofest)

Two years later the veteran radio actress Joan Tompkins, the best-remembered Nora, succeeded Holland. She carried the part almost to the end of the run. Tompkins also played the long-running role of Norine Temple, Ellen Brown's best friend, in *Young Widder Brown*. Earlier she originated the title role of *Lora Lawton*. She had recurring roles on *Against the Storm, Big Sister, David Harum, Our Gal Sunday* and *Your Family and Mine*. Her soft-spoken, polished portrayal of Nora marked her as one of the leading ladies of daytime serials.

In her book *Tune in Tomorrow*, Mary Jane Higby, another legendary serial heroine, recalled being an aspirant in what she claimed was "the last of the great radio auditions." In the late 1950s Joan Tompkins surmised that the fortunes of broadcasting's future would be made in California, not New York. Wanting a stake in that action, she notified CBS that when her contract expired, she wouldn't renew. She planned to seek her place in the sun.

The big audition to replace Tompkins drew 84 candidates for the role of Nora Drake. Earlier, Mary Jane Higby had weathered the long-expected cancellation of her own protracted ABC series, *When a Girl Marries*, where she had played the feminine lead of Joan

Davis since 1939. Now Higby was to compete with scores of others for daytime radio's final coveted prize.

Higby's account of that audition offered insights into what was involved in acquiring a part in soap operas. Anxiously she awaited a phone call telling her she had won the part outright. When a call finally came, it wasn't what she expected: she had made the first cut and had to return to the studio to face a second large audition. She was eventually selected and carried the lead for the serial's final months. Getting there, she intimated, wasn't half the fun!

Shortly after joining the show, Higby recalled an incident that gave her cause for personal reflection. A quarter of a century earlier, she had been sitting by herself, virtually unnoticed, on the stage of a live broadcast of the *Kraft Music Hall* starring Bing Crosby. Momentarily she would have a turn at making a pitch for the sponsor's cheese. On joining the *Drake* cast, years later, she was bewildered to hear the serial's opening plug—then on tape—for Chesterfield cigarettes. It wasn't the sponsor that got to her, it was *who* was chanting "Sound off! Sound off! Sound off for Chesterfield!" In the twilight of the industry, Bob Hope and Bing Crosby were crooning the commercials! In some kind of misplaced irony, *she* was the star and Crosby was selling the sponsor's product for *her*! Things had certainly come full circle.

Alan Hewitt played Ken Martinson for the full run of *This Is Nora Drake*. He also appeared in the serials *My Son and I* and *The Romance of Helen Trent*. Hewitt died at age 69 on November 7, 1986.

Although *Drake* debuted on NBC, for most of its life it was heard on CBS. For a year, in 1948–49, it was one of a handful of soap operas for which its sponsor agreed to underwrite a broadcast on dual networks.

Announcer Bill Cullen became one of broadcasting's most versatile performers, gaining a reputation as TV's most prolific quizmaster. He emceed or appeared as a recurring panelist on almost two dozen daytime game shows from the 1950s to 1980s. The affable man with the horn-rimmed glasses and the elfin grin had an enthusiasm for his work that came off as contagious. Yet a message he read for the sponsor one day in the late 1940s on *This Is Nora Drake* would have been challenged by a more liberated audience a half-century later. The copy read: "Each month more than a million women use Toni home permanents—schoolgirls, secretaries, housewives—women with no more experience or training than *you* have!" Though we may be sure his words weren't intended to be condescending—and may not have been perceived that way in 1948—Cullen's remarks would in no way amuse women if read over the air today. The anticipated storm of protest that might result could lead to strong reprimands and perhaps termination for those responsible. Foote, Cone and Belding was surely working in a kinder, gentler, more accepting age (except, perhaps, of women).

In *This Is Nora Drake*, fans met a professional career woman who was able to set occupation and personal life against a backdrop of romantic triangles, intrigue and evildoers. Her resilience allowed her to withstand the setbacks that would have routed most others in similar surroundings. Even though all of it was an illusion, of course, housewives, secretaries and schoolgirls by the droves were enthralled by it—and sales of home permanents soared.

27
Today's Children
(A Bridge Over Troubled Waters)

Déjà vu (n.): Something already seen; an illusion that one has previously had an experience that is new. Some listeners must have experienced déjà vu while hearing this show. The premise, the characters and the locale must have seemed more than vaguely familiar. Even the names of the characters were virtually the same as names they had heard earlier. What in the world was going on? As it turned out, Irna Phillips, who created this show in 1932, was also the author behind *Painted Dreams*, a serial introduced to a Chicago audience in 1930. Scholars have often regarded *Dreams* as the very first daytime drama by installment. But Phillips and her employer soon ran into legal difficulties concerning who owned the material she had written. Getting nowhere with it, she resigned her job and took her ideas to a competing station. There she created an almost identical series, which was picked up by NBC Blue for nationwide airing. Set in an urban ethnic community in Chicago, the drama originally revolved around a tightly knit Irish-American family headed by a strong, widowed matriarch who imbued her brood with ageless moralistic messages. It later evolved into a German-oriented family epic set in the same neighborhood. Having little elsewhere to turn, daytime audiences made the program an instant hit, and it remained at that level for four years, until Phillips abruptly withdrew it. She returned the drama to the air after it had been absent for a half-dozen years, but it never achieved the prestige it had earlier enjoyed. The series was one of the first to exploit the premium request for a memento, a model for many shows that followed.

Producer: Carl Wester
Directors: Bob Dwan, Axel Gruenberg, George Fogle
Writer: Virginia Cooke, Irna Phillips
Announcer: Louis Roen
Mother Moran: Irna Phillips
Eileen Moran: Fran Carlon, Ireene Wicker
Frances Moran Matthews: Bess Johnson, Sunda Love
Mama Schultz: Virginia Payne
Papa Schultz: Murray Forbes
Others: Edith Adams, Ernie Andrews, Bob Bailey, Jeanne Bates, Herb Butterfield, Harriet
Cain, Marjorie Davies, Patricia Dunlap, Jack Edwards, Jr., Willard Farnum, Laurette

Fillbrandt, Joe Forte, Margaret Fuller, Betty Lou Gerson, Jo Gilbert, Lucy Gilman, Robert Griffin, Clarence Hartzell, Wilms Herbert, Milton Herman, Raymond Edward Johnson, Helen Kane, Lois Kennison, Rupert LaBelle, Forrest Lewis, Frank Lovejoy, Judith Lowry, Jean McGregor, Marvin Miller, Betty Moran, Gene Morgan, Parker O'Malley, Ethel Owen, Frank Pacelli, Gale Page, Irna Phillips, Ed Prentiss, Edwin Rand, Ruth Rau, Michael Romano, Nanette Sargent, Everett Sloane, Olan Soule, Fred Von Ammon, Willard Waterman, Donald Weeks, Walter Wicker, Parker Wilson, Seymour Young, more

Theme: "Aphrodite" (Goetzl); "Autumn Nocturne"

Sponsors: General Foods sponsored this series on Chicago's WMAQ from October 1932 until it reached network status. (It had begun on June 16, 1932, as a sustainer.) From Sept. 11, 1933, to Dec. 31, 1937, Hutchinson Advertising bought the show for another consumer foods packager, Pillsbury Co. (flour, cake mixes, etc.). After an absence of several years, the show returned on Dec. 13, 1943, sponsored by a third food competitor, General Mills, Inc. (flour, cake mixes, cereals, biscuits, etc.) until June 2, 1950.

Ratings: After the serial resumed, audiences never equaled those of earlier years (when the show had captured first place). The novelty of such programming had passed by then, and there was greater competition for people's time and more programs to select from. High: 6.9 (1944–45); low: 4.2 (1947–48); median: 5.3 (based on 1943–50 figures; earlier numbers unavailable).

On the Air: Sept. 11, 1933–May 29, 1936, NBC Blue, 10:30 a.m. ET; June 1, 1936–Dec. 31, 1937, NBC, 10:45 a.m.; Dec. 13, 1943–Nov. 29, 1946, NBC, 2:15 p.m.; Dec. 2, 1946–May 28, 1948, NBC, 2:00 p.m.; May 31, 1948–June 2, 1950, NBC, 2:30 p.m.

And today's children, with their hopes and dreams, their laughter and tears, shall be the builders of a brighter world tomorrow.

— Epigraph to *Today's Children*

The history of *Today's Children* may be traced to the origins of soap opera and earlier. The program's ancestry is nothing short of amazing, for this single series directly figures into the lineage of several of its contemporaries. Very few serials, if any, could have had the interaction with, input from or influence on as many as five other daytime series. *Today's Children* achieved such distinction.

The time line that follows documents the heritage of this extraordinary drama. Succeeding explanations more adequately clarify how a single program had such choice opportunities to connect with so many of its peers.

• 1930: *Sue and Irene.* Even before radio serials existed, the doyenne of daytime drama and creator of *Today's Children* was at work earning credentials and experience as a dramatist on this program at a local radio station.

• October 20, 1930–1933; October 10, 1933–February 2, 1934; December 30,

1935–September 28, 1936; April 29, 1940–November 20, 1940: *Painted Dreams*. What is considered broadcasting's earliest true serial received mixed reviews in several attempts out of the starting gate; the forerunner of *Today's Children* would offer an engaging model for hundreds of serials to follow.

• June 16, 1932–September 8, 1933; September 11, 1933–December 31, 1937; December 13, 1943–June 2, 1950: *Today's Children*. A local drama with its roots in two predecessors became a national success. Withdrawn while riding the crest of popularity, it returned to the air after an absence of a half-dozen years. Thus, it satisfied listeners for several years more while lending characters and borrowing from those in other series.

• January 3, 1938–September 25, 1942; June 5, 1944–May 28, 1948: *Woman in White*. The *Today's Children* troupe would appear on the very first show of this replacement series in a unique transition experiment.

• June 29, 1942–December 10, 1943: *Lonely Women*. Although this drama didn't last long, it left off where *Today's Children*, by then a returning favorite, was to pick up.

• January 25, 1937–present (with interruptions): *The Guiding Light*. Interaction between the casts of some of the aforementioned was to be the name of the game on this most durable serial. It even took over the jarring theme song, Goetzl's "Aphrodite," discarded by *Today's Children*.

We have already observed that Irna Phillips, who would create so many successful radio and television dramas, was a schoolteacher who strolled into Chicago's WGN one day in 1930 looking for work. She was hired as an actress, but her talents were soon recognized beyond speaking parts. In an early experiment she played Sue in the series *Sue and Irene* while another former teacher, Ireene Wicker, played Irene. Together, the pair provided all of the voices. Stations weren't yet into hiring large casts for such trivial chatter.

Geared to a daytime audience, which most assuredly meant housewives, *Sue and Irene* may have been WGN's initial (and weak) attempt at drama by installment. The show was on the air for Lever Brothers' dishwashing and laundry detergent, Super Suds. The two women's simple on-air dialogue, though conversational in tone and a far cry from what would develop, undoubtedly confirmed a speculation that the powerful station's management harbored before Phillips' arrival: there was a highly receptive audience for some type of serialized fiction among daytime radio listeners.

This undoubtedly started the wheels turning in Irna Phillips' mind. It wouldn't require any nudging from management to dissatisfy her with the status quo. Persistently she approached WGN officials, asking for a greater share of the station's acting and writing responsibilities. Within three months she was given a chance to draft a fortnight's worth of scripts for a serial revolving around an Irish-American household.

The cast, soon expanded, initially included a matriarch, a daughter and a friend of the daughter. When the show was ready to audition, however, potential sponsors were reluctant to underwrite such an untried project. Undaunted, station management launched the program on a sustaining (or unsponsored) basis. Titled *Painted Dreams,* the fictional account appeared for a year without benefit of sponsorship, airing new episodes six days a week. In October 1931 it was sold to a Chicago-based meatpacker, Mickleberry Products Company.

Irna Phillips was assigned to write the drama and play dual roles in it, something *Sue and Irene* had conditioned her for. As the elderly, widowed Mother Moynihan, she became a kindly, philosophical, all-wise protagonist coping with the realities of the Depression era.

Her single goal in life was to ensure the ultimate happiness of her grown children. The simple message of the drama was that marriage, love and motherhood offered the greatest achievement and destiny any female could hope to experience. Most of the action occurred in an urban Chicago neighborhood where the Moynihans lived.

Not surprisingly, Ireene Wicker was featured in the *Painted Dreams* cast, playing the part of Mother Moynihan's daughter, along with several other roles. Lucy Gilman, Kay Chase, Alice Hill and Olan Soule were also among those in the troupe. A conspicuous sidelight was that Frank Hummert — whose name would be identified with an assembly line turning out more daytime radio serials than anyone else — produced *Painted Dreams* for his most formidable soon-to-be competitor, Irna Phillips. The show wafted onto the air with "I'm Yours" as its musical theme.

The most noteworthy detail about *Painted Dreams* is not who played the parts or what the story was about or who produced it or even the degree of success it enjoyed. Its ultimate contribution to soap opera is that it is generally believed by most students of the genre to be the very *first* serial — the first to appear via any electronic media. Other similar broadcast features achieved network status before *Dreams* aired on CBS on October 10, 1933. But *Dreams* was heard (in 1930) on a local station long before its rivals and eventually catapulted to a national audience. Before that, however, some legal maneuvers occurred that would affect the rights of all future serial authors and the ultimate ownership of the materials they created. It began when Phillips requested the rights for *Painted Dreams* from her employer, WGN, so that she could take the program to a network for national airing. She believed the show to be hers to do with as she saw fit. But the station refused, claiming the program was conceived under the station's direction and guidance.

In 1932 Phillips resigned from her post at WGN and filed a chancery suit against her former employer, seeking to prevent anyone else from using "her" material. Phillips had "never relinquished to defendants (WGN), by contract or otherwise, her author's property rights in her creation which consisted of the intangible common-law right of proprietorship — not in the *general or basic idea* — but in the *set-up*, the *scene*, and the *characters*, which she alone worked out and into which she had breathed her created brain conceptions,"[1] her attorneys argued.

The unsettling and profoundly influential dispute over copyright ownership of broadcast material would drag on in the courts for more than eight years. By 1941, when the case was ultimately adjudicated, the situation had become a matter of principle in essence, certainly more symbolic than real. Not until the Illinois state court sided with WGN did Phillips relinquish her hard-fought attempts to maintain ownership of the child to which she had given birth — the world's *first* soap opera. (Meanwhile, WGN had continued broadcasting *Painted Dreams* with another writer and cast. On October 10, 1933, the station allowed CBS to pick up the series for nationwide airing. But the ratings were so poor that it left the air in a scant 16 weeks, on February 2, 1934. It returned for a couple of subsequent, short-lived stints — one on MBS, the other on NBC Blue — but the show never regained the promise it had demonstrated to an early Chicagoland following.)

Despite her legal setback, which would occur nearly a decade later, the indomitable Irna Phillips, fully confident by 1932 of her own creative talents and abilities, determined she wouldn't be thwarted by an ongoing feud with a former employer. There was more than one way to tame a lion; she would prove it.

Bravely, Phillips carried forward by creating a "new" show while borrowing heavily from *Painted Dreams*. In fact, her second serial—*Today's Children*—came off sounding like a virtual carbon copy of the first. Its locale was Hester Street in Chicago, where stories of a cross-section of neighborhood families intertwined.

Its principal action centered around an Irish-American family headed by a widowed matriarch. Sound familiar? Mother Moynihan, in this series, became Mother Moran, portrayed by none other than—can you guess?—Irna Phillips, who also played the part of Kay Norton, Mother Moran's adopted daughter. What was the same character's name in *Painted Dreams*? Sue Morton. (Notice the similarity. Was this only a coincidence?) Meanwhile, daughter Eileen (Irene in *Painted Dreams*) was portrayed by—who else?—Ireene Wicker. Even Mother Moynihan's dog, Mike, who barked to protest the occasional profuse nature of his mistress' homespun philosophy, appeared in the new series, this time as Mickey. But Phillips wasn't left barking up a tree on *Today's Children*: Whereas she had voiced the animal's barks on *Painted Dreams*, a mechanical device, prompted by a sound effects specialist, supplied them on cue on *Today's Children*. The funding was obviously a little more liberal for this show. Even the message of the new show was the same as that of its predecessor: marriage is woman's finest career; nothing must deter her from reaching her ultimate reason for existence. (Ironically the serial's creator, Phillips, was never married.)

The dialogue on one show was similar to that which listeners heard on the other. When, for instance, eldest daughter Frances, who aspired to be a great artist, grumbled that matrimony shouldn't dissuade her from "the realization of the dream that I've been painting almost all my life," Mother Moran typically advanced an admonition that sounded as if it came from Mother Moynihan: "When you're paintin' your dreams, be careful of the colors you're goin' to be usin', 'cause sometimes you make a mistake, and the colors that you think are goin' to look good don't look so good in the finished picture. Now, Frances, darlin', let me be sayin' just one more thing to ya. There are three colors that have stood the test of all time. They are the colors that are the foundation of all dreams of all the men and women in the world: The colors of love, family, home."

Moralizing to a feminist on another episode, Mother Moran cautioned, just as Mother Moynihan might have said: "In your plan, women wouldn't be havin' time to be havin' children and keepin' a home.... I'm thinkin' that a country is only as strong as its weakest home. When you're after destroyin' those things which make up a home, you're destroyin' people." It would have been difficult for many homemakers—the bulk of Mother Moran's faithful fans—to object to sentiments such as those.

By the time *Painted Dreams* finally arrived before a national audience over CBS, *Today's Children* had already garnered a loyal following on NBC Blue due to the favorable circumstance of a month's head start. CBS's listeners outside the reach of WGN, where *Painted Dreams* had been airing for three years, must have felt that the show was an imitation of a very similar story line they were already hearing over NBC Blue. Irna Phillips took some consolation, perhaps, in the fact that although her former show badly trailed the one on which she now focused, the notoriety from the former show must have enhanced, not diminished, her image as a competitive daytime programming developer.

Undoubtedly as a result of her legal melee, Phillips became a rather astute businesswoman. She established her rights to the material she created, beginning with *Today's Children* and continuing with all subsequent series she created. She also turned down an offer to work for WGN's chief competitor, WMAQ, preferring to act as an independent producer. For four months she bore the full expenses of producing *Today's Children* until a sponsor could be signed.

By that time the idea of enticing new listeners and retaining present ones through premium offers had been tested. As early as the broadcast of August 3, 1932, Mother Moran's announcer was touting a family photograph, sent free with a simple postcard request. (The idea of labels, box tops and coins in exchange for a souvenir hadn't been fully developed yet.) According to Phillips, the response to that plea netted 10,000 requests. Apparently it was enough to convince a sponsor, for two months later General Foods signed to underwrite the program on WMAQ.

After *Today's Children* aired for a few months on NBC Blue, the listeners were told that in return for a flour label, Pillsbury (the show's first network sponsor) would send a brochure recalling the history of the Moran family. Within a few weeks, in excess of 250,000 labels arrived. The trade publication *Broadcasting* subsequently observed: "The amazing allegiance of hundreds of thousands of women not only to the members of the cast but to Pillsbury products is a constant source of wonderment even among those professional people who for years have been working with radio."[2] It need not have been; the intense loyalty that listeners felt toward such daytime series was indicative of the marketing ability of these dramas. That fact was proven by scores of similar ventures. Pillsbury offered new souvenir family albums of the Moran clan annually.

By the late 1930s, *Children* had become the most popular soap opera on the air. Why, then, would its creator suddenly withdraw it? The answer is simple: Phillips' own mother had been the inspiring catalyst for many of the ideas the writer used to plot the show. Despite a plea from Pillsbury, on the death of Phillips' mother in 1937, the author decided to pull the top-rated series from the daily lineup.

She didn't leave Pillsbury empty-handed, however. The grandame of soap opera had developed an intense interest in the professional person as a fascinating source for absorbing action and dialogue. It was a formula that worked exceedingly well and signified much of the fictionalized characterization that she developed in the remainder of her career. Phillips trotted out a replacement series, *Woman in White,* centered in a small hospital. Pillsbury bought it, and that drama soon reached the pinnacle of popularity among daytime listeners.

To introduce it, Phillips crafted a simple, ingenious device that would carry listeners from one show to the other without losing a large segment of the audience. More than a decade later she would employ a variation of this idea to create awareness for *The Brighter Day,* her last major radio serial. *Day* was introduced when one of its major characters appealed to the heroine of *Joyce Jordan, M.D.,* the departing series, for professional help during *Jordan's* ending episodes.

The final 15-minute broadcast of *Today's Children* aired on Friday, December 31, 1937. But in a stroke of brilliancy Phillips brought the cast back to the microphone on Monday, January 3, 1938, at its same quarter-hour — the segment appearing as *Woman in White* in newspaper radio listings across the country. On that day, Mother Moran called her little family around her to announce the engagement of two of her "children" — adopted daughter Kay Norton and Bob Crane. Celebrating the impending nuptials with a cake, undoubtedly made with Pillsbury's Sno Sheen cake flour (the sponsor's product), Mother

Moran gaily sang: "A cake ta bake, and a floor ta sweep … And a tired little babe ta sing ta sleep; What does a woman want more than this? A home, a man and a child to kiss."

Phillips simply couldn't overlook a final opportunity to state once again the point of her departing series. But Mother Moran also had another message, which she pointedly shared with listeners: that each of her children was on the right path. Kay gave this explanation: "Mother Moran, somehow I think that your friends should know that your wise teachings over the past five-and-a-half years have given each of your *Today's Children* a foundation that nothing can destroy. You've shown us a road on which we know that our footing is sure." Her fiancé opined: "I'm a comparative newcomer as one of *Today's Children*, but I too would like to say to the friends of *Today's Children* that I feel sure that each one of us … will be able to meet any situations through what we've learned from the teachings of a woman who has reared her family … with an understanding and a sympathy that can't fail…, no matter what the future may hold."

Mother Moran thanked each one by name, declaring: "I feel that my work is over and I have indeed been repaid ta the fullest." Turning to the fans tuning in, she made the transition to the successor series, *Woman in White.* The announcer introduced the new soap opera by its title, its theme came up and he read the show's epigraph: "I expect to pass through this life but once. If, therefore, there is any kindness I can show, or any good I can do to any fellow, let me do it now, for I shall not pass this way again." Music up and out. A new drama had begun. *Today's Children* was gone but not quickly forgotten.

By then Irna Phillips had already become widely recognized for her contributions to drama by installment. With the successful entries *Today's Children*, *The Guiding Light* and *Road of Life*, in 1937 she was already a major player in the high-stakes production of daytime radio programming.

In 1942 she unveiled yet another drama titled *Lonely Women*. It was set in a New York hotel catering exclusively to women — women primarily waiting for their husbands and boyfriends to return from World War II. The series focused on the "universal cry of womanhood — loneliness," which was irritated by the elements of battle. The plots followed women who felt exiled by their separation while attempting to find companionship and meaning in an environment robbed of its young men by the ravages of war.

The serial introduced several figures who became noteworthy if only because they appeared in a subsequent series that displaced *Lonely Women* 18 months later. Those characters were simply carried over to a continuing version of *Today's Children*. On December 13, 1943, as *Lonely Women's* popularity declined, *Today's Children* returned. While *Children* was then written by Virginia Cooke, its plots were developed by Irna Phillips. And it carried the same themes of family love and togetherness that had been its hallmark six years earlier.

The returning *Children* had at least two advantages: a substantial, devoted following from when it was last broadcast; and principal characters from a story line (*Lonely Women*) already familiar to listeners in that same quarter-hour. Featured in the renewal was a German family — the Schultzes. The parents were played by Murray Forbes and Virginia Payne (both appeared for 27 years on *Ma Perkins*), and the children were played by Betty Lou Gerson and Ruth Rau (Marilyn), Patricia Dunlap (Bertha), and Ernie Andrews (Otto). Another son, Joseph, supposedly died in the war. Imagine the family's surprise when Joseph's war buddy Stone arrived in the Schultzes' Chicago neighborhood pretending to be Joe. In an attempt to ingratiate himself, Stone explained that plastic surgery had rebuilt his war-torn face. The love-starved GI was welcomed by the Schultzes. But he soon found his intentions and cover compromised when feelings for his unattached "sister" Bertha went beyond sibling affection.

Meanwhile, a similar incident was being played out on *Ma Perkins*. (Recall that Mr. and Mrs. Schultz were portrayed by two principals of the *Perkins* serial.) When Ma's son, John, was killed in the war, a young man who looked enough like John to have been his identical twin turned up in Rushville Center. Although this family knew that Joseph (ironically, the name of the deceased son in *Today's Children*) was *not* their son and sibling, his features and gentle spirit were constant reminders of the young man they had lost — so much so, in fact, that Ma invited Joseph to live in their home and occupy John's room. He even took John's old job. Was this oddity simple coincidence between the two serials? It certainly appeared as if the Hummerts were listening to Irna Phillips' dramas, or vice versa, for some plot line fodder.

A short time after *Today's Children* resumed, Phillips decided to pursue an idea that called for scheduling a trio of her popular serials in a unique NBC block. Programmed adjacent to one another, *The Guiding Light* (2:00), *Today's Children* (2:15) and *Woman in White* (2:30) were collectively referred to as the General Mills Hour. (There was a fourth NBC quarter-hour sponsored by General Mills at 2:45, *The Light of the World*. Introduced as a Hummert production, it was based on biblical character portraits instead of contemporary open-ended tales.)

The three Phillips dramas in the "Hour" block employed a common announcer who introduced each one daily. Also, cast members frequently interacted with those of all three serials. As a part of this unique concept, the U.S. Office of War Information worked with Phillips to present a half-hour broadcast in May 1945 on behalf of national relief efforts. Through a combined story line on *Today's Children* and *Woman in White*, the one-time effort attempted to gain empathy from listeners in rehabilitating wounded war veterans.

In 1946 the General Mills Hour was involved in yet another "experiment." The advertising agencies still almost single-handedly controlled the washboard weepers. Whereas the soap operas had flourished in Chicago in the 1930s, toward the end of that decade and in the early part of the 1940s the ad agencies began to transfer production of their dramas to New York City. There they could take advantage of a larger talent base and be in closer proximity to network (and some agency) headquarters.

But General Mills decided to move that firm's block of afternoon serials to new production facilities in Hollywood, California. West Coast talent would then be available to their shows. Its first serial to move West, in July 1946, was *Masquerade*, a new Phillips' series supplanting *The Guiding Light*. *Light* was discontinued by General Mills and temporarily left the air as the result of the legal dispute over its origins. (Phillips was certainly becoming an old hand at courtroom imbroglios!) Soon, *Woman in White* and *Today's Children* were also dispatched to the West Coast.

Today's Children was a bridge over troubled waters between several daytime dramatic series, interrelating locales, story lines, characters (including several with similar names), actors, writers, producers, sponsors and time periods. Having originated from a controversy surrounding broadcasting's reputed first soap opera, its importance in the annals of daytime radio's history can't be easily dismissed. Although its popularity faded in the comeback years, in its glory days *Today's Children* rode the crest of a tide that held the daytime faithful glued to their sets. Despite her legal troubles, could Irna Phillips have asked for anything more?

28
Wendy Warren and the News
(Reports from the Women's World)

Critics found less to fault in this soap opera than in most others because it sustained a note of realism that many of its contemporaries didn't enjoy. A daily news broadcast within its confines added an air of legitimacy to the story line. The fact that the protagonist's career in journalism embraced electronic and print media required the action to reflect the day on which it was heard, unlike activity airing on peer dramas. Thus, 24 hours in the plot elapsed between one broadcast and the next. Weekends were just that: on Fridays, the heroine often told of her plans for Saturday and Sunday; on Monday, she recalled conversations she had had and places she had been in the interim. There was an occasional flashback sequence so that listeners could hear some important development that had transpired since Friday. It was a distinction that set this soap opera apart from the pack. Aside from that, the drama pursued issues not just of the heart but of intrigue and suspense. Wendy and her cohorts found themselves in a crusading mode, literally fighting against subversive forces that threatened to curtail our freedoms and bring down our government. The authors, Frank Provo and John Picard, turned out some of the best scripting among daytime dramas. Their uncanny ability to hold audiences with suspenseful verbiage contributed immeasurably to the popularity of this midday thriller.

Producer: Benton and Bowles advertising agency
Directors: Hoyt Allen, Allan Fristoe, Tom McDermott, Don Wallace
Writers: John Picard, Frank Provo
Music: Clarke Morgan
Sound Effects: Hamilton O'Hara
Announcer: Hugh James (as Bill Flood)
Wendy Warren: Florence Freeman
Newscaster: Douglas Edwards (as himself)
Gil Kendal: Les Tremayne
Mark Douglas: Lamont Johnson
Anton Kamp: Peter Capell
Don Smith: John Raby
Sam Warren: Rod Hendrickson
Aunt Dorrie: Tess Sheehan

Others: Vera Allen, Horace Braham, Anne Burr, Jane Lauren, Guy Spaull, Lotte Stavisky, Meg Wylie, more

Theme: "My Home Town" (Morgan)

Sponsors: From June 23, 1947, to Sept. 17, 1954, Benton and Bowles governed this serial for General Foods Corp. (largely for Maxwell House coffee but also for Baker's coconut, Gaines pet foods, Post cereals and other brands). The series' time was purchased by Procter & Gamble for several months starting on Sept. 30, 1954, for a variety of household and personal-hygiene products. In its final three years the show was sold under multiple sponsorship.

Ratings: High: 10.2 (1949–50); low: 3.9 (1955–56); median: 6.4 (figures for 1947–56 seasons).

On the Air: June 23, 1947–Nov. 12, 1958, CBS, 12:00 noon ET.

Legendary actresses Lucille Wall and Florence Freeman seemed to be playing a humorous radio quiz, *Can You Top This?*, although in their case it was no laughing matter. Wall simultaneously played the heroines on two serials, one for more than a decade (*Portia Faces Life*), the other for 15 years (as Belle Jones on *Lorenzo Jones*). Although a man (the actor Karl Swenson) theoretically played the lead in the latter series, Wall dialogued with him daily. (Earlier, from 1938 to 1940, she was the female lead in a third serial, *Your Family and Mine*.) Freeman, meanwhile, eclipsed Wall's record: she appeared as the inimitable title character of *Wendy Warren and the News* for its full run of more than 11 years; and for almost 16 years she was the heroine of the late-afternoon romantic odyssey *Young Widder Brown*.

Whereas several other actresses were heroines in two, three, four or more shows, none achieved similar levels of longevity in dual series. An extensive glimpse into Freeman's life will shed some revealing insights into the personal and working careers of a typical daytime soap opera lead. Born on July 29, 1911, in New York City, Freeman prepared herself at Wells College of the State University of New York and Columbia University for a career in education, earning a master's degree from the latter. After teaching English for a while she settled in the environs of New York with her husband. He was a rabbi, professionally serving as the spiritual head of his temple. At Jersey City, New Jersey, across the river from the Big Apple, the couple raised a family of two daughters and a son. Freeman was extensively involved in family activities but didn't limit herself to those in her "off hours." She typically gave many hours each week to the concerns of temple members and temple functions while volunteering additional time to charitable causes like the Community Chest and Red Cross drives. She was a member of the National Board of Temple Sisterhoods. Throughout the years she was playing on daytime radio, she invested herself in such efforts. When a serial heroine or hero left the microphone, she or he often lived a life fairly reminiscent of that led by many in the radio audience.

Freeman's pilgrimage from private life to professional career fills in some gaps in how daytimers became established in the business. In 1933 she was hired by New York's

WMCA to be available day or night, seven days a week, for $50 weekly. This was during the depths of the Depression, and she considered herself "very fortunate" to have gained a job when so many people were losing theirs.

Her interest in radio acting prompted her husband to suggest that she purchase a copy of the entertainment trade publication *Variety*. It would provide information on the advertising agencies that produced radio shows. In a late 1997 interview with this author she chuckled, "I had never heard of *Variety* before." She bought it and studied it intensely.

Locating an agency on the city's west side and another on Madison Avenue, Freeman sallied forth, with a nickel in hand for bus fare and a transfer to get to the east side. At the west-side agency, an advertising executive arranged an audition for her with Edwin Wolfe, an NBC director. "If you're any good," he assured her, "you have a job on the *Madame Sylvia of Hollywood* program." Freeman later recalled: "From that time forward I worked every week for more than twenty years."

She did the speaking voices of Gladys Swarthout and Helen Jepson of the Metropolitan Opera Company. She worked the nighttime shows, appearing on Paul Whiteman's musical program in short sketches with, among others, Bing Crosby, Max Baer and the renowned Russian actress Alla Nazimova.

For several years in the early 1940s Freeman played in the situation comedy *Abie's Irish Rose*. She was the female lead in the serial *Dot and Will* (1935–37) and the lead in *A Woman of America* (1943–46). But the dual roles for which she will always be remembered were as the scorned lover, Ellen, in *Young Widder Brown* (1938–54) and as news journalist Wendy Warren (1947–58). In all, she acquired the heroine roles in four soap operas, for a combined total of more than 31 years.

In the years she appeared as Wendy and Ellen, Freeman's daily schedule called for her to leave home at about 9:30 a.m. each day, traveling by train. That would put her at the CBS studios in time for *Warren* rehearsals, which started at 10:30. After this broadcast ended at 12:15, unless she had luncheon appointments with writers, directors or publicity agents, her time was her own for leisurely dining and shopping. At 3:45 p.m. she reported to NBC for rehearsals for *Young Widder Brown,* which went on the air at 4:45 during most of its run. (It moved to 4:30 in the 1950s.)

She jealously guarded her time for family and volunteer commitments, spending evenings helping her children with their homework as necessary. Freeman refused to accept radio performances on weekends and relinquished her role in *Young Widder Brown* on January 15, 1954, due to family concerns, including aging parents living in Florida. She confessed to this author that of all the parts she played, Wendy was easily her "favorite," due to its sense of immediacy and realism; it was "in touch" with what was going on in the world. After 16 years of Ellen Brown's on-again, off-again romance with Anthony Loring, she noted: "I saw where that was headed too and decided I'd had enough."

In late 1948, little more than a year into the *Warren* series, readers of a national fan magazine voted Freeman their favorite daytime serial actress.[1] For many years the actress and her husband lived in a Florida senior citizens' residence, where Freeman played bridge with other tenants several nights a week. At his death in 1998, she returned north.

Wendy Warren and the News combined a fictionalized plot with one in real life. Daily it began with a live broadcast of current events, followed by a continuing narrative like those on other daytime serials. This had the effect of moving the story along at a much faster pace than that of any of its peers.

This soap opera was, in essence, creating action in real time. Its counterparts could take weeks to progress from breakfast to lunch through elongated circumstances. On *Warren*, because every single day was a *new* one, virtually everything in the story line occurred on the day it was broadcast. Although that meant there was no action on Saturdays and Sundays because the show was silent, it made use of flashback sequences and dialogue references at appropriate intervals.

This netted the very positive result of injecting believability into the plots. The action suggested that this serial was on a mission with someplace to go. Skeptics who saw all daytime dramas as the same — ensuring that their fans could randomly miss a few episodes and it wouldn't make any difference because the story line moved slowly anyway — found out differently here. Missing a week often required more than minimal catching up. Forfeiting a day meant losing 20 percent of the plot development for the week. Ultimately the serial's contributions dignified the genre while giving the critics less to chastise.

The drama was one of three to occupy a single quarter-hour time period in runs exceeding a decade. (The others were *Our Gal Sunday* and *Stella Dallas*.) *Wendy Warren and the News*, however, appears to have been the only durable serial to have cast every role only *once*.

Its theme song, written by organist Clarke Morgan, may have been the only soap opera tune to receive so much acclaim that it was turned into print. Notoriety for "My Home Town" resulted in the melody being published and distributed in sheet-music form. Few, if any, other serial themes created for shows received that kind of exposure.

The origins of the serial indicate it was on a course toward distinction from its start. Throughout much of the 1930s and 1940s, America's musical sweetheart, Kate Smith, affectionately called "the Songbird of the South," was featured in several formats on daytime network radio. For nine seasons, beginning in 1938, she reigned as the unchallenged queen of the midday ratings. Her fifteen-minute CBS show, *Kate Smith Speaks*, aired at high noon. It offered the sponsor, General Foods Corporation, a choice method of delivering its commercial messages. Smith's series, the focal point of a phenomenal sale of U.S. war bonds, presented features of special interest to women as well as an occasional song sung by the show's star.

Nothing lasts forever, however. In due time even General Foods determined that it might be wise to try a new format at that auspicious hour. Smith's ratings were still quite high, 6.2 in early 1947, although they had been up to 8.9 a few years before. Given the star's promising continued success, the decision was made to shift her show to MBS rather than withdrawing it altogether. It would be a welcome addition to a smaller network. The star's recognition, her fans and her talent could probably improve the fortunes of that web's daytime programming too. And her show would remain at noon without missing a broadcast. Thus, the popular entertainer moved to Mutual, remaining there for four years under participating sponsorship.

CBS program executives were left scrambling for a replacement that could maintain the long-standing appeal that Smith had achieved. They sought to retain the audience by keeping some of the attributes that had made Smith's program of particular interest to women. Simultaneously, they hoped to draw an even larger audience, including men.

That's when someone came up with the untried formula of a capsule of the day's news events paired with a feature for women within the context of a soap opera. The heroine's story would then follow the news. The idea was so novel that the network brass agreed it just might work.

Wendy Warren and the News debuted on June 23, 1947, sponsored by General Foods (for Maxwell House coffee), Smith's recently departed client. It arrived to the rush of a frantic burst of telegraph keys, those keys sounding strangely like an automatic coffee percolator just starting to perk. The basso profundo of broadcasting's Hugh James became synonymous with the opening. As the serial's announcer, he used the pseudonym *Bill Flood*. Flood barked the line he would repeat for years: "Maxwell House ... the coffee that's always [or, as Flood stated it, *ul*-ways] good to the last drop, brings you *Wendy Warren and the News*." The rapid-fire clicking of the telegraph noise was abruptly silenced, and Florence Freeman articulated decisively: "Hello folks, this is Wendy Warren with news reports from the women's world. But first, here's Douglas Edwards with the latest headlines." The acclaimed CBS correspondent proceeded to read the day's top events in capsule form.

"The government rested its case this morning in the Alger Hiss perjury trial," he launched the newscast one day in the summer of 1950. Edwards went on to state that on Capitol Hill, the House Veterans Committee would probably consider a multibillion-dollar bonus bill for World War II veterans. Meanwhile, the Labor Department reported an employment slump in manufacturing industries while in Pittsburgh pressure was being applied by the Steel Union to get a major firm in that industry to bargain on pensions. In Paris foreign ministers remained deadlocked over a working plan for Germany and an Austrian peace treaty, complicated by Russia's refusal to guarantee the West free access to Berlin. And a church-state conflict in Czechoslovakia had risen to new proportions with the Catholic archbishop virtually a government prisoner. "And now, Wendy, what's the news today for the ladies?" Edwards inquired.

"Well Doug," replied Freeman as reporter Wendy Warren, "the dean of Sweetbrier College, Dr. Mary Eli Lyman, will become one of the first women ever to hold a full professorship in an American theological school when the 1950 academic year begins. Dr. Lyman has been elected as the very first woman faculty member of Union Theological Seminary in Manhattan, New York.

"Fall fashion previews show that pockets of all kinds and sizes will be a leading feature in milady's wardrobe. Fall collections show pockets not only for daytime but evening clothes as well.

"When a gunman entered the Pontiac, Michigan, home of Mrs. M. Russell Coile yesterday and demanded money, this quick-witted housewife handed the bandit a ham sandwich instead. He was so surprised he gulped it down and fled."

Telegraph keys popped. Wendy acknowledged: "And now, here's Bill Flood with a word for you." The keys abruptly halted again. James (alias Flood) eased into his first commercial for Maxwell House, reminding listeners the coffee was "*ul*-ways good."

Following the plug, the keys rattled again. After a few clicking sounds, Wendy advised: "Off the air!" Then she said "good-by" to Flood (who was then transformed into narrator), and she entered her own mythical world of soap opera. About five minutes had elapsed since the start of the quarter-hour.

Professionally, Wendy went from her stint as a midday radio news reporter to a

Picnicking by the lake in New York's Central Park, CBS newsman Douglas Edwards and actress Florence Freeman, heroine of *Wendy Warren and the News,* enjoy a warm day in the summer of 1950. As Wendy Warren, Freeman provided genuine reports during Edwards' midday headline capsules. (Courtesy of Florence Freeman)

correspondent for the fictitious *Manhattan Gazette.* She came by her journalistic interest naturally; her widower father, Sam Warren, was the longtime editor of a neighboring newspaper, the *Clarion,* in the small community of Elmdale, Connecticut. Sam was a crusading scribe who at home was constantly clucked over by his matronly sister, Dorrie ("Aunt Dorrie" to Wendy).

In her frequent visits to their home, Wendy found calm from the harried demands of big-city life. She often spent weekends there, relishing the opportunity to seek out the quietness of its placid tranquillity. It was like "a million miles" separating her from her cares and frustrations in New York City.

The very nature of her work, and perhaps something in her own genes, gave Wendy exceptional chances to be involved in battles of her own. Several of her assignments proved to be dangerous. Tireless fellow crusader Anton Kamp fought alongside her for just causes. He bore a thick accent, having migrated to the United States while fleeing internal foreign aggression.

Together they sought to expose an international ring of global oppressors who were determined to silence free-speaking sorts. Left unchecked, these underworld figures threatened to invade and control our nation's security. The action delivered some rather chilling moments. No specific nations were mentioned from which these demonic forces emanated. But the listener took it on good faith that the evil intentions of such planetary hooligans were authentic. If Wendy and Anton weren't successful, all hell could break loose for America.

On April 15, 1949, the pair dined together, then attended a symphony concert led by an intriguing guest conductor from Anton's mysterious overseas homeland. The maestro, Ferdinand Varner, had been Anton's friend 15 years earlier. By then, however, Anton admitted that Varner was "spinning a dark web." As the duo sat in the audience waiting for the concert to begin, they passed the time with this exchange:

> ANTON: At times, I shall point out to you certain people … people important to the movements we are fighting. Do you understand?
>
> WENDY: Yes.
>
> ANTON: When I do, I shall use a sort of code. Instead of telling you, uh, "There goes Madam X, a spy working against our government," which sounds ridiculously melodramatic, I shall simply say, "There is one of those *interesting* people."
>
> WENDY: I'll remember.
>
> ANTON: If we should happen to be overheard, it makes no difference. The only reason I'm talking to you now in this way is that the people to my left are late….
>
> SFX: Audience applause
>
> WENDY: (Applause under) Oh, Varner is coming out. Has he changed since you saw him last?
>
> ANTON: (As applause begins to subside) I do not wish to say. Wendy, do you see that handsome dowager in the first box on the right?
>
> WENDY: Yes, she's been inspecting us through her opera glasses ever since we came in. I … I suppose I have met her, but I … I can't think who she is.
>
> ANTON: She is one of those *interesting* people!

If you liked people who spoke in riddles, you'd have been fascinated with this soap opera. Sometimes it was a challenge just to figure out the message being conveyed.

Following the musical performance, Wendy and Anton went backstage to congratulate the maestro. Anton had not seen Varner since parting from their native land more than a decade earlier. In a brief conversation, he and Wendy learned that the conductor had spent four years in a concentration camp.

For more than a year, announcer Flood would summarize events that delved into the eerie darkness of this intense espionage campaign. The synopsis below occurred after an encounter between Wendy — by then wiser about the enemy and its insidious intent — and some agents. Flood recapped: "Throughout this meeting, there's a part of Wendy that watches the scene and all its ugly implications, a silent observer … cool … poised … calculating…, that knows no fear, no hesitation … that knows that if she betrays the slightest weakness now, the cause for which she and Anton are fighting will be irrevocably lost!"

It was heavy stuff, and it probably attracted and kept tens of thousands of male lis-teners involved with the serial's plot following the newscast — just as it was designed to do. Even unbelievers could get caught up in such matters as conspiracy against our government and international espionage. This was the matter from which good drama was made. With a new chapter unfolding every day, turning it off was even more difficult.

There was also a romantic element in *Warren*. Most of it didn't surface until the 1950s, after some menacing types had been quelled. Playwright Mark Douglas was Wendy's longtime beau. Engaged before the war separated them, he later married Nona Marsh. Like most other first marriages on soap operas, theirs wasn't a good one. At about the time Wendy reentered the picture, the Douglases had decided to split.

Not surprisingly, passion resurfaced between Mark and Wendy. But on the very precipice of divorce, Nona appeared to Wendy to say that she was pregnant and wouldn't be leaving Mark after all. Stunned beyond belief, Wendy was still able to hold her emotions in check. In an effort to be considerate, a trait she demonstrated again and again, Wendy agreed to help Nona reestablish her marriage with Mark.

Wendy's personal troubles were complicated by professional ones when a new man-aging editor arrived at the *Manhattan Gazette*. Don Smith's gruff exterior and sarcasm infu-riated her. She had many unpleasant exchanges with him yet was able to partially break through his rough exterior. Having once again lost Mark, she saw in Smith at least a tem-porary answer to her long-denied quest for romance. In a liaison drifting toward wedlock, their relationship suffered a setback when Kay Clement took a tumble for him. Gossip columnists immediately paired off Smith and Clement, a financial backer of the *Gazette*. Wendy was soon displaced.

Suddenly, Smith proposed immediate marriage to Wendy. Had his request arrived earlier, her answer would have been yes. But by then she was confused. His interest in her had taken a sharp nose-dive. In the end, she decided to brush him off.

Other factors were at work in the story line. Wendy's doting father, Sam, suffered a heart attack and went to a sanitarium for several months of recuperation. Aunt Dorrie, having little else to do, went to New York to housekeep for Wendy.

Mark Douglas, Wendy's twice-lost first love, reentered the picture, by then suffering amnesia, a ploy of many serials. As Wendy continued to hold a soft spot in her heart for Mark, she grieved over his mental lapses. She cared for him, did all she could to comfort him and patiently helped him piece together much of what he had forgotten. After an extended time of specialized treatment, Mark returned to the farm he loved. Wendy made many trips there to help him over his prolonged crisis.

Suitor number three, millionaire publisher Gil Kendal, entered the plot about then. Though often appearing to others as a rather heartless boor, he never did so to Wendy. At last she decided to cast her lot with him. But when she said "yes" to Gil, she resigned herself to a life "unhappily ever after." By 1954 he suffered an emotional setback. She spent months nursing him to health after *his* general mental confusion.

The pair went into oblivion facing the usual thread of marital discord. Wendy's cru-sading spirit still attempted to right the wrongs while fighting off evil mobs determined to undermine a peaceful environment.

The program's authentic newscaster, Douglas Edwards, was born on July 14, 1917, at Ada, Oklahoma. At age 15 he was on the air at a 100-watt station at Troy, Alabama. His formal education included the University of Alabama, Emory University and the University of Georgia while he worked part-time at Atlanta's WSB and other local stations. He was hired by Detroit's WXYZ and moved to CBS in 1942. Near the end of World War II he was added to Edward R. Murrow's London staff. Edwards covered political conventions in 1948, and CBS tapped him to anchor TV's first nightly network newscast (*Douglas Edwards with the News*). His daily radio newscasts continued until his retirement in 1988. Edwards died on October 13, 1990, at Sarasota, Florida.

Hugh James (Bill Flood) was a busy broadcasting personality too. Born in Bronx, New York, on October 13, 1915, he decided while in high school to make radio his career. From an NBC page, he advanced to giving tour guides and to delivering on-air station breaks. At age 20 he was an NBC staff announcer at Philadelphia; he then moved to Washington, D.C. He broadcast the second-term inauguration of President Franklin Roosevelt in 1937 and returned to New York in that year to announce the nightly newscasts of Lowell Thomas.

For 15 years he announced four daily network shows. His assignments included *Famous Jury Trials, House in the Country, The Parker Family, The Second Mrs. Burton, When a Girl Marries, Star for a Night, The Right to Happiness, True Detective Mysteries, Three Star Final* and *Big Town.* James' most renowned duty was for *The Voice of Firestone,* in which he combined roles of host and announcer. The program was on radio weekly for many years and later was simulcast on television. His strong baritone voice worked well in commercials and in introducing the musical selections. He once professed, "Sincerity is the most important quality an announcer can possess."

Occasionally fans of some radio series became so wrought up in the action that they had difficulty separating truth from fiction. This was usually manifest in the form of good-natured advice that the actors received in written communications. Some heroes and heroines read through large stacks of mail suggesting that they be wary of certain individuals in the story line. Sometimes a letter writer urged one to choose a particular suitor over another. Others sent names for the babies of expectant parents in a radio drama.

Once in a while, however, attempts at interaction with a star went further, and occasionally things between fans and their idols simply got out of hand. This happened to Florence Freeman. Daily she appeared in two separate facilities. Following her midday stint at CBS as Wendy Warren, she crossed over to NBC for her late-afternoon performance as Ellen Brown. On *Warren* she played a real newscaster, then a columnist on a mythical newspaper.

Somehow one female listener identified in a very strange way with Freeman's role, convincing herself that Freeman was "out to get" her. She wrote the actress communications stating her convictions in no uncertain terms. "I'm on to you, you bitch!" she exclaimed in one note. "If you mention my name in your filthy column, you'll be sorry for it!" Eventually the woman began lying in wait for Freeman outside the CBS studios. When she stalked her from CBS over to NBC one day, Freeman appealed to *Warren's* advertising agency, Benton and Bowles. A uniformed policeman was immediately assigned to protect her and was on duty as her personal bodyguard for three weeks. Freeman's stalker apparently got the message and was never heard from again.

Fan magazines naturally identified with Wendy Warren's abilities as a communicator. She was asked to write features for several of the slick publications. One, *True Experiences,* carried a monthly column called "Woman's World" supposedly authored by Warren. In reality, of course, it was contributed by a periodical staff member. Such diversions raised the level of interest in both the program and the magazine.

In *Wendy Warren and the News,* radio produced a hybrid show between fact and fiction — often making the part that was never intended to be believed sound as if, in reality, it could be accepted too. Seeking to carry on a tradition of high ratings garnered by the inimitable Kate Smith, CBS took a gamble that something as farfetched as this mixed bag would not only hold the audience but build on it. The wager paid off.

Freeman, the series lead from start to finish, gave *Warren* an immeasurable advantage. As she read those sometimes brilliant lines offered by John Picard and Frank Provo, her delivery transmitted a sincerity that spoke volumes about her own acting qualities. At the appropriate time, anguish would resonate from her lips, allowing her to identify with characters in crisis while flawlessly conveying empathy. In lighter moments, she could chuckle on cue and the laughter came across as genuine, never contrived. Few dispatched meaning as well as she, no matter what a script required.

There had to be a *reason* Freeman tasted the flavor of such heady success. Could it be that perhaps — just perhaps — she was better at playing a soap opera heroine than just about everybody else?

29
When a Girl Marries
(Follow Your Heart)

Writer Elaine Carrington's tribute to "everyone who has ever been in love" was fraught with amnesia, vast gaps in social strata, infidelity, murder, suicide, separation and the usual barrage of tricks that most soap opera heroes and heroines encountered. Despite that, for much of the air life of *When a Girl Marries*, the central figures — Joan and Harry Davis — remained true to their common values and, thus, to one another. For a dozen years their story became one of the most popular in serialdom, at times drawing more listeners than any other daytime radio feature. It began as Harry Davis, a young, poverty-stricken law graduate, interrupted the wedding plans of Joan Field, a debutante not firmly committed to her intended. Love at first sight resulted for both Joan and Harry. The reaction — and interaction — of their friends and families was the basis of their story. On their way through life they became parents of two children, gained practical advice from Harry's mother and brushed against the traumatic struggles of companions. Carrington wanted her serials to be believable; she wanted to place actors in situations that could realistically occur to people whom the listener knew. *When a Girl Marries* followed that pattern — in the years she wrote it, at least — although more drama occurred in the lives of the Davises than anybody could expect to confront in a lifetime. No one would have listened, of course, had there been less of it.

Producer: John Gibbs
Directors: Oliver Barbour, Tom Baxter, Olga Druce, Scott Farnworth, Charles Fisher, Maurice Lowell, Kenneth W. MacGregor, Tom McDermott, Art Richards, Warren Somerville, Theodora Yates
Writers: LeRoy Bailey, Elaine Sterne Carrington
Music: Richard Leibert, Rosa Rio, John Winters
Sound Effects: Fred Cole, Keene Crockett, David Gaines
Announcers: George Ansbro, Frank Gallop, Don Gardiner, Hugh James, Dennis King, Wendell Niles, Dick Stark, Charles Stark
Joan Field Davis: Noel Mills (May–November 1939), Mary Jane Higby (1939–57)
Harry Davis: Whitfield Connor, Robert Haag, John Raby, Lyle Sudrow
Lily: Georgia Burke
Sammy Davis: Dolores Gillen

Mother Davis: Marion Barney
Mother Field: Frances Woodbury
Others: Jone Allison, Jack Arthur, King Calder, Peter Capell, Staats Cotsworth, Toni Darnay, Jeannette Dowling, Helene Dumas, Audrey Egan, Michael Fitzmaurice, Anne Francis, Wynne Gibson, Eunice Hill, Ed Jerome, John Kane, Richard Kollmar, Joe Latham, Paul McGrath, John Milton, Ethel Owen, Madeleine Pierce, William Quinn, Kay Renwick, Rosemary Rice, Edgar Stehli, Maurice Tarplin, Joan Tetzel, Gladys Thornton, Gertrude Warner, Karl Weber, Ethel Wilson, Irene Winston, Frances Woodbury, Eustace Wyatt, more

Theme: "Serenade" (Drigo)

Sponsors: Benton and Bowles brought this serial to radio for the Prudential Life Insurance Co. When Prudential canceled on Aug. 22, 1941, the series left the air. It returned five weeks later for General Foods Corp. as a commercial vehicle for Baker's chocolate and coconut, Calumet baking powder, Maxwell House coffee, Sure-Jell ("The powdered pectin product that takes the guesswork out of jams and jelly-making"), Swans Down cake flour and other kitchen aids. General Foods canceled on June 29, 1951; the series was carried on a sustaining basis for 12 weeks; and General Foods renewed sponsorship, underwriting it from Sept. 24, 1951, to March 28, 1952. It left the air for eight months, returning for Durkee Foods (mayonnaise and other products) from Nov. 17, 1952, to May 29, 1953. It then left the air for seven months, returning Jan. 4, 1954, through April 1, 1955, for the Carnation Co. (chiefly for evaporated milk). After that, until the end of the run, the show was sold to multiple sponsors.

Ratings: Despite frequent network shifts and its on-again, off-again status, this series collected some of the best numbers in daytime radio. The actress playing the heroine, Mary Jane Higby, claimed it held "the highest rating on the air for five consecutive years." Its peak, 9.2, occurred in 1944–45; it fell to 2.1 in 1951–52. In 17 seasons the drama topped a lofty 7.0 nine times. But in its final six seasons the program never recaptured the luster of its glory years, boasting a high of 4.0 only once (1954–55).

On the Air: May 29, 1939–July 28, 1939, CBS, 2:45 p.m. ET; July 31, 1939–Aug. 22, 1941, CBS, 12:15 p.m.; Sept. 29, 1941–June 29, 1951, NBC, 5:00 p.m.; July 2, 1951–Sept. 21, 1951, ABC, 11:30 a.m.; Sept. 24, 1951–March 28, 1952, ABC, 11:15 a.m.; Nov. 17, 1952–May 29, 1953, ABC, 10:45 a.m.; Jan. 4, 1954–Aug. 30, 1957, ABC, 10:45 a.m.

This is the story of Joan Field, a young girl who came to know that love can be stronger and finer than anything else in the world. Perhaps you yourself can remember the thrilling, heartbreaking days that now are hers—and the hopes and dreams and struggles that every young couple experiences before that day of all days—When a Girl Marries.

— Epigraph to *When a Girl Marries*

In her moving first-person account of the Golden Age of radio, actress Mary Jane Higby tells about her first day on the job as heroine in *When a Girl Marries* (a title shortened to

Wag'em by cast members).[1] For several weeks there had been lots of secrecy afoot at CBS as director Ken MacGregor sought to replace the series lead in hopes of boosting the fledgling drama's ratings. The serial had been on the air but a few months, and early listener response had been passive. MacGregor knew that if something wasn't done quickly, *When a Girl Marries* would meet the fate of many of its contemporaries, leaving the air after a very brief spell.

Believing a change at the top was in order, MacGregor auditioned for a replacement, never telling the actress (Noel Mills) who was playing the heroine about his intentions. In the end he selected Higby, who signed a union minimum contract of $21 per episode — her guaranteed security for 13 weeks.

In some detail she related her first appearance at the CBS studio. Although she was tense, as might be expected, others sought to put her at ease during rehearsal for the show's live 15-minute performance. Following rehearsal, in the brief moments before going on the air, Higby calmed herself by sitting down on a folding metal chair. She opened her suit jacket and let it hang loose. Oblivious to everything else, she wanted to retain the mood set in rehearsal, so she kept her face buried in her script. Announcer Frank Gallop began the lead-in for the day's dramatic action, featuring dialogue between the characters of Joan and Harry.

Seeking some reassurance from her friend Ken MacGregor, Higby momentarily looked up into the studio control booth. MacGregor was there all right. And behind him stood Noel Mills, the girl she was replacing, her eyes brimming with tears and her cheeks swollen. Under that kind of pressure and with her cue rapidly approaching, Higby attempted to stand and couldn't. Her belt buckle had wedged between the seat and back of her chair, and she was unable to free herself.

The sound effects technician, David Gaines, saw what was happening and rushed to her side. He couldn't free her either. By then, Gallop had arrived. He whispered for her to get up. "With the tall dignified announcer holding the chair pressed to my buttocks and Dave still fumbling with the belt, the three of us shuffled across the highly waxed floor to the microphone," she recalled.

The mood MacGregor had sought to create dissipated. Higby wished she could have been anyplace else. Somehow she got through the broadcast without a flaw. By the time it was over, her predecessor had departed. More than a quarter of a century later, Higby remembered it as "the longest broadcast of my life."

It was not a particularly auspicious beginning for what turned out to be one of the longest heroine tenures in soap opera. Higby remained with the drama through four cancellations, including the last one, on August 30, 1957. Her memoirs, first published in 1966, are an insightful, often comedic treatment of backstage life at the radio soap operas. She details how an obscure, determined young actress climbed the ladder of success to its highest rungs. She also reaped the good fortune of being in the right place at the right time.

Born in St. Louis on June 29, 1909, Higby appeared in a few silent films at about ten years of age. Her father, a movie director, moved the family to the West Coast early in her life. She began appearing on radio series airing from Hollywood while she was in her early 20s; these included *Shell Chateau, Hollywood Hotel, Lux Radio Theatre* and *Parties at Pickfair.* A few years later she packed her bags and moved to New York, correctly surmising that opportunities in network radio were much greater there.

Higby's radio credits would eventually include roles — some of them running for several years — on *David Harum; Thanks for Tomorrow; The Romance of Helen Trent; Grand Central Station; Five Star Matinee; Joe Palooka; This Is Nora Drake; John's Other Wife; Joyce Jordan, Girl Interne; Linda's First Love; Listening Post; The Mysterious Traveler; Nick Carter, Master Detective; Perry Mason; Stella Dallas; The Story of Mary Marlin* and *Mr. Keen, Tracer of Lost Persons.*

As a promotional gimmick, in the mid–1950s one of the consumer fan magazines included a monthly advice column that was supposedly authored by Mary Jane Higby. "Each month," a disclaimer stated, "Joan Davis will answer your question on any problems concerning marriage, except problems of health or law." Readers who submitted concerns that she selected for answering, and those who gave the best answers "chosen by Joan Davis" to concerns that had been published earlier, earned $25 for their trouble.[2] It was pure schmaltz, but it kept the subscribers reading and the listeners tuning in to the soap opera.

In 1969 Higby told this author that she kept in touch with many peers from her days of playing in the serials. She visited with several frequently. And just as some of her contemporaries did, she enjoyed appearing on

Mary Jane Higby went to New York with one avowed purpose: to become a soap opera queen. She achieved it, winning the heroine's role on one of the longest-running serials, *When a Girl Marries.* Her autobiography offers insight into life as a serial luminary. (Photofest)

interview programs to talk about the Golden Age of radio. Married in 1945 to radio actor Guy Sorel, Higby returned to the screen in 1970 in a highly acclaimed portrayal of a 66-year-old widow in *Honeymoon Killers.* She died on February 1, 1986, in New York.

Nothing has been preserved about Noel Mills, whom Higby replaced on the series, besides her brief stint on *When a Girl Marries.* Regretfully, she vanished as quickly as she appeared.

Four actors portrayed the role of Harry Davis, Joan Davis' husband. John Raby, the first, is perhaps best remembered, for he played it twice. His radio credits include *House in the Country; Amanda of Honeymoon Hill; The Brighter Day; Joyce Jordan, Girl Interne; Nick Carter, Master Detective; Our Gal Sunday;* and *Wendy Warren and the News.* Raby acted on one of TV's first serials, *A Woman to Remember,* which lasted for almost five months on the Dumont network in 1949. He died in 1975.

He was succeeded as Harry Davis by Robert Haag, who appeared in *Death Valley Sheriff, Death Valley Days, Young Doctor Malone* and *Young Widder Brown.* Whitfield Connor, another successor, had no other known radio credits but played Mark Holden in TV's *The Guiding Light* (1955–59). He died on July 23, 1988, at age 72.

The final Harry Davis, actor Lyle Sudrow, remained busy on *Special Agent, House in the Country, The Guiding Light, The Mysterious Traveler, Portia Faces Life* and *Road of Life.* He was the original male lead in the TV version of *The Guiding Light,* playing Bill Bauer from 1952 to 1959.

When a Girl Marries was created and originally written by Elaine Sterne Carrington, the author of several popular dramas. She turned the writing of this one over to LeRoy Bailey in the 1940s. Bailey had written an earlier soap opera that had also featured Mary Jane Higby in the lead, *Thanks for Tomorrow.* Higby played a blind pianist there. When it came time for the piano to be heard, Paul Taubman was at the keyboard. Something about that arrangement seemed fair enough. On *Shell Chateau,* Higby was the spoken voice for opera singer Nadine Connor. Go figure.

When a Girl Marries was purportedly a love story despite its tendency to dip into other matters. When it originated on May 29, 1939, the protagonist, Joan Field, was single. The reader is probably already aware that as a rule, young girls didn't make successful heroines on soap operas. Marriage, widowhood or divorce was virtually a prerequisite for those serials that enjoyed commanding audiences. A heroine who was single at the launch of a new drama wasn't likely to remain so for very long. (The title character in *Rosemary* is a good example.) It took Joan Field only 133 episodes — 26 weeks — to get to the altar. Somehow, homemakers resonated with women who had been married at least once, and the producers weren't inclined to break with a proven formula.

Producers Frank and Anne Hummert favored a fair number of their serials with the presupposition of taking a young woman from the sticks and marrying her to a man of prosperity, culture, education, influence and social status. But Elaine Carrington decided to reverse the trend. In *When a Girl Marries,* it was the male member of the duo who came from the wrong side of the tracks. For years he would harbor a feeling of being beneath his spouse's aristocratic caste, even after becoming moderately successful in law. (He obviously achieved *something*— for several years the Davises could afford a black maid, Lily, one of a dying breed in soap opera.)

The serial offered an interesting hypothesis, and it obviously struck a note with the women at home. The story began when young Harry Davis, who had recently graduated from law school, dropped in unexpectedly at the home of Sam Field, Stanwood's leading attorney, to ask for a job. Harry, who had grown up on the opposite side of town in a life of poverty, was raised alongside a younger brother by his working mother. With no discernible outside interests, the mother had doted on her two sons.

On this occasion Harry found himself in the midst of a formal dinner party at which Sam Field intended to announce the engagement of his eldest daughter, Joan, to wealthy Phil Stanley. Harry's timing, it turned out, could not have been more propitious. When his and Joan's eyes initially met, both felt love at first sight. The reaction between them was so striking, in fact, that her parents and her younger sister, Sylvia — and Phil himself, for that matter — recognized it. The engagement announcement was postponed.

Harry went to work in Sam Field's office. In a short while he proposed marriage to Joan. In early December 1939, in an exquisite garden on the Field estate, Joan and Harry were wed. Meanwhile, out of jealous pretense, Phil Stanley proposed to Eve Topping to show Joan that he could succeed without her. Even though Phil didn't love Eve, Eve told him: "I just happen to be head over heels in love with you…. I think I can love enough for both of us." The pair eloped.

Elaine Carrington flaunted her ability to appall any agency or network brass that might attempt to limit or intimidate her. On one occasion Benton and Bowles constructed an elaborate and very expensive papier-mâché model of Stanwood, the fictitious town in which Joan and Harry lived. Inviting Carrington to view it, agency executives pointed out that the model would help them know at once if any positional errors were occurring in her scripts. Carrington gave tacit approval of the concept before moving on.

That wasn't the end of it, however. Within a few weeks Harry — by then on the road to becoming successful in law practice — purchased a farm in nearby Beechwood (notably, a town *without* a papier-mâché layout). Ostensibly because he feared the social whirl of Stanwood would threaten his marriage, due to the wide chasm between their backgrounds, Harry moved his wife to the Beechwood farm. She soon presented him with a son, Sammy. (At least two members of that family had what were, or would later be, recognized by the public as famous names — Joan Davis and Sammy Davis. Certainly, producers had no problem giving serial characters such widely recognized names. The female lead in *Big Sister* was married to John Wayne, for instance.)

Harry's ongoing concerns about his origins continued to plague him, striking an empathetic chord with Betty MacDonald, his secretary. She had been more than a little perturbed when he had announced his engagement to be married, although she had tried to hide it. Betty had obviously done some wishful thinking of her own, and her hopes and dreams thus far simply hadn't worked out.

At a party one night Joan saw for herself what her neighbor and intimate friend Irma Cameron had been warning her about: there was Betty in an embrace with Harry. Totally bewildered and hurting, Joan carried Sammy back to Stanwood to her parents' home to live. A short time later a second child, a daughter whom she named Hope, was born. Joan found a job and remained in numbed depression for years.

Meanwhile, Joan's friend Irma was attracted to Steve Skidmore and eventually fell deeply in love with him. But Harry's secretary, Betty, who had broken up his marriage, again intervened, taking Steve from Irma and wedding him.

Some years later, as Joan dragged herself home from work one evening, she observed Harry and Betty standing on the sidewalk. Sammy was with them. In horror, Joan saw that her son was in the path of an oncoming truck. Unable to move, she watched as Betty — in one desperate act of honor — shoved Sammy out of the way, sacrificing her life for his.

That was not the end of it, however, for Betty left a legacy of trouble. A few episodes later a cousin, who bore an uncanny resemblance to Betty MacDonald and had the similar name of Betty Scofield, arrived. Not long afterward she was murdered in the Davis barn. So damning was the evidence pointing to Harry that he was accused, tried and convicted of the crime. (Like Dr. Anthony Loring in *Young Widder Brown*, Harry had a penchant for being falsely accused of murder. On a later occasion a revengeful alcoholic was passionately jealous of Harry. In a deceptive ploy, this scoundrel arranged for his suicide to look like murder, leaving clues to ensure that suspicion fell on Harry. Even the dead seemed out to get poor Harry!)

As Harry awaited sentencing for killing Betty Scofield, the courtroom was stunned by a surprise confession from Steve Skidmore. He had seen Scofield at the barn; her resemblance to his late wife had upset him so much that he had begun to choke her, then fainted. When he came to, she was dead.

It took Joan Davis to unravel the mystery. She discovered that an unsavory Robert Nobel — who despised Scofield — had come on the scene in the barn during those moments. Witnessing Steve's feeble attempts to kill Scofield, Robert finished the job after Steve passed out. The charges were dropped against Steve; Robert was indicted and convicted; and Steve and Irma Cameron were married at last. They too purchased a farm but suffered through financial reverses and eventual bankruptcy.

In another sequence, Harry became the legal counsel for a fictional factory during World War II. As such, whenever he could find an occasional group of slackers, he used the opportunity to deliver patriotic speeches about sticking to the job. In this way *When a Girl Marries* did its part to contribute to the at-home war effort. John Raby, who portrayed Harry, also left the series in late 1942 after his call-up to service with Uncle Sam. He returned to the drama in his old role following his release.

Harry's mother, referred to as "Mother Davis" in the story line, frequently philosophized on her positive assessment of life. Her part was played by actress Marion Barney, who simultaneously played prominent mother/mother-in-law roles in two other Carrington serials: *Pepper Young's Family* and *Rosemary*. Mother Davis's other son, Tom, who was in high school when Harry and Joan married, never aspired to the lofty challenges of his older brother. Preferring to wallow in a state of semi-impoverishment, he was satisfied as a garage mechanic. However, he was somehow able to amass at least some financial assets, which he loaned to his brother in Harry's time of dire straits.

In the late 1940s Harry disappeared in New York City while suffering amnesia. Like Lorenzo Jones, Harry wandered the streets of the Big Apple during his memory loss. And like Lorenzo, Harry almost made it down the aisle with another woman (Angie Jones) while still married to someone else.

After his memory returned and Harry and Joan were reunited, the wealthy mother of Phil Stanley (the man whom Joan had originally planned to marry) bequeathed a large sum of money to Anne Dunn. Into Joan's hands, however, Mrs. Stanley placed the power to determine whether Anne was spending the proceeds wisely. If she wasn't, Phil was to receive the balance. Joan saw Anne wasting her income riotously and gained Anne's enmity when she carried out Mrs. Stanley's command. Anne subsequently turned her estate into a luxury club and was elated when Angie Jones, Harry's unfulfilled lover from New York, agreed to come to Beechwood as her dining-room manager. This stirred up trouble between Joan and Harry, precisely what Anne intended.

After that issue was resolved, Joan became temporarily paralyzed in an accident, pushing Harry into serious financial hardship. Borrowing heavily from his brother to pay for Joan's hospitalization, Harry became embroiled in a family feud as Tom's wife, Lola, a high school dropout, prodded both men for immediate restitution of the funds.

By 1952 Joan was attempting to salvage her sister Sylvia's unraveling marriage. At the same time Harry sent his family to Paris, hoping they would avoid a scandal he was caught in with Claire O'Brien. Normalcy for them, it seemed, was a continuing series of curious misfortunes.

Higby noted that the mournful malaise that accentuated the dishpan dramas was systematically relieved every 12 and a half minutes by the joviality of a sales plug — that is, everywhere except on *When a Girl Marries* in its first two years, when the sponsor was the Prudential Life Insurance Company. She and John Raby, as the happy couple, bubbled over with young love and faith in the future, she recalled, routinely followed by Frank Gallop's dispensing of large doses of gloom. Engaging in Hamlet-like soliloquies, Gallop wondered aloud what would happen to the happy family if the wage-earner was suddenly snatched from their midst. Thankfully, the doomsayer stayed with CBS when the program transferred to NBC. There Charles Stark brightened the commercial messages as he raved about Baker's chocolate on behalf of General Foods.

The parallels between *Today's Children* and its predecessor, *Painted Dreams*, had implications for *When a Girl Marries* too. In the previous dramas, author Irna Phillips had cast her characters in settings that were so similar they were practically identical. She also gave them names that were virtually the same. More than 14 years after *When a Girl Marries* went on the air, Elaine Carrington decided to create a televised serial based on its early radio scripts. She called it *Follow Your Heart*. The show debuted on NBC-TV on August 3, 1953, but was gone by January 8, 1954. Here, as in the original, the basic premise was that of a prosperous socialite girl meeting a poor but promising boy. Could they, from such different worlds, find happiness together?

Julie Fielding (notice the similarity in names here) lived with her younger sister and her mother, who was estranged from Julie's father, in Ardmore. As the story began, Julie's engagement to wealthy Harry Phillips (again, notice the name!) was to be announced at a party — even though Julie still had her doubts. She had known Harry all her life. "It would be a lot more fun," she wistfully mused, "to be marrying a stranger ... somebody I didn't know a thing about ... somebody I fell head over heels in love with ... madly ... frantically in love." Sound familiar?

When dashing young Peter Davis (now the names are *really* sounding familiar) arrived at her home on the evening of the engagement party, it was the result of a mix-up. He was keeping an appointment with Julie's father about a job interview, having gotten Sam Fielding's address from the telephone book. But after 15 years of separation from Sam, Mrs. Fielding had never taken the telephone number out of his name. This gave Julie and Peter an opportunity to meet — love at first sight again — and she offered to drive him to her father's hotel.

Julie's father subsequently hired Peter; Georgie MacKenzie, the daughter of Peter's landlady, fell hopelessly in love with Peter; Julie and her mother split over Mrs. Fielding's impression that Julie was making a serious mistake in rejecting Harry Phillips; Julie moved out and took a room at Mrs. MacKenzie's boardinghouse, which, of course, gave Georgie fits; and the show was canceled. It was an interesting hypothesis. Even though it didn't work a second time (viewers preferred the competing *Strike It Rich* on CBS), imitation — even by the same creative genius — was unquestionably the ultimate form of flattery.

When a Girl Marries appeared on three radio networks. Following an initial two years at CBS, after an absence of five weeks it continued for another decade at NBC. ABC, meanwhile, had abandoned soap operas altogether in the early 1940s. (Even when ABC again broadcast soap operas, the network refused to include the form in its daily television logs for another decade.) But in the autumn of 1951 ABC programmers did an about-face, making a strong bid to regain the daytime audiences they had discarded during World War II. They returned as many as a dozen serials to the schedule, most of them revivals of previously popular daytime dramas that were then off the air: *Against the Storm, Joyce Jordan, M.D., Lone Journey, The Story of Mary Marlin* and *Valiant Lady*. To this group ABC was able to add the long-running *When a Girl Marries*, acquired from NBC.

But listeners weren't ready to leave favorite, long-established soap operas that were still running on other radio networks. And of course, by then new ones were beginning to pop up on television. Thus, ABC's ratings-building ploy was a miserable disaster. Within a few months, most of that network's serials were gone, this time for good. *When a Girl Marries* was, by 1953, ABC's sole open-ended survivor.

During the drama's last six years, all at ABC, the program was canceled three times. In total, it was off the air for nearly a year and a half of its 18-year run. What had opened with tremendous promise and had evolved into a "tender, human story of young married life, dedicated to everyone who has ever been in love," ended in a debacle. Only a tiny fraction of the show's once mighty audience still tuned in every weekday morning. It was a sad commentary on a major soap opera, as well as on a once proud tradition that was rapidly approaching a dismal end.

30
Young Doctor Malone

(A Page from a New Chapter)

With a Dixieland jazz band belting out the early notes of "Alexander's Ragtime Band," this saucy little drama bounced riotously onto the airwaves in the early afternoon plugging Crisco, the sponsor's "all-vegetable shortening." It was one of the better-written, better-acted and better-directed medical dramas and lasted until the final day of radio soap opera broadcasts. Set in the mythical hamlet of Three Oaks, the serial concerned Dr. Jerry Malone and his trials and tribulations with two wives. (Let's face it: one woman simply couldn't satisfy the serial heroes who chose medicine for an occupation. *Road of Life's* Dr. Jim Brent and *Big Sister's* Dr. John Wayne had two wives each; *This Is Nora Drake's* Dr. Ken Martinson was miserable with his one and sought Nora from the day of his nuptials; and bless him, Dr. Anthony Loring, Ellen's suitor in *Young Widder Brown*, married twice and pursued Ellen for nearly two decades as a third victim. Why should Dr. Malone be different?) Like the others, he made a poor choice on his first trip to the altar but rectified it the second time around. His new wife grew fond of his grown daughter, on whom he doted. In addition to the narrative's domestic side there was a strong tie with health care in which the young intern-turned-doctor-turned-hospital-administrator grew into a highly respected professional.

Producer-Director: Ira Ashley
Producers: Minerva Ellis, David Lesan, Basil Loughrane
Directors: Stanley Davis, Walter Gorman, Fred Weihe, Theodora Yates
Writers: David Driscoll, Julian Funt, Charles Gussman, David Lesan, Irna Phillips
Music: Charles Paul, John Winters
Sound Effects: Jerry McCarty, John McCloskey, George O'Donnell, Hamilton O'Hara, Walter Otto
Announcers: Sy Harris, Ted Pearson, Ron Rawson, Peter Thomas
Dr. Jerry Malone: Alan Bunce (1939–43), Carl Frank, Charles Irving, Sandy Becker (1947–60)
Ann Richards Malone: Elizabeth Reller, Barbara Weeks
Tracy Adams Malone: Jone Allison, Joan Alexander, Gertrude Warner
Jill Malone: Joan Lazer, Madeleine Pierce, Rosemary Rice
Others: Vera Allen, Ray Appleby, Frank Ayres, Joan Banks, Tony Barrett, Richard Barrows,

Frank Bealin, Martin Blaine, Naomi Campbell, Pattee Chapman, Jeanne Colbert, Nancy Coleman, Richard Coogan, Lester Damon, Helene Dumas, Isabel Elson, Elspeth Eric, Ethel Everett, Robert Haag, Larry Haines, Franc Hale, Ray Hedge, Tommy Hughes, Donna Keith, Arnold Korff, Berry Kroeger, Bill Lipton, Jack Manning, Ian Martin, M. McAllister, Paul McGrath, Janet McGrew, Sellwin Meyers, Ethel Morrison, Herbert Nelson, Eleanor Phelps, William Podmore, Betty Pratt, Katharine Raht, Amanda Randolph, Billy Redfield, Bartlett Robinson, Tess Sheehan, Joy Terry, Barry Thomson, James Van Dyk, Evelyn Varden, Ethel Wilson, Bernard Zanville, more

Theme: Original composition (Winters)

Sponsors: After this serial prevailed in a sustaining mode for five months, Benton and Bowles purchased it for General Foods Corp. (Post cereals and other edibles), April 29, 1940–Jan. 5, 1945. Procter & Gamble (P&G) added a second daily airing Aug. 31, 1942–Jan. 1, 1943. From April 2, 1945l, to June 24, 1955, P&G underwrote it primarily for Crisco shortening and later for Joy dishwashing liquid ("Liquid Joy makes dishwashing ... almost nice," announcer Ron Rawson assured listeners) and various detergents. Beginning on July 18, 1955, the show was sold to the Gillette Co. for Toni home permanents and other hair-care products. In its final years the drama was under multiple sponsorship. One of its major clients was the Staley Corp. for Sta-Puf laundry starch, fabric softener and related commodities. Other regulars were Campana skin cream, Scott paper products, Dr. Caldwell's senna laxative and 4-Way cold tablets.

Ratings: High: 8.5 (1940–41); low: 4.7 (1955–56); median: 6.2. In 15 seasons it dipped below a benchmark 5.0 only once (figures for 1940–56 inclusive).

On the Air: Nov. 20, 1939–April 26, 1940, NBC Blue, 11:15 a.m. ET; April 29, 1940–Jan. 5, 1945, CBS, 2:00 p.m.; Aug. 31, 1942–Jan. 1, 1943, NBC; April 2, 1945–Nov. 25, 1960, CBS, 1:30 p.m.

They're ... cookin' with Crisco,
From New York to Frisco...
Pies are so flaky, cakes are so light;
Fried foods digestible, with Crisco they're right...
So-o-o-o, keep on cookin' ... with Crisco!
— Commercial jingle at sign-off of *Young Doctor Malone*

About half of *Young Doctor Malone*'s 20 years on the air was underwritten by Procter & Gamble. While not all of that decade was the exclusive domain of a single product, the serial and its durable sponsor, Crisco, will likely remain inextricably linked in its fans' minds forever.

The tie between the all-vegetable shortening and the long-running drama is one of marketing's superlative daytime achievements. For millions who listened daily, the years of repetition of *Malone*'s catchy commercial jingle, played to an upbeat Dixieland-jazz rendition of "Alexander's Ragtime Band," made it a memorable success. A high percentage of the fans, if asked to identify the sponsor now, would surely name Crisco. Such recognition was an advertising agency's answer to prayer.

In its P&G years, the show featured a stunning opening:

> MUSIC: Seven notes played brightly on Dixieland trumpet, up
> the scale
> MALE VOCALIST: (Over organ and trumpet, down the scale)
> C-R-I-S-C-O...!
> ANNOUNCER: It's Crisco's ... *Young Doctor Malone*!
> MUSIC: Organ segues into a few notes of theme
> CAST MEMBER: (Few lines lifted from that day's dialogue)
> ANNOUNCER: This is a page from a new chapter in the lives of
> Ann Malone and her husband, Jerry, written by Julian Funt.
> We'll return to the Malones in just a moment.

At the end of each episode, following the final commercial, the announcer said farewell, bidding the audience: "Listen again tomorrow to *Young Doctor Malone* and all the other Three Oaks people who are brought to you by pure, all-vegetable Crisco. Now, this is Ron Rawson reminding you...." A male singer then cranked up the Crisco Dixieland-jazz ditty featuring the lyrics quoted at the start of this chapter.

The similarities between this serial and several of its peers are striking:

• The protagonists here and in *Road of Life* were both physicians, and both were estranged from their wives of many years. After years of emotional separation, the spouses died. The central characters were then free to remarry into happy, healthy relationships. Both did.

• Just as in *The Second Mrs. Burton*, the leading man had a dominant mother who injected herself and her ideas into everybody's lives.

• The male leads on *Rosemary, Big Sister* and *Young Doctor Malone* indicated preferences for the big-city life of New York City over their less-glamorous existences in small-town America.

• Like Aunt Jenny, who entertained announcer Danny Seymour in his daily visits to her kitchen on behalf of sponsor Spry, Dr. Malone had a similar conspirator in Bess Pringle. Three Oaks' mythical monarch of culinary arts served up a piece of freshly baked apple pie or another delicacy (made with Crisco) to son-in-law Tom Baugh whenever he stopped by.

Jerry Malone was at the apex of the Malone story. At its start he was a young physician at Three Oaks Medical Center. For argument's sake, let's assume that after college and years of formal medical training and residency he was, perhaps, 32 years old when he arrived in Three Oaks in 1939. If that assumption is valid, he would have been in his early to mid–50s by the time he left the air in late 1960. Was he still *young* Doctor Malone? Lest we forget, even the enchantingly desirable, constantly stalkable, forever chaste Helen Trent was seeking a life partner at a scant 62 when her show left the air — a mere babe in arms! In radio, "looks" could be deceiving (at least, until one did the math).

Three Oaks: where was that fictional hamlet to which Malone had moved? Daytime radio theorists suggested it lay somewhere between New York and Illinois. They based this on an occasional dialogue reference to seasonal changes and a prevailing preference for a widely practiced dialect. In no way, of course, did this limit a listener from establishing

Three Oaks wherever he or she wanted it to be. That was one of the great characteristics of the theater of the mind.

In the early days of the serial, Malone had a matronly housekeeper named Penny. He suffered the misfortunes that came with having a well-intentioned, overly protective mother, "Mother Malone," who was the town busybody too. He was often embarrassed when her overbearing instincts caused her to dip into his affairs.

A bachelor then, he soon began dating his charming registered nurse, Ann Richards. In those days the actress who played her achieved the dubious honor of reading long commercials while in character. Introduced to listeners as Ann Richards, she'd speak authoritatively, citing the attributes of Post 40% Bran Flakes, an almost unheard-of phenomenon for a serial actress today. In that era, however, it was common practice for performers — including those whose real names the audiences didn't know — to wax eloquently about the wares that were paying their salaries. This was supposed to make the sponsor's product more appealing and even credible.

Richards and Malone were wed early in the series. They soon had a daughter, Jill, who grew up to become the apple of her father's eye. Over the years it was obvious that Jill and her father got along better than her parents did. As the story progressed, Jerry encountered the typical misfortunes that beset most soap opera leads. Shot down over Germany and presumed dead during World War II, he returned home and became involved in a murder trial. Later, he recovered from a temporary crippling affliction. Having gained substantial experience and credentials, he was elevated to the position of medical director.

Jerry and Ann, much like the Brents in *Road of Life*, became career-driven to the point that success at any price seemed paramount. Jerry was consumed with an overwhelming passion for the Three Oaks Medical Center. Ann's impetuous jealousy showed, meanwhile, as she climbed her own career ladder. As a result, their personal relationship deteriorated.

Jerry eventually left Three Oaks to join a medical research institute in New York City. There his life became entwined with the seductively attractive yet domineering Lucia Standish, an extremely powerful woman. She exerted her influence to have Jerry appointed director of the institute, while in Three Oaks, Ann was also moving up. Jerry's philanthropic lawyer, Roger Dineen, husband of Ann's best friend, Lynne, named her as superintendent of the Dineen Clinic. Jerry and Ann had reached pinnacles of success in their professional lives.

By the late 1940s wealthy Three Oaks industrialist Sam Williams and his son, Gene, were both romantically pursuing Ann. For a while, she held them at bay. As these suitors were frequently engaged in tempestuous quarrels, Ann was drawn into the fray as a mediator.

The Malones' separation, while originally expected to be only temporary, took on degrees of permanency as time passed. Realizing that their marriage was hanging by a thread, Ann took a pride-destroying trip to New York City, hoping for reconciliation. It was not to be. She returned to Three Oaks less confident about their future as a couple.

Lucia's almost total domination of Jerry noticeably affected his speech and thinking. While the Malones verbally manifested their love for one another, Ann correctly perceived that Lucia's control over Jerry was preventing any attempt to reconcile. Accordingly, she insisted that Jerry resign from the institute and return to Three Oaks. Jerry refused, blinded by the glamour of his work and the domination of Lucia Standish.

By 1950 the Malones' marriage had reached such an impasse that a national fan magazine featured a writing competition based on their dilemma.[1] The object was to submit an appropriate answer to the question: "Should a threatened marriage be held together for the sake of the child?" Details were recounted in print. Replies were solicited. A short time later, $25 was awarded to a reader in Roslindale, Massachusetts who suggested that Ann persist in her marriage — "be patient and present," recommended the letter writer — or Lucia would ultimately win Jerry. Runner-up prizes of $5 each were awarded to writers of the next five "best" letters.

As a divorce from Jerry and marriage to Sam Williams seemed imminent, Ann learned that Jerry had vanished from work and home in New York. Having at last become totally disillusioned by some of Lucia Standish's actions, Jerry turned his back on everything she had helped him achieve. He intended to start over again. Oblivious to the fact that he had recently become the romantic object of a colleague's wife, Jerry retreated from Lucia's clutches to the "safe haven" afforded by that colleague's home!

Increasingly apparent was the fact that this man — a professional to whom many turned for refuge — could not shake the personal problems that hounded him. Therefore, the Malone story was viewed as "dreadfully morbid in outlook."[2] For most of its years — until Jerry's second marriage, at least — that assessment was on target.

Ann Malone eventually died. For a while the disciplined physician tried to lose himself in his work. Finally, by 1954 he had made significant strides in recovery and was ready to move on. Content with the knowledge that Jill was healing satisfactorily after the loss of her mother, Jerry began to date again. The young woman he was attracted to, Tracy Adams, would ultimately prove to be a godsend.

Over time Tracy and Jerry fell in love and were married. From the outset the couple was able to cope with life's dilemmas much more amiably than Jerry and Ann had. And for the first time in more than a decade, Jerry seemed virtually at peace with the hand life had dealt him.

Four actors portrayed Jerry Malone: Alan Bunce, Carl Frank, Charles Irving and Sandy Becker. Bunce is forever etched in listeners' minds as the lovable, henpecked husband on two comedy series, *Ethel and Albert* and *The Couple Next Door*. The latter, departing on the day radio serials died, had begun in 1935, though it wasn't broadcast continuously. Bunce was in the cast, but he and writer-actress Peg Lynch didn't "star" in the series until 1957. They played Ethel and Albert Arbuckle from 1944 to 1950 on radio. From 1950 to 1952 they appeared in a segment of *The Kate Smith Hour* on daytime TV called *The Private Lives of Ethel and Albert*. That was spun off into a nighttime sitcom on NBC-TV (1953–56).

Born on June 28, 1908, at Westfield, New Jersey, Bunce appeared in 35 stock productions and on Broadway. He costarred with his wife, Ruth Nugent, in *Dream Child*, a play written by her father, J. C. Nugent. Bunce played genial Governor Alf Smith in *Sunrise at Campobello*. His radio credits included recurring roles in *Hello, Peggy* (he was the male lead), *Home of the Brave*, *John's Other Wife*, *Pepper Young's Family*, *Young Widder Brown*, *David Harum* and *Joyce Jordan, Girl Interne*. Bunce died in New York City on April 27, 1965.

Carl Frank was a versatile performer, announcing *This Is Your FBI*, cohosting *What's My Name?* and playing the male lead in *Betty and Bob*. He regularly appeared in the casts of

Columbia Presents Corwin, The Court of Missing Heirs and *Whispering Streets.* He had the title role in *Buck Rogers in the Twenty-Fifth Century* and a running part in *Your Family and Mine.* From 1949 to 1957 he was Uncle Gunnar Gunnerson on one of TV's first live dramatic series, *Mama.* Frank died on September 24, 1972, at age 63.

The equally talented Charles Irving hosted *Coronet Quick Quiz,* directed *This Is Nora Drake,* had a running part in *Bobby Benson's Adventures* and announced several series: *The Breakfast Club, The Henry Morgan Show, Those Websters* and *The Fat Man.* He died on February 15, 1981, at age 68.

The role of Jerry Malone is most intimately identified with Sandy Becker, who performed it in the final 13 years of the serial. Becker appeared in *Treasury Agent* and *Life Can Be Beautiful* while announcing *Backstage Wife, The Shadow* and *Stepping Out.* After radio he provided voice-overs on a trio of weekend TV children's cartoon series: *King Leonardo and His Short Subjects* (1960–63), *The Underdog Show* (1966–68) and *Go Go Gophers* (1968–69). He died on April 9, 1996, at age 74.

As Young Doctor Malone, the part for which he is best remembered, Becker gained name recognition among daytime radio fans. He brought a kind of subtle authority to the role while maintaining a sympathetic understanding of the plight of others. In *Malone's* later years, Becker offered a convincing level of dignity in a larger context of the counseling that he seemed destined to play in the lives of the drama's characters.

Veteran radio actresses Elizabeth Reller and Barbara Weeks took the part of Ann Richards Malone. Reller was the Armstrong Quaker Girl on *The Armstrong Theater of Today,* occasionally appeared in the casts of *The Amazing Mr. Smith* and *The Man Behind the Gun* and played the female leads in both *Betty and Bob* and *Michael and Kitty.* She carried major roles in *Doc Barclay's Daughters* and *Portia Faces Life.* Weeks had the title role in *Her Honor, Nancy James,* was the female lead in *Meet the Dixons,* often appeared on *Philip Morris Playhouse* and had recurring parts on *We Love and Learn* and *The Open Door.* She died on July 4, 1954, at 47.

The part of Tracy Adams Malone, Jerry's second wife, was played by three actresses who were all well-known in radio theater: Jone Allison, Joan Alexander and Gertrude Warner. Allison played the lead in *Hearts in Harmony.* She had recurring parts in *The Aldrich Family, Brave Tomorrow, The Guiding Light, Home of the Brave, Rosemary, When a Girl Marries* and *Casey, Crime Photographer.* Following the 1952 debut of *The Guiding Light* on TV she briefly acted in her long-running radio role of Meta Bauer. Joan Alexander is best recalled as Perry Mason's longtime cohort, Della Street.

Gertrude Warner may have played the leads or female leads in more dramas than any other actress. Her credits include *Against the Storm, Beyond These Valleys, Brownstone Theater, Ellen Randolph, Joyce Jordan, M.D., The Man I Married, Modern Romances, Mrs. Miniver, Perry Mason, The Shadow* and *Whispering Streets.* Adding *Young Doctor Malone,* she acquired at least a dozen such roles. She was in *Dangerously Yours* and *Ethel and Albert* and had running parts in *City Desk, David Harum, Ellery Queen, The Right to Happiness, When a Girl Marries* and *Valiant Lady.* For a brief time in 1960 she appeared in TV's *As the World Turns.* Warner was born on April 2, 1917, at West Hartford, Connecticut, and launched her career at Hartford's WTIC. In later life she taught acting at Oberlin College and the Weist-Barron School. She died on January 26, 1986.

Young Doctor Malone was one of a handful of radio serials to make it to television.

The lead of *Young Doctor Malone* was portrayed for 13 of its 21 years by Sandy Becker. The physician mellowed over the years, becoming a strong counselor figure near the serial's end. As the series left the air in 1960, Becker claimed the departure was the "saddest" of the experiences he and the radio audience had shared. (Photofest)

Unlike all but a couple of the others, it enjoyed a successful run of a few years on the small screen. (Its characters were introduced in the final few episodes of the drama it replaced, *Today Is Ours*, which survived for only six months. Such crossover introductions worked successfully for Irna Phillips for the debuts of two radio serials, *Woman in White* and *The Brighter Day*. She created the televised version of *Young Doctor Malone*. Julian Funt and David Lesan, who had written the radio play, had cocreated the departing *Today Is Ours*.) The half-hour *Malone* TV presentation debuted on NBC-TV on December 29, 1958, at 3:00 p.m. It moved to 3:30 p.m. on October 1, 1962, and was withdrawn on March 29, 1963.

Only the principal characters' names transferred to the TV format: Jerry, Tracy and Jill. David Malone, a son who wasn't in the radio drama, became the new central character. Three Oaks Medical Center was gone; David practiced medicine at Valley Hospital, in Denison, Maryland. While attempting to live up to his father's sterling reputation, he resigned himself to being chased by several women. He finally married one, only to be accused of killing her mother. His sister, Jill, was tried for killing her husband; the siblings were exonerated, but mayhem and murder ruled the airwaves, unlike the quiet little drama on radio where a difference of opinion stirred a tempest in a teapot.

Young Doctor Malone was one of four open-ended dramas canceled on soap opera's final fateful day on radio, November 25, 1960. Only a few days earlier, a prominent member of the Three Oaks Medical Center board had attempted to force Dr. Ted Mason to resign as director. Presumably, this would have cleared the way for Jerry Malone to return to the post that — years before — he had held, before his move to New York City. But Jerry refused to accept an offer to be reinstated. Mason breathed a sigh of relief. However, after Mason's untenable position was made clear, Mason voluntarily resigned and called Jerry, urging him to reconsider. Jerry accepted and made plans to return to Three Oaks.

On another front, wedding plans between young Warren Scott (nicknamed "Scotty") and Jerry's daughter, Jill, were proceeding, despite open hostility from Scotty's jealous mother. In a final try to effect a reconciliation, Jerry visited Mrs. Scott, urging her to sanction her son's marriage by attending the nuptials the next day. In the series' final moments, Mrs. Scott broke down and relented. As the show left the air, Jerry seemed headed toward the eternal bliss that had eluded him for a couple of decades.

Listeners who lingered over years of absorbing story plot must have felt that their drama — a favorite of millions — was being rushed aside by CBS on that last broadcast. Tying up the details was performed quickly. The obvious intent was to neatly extinguish the years of conflict and to do so rapidly so that affiliate stations could have more time to sell to advertisers, boosting bottom-line revenues.

After the opening commercial and an initial scene on November 25, 1960, a commercial break interrupted the plot. Announcer Peter Thomas, in a moving farewell from a long-time sponsor, brooded.

> Today marks the end of an era for all the friends of Young Doctor Malone because this fine program goes off the air with this broadcast. Sta-Puf laundry rinse is proud to include itself among those loyal friends, since Sta-Puf has sponsored the program for a long, long time. Yes, the Staley folks are sorry to say "good-by" to the show that's ending, but we feel that through it we've made wonderful friends all over America.

> And we sincerely hope that pleasant relationship will continue.
> We appreciate your loyalty, just as you have ours…. And now
> for S-T-A-P-U-F, a regretful "good-by" to Young Doctor Mal-
> one.

An organ bridge returned listeners to the final scene. Following a concluding commercial, the announcer attempted to tie up the loose ends as the show's familiar theme languished in the background.

> This is Peter Thomas. As the current series of Young Doctor
> Malone comes to a close, we leave Jill on the eve of her wed-
> ding day happy in the knowledge that Scotty's mother at last
> has given her blessing. As for Jerry, the weeks that lie ahead
> will be challenging ones as he must resume the responsibilities
> of directing the clinic. But with the encouragement, love and
> support of Tracy, Jerry will go forward in new paths of service.

The organ abruptly ground to a halt. Appropriately, Sandy Becker, who had played the role of Malone for most of the run, addressed the listeners as himself.

> Friends, this is Sandy Becker. For the past many years we've
> had numerous experiences together, and today we share the
> last, and for me — the saddest. It's the one which ends with the
> final farewell. I take great comfort in knowing that for these
> many years we've provided you with pleasurable listening. On
> behalf of the cast, Ira Ashley, our producer-director, and
> David Lesan, our writer, a very heartfelt "thank-you." And
> "good-by."

In the seconds before the music resumed and an unidentified network announcer hastily broke in, you could almost hear the sobs you knew were there. Without taking a breath, however, the announcer offered this salacious pronouncement, obviously intended to be welcomed news: "Next, *The Second Mrs. Burton.* Monday, CBS news goes double for you to ten minutes an hour weekdays on the CBS Radio network." Hot dog!

With apologies to Charles Dickens, who wrote the words a century earlier, it was "the best of times" for the affiliates, "the worst of times" for serial lovers. Devotees of daytime drama saw it as "the age of foolishness, … the epoch of incredulity, … the season of Darkness, … the winter of despair."[3]

Ten minutes of news instead of *Young Doctor Malone* — it was the pits.

31
Young Widder Brown
(The Age-Old Conflict)

How could a widowed mother allow her "two fatherless children" to spend decades deciding her fate, placing a hex on suitors they considered unworthy of their mom's hand? Such a supposition, coupled with amnesia, blindness, murder and mayhem of many sorts, destined Ellen Brown to spend decades in unfulfilled desire. Pursued by several handsome, brilliant and eligible bachelors, Ellen was careful to choose suitors who exhibited stability and promise. Unlike the deranged chaps that plagued several other serial heroines, Ellen's men were likely to be professionals — physicians and lawyers. But producers Frank and Anne Hummert had a flair for creating obstacles that would prevent any of her long-term entanglements from reaching the altar. Engagements were frequently broken while the heroine pondered her fate. Even when every possible roadblock to marriage appeared to have evaporated, this enterprising young woman — who ran a tearoom for a livelihood — encountered yet other immovable objects that kept her from reaching any wedding chapels. Ellen could easily be considered radio's second-most-sought-after widow, following Helen Trent. Helen shared similar frustrations for 27 years, although most of *her* admirers were plain and simple lunatics. In a series titled *Young Widder Brown*, it should have been clear to listeners that matrimony would never win out. If it had, the premise on which the soap opera was built would die, and the title would have no value. The serial was classic matinee misery, and circumstances dictated that it could never be otherwise.

Producers: Frank and Anne Hummert
Directors: Martha Atwell, Richard Leonard, Ed Slattery
Writers: Jean Carroll, Lawrence Hammond, Frank and Anne Hummert, Elizabeth Todd
Music: John Winters
Sound Effects: Ross Martindale
Announcer: George Ansbro
Ellen Brown: Florence Freeman (1938–54), Wendy Drew (1954–56)
Anthony Loring: Ned Wever
Herbert Temple: Eric Dressler, House Jameson, Alexander Scourby
Norine Temple: Joan Tompkins
Maria Hawkins: Lorene Scott, Agnes Young, Alice Yourman
Victoria Loring: Riza Joyce, Ethel Remey, Kay Strozzi

Janey Brown: Marilyn Erskine
Mark Brown: Tommy Donnelly
Peter Turner: Clayton (Bud) Collyer
Others: Charita Bauer, Arline Blackburn, Horace Braham, Alan Bunce, Sarah Burton, War-
ren Colston, Jane Erskine, Toni Gilman, Robert Haag, Louis Hall, Joy Hathaway, Tom
Hoier, Irene Hubbard, Tommy Hughes, Ethel Intropidi, Bennett Kilpack, Ray Largay,
Athena Lorde, Frank Lovejoy, John MacBryde, Florence Malone, Jimmy McCallion,
Bess McCammon, Eva Parnell, Elaine Rost, Virginia Routh, James Sherman, Helen
Shields, Muriel Starr, Lili Valenti, Dick Van Patten, more

Theme: "In the Gloaming"; "Wonderful One"

Sponsors: Blackett-Sample-Hummert brought this serial to radio as a sustaining feature.
After 16 weeks the quarter-hour was sold to Sterling Drugs, initially to advertise Bayer
headache remedies. For most of the soap opera's life, however, it was a commercial
vehicle for Sterling's Phillips' Milk of Magnesia product family (laxatives, dentifrices
and face creams). Other commodities from Sterling's vast arsenal of personal and clinical goods (like Double Danderine shampoo and Haley's M-O mineral emulsion oil)
were plugged. When Sterling withdrew sponsorship in 1954, the Gillette Co. bought
into the show on behalf of Prom home permanents, White Rain shampoo and other
hair-care preparations. Gillette relied on the widely recognized voice of radio actress
Ruth Warrick as spokeswoman for its Prom commercials. Near the end of the run, the
series was once again broadcast as a sustaining feature.

Ratings: High: 8.6 (1942–43); low: 2.6 (1955–56); median: 6.4. In 18 full seasons, this serial
dropped below 5.0 only twice, in its first and final years on the air. For two-thirds of the
serial's life (12 seasons), numbers exceeded 6.0; in two-thirds of those years (eight seasons), they were above 7.0.

On the Air: June 6, 1938–Sept. 23, 1938, MBS, 4:00 p.m. ET, titled *Young Widder Jones*;
Sept. 26, 1938–June 2, 1939, NBC, 11:30 a.m., retitled *Young Widder Brown*; June 5,
1939–March 23, 1951, NBC, 4:45 p.m.; March 26, 1951–Jan. 6, 1956, NBC, 4:30 p.m.;
Jan. 9, 1956–June 22, 1956, NBC, 4:15 p.m.

Again we present the moving human drama of a woman's heart and a mother's love—Young Widder
Brown. *In the little town of Simpsonville, attractive Ellen Brown, with two children to support, faces the
question of what she owes to them and what she owes to herself. Here's the story of life and love as we all
know it.*

— Epigraph to *Young Widder Brown*

Well, this was life and love as we might have known it if our widowed mothers had been
pursued by an endless stream of suitors, several with the patience of Job. These guys would
keep waiting forever.

It must have seemed awkward to faithful listeners of *Young Widder Brown* that, at
times, Ellen's failure to gain the permission of her offspring to marry was the sole reason

she couldn't fulfill the dictates of her heart. When the writers temporarily exhausted all other credible excuses for detaining her and her beaus from the altar — trials for murder, temporary blindness, amnesia and the like — they pulled out the time-honored "children's approval" subterfuge. No matter how sterling the qualities or how close the resemblance to saintliness, a candidate for stepfatherhood couldn't get to first base on this serial if Mark and Janey Brown — Ellen's "fatherless children" — turned thumbs down on him. Here, where children were often "seen but not heard," especially so in the final decade, Ellen "reported" their verdicts to other characters (and thus, to the listening audience).

Sometimes it seemed the little devils were hell-bent on preventing their mother from attaining any sustained happiness. Ellen had to work outside the home in an era in which nearly all women remained at home raising their children. Though she never would have admitted it, her charges were overbearing, selfish brutes who destroyed every chance she had to improve the family's material lot in life.

The observation was made earlier that if Helen Trent was 35 years old at that soap opera's inception (as her serial's epigraph suggested), she would have been at least 62 when she left the air 27 years later. By that same logic, Ellen Brown, in her early 30s when *her* series began, could easily have been 50 or older when *she* departed the airwaves 18-plus years later. Consider this: if Janey had been six and Mark four when *Young Widder Brown* debuted, and that certainly seems reasonable, then by golly their mom was still checking with them about potential stepdaddies when they were 24 and 22, respectively! Ellen appeared to be slow in figuring out the announcer's admonition about "what she owes to herself."

Young Widder Brown was accredited as "some of the most excruciating radio torture ever devised."[1] Before it was over, Ellen not only was thwarted in romantic endeavors at every turn but also suffered frequent indignities at the hands of two matronly women who were related to her most beloved suitor. On dual occasions she agonized over murder trials in which her intended was falsely accused and had to prove his innocence. She encountered a boatload of physical disabilities — an airline crash nearly killed her, leaving her with absolute memory loss, the bane of soap opera heroes and heroines for decades. A few years earlier she experienced total blindness, brought on by an allergy to chocolate cake. (That malady received a quick cure when a cake-flour sponsor for the network complained.)

All of her misfortunes would have dashed the hopes of a lesser woman. But not this one. She was, as her most persistent beau informed her, "a girl in a million," for adversity never overcame her. Ellen's optimism, her indomitable spirit, her attitude of caring for others even in the face of crushing defeat allowed her to positively react to life's sorrows when they seemed almost beyond human endurance. While her serial offered lots of "excruciating torture," Ellen's fans must have remained hopeful, marveling at her willingness to look for a silver lining in every dismal encounter.

Few of the faithful will recall that Ellen Brown's serial was launched under another handle. After 16 weeks of broadcasting as a sustaining feature on Mutual, *Young Widder Jones* was sold to Sterling Drugs for airing on the NBC network. At that juncture, producers Frank and Anne Hummert faced a small crisis with their fledgling serial assigned to the 11:30 a.m. quarter-hour. Perhaps at the request of Sterling Drugs, the Hummerts planned to bring another successful Sterling-sponsored late-afternoon serial forward, creating the nucleus of a block of Sterling serials on NBC. The soap opera to be moved to the morning lineup was *Lorenzo Jones*, which was to be transferred to the 11:15 quarter-hour, adjacent to *Young Widder Jones*.

With back-to-back serials both carrying the name *Jones* in their titles, listeners might think that Ellen and Lorenzo were somehow related (other than by sponsorship), creating an awkward dilemma. The solution: the Hummerts elected to change the surname of the newer, less established *Young Widder Jones*. (The shift turned out to be fortuitous: a short while later both serials were paired at new times, *Lorenzo Jones* at 4:30 and *Young Widder Brown* at 4:45 on NBC, where they remained together for another dozen years. By then Sterling had purchased the entire hour on NBC between four and five o'clock for a block of serials.)

Brown was among several dramas to switch its theme songs. It may have been the last of the radio soap operas, in fact, to change its melody, only a few years shy of cancellation. For most of its life this serial was introduced by an organ rendition of "In the Gloaming." But by the early 1950s the show wafted onto the air to the strains of "Wonderful One," a tune already familiar to many in the audience. The drama's opening epigraph was dramatically edited too, pared to a simple phrase:

> The National Broadcasting Company now brings you *Young Widder Brown*, the story of attractive Ellen Brown with two fatherless children to support — the story of the age-old conflict between a mother's duty and a woman's heart.

There were still no limits on the offspring: Mark and Janey could determine their mother's fate without restraint.

Ellen Brown's husband had died sometime before the series reached the air, leaving her to raise a young boy and girl by herself. She was not alone on radio in this regard. Matriarchy prevailed in households headed by the heroines of *Margo of Castlewood*, *My Son and I* and *Manhattan Mother*, short-lived serials appearing in the late 1930s. Ma Perkins and the heroines of *Painted Dreams* and *Today's Children* also headed fatherless families, as did the mother of Rosemary. Even Carolyn Nelson of *The Right to Happiness*, radio's most married heroine, went for several years as a single mother between husbands three and four. Each of these women exuded remarkable confidence and ability, coping with whatever life handed her, possessing the fortitude to provide for her family's material as well as emotional needs.

While the hypothesis of *Young Widder Brown* dealt with the obstacle course that prevented Ellen from achieving a second marriage, along the way it also allowed her to become an astute businesswoman. To sustain her family she was able to purchase a tearoom in the midwestern hamlet of Simpsonville, somewhere in the not-too-distant vicinity of Chicago. Once again she had plenty of company among her peers. Several women on other dramas introduced in the 1930s demonstrated their prowess at running small business ventures. On the death of *her* husband, Ma Perkins took over the operation of his lumberyard. Brenda Cummings, heroine of *Second Husband*, and Stella Dallas both ran successful sewing shops. The title character on *Jenny Peabody* was the proprietress of a minor hotel. *Manhattan Mother's* central figure became a noted businesswoman. The protagonist in *Kitty Keane, Incorporated* managed her own detective agency. And on *Arnold Grimm's Daughter*, Connie Tremayne ran a lingerie emporium. All were enterprising and at least modestly successful entrepreneurs.

With two fatherless children to support, a woman couldn't be uncertain about her intended. Ellen Brown (Florence Freeman in the title role of *Young Widder Brown*) and her long-suffering suitor Anthony Loring (played by Ned Wever) spent many a dismal day managing to avoid the altar. (Courtesy of Florence Freeman)

The objects of Ellen Brown's affection, aside from her offspring, were several. In *Brown's* earliest years Dr. Peter Turner became her most unflagging suitor. He was a physician at Simpsonville's Health Center Hospital. At about the same time, attorney Herbert Temple — who was destined to become Ellen's lifelong admirer and friend but never her spouse — entered the competition for her hand. He had the good sense, after a sustained period, to realize she would never be his and dropped out. Did he, perhaps, sense the overwhelming power of Ellen's children?

At any rate, a win-win situation resulted, and he remained a major character in the drama until the end. After withdrawing from the fray, Herbert moved on with his promising legal career. In an interesting turn of events Norine, the woman he married, became Ellen's best friend and confidante. To Norine alone Ellen bared her soul on life's foibles, revealing her innermost thoughts.

Ellen also maintained a friendship with Maria Hawkins, who often helped her out at the tearoom and looked after her children. But Maria was universally viewed as the small-town gossip; it would have been difficult under the circumstances for Ellen to have developed with her a rapport similar to the one she was able to maintain with Norine. Norine knew how to keep secrets, and she was unwavering in her defense and support of Ellen Brown, no matter what.

Eventually, Peter Turner also grew weary of some perceived fickleness in Ellen. He too departed for other pastures. His replacement, beginning in 1940, was Dr. Anthony Loring, who would influence both Ellen and this serial for the next 16 years. Ruggedly handsome, the personable young medical intern with the discerning mind would in time grow to love Ellen Brown more than life itself. Although there would be others with designs on her, Anthony became her most persistent admirer.

They were engaged to be married on several occasions, only to have their hopes tested by outside forces. Sometimes Ellen delayed, awaiting Janey and Mark's approval of a man who adored them and never gave them cause to dislike or distrust him. Certainly the "age-old conflict between a mother's duty and a woman's heart" was never better demonstrated than here. Third parties frequently intervened too, forcing a breakup of the lovebirds so that outsiders could attempt to achieve their own ends.

In the spring of 1949, Anthony believed that Ellen had died in an airplane disaster. What he didn't know, and wouldn't learn for a while, was that she had survived but suffered amnesia. She became the victim of one of this serial's few deranged men, David Blake, who held her captive in a secluded hillside refuge. (Doesn't this sound like some of the maniacal encounters that contemporary heroine Helen Trent endured?) Anthony later learned that Ellen was alive, but on her rescue — he realized his own agony was far from over: she had no memory of any prior relationship with him. Instead, she acknowledged her interest in a new suitor, David Campbell. In the meantime young Angela McBride entered the story line, and it became apparent rather quickly that she saw husband material in Anthony.

When the physician made a strong appeal to Ellen to help her recall their affectionate past, Ellen's memory was mysteriously restored. But Angela, dissatisfied with that turn of events, decided that if Anthony couldn't be persuaded to leave Ellen, then Ellen would have to be destroyed. To accomplish her mission she arranged the death of Amanda Cathcart, David Campbell's neurotic sister. Initially it appeared that Amanda had died from an automobile accident in which Ellen Brown (who else?) was driving. But when an eyewitness,

Bruce Weldon, came forward and reported that Angela — not Ellen — was at fault, Ellen's freedom was ensured. She could get on with her marriage to Dr. Loring at last! But then, Bruce admitted that *he* was deeply infatuated by Ellen's charms.

After more than a dozen years following the death of her husband, Ellen was told by unscrupulous charlatans that he was still alive and living in Chicago. (A similar sequence occurred to *Rosemary's* mother, it may be recalled.) Going to the Windy City to verify their claim, she fell under the spell of a ruthless man posing as her husband, William. He and an accomplice outlined a scheme that would provide a large sum of cash for Ellen, provided she would agree to marry and then divorce "William." High-principled Ellen, of course, refused. But with only Norine Temple, back in Simpsonville, aware of where she had gone alone, Ellen was left at the mercy of the two by-then desperate men.

In another prolonged sequence, a wealthy widower, Horace Steele, and his flighty teenage daughter, Jacqueline, moved to Simpsonville in 1951. They brought with them enough trouble to nearly destroy Ellen's and Anthony's lives. The couple had broken their engagement — again — shortly before the Steeles arrived. The unrest began when Horace fell head over heels in love with Ellen. Anthony bitterly resented Horace's intrusion, naturally.

Things heated up when a New York socialite, Lita Haddon, moved to town a short time later. As soon as she learned that her old flame Horace had the hots for Ellen, she unequivocally informed Ellen that *she* — Lita — would marry Horace. She threatened Ellen, warning her that disaster would follow if Ellen pursued a friendship with Horace. Prompted by Lita's jealousy, Horace asked Ellen to marry him. A short time later Anthony was summoned to the Steele home and found Horace shot to death. An uncontrollable Lita confessed to the crime.

Ellen's enormous capacity for tenderness and compassion came through once again, as listeners overheard this conversation:

> ELLEN: (Speaking of Jacqueline) ...She had some justification for blaming me for Horace's death.
> ANTHONY: Oh rubbish, dear.
> ELLEN: At 19, your father is shot down by a madwoman — do you think you have much time for reasonable thought? I don't.... Poor Anthony...! (With sincerity) Heaven help that poor mad creature! ...Oh Anthony, who cannot believe that we work out our punishments right here on earth when they look at Lita Haddon ... when they see her ... when they hear her crazy cries?
> ANTHONY: You have something there, dear.
> ELLEN: I know ... I know I have. Anthony, you'll have to be very sure that she gets the best psychiatric attention ... you, you owe that.
> ANTHONY: To whom do I owe it?
> ELLEN: To the faith that Horace Steele had in your honor, Anthony. We ... we owe it ... to ... to the fact that we were his friends ... and he counted on us for help. Now ... now we have to look after Lita and Jacqueline. Lita ... because she may turn on Horace's daughter; Jacqueline ... well, Jacqueline's had enough!
> ANTHONY: You're a girl in a million, darling!

And she was. Soft-spoken Ellen daily said to homemakers: "It's all right to put others' feelings, needs and wants ahead of your own." In that short piece of dialogue, Ellen expressed concern for the victim's kin, for the man who had witnessed the murder, for the murderer and for the memory of the victim, to whom she believed she and Anthony owed a debt. She said not a word about her own good deeds; Ellen Brown was the personification of righteousness, never slipping out of character. (Norine Temple sometimes referred to her as a "saint.")

Unfortunately, Anthony and Ellen would soon discover how vindictive the deranged Lita Haddon could be. Knowing Ellen's deep feelings for Anthony, Lita quickly recanted her confession, offering a sworn statement accusing Anthony of murdering Horace Steele in a jealous rage over Ellen. As a result, Anthony stood trial for murder. Eventually, thanks in part to Ellen's perseverance, he was cleared when evidence surfaced proving that Lita Haddon had killed Horace, as she had initially confessed. But it was an ordeal in which the outcome was at times uncertain, and it took a toll on Anthony and Ellen.

The following year Anthony seemed hopelessly embroiled in a controversial effort to prove that a brief marriage in his younger days had been legally annulled. A drawn-out sequence left him so weak that he appeared to have lost all hope of marrying Ellen. Ellen was bewitched, bothered and bewildered by this startling revelation from Anthony's past. And consequently Dudley Collins, who investigated the records of Anthony's marriage and annulment, used the opportunity to pursue his own romantic interest in Ellen.

The final dimension in the series' major plot developments — one that continued for the last three years that *Brown* was on the air — revolved around Millicent Randall. The vampish Millicent, eager to get her hooks into successful surgeon Anthony Loring, persuaded him to believe a lie she told about Ellen. Turning his back on the love of his life after 13 years, Anthony married the scheming Millicent, only to learn that she had tricked him. In the meantime Ellen, believing her opportunities with Anthony were gone forever, weighed a marriage proposal from Michael Forsythe, who had badgered her for months. She put him off for a while but eventually accepted. This must have come as a shock to the faithful listeners, for she had been unable to make a lasting commitment to several men over much longer periods of time.

Meanwhile, Millicent stood squarely in Anthony's way of freedom and happiness, unwilling to give him the divorce he desperately sought. Ellen, on the other hand, was unable to proceed with her wedding plans with Michael when she realized that Anthony was the only man she had truly loved since her late husband died.

The character of Victoria Loring, Anthony's sister, was also prominent in the story line during this period. She was to Ellen Brown what Dick Grosvenor's mother was to Stella Dallas throughout that drama's long run: a self-serving, wealthy, pompous woman whose all-consuming passion was to destroy any chance the lovers might have for sustained happiness.

For little apparent reason, Victoria left no stone unturned in carrying out her vendetta against Ellen — day after day, week after week, month after month, year after year. In the serial's fading days she occasionally linked up with Anthony's wife, Millicent, in joint efforts to remove Ellen from their lives. Never did two women connive more brazenly to destroy a single individual than this pair. Kind, compassionate Ellen, who invariably looked on the cheerful side of everything, was one of soap opera's long-suffering martyrs.

The abuse she took at the hands of such detractors was some of the most unpleasant any heroine ever faced.

Millicent met an untimely death in the autumn of 1955. And for the second time in less than five years, Anthony stood trial for a murder he didn't commit. For months he faced an endurance test, and it genuinely appeared that he might lose. In the end Ivan Mansfield, whom Millicent had hired as an intervention in Ellen and Anthony's relationship, was revealed as her killer.

As the serial wound down, the evil hand of Millicent Loring reached out from the grave to dispel hopes of lasting peace for her husband and Ellen Brown. On the condition that Ellen agree never to marry Anthony, Millicent's will stipulated that Ellen would receive a quarter of a million dollars. At first Anthony believed Ellen might accept the offer. Even when her durable lover couldn't recognize her intents, the listeners knew better; it would have been completely out of character for her to have taken the money and run.

There was just time for one final play for Anthony. Ellen's loathsome cousin Isabel Jennings arrived in Simpsonville and put her designs on the doctor. At the time, she was seeking a divorce from her husband, and she named Ellen as an adulteress prompting that action. Anthony, ever the cautious one, deliberated over this news right down to the final broadcast day. Ellen, meanwhile, had had enough. She decided to leave Simpsonville and never return, taking her children to Chicago to live, at least until she established roots somewhere else. She sold her tearoom and gathered her family and possessions.

Moments before the serial ended, Anthony came to his senses and raced over to intervene, offering an apology and asking her to change her mind. Ellen admitted: "All along I was praying in my heart that you'd come here and stop me from going away." Anthony felt that the battle had been won when she added: "Just hold me close … and don't ever let me go." Instead of driving her to the airport, he told her he would take her to purchase a marriage license (with or without Mark and Janey's consent this time).

The Hummerts were shrewd operators, however, always thinking ahead. Hoping that one day the series might return to the air, they weren't about to let that elusive knot be tied while the drama was still *on* the air. If *Brown* was ever summoned for a return, an automobile wreck or a dozen other plausible excuses could prevent Ellen and Anthony from reaching matrimony.

If any of this sounds familiar to those who listened to more than one daytime drama, it should. During the lunch hour shared by millions of Americans, serial addicts tuned to an almost identical strategy being played out on CBS — this one lasting for 27 years. At 12:30 p.m. poor Helen Trent was desperately pursued for nearly three decades by suitor Gil Whitney, who — like Anthony Loring — was also a professional. (Whitney was a lawyer.) Just when it appeared that every possible barrier that had kept Helen and Gil from the altar had been forever put to rest, one of them would fall victim to amnesia or be accused of a dreadful crime or have to fight off a third party for the other's affections.

Anyone following the plights of Helen and Ellen (even their names were similar!) could think that the scripts were written, directed and produced by the same people. They were. The Hummerts, whose assembly-line factory was responsible for both serials, frequently rotated writers and directors among their various properties. Thus, it was no coincidence that these two heroines labored under a similar premise.

Through January 15, 1954, the part of Ellen was played by Florence Freeman, who was also the heroine of *Wendy Warren and the News* during that series' long run. Freeman relinquished the role of Ellen ostensibly because she wanted to spend more time with her family. Her father was gravely ill, and her mother needed support. She confided to this author that she had also grown weary of the repetitive plots that the Hummerts recycled for the *Brown* series. After almost 16 years, she decided she had had enough.

Radio biographers have been unintentionally silent in providing details about the life of Freeman's successor as Ellen Brown. Wendy Drew, who played the heroine until the series left the air two and a half years later, subsequently gained the role of Ellen Lowell in one of TV's first 30-minute soap operas, *As the World Turns.* In private life, after marrying photographer Kenneth Heyman, Drew left that series in 1960 to raise a family. Aside from that, no other details on her contributions are available.

The Hummerts preferred to downplay the individuals who labored for them as writers, actors and directors. Few in their employ could ever reach the point of thinking more highly of their efforts than the Hummerts intended. Yet in *Brown's* latter days, a rather nondescript epigraph at the end of each day's episode was expanded to credit several individuals who shared in the performance.

> *Young Widder Brown* is from the original radio play by Frank and Anne Hummert and is produced under their supervision. Dialogue by Jean Carroll; directed by Richard Leonard. Wendy Drew plays Ellen Brown and Ned Wever is Anthony Loring. Today's episode of *Young Widder Brown* was brought to you by the National Broadcasting Company. George Ansbro, speaking. *Young Widder Brown* will be on the air at this same time tomorrow.

What prompted the changes? Perhaps it was a small reward to hangers-on as the Hummerts saw their vast radio enterprise crumbling. Offering performers this recognition may have been some inducement to keep certain personalities loyal to Air Features, Inc., their production house. The change came at a time when more tempting opportunities were compelling some to abandon radio for television. Whatever the reason, it was almost a 180-degree turn from the Hummerts' past modus operandi. The timing was unfortunate in that for all the years Florence Freeman played the lead, she was never credited on the air.

Announcer George Ansbro remained with the program from its inception to its demise. Each day at the conclusion of the action and dialogue, he would ask several thought-provoking questions designed to get listeners thinking about subsequent episodes. Invariably, his final question concluded with the words *Young Widder Brown.* This was the same pattern followed by another Hummert serial: its announcer ended each day's chapter with pointed missives concluding with the words *Our Gal Sunday.* Ansbro posed questions such as: "What implications does this shocking revelation have in store for Anthony and Ellen? How will it affect their relationship with young Muriel Swarthmore? In reality, will the confirmation given by Herbert Temple allow things to ever be the same for *Young Widder Brown*?"

That finish took a greater sense of urgency in the serial's latter days, at times seeming more like a commercial than an extension of the story line. Ansbro offered these lines on December 22, 1955: "For the second time Victoria has brought up Ivan Mansfield's name.

Just what is her sudden interest in this treacherous artist? And in the back of her mind, does she hope to use him in a plan to save Anthony Loring? Will Victoria reveal her plans to Ellen tomorrow at this same time on *Young Widder Brown*?" You could bet money on it: things had reached a frantic state as every tool in radio's promotional arsenal was being employed to fend off the encroaching TV. Sadly, some of the theater of the mind's aura had already slipped away.

From its introduction in 1940, the part of Anthony Loring was portrayed by Ned Wever, as talented a musician as he was an actor. He wrote the lyrics to several popular songs, among them "Spellbound," "I Can't Resist You," "Trouble in Paradise" and "Trust in Me." This native New Yorker, born on April 27, 1902, attended Princeton, where he took an interest in music and theater, writing songs and skits. In that institution's prestigious Triangle Club, noted for its original musical comedies, he acted in principal roles and became the group's president. During his senior year he wrote a book, lyrics and music and acted in and directed the club's production of *They Never Come Back*.

A short time after graduation, Wever was cast in a major Broadway role in *The Fan*. He went on to appear in *Lady, Be Good* and *The Great Gatsby*. He soon found himself playing alongside Paul Kelly, Grace George, Melvyn Douglas and other legendary thespians of the era. He composed show tunes for Broadway productions featuring Billy Rose and Ed Wynn. And when he was on stage, he was often cast in the parts of detectives and heavies.

It seemed natural, then, that when he joined CBS in the early 1930s, he landed leads in *True Detective* and *The True Story Hour*. This opened the door for the leads or the male leads in *Dick Tracy, Bulldog Drummond, Lora Lawton, Angel of Mercy, Manhattan Mother* and *Two on a Clue*. He appeared regularly, often with running roles, in *Little Italy, Under Arrest, The Wonder Show, Grand Central Station, Perry Mason, My True Story, The Cavalcade of America, Mystery Theatre, Betty and Bob, Big Sister, Pages of Romance, Valiant Lady, Her Honor Nancy James* and *Mr. Keen, Tracer of Lost Persons*.

Wever was voted "Favorite Daytime Serial Actor" in 1949 by readers of a popular fan magazine. That same year the fans elected Florence Freeman (Ellen Brown and Wendy Warren) their "Favorite Daytime Serial Actress."

When East Coast career opportunities began to dwindle, Wever and his wife and two daughters moved from their Old Greenwich, Connecticut, home to a new life in California. He went on to appear on the big screen in *The Prize* and *Some Came Running* and on the small screen in 70 TV productions including *Get Smart* and *Bonanza*. He died on May 6, 1984, in Laguna Hills, California.

Wever sometimes used certain occasions to defend what he did for a living. Critics of radio drama, and particularly soap operas, were often merciless in condemning the serials. Wever, who admitted that he bristled when he heard what he labeled shallow thinking, said he regarded playing in the serials to be a privilege. In a published account, he stated: "I maintain that, by and large, *Young Widder Brown* is as well-written as any drama on the air. As Doctor Loring, I've had scenes in it that I'd be pleased to play on Broadway. Let's be discriminating. Let's judge radio programs on their merits."[2]

The announcer on *Brown* remained with the series for the entire run. George Ansbro, a native of Brooklyn, New York, was born on January 14, 1915. Introduced as a boy soprano to radio, he had trekked one day in 1927 to New York's WJZ, where a pal was appearing on *The Milton Cross Children's Hour*. Ansbro auditioned and was accepted for the show. In

1931 he became an NBC page and tour guide. Without pay, he commuted regularly to WAAT in Jersey City to practice his skills as an announcer. By 1933 he was the memorable master of ceremonies on "The Brass Button Revue," a program of NBC page talent. A year later, at age 19, Ansbro was promoted to junior announcer.

His announcing credits are legion: *Mrs. Wiggs of the Cabbage Patch, Omar the Swing-maker, Waltz Time, Pick-A-Date with Buddy Rogers, Manhattan Maharajah, Sunday Sere-nade with Sammy Kaye, Lowell Thomas and the News, Go for the House, Dorsey Brothers, Chaplain Jim, Ethel and Albert, Home Sweet Home, Singo, When a Girl Marries, Ladies Be Seated, What Makes You Tick?* and *Mr. Keen, Tracer of Lost Persons.*

Ansbro was the only announcer to stay with one soap opera for an entire run lasting 18-plus years. When the Federal Communications Commission in 1942 ordered the split of the NBC Red and NBC Blue networks into separate ownership, he remained on *Brown* under the terms of the separation. He also gained the distinction of being the final announcer with dual ABC and NBC affiliation. In January 1990, on retirement, he was rec-ognized as the oldest employee, in terms of service (59 years), of all the networks. A month earlier he had retired from 24 years of hosting a weekly ABC discussion series, *FBI Wash-ington.* In the late 1990s, Ansbro is still making public appearances at vintage radio club conventions. At those events he announces re-creations of some of the shows on which he originally appeared.

When *Brown* left the air for the last time on June 29, 1956, it must have been a sad day for Ansbro, Wever and a handful of others who had been with the serial since its earli-est days. But there were no tearful good-byes, at least not on the air. Ansbro merely told the fans at home: "This concludes the present series of *Young Widder Brown* broadcasts." He said nothing more. There would always be the hope — among the producers, the cast and the fans — that the crew would return. On this depressing day in June, however, that likeli-hood seemed about as promising as the elusive nuptials of Anthony Loring and Ellen Brown.

Epilogue

For of all sad words of tongue or pen,
The saddest are these: "It might have been!"
— John Greenleaf Whittier, *Maud Muller*

When the Thanksgiving feast was over at Ma Perkins' house in 1960, millions of faithful listeners felt utterly dispossessed. Soap opera had extended the promise of immortality and eternal return — on the same station, at the same time, tomorrow. Now it was reneging on its covenant pledge. Rushville Center and Three Oaks and Simpsonville and Fairbrooke and dozens of other mythical hamlets disappeared as if they had never existed. Worse, their inhabitants — who for many listeners seemed more like friends, neighbors and relatives than mere acquaintances — also evaporated into thin air. In fact, their existences wouldn't be acknowledged ever again on the very stations that had aired them for so long!

How could any justification be made to those legions of fans who had composed the audiences of their local stations for all those years? And how could anyone responsible for this debacle be trusted again with any real sense of credibility? Such lingering questions must have filtered through the agony and anger that the disenfranchised felt on that awful day when radio drama died.

Actor Les Tremayne would note in 1988 that the unfortunate part was that the end didn't have to come. Radio drama in other countries, he observed, continued broadcasting after the advent of TV. Vast audiences, including convalescents, the aged, the blind and all who get starry-eyed when they talk about "those days," were simply left mired in an abysmal swamp.

But there was another, less obvious reason why those people were left in the lurch. The affiliates, who had lobbied hard to force the networks to release more time for local programming, were victors in a final battle. In mid–August 1960, CBS — the only network still airing serials — announced it would pare back its daytime schedule on November 25, discontinuing its last few dramas.

Thus, for economic greed, the radio serials were dismantled — and simultaneously joined the sphere of national folklore.

Ah, but while they lasted...!

Oh! scenes in strong remembrance set!
Scenes never, never to return!
— Robert Burns, *The Lament*

Appendix A:
Soap Opera Firsts,
Lasts and Mosts

First Daytime Serial
Painted Dreams (debuted October 20, 1930, on Chicago's WGN)

First Daytime Network Serial
Clara, Lu 'n' Em (shifted from evening by NBC Blue on February 15, 1932)

First Smash Hit on a Network
Just Plain Bill (debuted September 19, 1932, on CBS)

Radio's Most Durable Open-Ended Serial (Number of Broadcasts)
The Romance of Helen Trent (7,222 broadcasts, 26 years, 11 months)

Radio's Most Durable Open-Ended Serial (Debut to Cancellation)
Ma Perkins (27 years, 3 months, with some interruptions, 7,065 broadcasts)

Most Durable Closed-End Serial
Aunt Jenny's Real Life Stories (19 years, 10 months)

Broadcasting's Most Durable
The Guiding Light (debuted January 25, 1937, with some interruptions)

Most Dual Broadcasts
Road of Life (9 years on the air twice daily, CBS and NBC)

Most Broadcasts per Day
Pepper Young's Family (three times a day in 1937–38 on NBC Blue, MBS and NBC)

Most Durable in Single Time Segments
Our Gal Sunday (21 years, 9 months, at 12:45 p.m. ET on CBS)
   First Runner-up
   Stella Dallas (17 years, 7 months, at 4:15 p.m. ET on NBC)
   Second Runner-up
   Wendy Warren and the News (11 years, 5 months, at 12 noon ET on CBS)

Local Station Premiering Most Daytime Serials Moved to Network
WGN, Chicago (7 series)
   Runner-up
   WLW, Cincinnati (4 series)

Most Repeated Premise
Marrying an ordinary girl to wealth or prominence; often she would spend the rest of her days fighting off vixens who found her spouse irresistible (*Amanda of Honeymoon Hill, Backstage Wife, Betty and Bob, Linda's First Love, Lora Lawton, The Man I Married, Modern Cinderella, Our Gal Sunday, Peggy's Doctor, Rich Man's Darling, The Story of Mary Marlin, The Strange Romance of Evelyn Winters*)

Most Mailhook Plot Integrations
David Harum (profuse references to premium offers by the series characters)
   Runner-up
   Lora Lawton (same sponsor and ad mogul)

Opposite: Best-looking radio stars: this bevy of beauties, all radio soap opera queens, gathered for a 1956 telecast of *The Ed Sullivan Show.* (Courtesy of Florence Freeman)

Most Obvious Copycat Series
Today's Children (almost identical story line, locale, characters and theme of *Painted Dreams*; same creator)
   Runner-up
   The Woman in My House (numerous similarities to *One Man's Family*; same creator)

First Spin-Off Series
The Guiding Light spun into *The Right to Happiness* in 1939. Other spinoffs: *Hilltop House* into *The Story of Bess Johnson* (1941); *Big Sister* into *Bright Horizon* (1941)

Most Title Identifications
Pepper Young's Family (a.k.a. *Red Adams, Red Davis, Forever Young*)
   Runner-up
   We Love and Learn (a.k.a. *As the Twig Is Bent, The Story of Ruby Valentine*)

Most Durable Sponsor-Serial Relationship
Procter & Gamble for *Ma Perkins* (23 years, 3 months, including 7 years of dual broadcasts)

Series with the Highest Writing Honor
Against the Storm by Sandra Michael; *One Man's Family* by Carlton E. Morse (winners of the Peabody Award, the most distinguished literary achievement in radio)

Series Last Aired on a National Radio Network
The Second Mrs. Burton (Nov. 25, 1960, CBS)

First Televised Serial
Big Sister (1946, one time)

First Radio Title Transplanted to Television
The Guiding Light (first aired on CBS television on June 30, 1952, and still running). Others that made the transition from radio to television included *Valiant Lady* (Oct. 12, 1953–Aug. 16, 1957, CBS); *The Brighter Day* (Jan. 4, 1954–Sept. 28, 1962, CBS); *One Man's Family* (Mar. 1, 1954–Apr. 1, 1955, NBC); *Portia Faces Life* (Apr. 5, 1954–July 1, 1955, CBS); *Road of Life* (Dec.13, 1954–July 1, 1955, CBS); *Kitty Foyle* (Jan. 13, 1958–June 27, 1958, NBC); and *Young Dr. Malone* (Dec. 29, 1958–Mar. 29, 1963, NBC).

First Soap Opera Story Line Reprised on a Television Serial
When a Girl Marries, the early scripts of which were reprised on *Follow Your Heart* in 1953.

Another radio soap that saw television air time was *One Man's Family*, reprised on a television series of the same name.

Creators of Largest Volume of Serials (Duo)
Frank and Anne Hummert (60+ shows, more than 40 of those serials)

Creator of Largest Volume of Serials (Individual)
Irna Phillips (9 on radio; 9 on television; through protégés influenced 6 more on television)

Most Prolific Serial Writer
Robert Hardy Andrews (from 1932 to 1942, wrote 4–7 shows exceeding 100,000 words weekly)

Actress with the Longest Tenure as a Radio Heroine (Career)
Florence Freeman (31+ years in *Dot and Will, Young Widder Brown, A Woman of America, Wendy Warren and the News*)

Actress with the Longest Tenure as a Radio Heroine (Single Role)
Virginia Payne (27 years, 3 months, as *Ma Perkins*)

Actress Performing in Greatest Number of Serials
Ethel Owen (15 serials)

Actor with the Longest Tenure as a Serial Hero (Career)
Murray Forbes (29+ years as male leads in *Ma Perkins, Lonely Women, Today's Children*)

Actor with the Longest Tenure as a Serial Hero (Single Role)
Murray Forbes (27 years, 3 months, as Willie Fitz in *Ma Perkins*)

Actor Performing in Greatest Number of Serials
Marvin Miller (15 serials, some as an actor, some as announcer)

Announcer with the Longest Tenure on a Single Serial
George Ansbro (18 years, *Young Widder Brown*)

Most Married Heroine Carolyn Allen (4 times in *The Right to Happiness*)

Appendix B:
Adult Weekday Radio
Serials by Year of Debut

Note: This appendix covers a wider range of serials than is profiled in the preceding chapters. Serials are alphabetically arranged within each year. Debuts sometimes occurred on single or regional stations before national airing. Some early dramas were nighttime features long before emerging on weekday (Monday-through-Friday or Monday-through-Saturday) radio schedules. The juvenile serials (e.g., *Jack Armstrong, Little Orphan Annie, Tom Mix, Sky King*) are not included because they were not targeted for audiences beyond the childhood and early teen years. Series titles appearing in boldface are highlighted in separate chapters in this volume.

Soap Opera Forerunners: These successful serialized programs were aired at times other than on weekday daytime schedules: *Sam 'n' Henry* (1926 premier), *The Smith Family* (1927), *Amos 'n' Andy* (1928), *Moonshine and Honeysuckle* (1930).

1930 (2)
The Life of Mary Sothern (WLW, Cincinnati)
Painted Dreams (WGN, Chicago)

1931 (4)
The Gumps (WGN, Chicago)
The Life of Irene Castle (syndicated)
Miracles of Magnolia
The Stolen Husband

1932 (7)
Betty and Bob
Clara, Lu 'n' Em (1930 evening debut, WGN, Chicago)
Judy and Jane (Midwest region only)
Just Plain Bill
Red Adams (evolved into *Red Davis* in 1933)
Today's Children (WMAQ, Chicago; copy of *Painted Dreams*)
Vic and Sade

1933 (4)
Easy Aces (1930 evening debut, KMBC, Kansas City)
Ma Perkins (WLW, Cincinnati; then NBC)

Marie, the Little French Princess
The Romance of Helen Trent

1934 (5)
Dreams Come True
Home Sweet Home
Peggy's Doctor
Song of the City
The Story of Mary Marlin (WMAQ, Chicago)

1935 (13)
Bachelor's Children (WGN, Chicago)
Backstage Wife (a.k.a. *Mary Noble, Backstage Wife*)
The Couple Next Door (WGN, Chicago)
David Harum (WOR, New York)
Dot and Will
Five Star Jones
Girl Alone (local series; NBC in 1936)
The Girl Next Door
Happy Hollow (1929 evening debut, KMBC, Kansas City)
Molly of the Movies
Mrs. Wiggs of the Cabbage Patch

The O'Neills (1934 evening debut)
We Are Four (WGN, Chicago)

1936 (14)
Big Sister
Dan Harding's Wife
Foxes of Flatbush
The Goldbergs (1929 evening debut, WJZ, New York)
Hope Adams' Romance
Houseboat Hannah (syndicated; NBC in 1938)
The Johnson Family (WLW, Cincinnati; then MBS)
John's Other Wife
Love Song
Modern Cinderella (WGN, Chicago; then CBS)
Pepper Young's Family (debuted as *Forever Young*)
Rich Man's Darling
Trouble House (portion of *Heinz Magazine of the Air*)
Way Down East

1937 (18)
Arnold Grimm's Daughter
Aunt Jenny's True Life Stories (a.k.a. *Aunt Jenny's Real Life Stories*)
Carol Kennedy's Romance (portion of *Heinz Magazine of the Air*)
Follow the Moon
The Guiding Light
The Heart of Gold
Hello, Peggy
Hilltop House
Jenny Peabody
Kitty Keene, Incorporated
Lorenzo Jones
Myrt and Marge (1931 evening debut)
The Old Homestead
Our Gal Sunday (evolved from *Rich Man's Darling*)
Pretty Kitty Kelly
Road of Life
Scattergood Baines (West Coast region)
Stella Dallas (WEAF, New York)

1938 (19)
The Carters of Elm Street (Chicago area)
Central City
Doctor Kate
Her Honor, Nancy James
Jane Arden
Joyce Jordan, Girl Interne (a.k.a. *Joyce Jordan, M.D.*)

Life Can Be Beautiful
Madame Courageous
Margo of Castlewood
Midstream (WLW, Cincinnati)
Mother-in-Law
Stepmother (a.k.a. *Kay Fairchild, Stepmother*)
Terry Regan, Attorney at Law
This Day Is Ours
Those Happy Gilmans
Valiant Lady
Woman in White
Young Widder Brown (debuted as *Young Widder Jones*)
Your Family and Mine

1939 (25)
Adopted Daughter (regional)
Against the Storm
Beyond These Valleys
Brenda Curtis
By Kathleen Norris
The Career of Alice Blair (syndicated by WOR, New York)
Caroline's Golden Store
Doc Barclay's Daughters
Ellen Randolph
Harvey and Dell
The Life and Love of Doctor Susan
Linda's First Love (syndicated)
Manhattan Mother
The Man I Married
Meet Miss Julia
Meet the Dixons
My Son and I
Orphans of Divorce (launched in evening; moved to daytime)
The Right to Happiness (*The Guiding Light* spin-off)
Society Girl
Thunder Over Paradise
The Trouble with Marriage
When a Girl Marries
Woman of Courage
Young Doctor Malone

1940 (13)
Amanda of Honeymoon Hill
Charlie and Jessie
Dearest Mother (syndicated)
Friend in Deed
I Love Linda Dale
Kate Hopkins, Angel of Mercy
The Light of the World
Lone Journey

Martha Webster (a.k.a. *Life Begins*)
Mother o' Mine
Portia Faces Life (KTSA, San Antonio; then CBS)
This Small Town
We, the Abbotts

1941 (18)
As the Twig Is Bent (syndicated)
The Bartons,
Bright Horizon (*Big Sister* spin-off)
Edith Adams' Future
Front Page Farrell
Helen Holden, Government Girl
Helping Hand
Helpmate
Home of the Brave
House in the Country
I'll Find My Way
In Care of Aggie Horn
Into the Light
Mary Foster, the Editor's Daughter (syndicated; then MBS)
The Mystery Man
Stories America Loves
The Story of Bess Johnson (*Hilltop House* spin-off)
We Are Always Young

1942 (11)
The Andersons
Aunt Mary (West Coast region; MBS in 1946)
Chaplain Jim, U.S.A.
Jane Endicott, Reporter
Kitty Foyle (evolved from *Stories America Loves*)
Little Women
Lonely Women (segued into reincarnation of *Today's Children*)
Second Husband (1937 evening debut)
Second Wife (West Coast region)
Snow Village Sketches (1936 evening debut)
We Love and Learn (succeeded *As the Twig Is Bent*)

1943 (10)
American Women
Brave Tomorrow
Dreft Star Playhouse (a.k.a. *Hollywood Theatre of the Air*)
Lora Lawton
Now and Forever
The Open Door
Perry Mason
Sweet River

This Life Is Mine
A Woman of America

1944 (7)
Ethel and Albert
Rosemary
The Strange Romance of Evelyn Winters
Tena and Tim (mid–1930s debut in syndication)
This Changing World
True Confessions
Two on a Clue

1945 (3)
Barry Cameron (a.k.a. *The Soldier Who Came Home*)
The Story of Sandra Martin
A Woman's Life (evolved from *Bright Horizon*)

1946 (3)
Masquerade
Rose of My Dreams
The Second Mrs. Burton (evolved from *Second Wife*)

1947 (5)
Katie's Daughter
Song of a Stranger
The Story of Holly Sloan
This Is Nora Drake
Wendy Warren and the News

1948 (1)
The Brighter Day

1949 (3)
Dorothy Dix at Home
Marriage for Two
Second Spring (syndicated)

1950 (1)
Nona from Nowhere

1951 (3)
Doctor Paul
King's Row
The Woman in My House

1952 (1)
The Doctor's Wife

1954 (3)
Ever Since Eve
Hotel for Pets
Michael Flagg, M.D.

1955 (1)
The Story of Ruby Valentine (evolved from *We Love and Learn*)

1956 (1)
Five Star Matinee

1957 (2)
The Affairs of Doctor Gentry
One Man's Family (1932 evening debut, KGO,
    San Francisco)

1958 (1)
Real Life Stories

1959 (1)
Whispering Streets (1952 debut

as daytime complete-story drama)

1960 (1)
Best Seller

Unsubstantiated Year of Origin (5)
Dodsworth
Grandma Travels (syndicated)
Halfway to Heaven (syndicated)
Pages of Romance
Thanks for Tomorrow

Total: 205

Chapter Notes

Preface

1. Matelski, Marilyn J. pp. 36–40.
2. James Thurber, "O Pioneers!" *New Yorker*, May 15, 1948, p. 34.
3. Ibid.
4. *The Great Radio Heroes*, p. 11.

Chapter 2

1. Soares, Manuela, p. 174.
2. Stedman, Raymond William, p. 280.
3. Edmondson, Madeleine, and David Rounds, p. 54.

Chapter 3

1. Poindexter, Ray, p. 93.
2. *Variety*, December 3, 1947, p. 25.
3. Warner, Lloyd and William Henry. "The Radio Daytime Serial: A Symbolic Analysis." *Genetic Psychology Monographs*, February, 1948, pp. 3–71.

Chapter 5

1. Higby, Mary Jane, pp. 133–134.
2. Soares, Manuela, p. 174.
3. Lackmann, Ron, *Remember Radio*, p. 37.

Chapter 6

1. *Radio Mirror*. December, 1941, p. 39.
2. DeLong, Thomas A., p. 64.
3. Higby, Mary Jane, pp. 201–202.

Chapter 7

1. Stedman, Raymond William, p. 316.

Chapter 8

1. *Radio and Television Mirror*. December, 1950, p. 40.

Chapter 9

1. LaGuardia, Robert, p. 20.
2. Higby, Mary Jane, p. 129.
3. Harmon, Jim, p. 176.
4. Dunning, John, *Tune in Yesterday*, p. 339.
5. Ibid., p. 338.
6. Stedman, Raymond William, p. 256.
7. *Variety*. July 23, 1941, p. 46.
8. Carskadon, Tom. "Restoring Cinderella." *Radioland*. February, 1935, p. 64.

Chapter 10

1. LaGuardia, Robert, p. 33.
2. Stedman, Raymond William, p. 315.
3. MacDonald, J. Fred, pp. 142–143.
4. *Radio Mirror*. February, 1947, p. 41.

Chapter 13

1. Stedman, Raymond William, p. 312.

Chapter 14

1. Stumpf, Charles K., p. 17.
2. LaGuardia, Robert, p. 6.

3. Dunning, John, *Tune in Yesterday,* p. 383.
4. Harmon, Jim, p. 178.
5. Lamparski, Richard, p. 111.
6. *Variety.* April 19, 1944, p. 24.
7. Edmondson, Madeleine, and David Rounds, p. 238.
8. Schisgall, Oscar, pp. 123–124.
9. Allen, Robert C., p. 117.
10. Editors of *Advertising Age,* p. 18.
11. "Life with Ma." *Time.* August 26, 1957, pp. 41–42.
12. Allen, p. 126.
13. *North American Radio Archives News.* Spring, 1996, pp. 33–34.
14. Higby, Mary Jane, p. 213.

Chapter 15

1. Morse, Carlton E., p. 3.
2. Ibid., p. 32.
3. Ibid., p. 34.
4. Slide, Anthony, p. 80.
5. Morse, p. xiii.

Chapter 16

1. Edmondson, Madeleine, and David Rounds, p. 55.
2. LaGuardia, Robert, p. 28.
3. LaGuardia, p. 10
4. Personal letter to author, November 18, 1958.

Chapter 17

1. LaGuardia, Robert, p. 23.
2. Stedman, Raymond William, p. 297.
3. DeLong, Thomas A., p. 5.
4. Wylie, Max, pp. 301–302.
5. DeLong, pp. 130–131.
6. Stedman, p. 297.

Chapter 18

1. *Encyclopedia of Consumer Brands,* Vol. 2, pp. 537–538.

Chapter 19

1. Lackmann, Ron, *Remember Radio,* p. 40.

Chapter 20

1. Edmondson, Madeleine, and David Rounds, p. 46.
2. Willey, George A. "End of an Era: The Daytime Radio Serial," *Journal of Broadcasting.* Spring, 1961, pp. 97–115.

Chapter 21

1. Gilbert, Annie, p. 70.
2. Ibid., p. 17.
3. LaGuardia, Robert, p. 29.

Chapter 22

1. *Life.* July 11, 1960, pp. 49–52.
2. Soares, Manuela, p. 177.
3. Stedman, Raymond William, p. 257.
4. Ibid., p. 321.
5. Dunning, John, *Tune in Yesterday,* p. 520.
6. Stedman, p. 258.
7. LaGuardia, Robert, p. 7.
8. Ibid., p. 8.
9. Dunning, *Tune in Yesterday,* p. 522.
10. Ibid., p. 521.

Chapter 24

1. Lackmann, Ron. *Same Time … Same Station,* p. 244.
2. Swartz, Jon D. and Robert C. Reinehr, p. 136.
3. Stumpf, Charles K., p. 22.
4. Buxton, Frank and Bill Owen, p. 200.
5. Stedman, Raymond William, p. 392.

Chapter 25

1. Stedman, Raymond William, p. 314.

Chapter 27

1. *Irna Phillips vs. WGN, Inc.*, Petition for Leave to Appeal, Supreme Court of Illinois, February Term, 1941, p. 10.
2. *Broadcasting*, March 1, 1925, p. 12.

Chapter 28

1. *Radio Mirror*, April 1949, p. 28.

Chapter 29

1. Higby, Mary Jane, pp. 112–15.

2. *Radio and Television Mirror*, January 1950, p. 43.

Chapter 30

1. *Radio and Television Mirror*, December 1950, p. 11.
2. Stedman, p. 389.
3. Charles Dickens, *A Tale of Two Cities*.

Chapter 31

1. Dunning, *Tune in Yesterday*, p. 660.
2. Ira Kanster "The Wever Way," *Radio and Television Mirror*, April 1949, p. 87.

Annotated Bibliography

To compile the data in this text, I heard literally hundreds and hundreds of tapes and recordings of radio serials, listening to some of them scores of times. I read and reread stacks of soap opera scripts, making voluminous notes as I went through them. In the process, I was acquiring an insatiable appetite for still more information. Legions of periodicals partially conquered the hunger, offering a wealth of anecdotes and little-known facts about the serials and the people who made them happen.

In addition, my secondary sources included newspaper clippings, magazine articles, items appearing in trade journals and vintage radio club newsletters. I specifically relied on *Broadcasting, Journal of Broadcasting, Life, Movie-Radio Guide, Newsweek, The New Yorker, New York Times, North American Radio Archives News, Radioland, Radio Mirror* and its successor *Radio and Television Mirror, SPERDVAC Radiogram, Time, True Experiences* and *Variety.* I also leaned heavily on unpublished compilations such as Jay Hickerson's "Necrology of Radio Personalities." I pored over tidbits of data supplied by interested friends and parties with whom I exchange, via computer, news about the hobby.

The primary research included interviewing a few of the living legends of radio soap operas. Extensive correspondence and telephone dialogues with these artists and other individuals on the fringes of the genre helped clarify and substantiate portions of the printed material and place it in proper perspective.

Finally, I scoured libraries in several major metropolitan centers in search of documents that would shed light on obscure details. The texts and materials that follow are those called on most faithfully. I commend them to the reader who, for reflective, nostalgic or scholarly purposes, desires to explore the subject further. The annotations may be helpful in classifying their content.

Allen, Robert C. *Speaking of Soap Operas.* Chapel Hill, N.C.: University of North Carolina Press, 1985.
    This is a scholarly approach to the genre, from formative days through the television era, given in easy-to-follow detail. The works of Irna Phillips are frequent examples, with four of her serial scripts included. The text makes a significant contribution for the serious student.

Anderson, Arthur. *Let's Pretend: A History of Radio's Best Loved Children's Show by a Longtime Cast Member.* Jefferson, N.C.: McFarland, 1994.
    Concerned with just one kids' show, this book nevertheless gives an eyewitness account of some of the actors who played on soap operas as juveniles and, later, as adults. Offering fresh insights into how a live dramatic program was produced, this book should appeal to those interested in varied forms of radio drama.

Buxton, Frank, and Bill Owen. *The Big Broadcast, 1920–1950.* 2d ed. Lanham, Md.: Scarecrow, 1997.
    In a sense, this is a "bible" of radio, providing fairly reliable descriptions, cast lists, epigraphs and obscure details on hundreds of programs, from music to comedy and everything in between. It is limited by the fact that its scope ends in 1950, a full decade before the end of radio serials.

_____. *Radio's Golden Age: The Programs and the Personalities.* New York: Easton Valley, 1966.
    A precursor to the authors' subsequent

editions of *The Big Broadcast*, this book filled an important void for hobby enthusiasts when it was first released. It also ignores scores of shows that debuted in the 1950s.

Castleman, Harry, and Walter J. Podrazik. *505 Radio Questions Your Friends Can't Answer.* New York: Walker, 1983.
 For the trivia buff, there's a lot of recall information here that can be applied in sharpening the senses about serials and other radio programming.

Chester, Giraud, Garnet R. Garrison and Edgar E. Willis. *Television and Radio.* 3d ed. New York: Appleton Century Crofts, 1963.
 The thoughtful broadcasting reader will find a wealth of intensive, easy-to-grasp documentation that will be useful for earnest research. A chapter on ratings systems is particularly insightful.

Copeland, Mary Ann. *Soap Opera History.* Lincolnwood, Ill.: Publications International, 1991.
 Strong pictures and verbiage relate the story of the televised serials, but there's little of value for radio enthusiasts beyond the introduction. Can this be a true interpretation of the volume's title?

DeLong, Thomas A. *Radio Stars: An Illustrated Biographical Dictionary of 953 Performers, 1920 through 1960.* Jefferson, N.C.: McFarland, 1996.
 DeLong offers a treasure chest of personalities in the industry, including birth/death dates and places, training, experience, honors and achievements in various mediums, outside interests and anecdotes — most never before published. Written in a lively style, the book includes photos of many of its subjects.

Dunning, John. *On the Air: The Encyclopedia of Old-Time Radio.* New York: Oxford, 1998.
 The definitive encyclopedia of American radio, from its beginning in the 1920s until the early 1960s. This 800-page reference work tops all others in providing more data on more shows than any other single source. It is an absolute must for vintage radio program aficionados.

_____. *Tune in Yesterday: The Ultimate Encyclopedia of Old-Time Radio, 1925–1976.* Englewood Cliffs, N.J.: Prentice Hall, 1976.
 Another of the "important works" on radio, this one offers vivid details behind the scenes of

most of the major series of the Golden Age and beyond. Programs are described by essays, some fairly brief and others quite extensive. Both the nostalgia buff and the serious student will profit and enjoy.

Editors of *Advertising Age. Procter & Gamble: The House That Ivory Built.* Lincolnwood, Ill.: NTC Business Books, 1988.
 This is an intriguing study of a firm that reached the pinnacle of the free enterprise system. Of interest to media fans will be P&G's marketing success story, including references to its predominance as a soap opera producer.

Editors of Moody's Investors Service. *Moody's Industrial Manual,* vol. 2. New York: Moody's Investors Service, 1978.
 A two-volume repository of corporate ownership in private business and industry in America, this work includes acquisitions and divestitures, officers, locations, brand names and the like. Also included are some of the sponsors of the daytime serials.

Edmondson, Madeleine, and David Rounds. *The Soaps: Daytime Serials of Radio and TV.* New York: Stein and Day, 1973.
 This excellent overview of the genre includes radio and TV serials through the publication date. Strong pictures, dialogue and heavy emphasis on Irna Phillips' works are included.

Encyclopedia of Consumer Brands, vol. 2. Detroit: St. James, 1994.
 This three-volume compendium of numerous brands and the firms that produce them includes many that underwrote the radio serials. The book gives interesting accounts of the application of both managerial and marketing expertise.

Gilbert, Annie. *All My Afternoons: The Heart and Soul of the TV Soap Opera.* New York: A&W, 1979.
 Another overview, this one is targeted at TV serials through the date of publication. A brief history with important references to radio is included. Irna Phillips claims the limelight, with the Hummerts mentioned only in passing.

Groves, Seli. *The Ultimate Soap Opera Guide.* Detroit: Visible Ink, 1995.
 Although this heavy paperback concentrates on present-day TV serials, it doesn't do so at the expense of their heritage. In a section on soaps' history, the author expounds on the radio

prototypes, then briefly examines more than 50 radio soap operas. Some of this information appears elsewhere.

Harmon, Jim. *The Great Radio Comedians.* Garden City, N.Y.: Doubleday, 1970.

Harmon provides an affectionate portrait of what made us laugh in radio's Golden Age. Of interest to soap opera fans are essays on *Lorenzo Jones, Vic and Sade, Easy Aces, One Man's Family* and *Ma Perkins,* some of them more melodramatic than funny.

_____. *The Great Radio Heroes.* Garden City, N.Y.: Doubleday, 1967.

This affectionate portrait of radio drama focuses in a serials chapter on *Stella Dallas, Our Gal Sunday, The Stolen Husband, Lorenzo Jones, Front Page Farrell, Ma Perkins, Vic and Sade, When a Girl Marries, One Man's Family* and more.

_____. *Radio Mystery and Adventure and Its Appearances in Film, Television and Other Media.* Jefferson, N.C.: McFarland, 1992.

The title is misleading; this book doesn't capitalize on the popular nighttime drama and adventure shows but on the late-afternoon juvenile adventure series (*Dick Tracy, Challenge of the Yukon* et al.). Despite that, serial fans will find references to several whose voices they heard for many years. TV, movies, print and other forms are related.

Head, Sydney W., and Christopher H. Sterling. *Broadcasting in America.* 4th ed. Boston: Houghton Mifflin, 1982.

This insightful treatise in easy-to-understand language is a sweeping, though comprehensive, overview of both radio and television mediums. The intellect will be rewarded with topical matters ranging from the origins of broadcasting to programming and audience measurement.

Hickerson, Jay. *The Ultimate History of Network Radio Programming and Guide to All Circulating Shows.* 3rd ed. Hamden, Conn.: J. Hickerson, 1996.

A valuable resource for every radio collector's shelf, this spiralbound log contains listings of more than 6,000 Golden Age programs. It includes sign-on and sign-off dates, stars, networks, sponsors, days and broadcast times. Updates in the form of supplements are available annually.

Higby, Mary Jane. *Tune in Tomorrow; or, How I*

Found The Right to Happiness with Our Gal Sunday, Stella Dallas, John's Other Wife, and Other Sudsy Radio Serials. New York: Cowles Education Corporation, 1968.

Although written in the first person more than three decades ago, this serial heroine's keen and often humorous observations are as timely now as then. She candidly tells of life backstage in a way others haven't, providing a rich reservoir of interesting detail along the way. This is a "must" for the serious student of the genre.

Hyatt, Wesley. *The Encyclopedia of Daytime Television.* New York: Billboard Books, 1997.

This inspired, delightfully written manual of TV, past and present, details hundreds of shows, with illustrations. In addition to cast lists, dates, times and networks, there are detailed accounts of plots and series backgrounds. Radio aficionados can trace careers of radio personalities into TV and shows that transferred from an audio to a visual medium.

Lackmann, Ron. *Remember Radio.* New York: Putnam, 1970.

Pictures and captions tell the story of radio's Golden Age. Not all shows are given, but a representative number are. The book includes brief vignettes on each radio serial at midcentury, plus the four network program schedules of that era.

_____. *Same Time ... Same Station: An A–Z Guide to Radio from Jack Benny to Howard Stern.* New York: Facts on File, 1996.

With brief essays on hundreds of personalities and programs, and with more than 100 excellent photos, this book received the wrath of critics for scurrilous contradictions and scores of errors, substantially diminishing it for use as a reliable source without validating the contents further.

LaGuardia, Robert. *From Ma Perkins to Mary Hartman: The Illustrated History of Soap Operas.* New York: Ballantine, 1977.

LaGuardia provides a concise photolog of soap opera, beginning with radio and continuing with TV. The chapter on radio documents the history of its serials with a lengthy narrative followed by pictures of cast members by year of series debuts. Though published more than two decades ago, the anecdotes and perceptive commentary still make valuable contributions.

Lamparski, Richard. *Whatever Became Of...?* First-Eleventh Series. New York: Crown, 1967–89.

This one-of-a-kind series presents short biographies on hundreds of famous personalities of yesteryear via pictures and verbiage. It includes a lot of material never before published.

MacDonald, J. Fred. *Don't Touch That Dial!: Radio Programming in American Life from 1920 to 1960.* Chicago: Nelson-Hall, 1991.
This is one of the better texts for the scholarly-minded enthusiast. The single chapter on soap operas is lengthy, filled with keen observations on how the genre influenced society. Most of the serials are delineated. Sensibly, it covers the entire time frame of the Golden Age.

Maltin, Leonard. *The Great American Broadcast: A Celebration of Radio's Golden Age.* New York: Penguin Putnam, 1997.
An impressive gift book for the nostalgia lover, this one attempts to cover it all yet makes few references to soap operas outside of *One Man's Family*. There's a noticeable bent toward West Coast personalities. Some material appears in other places. The text includes illustrations.

Matelski, Marilyn J. *The Soap Opera Evolution: America's Enduring Romance with Daytime Drama.* Jefferson, N.C.: McFarland, 1988.
A scholarly work focusing on the plots, characters, audience and trends in current televised serials. Brief examinations of several radio serials are provided, along with significant comparisons between TV and radio eras. Extensive research went into this project, including feedback from 600 viewers.

Modleski, Tania. *Loving with a Vengeance: Mass-Produced Fantasies for Women.* Hamden, Conn.: Archon, 1982.
This intellectual treatise explores popular culture — Harlequin romances, Gothic novels and soap operas — and its effect on women. A well-documented study contrasts the desires of the female reader/audience with the realities of circumstance. The serials chapter adds an important dimension of understanding for the genre's serious student.

Morse, Carlton E. *The One Man's Family Album: An Inside Look at Radio's Longest Running Show.* Woodside, Calif.: Seven Stones, 1988.
The true devotee of this long-running drama will probably think of this collection of pictures and copy as something akin to paradise. Included are historical highlights, biographies on cast members, four scripts, print ads, premiums

and behind-the-scenes data that only one closely connected with the show could provide.

Morton, Robert, ed. *Worlds without End: The Art and History of the Soap Opera.* New York: Harry N. Abrams, and the Museum of Television & Radio, 1997.
A fabulous assemblage of photographs and copy concerning radio and television serials, this would make a super gift book for any old-time radio buff who's caught up in the aura of daytime programming. Well-written and beautifully designed, it's a keeper.

Mott, Robert L. *Radio Sound Effects: Who Did It, and How, in the Era of Live Broadcasting.* Jefferson, N.C.: McFarland, 1993.
The behind-the-microphone scene is vividly described by a man who spent his career there. He introduces most of the professional radio sound specialists and tells of the shows they worked on while listing another group of obscure artists: the organists and other musicians. Heavy doses of anecdotes are right out of the pages of life.

Poindexter, Ray. *Golden Throats and Silver Tongues: The Radio Announcers.* Conway, Ark.: River Road, 1978.
Focusing on a single but important profession, the author provides a highly anecdotal, year-by-year, program-by-program account of how the network announcers earned their livelihoods. Brief glimpses into their history before network status are included.

Schisgall, Oscar. *Eyes on Tomorrow: The Evolution of Procter & Gamble.* Chicago: Doubleday/Ferguson, 1981.
Given the fact that P&G virtually built daytime radio for the networks, this 140-year history of P&G documents the firm's intensive advertising pilgrimage, including radio's important contributions. Soap opera played a major role.

Settel, Irving. *A Pictorial History of Radio.* 2d ed. New York: Grosset & Dunlap, 1967.
Excellent illustrations make this a poignant walk down memory lane. Beginning with the invention of radio and proceeding by decades from the 1920s through the 1960s, this is a loving portrait of an era that entertained and informed.

Slide, Anthony. *Great Radio Personalities in Historic Photographs.* Vestal, N.Y.: Vestal, 1982.
Celebrity-focused and alphabetically

arranged, these 235 black-and-white photographs and their captions chronicle the old-time radio years. The photos are generous-sized close-ups, adding to the life-size dimensions of those featured.

Soares, Manuela. *The Soap Opera Book.* New York: Harmony, 1978.

The radio serials are categorized by ethnicity, ordinary folks, women alone, super-heroines, medicos, highbrows and inspiration. Twenty-five radio serials are highlighted. The book is primarily about televised soaps, however, and approaches them from a topical context.

Stedman, Raymond William. *The Serials: Suspense and Drama by Installment.* Norman: University of Oklahoma Press, 1971.

The most insightful, accurate and authoritative chronicle yet, this priceless volume has long set the standard for serious exploration of the soap opera. A scholarly approach by an educator who devoted much of his life to discovering the true story, it provides valuable analysis and commentary on virtually all of radio's daytime network serials.

Sterling, Christopher H., and John M. Kittross. *Stay Tuned: A Concise History of American Broadcasting.* Belmont, Calif.: Wadsworth, 1978.

Taking a chronological approach to radio's history, this study starts before radio was invented and continues through 1977. As one would expect, there are several references to the soap operas.

Stuart, Mary. *Both of Me.* Garden City, N.Y.: Doubleday, 1980.

The autobiography of an early TV serial's heroine offers snapshots of how televised dramas got on the air in the 1950s. Along the way the author provides flashbacks to radio and its daytime "stars," some of whom transferred to her own long-running series, *Search for Tomorrow.*

Stumpf, Charles K. *Ma Perkins, Little Orphan Annie and Heigh Ho, Silver!* New York: Carlton, 1971.

This little book highlights dozens of soap operas and other shows. Even though much of the information is available elsewhere, this volume provides a composite sketch of the better-known serials while adding some lesser-knowns. A few pictures are included.

Summers, Harrison B., ed. *A Thirty-Year History of Programs Carried on National Radio Networks in the United States, 1926–1956.* New York: Arno Press and the New York Times, 1971.

The amount of effort that went into this reference is incalculable; nowhere has it been duplicated. The wealth of data it provides on programs, times, days and years of airing, sponsors and ratings is phenomenal. This may be the most important single reference work on radio.

Swartz, Jon D., and Robert C. Reinehr. *Handbook of Old-Time Radio: A Comprehensive Guide to Golden Age Radio Listening and Collecting.* Metuchen, N.J.: Scarecrow, 1993.

This volume is a highly readable collection of short narratives on hundreds and hundreds of programs. Importantly, it contains several other sections of merit, including a radio history, program category logs and emphasis on old-time radio collecting. The serious student and the nostalgia buff will love this.

Terrace, Vincent. *Radio Programs, 1924–1984: A Catalog of Over 1800 Shows.* Jefferson, N.C.: McFarland, 1999.

More shows are listed here than in any other published source — 1,835 of them, to be exact. The work includes 517 program openings and 243 closings, making it even more distinctive. Photos are limited but text is insightful.

Waggett, Gerald J. *The Soap Opera Book of Lists.* New York: Harper Collins, 1996.

Pointed exclusively toward TV serials, this book nevertheless includes some references to the radio serials and their personalities, although the number is minimal. The book is a trivia-lover's treasure chest.

_____. *The Soap Opera Encyclopedia.* New York: Harper Collins, 1997.

The author and publisher keep forgetting that before there was TV, there was radio. While the TV serials, past and present, are extensively examined, numerous cross-references surface about the radio soaps moved to TV and those individuals who took part in both mediums.

Wylie, Max, ed. *Best Broadcasts of 1939–40.* New York: Whittlesey House, 1940.

Actual scripts are included from dramatic productions deemed worthy of such designations. Some soap operas are included. This is one of a series of annual releases from that era.

Index

Note: **Bold** *numbers indicate pages with photos.*